Structure in Sculpture

The MIT Press
Cambridge, Massachusetts
London, England

Structure in Sculpture

Daniel L. Schodek

This book was set in Frutiger by Colotone Graphics, Inc. and was
printed and bound in the United States of America.

Library of Congress Cataloging-in-Publication Data
Schodek, Daniel L., 1941–
    Structure in sculpture / Daniel L. Schodek.
        p. cm.
    Includes bibliographical references and index.
    ISBN 0-262-19313-2
    1. Sculpture—Technique.   2. Artists' materials.   I. Title.
NB1170.S35 1992
731'.028—dc20   92-16904
                                              CIP

This book is dedicated to my mother in memory of my father

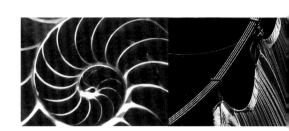

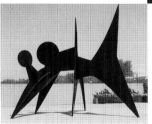

Contents

Acknowledgments

The ever-present support of Kay, Ned, and Ben Schodek deserves first and special mention. It is difficult to conceive how this book could ever have been completed without their special form of help, and certainly their forbearance. Additionally, Kay started the process of obtaining the many photographs that had to be acquired (meeting and talking with many delightful and helpful people in the process) and translating the text into a more readable form. If not for her help and encouragement at necessary times, a rather ragged manuscript and motley collection of photographs would undoubtedly still be in a disk somewhere in my computer. Others contributed as well. Jonathan Corson-Rickert's work sparked my immediate interest in the subject. I still remember his elegant fence sculpture. Roger Conover of the MIT Press proved willing to sponsor this unusual work and brought it over the necessary hurdles. Turning a rough manuscript and a series of digitized images into a printed book was a complex undertaking, and the efforts of Jeannet Leendertse and Matthew Abbate of the MIT Press are especially appreciated. A number of students—Austin Tang, John Leeke, Joe Kennard, BoHan Kim, Laura Campbell, Kathe Flynn, David Thal, Steve Raninger, Steve Atkinson, John Tong, and others—helped with finding examples, preparing illustrations, or tracking down elusive sculptors. Stephanie Goldberg picked up on the vexing task of obtaining formal permission to reproduce many of the photographs included. Henry Fernandez provided insights into some of the art historical aspects of the manuscript. The cooperation of organizations such as the Storm King Art Center, the Hirshhorn Art Gallery, and a number of other art centers and galleries is also greatly appreciated.

Introduction

This book deals with sculpture as a material construct. Drawing on straightforward physical principles of how sculptures stand and how material characteristics affect their shaping, the book illuminates the way these principles are reflected in specific works, either implicitly or as part of the sculptor's direct intent. In their simplest application, the theories presented here will help inform a sculptor whether a work proportioned in a certain way will overturn or not when set on a base, or whether a particular piece is big enough to support its own weight without bending excessively or even breaking off. But the ultimate aim is to demonstrate that a knowledge of structural considerations can have a positive potential for understanding the shaping of sculpture.

The book evolved over time and had many points of origin. On the one hand it is a response to the surprising paucity of studies treating sculptures from a technical perspective and seeking to understand them as either physical artifacts or manifestations of physical phenomena. To be sure, this line of inquiry is not wholly absent from the literature. The role and impact of technique and process considerations, for example, are largely understood, acknowledged, and documented. The same, however, cannot be said about structural considerations—a void this book seeks to fill. Some of the material in the book was drawn from the literature on preservation and restoration, and some of the chapters may be of interest to those in this field. But no rigorous attempt has been made to treat issues in the preservation or restoration of existing sculpture; rather, the intent is to provide an insight into how to prevent problems from occurring in the first place.

The book is also a response to an ever-increasing pragmatic need as more and more large-scale sculptures are placed in the public landscape. While it is often fashionable for authors and critics to deal with the conceptual rather than the pragmatic, sculpture has always had a comforting basis in reality. Something must be created, often an object must be made. Who makes it and how it is made can have an enormous impact on the character of the work itself—

particularly as the scale of the work increases. Certainly in large-scale works there is an increasing tendency and need for sculptors and professionals such as structural engineers, architects, or landscape architects to work together. Sculptures placed in public environments must be made safe. They must not collapse or overturn. It is not enough for a sculptor to assume that a large sculpture is safe; its safety must be known and demonstrable before it is built, or it may never get built. Explicit explorations of strength and stability are usually the province of the engineer and frequently entail significant impacts on the final form and shaping of a sculpture. Yet neither the sculptor nor the engineer knows very much about the other's profession. This book addresses technical issues of this kind directly in relation to sculptures. In this sense it is intended for an audience of sculptors, but also for architects and engineers who are often part of the design, review, and implementation process.

In addition to responding to these needs, the book reflects more personal concerns that were present at the moment of its conceptualization. There are many individuals who are structuralists by nature (not in Claude Lévi-Strauss's sense of the word but in the sense Gustave Eiffel might have given it), who are preoccupied with physical forms and seek to understand them in all of their dimensions, and who find what can only be described as delight in doing so. On this level the book is first and foremost the natural result of a structuralist's ever-consuming passion to look at all physical objects in the world, whether bird's wings or lampposts or sculptures, from a structural point of view, and to attempt to communicate this passion to others. A passion of this type is admittedly strange and may perhaps seem even bizarre to some. It has, however, an intellectual lineage. D'Arcy Thompson, for example, heroically summarized the work of many individuals seeking to understand the rationale for the shapes of plant and animal forms from a physical rather than a biological or evolutionary perspective in his 1917 classic *On Growth and Form*. Cannot sculptures be looked at purely in terms of their physical structure as well, and in a way that might well provide new insights into their form and shaping? Why not, after all.

How to think about the subject and organize a treatment of it proved far more difficult than meets the eye. A simple example might be of interest. In first conceptualizing this

book, I attempted to review existing physical classifications and/or morphological categorizations of sculptures, simply as a way of structuring both the book and the selection of sculptures to be discussed. But convincing classifications of physical forms are not to be found in the sculptural field. There is really very little of interest on this topic in the literature, since a purely physical perspective on form is not equivalent to classifications based on stylistic, cultural, or chronological concerns or intellectual movements. In a field like sculpture with its strong visual component, the absence of rigorous classifications by form, as at least one basis for discussion, is surprising. This book makes only marginal progress to remedy that situation. I have developed a simple structurally oriented classification so that the subject material can be dealt with in some coherent way, but my intent here has never been to develop classifications per se.

It should also be obvious by now that this book is not at all intended to be a treatise on science in art, attempting to draw parallels between the modes of inquiry prevalent in these two domains or considering a science-oriented perception of the world (in terms of values and objectives) as a basis either for existing art forms or for new movements. Rather, I have conducted a much more direct exploration of sculptures from a purely physical point of view, comparable to the analyses that could be made of any physical object. An attitude assumed through most of the book is that initially no value should be ascribed to any particular set of physical characteristics associated with a sculpture. I have attempted to restrict speculations and value-laden discussions to part 6 of the book, where license is assumed. This mode of inquiry, I believe, is a necessary precursor to any further debates that attempt to ascribe values to the sculptural facts thus uncovered. Such debates as currently occur often lack any real understanding of what it means to look at sculptures as physical objects, and as a consequence are often uninformed and thus uninteresting.

As a technique for conveying structural principles, I look at specific sculptures from a structural perspective. There is no implication, of course, that the sculptors themselves were somehow interpreting structure in their work. Similarly, the analyses shown are strictly my interpretation of how the structure of a particular sculpture works. Any book seeking to explore any class of objects from a structural point of view must necessarily and comprehensively address a known set of certain invariant principles (e.g., force composition and resolution, equilibrium concepts). I chose examples of sculptures that most clearly illustrate the specific points under discussion, with no particular thought to further consistency within the selection. Several works, notably Susumu Shingu's *Echo of the Waves* and *Gift of the Wind*, have been used as examples more than once in different parts of the book with respect to different issues. If the dispersed analyses are reassembled and read together, fairly complete and detailed case studies will emerge.

Given the principle of selecting examples primarily to elucidate structural phenomena, I made no attempt to limit the selection to the work of specific time periods or movements. In fact, when several equally useful choices existed, samples from different important attitudes or movements were rather arbitrarily selected. This was done to assure that the whole field was broadly covered and that the book would not be limited by seeming to be linked or relevant to only a specific class of sculpture. The collection of works discussed is consequently quite eclectic in nature.

Nonetheless, some apparent bias may appear to exist, since I quickly found that most of the works selected to illustrate specific structural theories did indeed come from one major movement—what has come to be known as "modern" sculpture or its immediate precursors or descendants. Certainly, sections of the text dealing with issues of precise balance found their clearest examples in the work of a few individuals—here Alexander Calder's mobiles provide such obvious examples that they simply cannot be ignored. For parts of the text dealing with sculptures based on repeating geometries, the clearest examples were also found in the modern movement. Plate and shell structures are largely associated with individuals such as David Smith or Anthony Caro. On the other hand, the best examples for an analysis of the human body (viewed as a structure) were found in the works of earlier periods. These trends are not in the least surprising. One reason for the prevalence of examples from modern sculpture and its precursors or descendants is its link with the rise of assemblage as a concept in sculpture. The emergence of the study of structural principles as an abstract field in the seventeenth through nineteenth centuries is also most closely linked with the rise of methods of building and bridge construction ultimately based on the thoughtful assemblage of elemental pieces

(although the principles are no longer restricted to such compositions).

Throughout, the book presents technical material drawing partly on mathematics and physics. I seek to convey basic structural principles in an instructive fashion, but this is not a "structures made simple" book designed for the lowest common denominator of readership understanding. An underlying premise in writing this book is that the audience consists of intelligent people who can deal with subjects at the level of complexity that is demanded by the issues involved and is intellectually satisfying. There have been highly debilitating trends in both the arts and the design professions toward making issues so simple that they become superficial; this is a particular problem in the treatment of technical subject matter. There *is* more to it, and individuals who want more are the targets for this book.

My intent is thus to treat the subject of structures in sculpture in a serious way so that a solid basis for further discussion can be established. A consequence of this decision is the adoption of at least some level of abstract notation for describing the physical principles and behaviors of concern. The use of symbols—and the associated connotation of "mathematics"—to describe physical phenomena do take some getting used to on the part of readers unaccustomed to this way of thinking. While I obviously feel that the value of this approach ultimately makes it worthwhile, the question remains whether the use of symbolic notations could have been avoided completely. After all, Galileo Galilei sought to describe the physical principles underlying the strength and shaping of physical objects via pure discourse (in the form of a master talking to his student) in his *Two New Sciences*. Try reading it. It is a marvelous work by a great mind. Still it becomes evident very quickly that the approach is cumbersome. It can take a student only so far before one realizes the desirability of recourse to symbolic manipulations as a way of concisely expressing very sophisticated and complex phenomena. This conciseness and ability to deal with complexities has always been the value of symbolic notation—a fact that has been amply demonstrated in many other fields. Nonetheless the value of presenting material in a purely qualitative way is equally clear. Given this dilemma, the approach taken in this book is to develop the presentation in parallel layers. Phenomena are described in a purely verbal way in the text. The same phenomena are then typically described in symbolic notation in technical footnotes. The latter often express more than the text descriptions, which are inherently limited by the restrictions of language. Any intelligent reader should be able to get something out of the text, and the more inquisitive will get even more out of the technical footnotes. The mathematics used is no more complex than basic arithmetic at the high school level. Nonetheless, the reader new to this kind of material should not think that any random page in the middle of the book can be easily read and understood without grappling with earlier parts. The theories and analytical principles are essentially cumulative in nature, and build on each other.

Material is also presented in increasingly complex ways, with explanations of particularly important phenomena appearing in different contexts and in different ways. It is probably best for a reader first to skip around through the text, getting familiar with the spirit of the treatment and a sense of the main concepts used (and developing a "need to know" about it), and only then start at the beginning for a more logical way of coming to grips with the material.

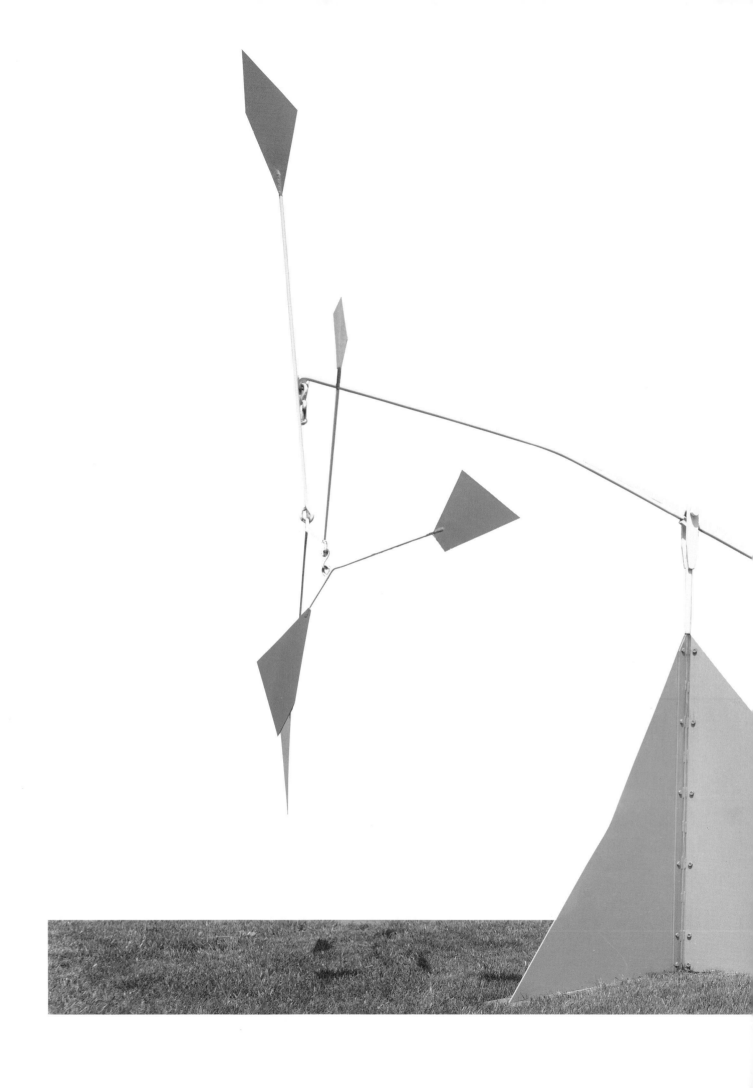

Structure in Sculpture: An Overview

(1)

Alexander Calder,
Mobile-Stabile.

1.0
Mark di Suvero, *Mother Peace.*

1 The Role of Structure in Sculpture

To say that this book is about "structure in sculpture" is easy. Explaining what is meant by this phrase is more difficult. Several writers have argued that if structure exists at all in sculpture it is probably a multilayered concept.[1] One layer is structure as a material construct of how sculpture stands, or its mirroring in specific ideas; another is structure as a part of the historical stylistic continuum of sculpture; another is structure as part of the communicative potential of sculpture. Of these, this book certainly deals with *structure as a material construct*, and, to a much lesser degree, with its mirroring in specific ideas. Certainly this specific conception of structure is more clearly linked with sculpture than with any of the other arts. Any realized piece of sculpture is a viable structure or it would not exist at all, yet the intent of sculpture is almost never purely structural. Intent and physical reality must coexist in a way that sets sculpture apart from painting or other art forms.

On Differing Attitudes

The structural precepts discussed throughout this book are concerned with why sculptures need to be shaped or proportioned in certain ways in order to have integrity as physical objects. The value of looking at sculpture in this light may not be quite obvious. After all, sculptors have been creating sensitive works from the very beginning—and others have been viewing them—without the benefit of any explicit intellectual understanding of forces and related concepts associated with the recent field of learning known as structural analysis and design. In some fields such as architecture, the role played by structure is more intrinsic and its form-generative potential is generally acknowledged. This is not the case in sculpture. But an appreciation of structural principles may well hold potential for improvements in either understanding or shaping sculpture now and in the future. The field of structures is young and its relation to sculptural activities largely unexplored.

It is useful to characterize the role of structure in sculpture in terms of its *generative, prescriptive,* and *prohibitive*

1
The following characterizations of "structure" are adopted from Jack Burnham's *Beyond Modern Sculpture* (New York: George Braziller, 1968).

potentials. That structural precepts may have a positive and broad role in generating forms is a theme that intrinsically underlies the remainder of this book. This fundamental theme will be returned to shortly. The use of structural precepts in a prescriptive sense—that is, to tell a sculptor what to do in a particular situation—will be seen to be neither a real possibility nor of any conceptual interest. This is not now, nor has it ever been in related fields, either a viable or a useful approach (despite the undoubted lingering hope on the part of some that such precepts will help provide "answers" in complex circumstances and ambiguous situations). The use of structural precepts in their prohibitive sense—that is, to tell a sculptor what may not be done—can ultimately contain a measure of truth if the precepts are selected to be used in this way. This view of structural and material concerns is pervasive in the literature but usually appears in a negative light, frequently taken to an extreme. Structural concerns are thus characterized as constraining influences, to be treated dismissively or argued passionately against by sculptors and critics alike.[2] This general attitude is curious and rather naive. Broadly defined material or contextual circumstances have long been part of the field of sculpture. Obvious material examples include limitations imposed by technique. Viewed differently, many of these constraints are in fact opportunities that have provided the essence of many fine sculptural traditions.

Sir Isaac Newton and his successors have simply articulated another contextual dimension that is relevant and that, at a minimum, must simply be respected. Sculptures as forms may well have been shaped to convey some meaning or other intent, but they can exist only in accordance with a largely known set of physical laws that received their first comprehensive postulation by Newton several centuries ago. A sculptor must operate within the context of these laws and may do so knowingly or unknowingly. For physical sculpture, a work not shaped or proportioned such that it exists in a state of equilibrium, for example, will simply fall over or otherwise collapse. It will do this no matter what the desires or artistic intents of the sculptor might be. A sculptor may seem to wish to explicitly contradict these physical laws—Barnett Newman's *Broken Obelisk* (fig. 1.1), discussed in detail in chapter 6, is an interesting case in point —but such works become portrayals of contradictions rather

1.1
Barnett Newman,
Broken Obelisk.

2
Sidney Geist in *Brancusi* (New York: Grossman Publishers, 1968) goes so far as to refer to materials in the work of Brancusi as serving as a simple "negative" principle (p. 159) that comes into play beyond their more or less useful or adaptable roles, which he did argue were treated feelingly.

than actual contradictions. Indeed, they may derive their positive essence from this condition (Newman's work is a good example). In any case, some intellectual understanding of the governing constraints associated with physical laws might be useful in both understanding and assessing such works, as well as in the more direct act of shaping them.

Returning to the positive generative potential of structural precepts, the fundamental or universal character of many of the principles discussed in this book has led many sculptors to use them—more or less consciously—as a direct inspiration for a work or more indirectly as a source of imagery. Obvious examples are provided in Alexander Calder's mobiles, which are clear and literal explorations of the concept of balance, one of the most important of all of the concepts discussed in this book. Richard Serra's *House of Cards (One Ton Prop)* (fig. 8.6) eloquently explores the concept of relational stability, although its ultimate intentions may lie elsewhere. Influences can be less direct as well. One such influence comes from reexamining strong forms originally developed for other uses. The basic principles discussed in this book are of general applicability to *any* physical form. As such they have been the basis for the shaping of physical forms in many different fields of endeavor, e.g., bridge design, aircraft design, building design. Some of these structural forms have been powerful sources of imagery in the works of many sculptors. Siah Armajani's reinterpretation of bridge forms is an obvious example, but works like *Midday* by Anthony Caro (fig. 9.8) also come close to the forms of structural design.

Despite these examples, I will argue more or less explicitly that sculptors have not yet fully explored the idea of structure as a theory of material placement in space, but have adopted only its imagery. In making this point, one must tread carefully. After all, thoughtful writers such as Jack Burnham have noted that "except for the matter of stability, structure is not the province of sculpture. While it may flirt with structural theory, sculpture becomes too literal and loses its validity once it merely interprets structure."[3] While such cautions are well taken, it is not at all obvious that the role of structure in sculpture is well enough understood for any well-reasoned position to be taken on its potential as a source of reference. Burnham did go on to argue that a more powerful attitude toward form-making would derive from an understanding of underlying scientific attitudes and

theories. This book seeks to provide a more rigorous basis for an inquiry into this point.

All in all, however, the fundamental view underlying this book is that the most powerful generative potential lies neither with literal explorations of structural principles (and certainly not with prescriptive approaches) nor with the use of structure as imagery, but with the complete assimilation of structural and material precepts in the minds and hands of a sculptor. At this higher level, they can inform the shaping of any object in a nonliteral and open way. In order to get to this level of assimilation, however, it is both useful and necessary first to treat the material didactically.

Structure versus Technique

To avoid a possible source of confusion, some terminology should be clarified at this point. Words like "technique," "technology," "structural," or occasionally even "scientific" are often used almost interchangeably in much of the available literature. But they really imply quite different perspectives. In this book, the term *technique* will be used in a limited sense in reference to the thoughtful use of processes and materials in making a sculpture, and not in the broader sense that includes informing intellectual ideas and precepts. A metal sculpture, for example, may be created as a whole unit by casting molten metal into a mold, or it may be assembled from discrete pieces by welding. Differences in the final form of an object due to different techniques may be quite radical, or essentially similar forms may be made using quite different processes. Normally the choice of *technique* used to make something creates both opportunities and constraints for the sculptor in the characteristics of the resulting form and its tactile qualities. Consequently, concern with technique has long been explicit in the field of sculpture (as the abundance of literature surrounding the topic surely confirms).

Structural concerns are quite different in nature from concerns of process-oriented technique. The theory of structures deals with the shaping of forms to meet certain objectives typically relating to the strength, stiffness, and stability of a physical object. Thus the theories presented here will not be explicitly concerned with how forms are actually produced or the implications of production processes, but rather with how forms and materials can achieve the required strength and stiffness—no matter what technique is used to make these forms.

Nonetheless there can be interdependences between technique and structure that are of real interest and are implicit in many stimulating works. Some sculptures have shapes that necessarily imply the use of certain materials because of their structural properties, and the use of these materials in turn implies certain production processes with their attendant implications of form and tactile quality. Newman's *Broken Obelisk* is inconceivable in a material such as stone, although it deliberately harks back to this primeval material. Its form is entirely dependent on the structural properties of steel and the associated fabrication process of welding. These interdependences are rich with form-generative possibilities.

On a broad level, the term *technology* is often used to describe the cognitive precepts and bodies of knowledge that are concerned both with process and with form, reflecting the interdependence of technique and structure.

The Importance of Scale, Process, and Communication Issues

This book explores the form of sculptures in a general way. The principles developed will be applicable to any work at any scale. Nonetheless, the issue of scale will constantly reemerge as pivotal. Simply put, structural concerns in small-scale works are invariably less of an issue than in large-scale works. The reasons for this hinge on relationships between the shape and absolute dimensions of an object, its related mass, and the forces and deformations developed within it. It will be seen that simple linear increases in the dimensions of an object are accompanied by far more rapid (or geometric) increases in the mass of the object and in accompanying forces and deformations. The bigger an object gets, the more influential on form become structural issues.[4]

The implications of these scale relationships are enormous vis-à-vis the act of proportioning physical objects. There are also other implications for the processes by which objects are designed and made. Small-scale works can result from the will and acts of single individuals. Structural concerns may or may not play an influential role, depending

3
Burnham, *Beyond Modern Sculpture*. Curiously, he seems then to accept kineticism and all sorts of other things with far briefer theoretical traditions as acceptable foundations.

4
This is a well-known phenomenon beautifully explored in D'Arcy Thompson's *On Growth and Form*, which asks for example why poodles have different proportions from elephants.

on the values and intents of the sculptor. The situation becomes quite different in really large-scale works. There is little doubt that structural considerations find their most explicit applications in the design of large-scale sculptures, especially those placed outdoors or those that move in some way. The design and placement of large-scale sculptures normally require close cooperation among sculptors, engineers, and public officials, since they often pose significant technical design and installation problems. Public authorities, such as building code officials, are in turn charged with assuring that the final works are indeed safe and do not pose any hazards to the public. The sculptor is legally required to design within the guidelines (often in the form of constraints such as are found in building codes) imposed by such authorities. These are difficult but important issues. Obviously situations of this type could easily compromise the artistic integrity of a work. On the other hand, the informed interaction among sculptors and others—professional architects and engineers, craftspersons and contractors—could well result in works that might positively transcend what any single individual might accomplish.

These issues are difficult to appreciate in the abstract. An example of how a complex and moderately large-scale sculpture came into being—Susumu Shingu's *Echo of the Waves* in Boston (fig. 1.2)—might prove useful. In 1976, the firm Cambridge Seven Architects designed a public plaza extending their design for the New England Aquarium of about twelve years before. In addition to serving over one million aquarium visitors a year, the plaza itself had become an important focus for public activity on the downtown waterfront. A main component of the design was a monumental piece of sculpture that was meant to move in response to the wind. With a full height of 65 feet, the sculpture would be visible from a nearby expressway and become an important landmark in Boston. Shingu designed *Echo of the Waves* for this setting. The sculpture is made of steel and fiberglass with a red enamel finish; its upper parts move in the wind. It is a highly complex sculpture that came about only after a long and difficult process involving at least eleven different fundamental participants, ranging from the client to the sculptor but including architects, engineers, fabricators, and others (see appendix 1).

The project was initiated as a gift to the Aquarium and the City of Boston by a private donor. The New England Aquarium contracted the architects to coordinate fabrication and installation. Representatives of the Aquarium attended design reviews to advise on the use of the plaza, monitored a budget allotted to the architects, and managed public relations from publicizing the effort as a major ongoing art work to opening ceremonies. The architects devised the spatial concept for the plaza and developed the idea to acquire a work by Shingu. Shingu was already well known for his work in Japan on wind-powered sculpture; the Aquarium piece was to be his first work in the United States. He developed a proposal for the piece and initially provided his own working drawings. The architects subsequently coordinated and supervised all aspects of the development, fabrication, and installation of the work, including engaging engineering consultants, managing the review process (including controlling costs and obtaining permits from the zoning department, building department, engineering department, and arts council), and arranging for fabrication and installation.

A consulting engineering firm engaged by the architect was initially given responsibility to review the original Shingu working drawings of the mast and T arm in particular, but found that the proposed design for the structure did not meet American building code standards for safety. Subsequently their duties expanded to designing several alternatives for the wind vanes. Their design and analyses showed that steel was both costly and not necessarily the best material for the sculpture.

For the sheathing, design criteria demanded that all materials and components have long-term failure-free operation with little maintenance or replacement. Translucency, abrasion resistance, and impact resistance were also considered important. The materials were not to discolor or structurally degrade due to ultraviolet light, salt water, local temperature variations, or other known environmental conditions. For maintenance reasons, integral rather than applied colors were preferred. For structural safety, notch sensitivity characteristics of the material were considered important. The materials were also to be cold-formable over a steel frame. The architects investigated several alternatives including a fiberglass cloth–teflon laminate used in microwave and aerospace design, an acrylic used in airplane windows, and a two-layered polycarbonate sheeting used in greenhouses. These were ruled out due to unsuitable

1.2
Susumu Shingu, *Echo of
the Waves.*

material properties. Ultimately, a fiber-reinforced plastic was chosen for the sheathing (the mast remained in steel). The material was manufactured for a roof and wall system—a stressed skin panel of sheet material bonded to an aluminum subframe and available in the approximate dimensions required. The company supplying the product, however, did not have the translucent material in stock and an opaque material was eventually used instead. Critical technical advice in specifying mock-ups of fiberglass skins, cost estimates, and connections in fiber-reinforced plastic were provided by yet another firm with expertise in composite materials and experience in the field of fluid dynamics as applied to windmill blades and boat hulls.

The engineering consultants also recommended additional studies on potentially destructive dynamic wind effects by a firm specializing in engineering research. This firm investigated special effects of wind loading and recommended many design changes, including the critical decision to make all parts of the upper structure rotate as a way of stabilizing it under certain wind conditions.[5] The engineering research firm also prepared computer analyses and structural drawings for the fabricators. Later they devised the application of strain gauges to the sculpture to verify assumptions about the dynamic loading. A specialist was engaged to address problems of bearings and mechanisms. The specialist designed all machining and bearings for the sculpture, including layout drawings of the steel structure, construction documents for the machining, and steel detailing for the bearings. He was responsible for the preliminary review of the entire project and was originally meant to be in charge of coordinating the fabrication, but was unable to assume this role due to liabilities involved.

By a bidding process, a firm was selected to be responsible for construction of the sculpture, including the finishing of components. The firm possessed an extensive background that included manufacturing Corvette auto bodies. At times design changes were proposed to simplify manufacturing, for example making an edge of the large wing of the sculpture a continuous curve rather than a series of segments. These proposals were always discussed with Shingu for final decisions. Three other organizations were also engaged—site contractors, site pavers, and riggers. The sculpture was successfully installed in 1983.

Throughout this involved process, the design of the sculpture underwent considerable change in material and detailing, although the concept remained essentially the same. The question naturally arises as to the sculptor's role in this process. The sculptor's role varied from simply approving design decisions that were already carefully thought out to consultation and direction. In some cases, he was asked for choice of paint samples or approval of a modification of a structural configuration; in others, he sent models or sketches to show how he wanted a piece resolved or to show his understanding of a change.

This particular example is not necessarily indicative of all sculptor/architect/engineer relationships, since the geographical separation of the participants clearly affected how the project proceeded. Different patterns of relationships, for example, would be seen in the cooperation among sculptors Siah Armajani and Scott Burton and architect Cesar Pelli in the work for the plaza on the North Cove in New York City; or in the execution of several of Richard Serra's larger works. But *Echo of the Waves* illustrates how complex bringing a large-scale project to fruition can actually be.

The need for good communication is obvious in this example. The positive benefits of engineers, architects, or public officials understanding what sculptors are seeking to achieve is clear. Sculptors unwilling or unable to understand the kind of framework in which they must act (or be able to adequately convey their intents to others) may find their works compromised by the dictates of others. That the responsibility for communication lies with all parties is obvious, but it is nonetheless always the sculptor with the primary vested interest in getting the work implemented. The obvious implication is that it might well be useful for sculptors to be able to meet these other individuals on their own ground and in their own language as a way of getting their works implemented. Many of the precepts discussed in this book are directed toward providing such a basis for communication.

1.3
Sol LeWitt, *Five Modular Units*.

5
The technical dimensions of this
decision are discussed in detail
in chapter 7. The engineering
research firm's evaluations were
also instrumental in the decision
to change the skin material
from steel to fiber-reinforced
plastic.

2 The Language of Structures

2.0
Christo, *Valley Curtain.*

Terms of Reference

One of the primary difficulties in beginning any discussion of sculptures from a structural perspective is simply that of settling on a language of communication. What words are used to describe forms from a structural point of view? What classifications exist? These are not inconsequential issues, for on the one hand a language of communication stems from a certain experiential base and related set of values, and on the other hand the language adopted affects perceptions of the world and how individuals act within it (or, in the case of sculpture, create forms within it). Since the field of sculptures has never really had a tradition of describing its forms from a structural perspective, there is no inherent experiential basis to draw upon and thus no special language exists.

The languages that do exist to describe structural forms invariably come from other disciplines that have long been preoccupied with the issue of structure in relation to the form of an object. The related fields of architecture and engineering provide ready examples; the languages they have developed for describing structural forms are very precise and detailed. Here there are words like *beam, column, truss, dome,* and the like, words summoning up specific images of structural elements that find widespread use as constituent parts of larger structural assemblies in both architecture and engineering. When used together to form a larger whole, these individual elements create artifacts such as bridges or building structures. As with any language, individual elements can also be arranged in different syntactical ways to convey meanings or intents that go beyond simple description. Indeed, it is exactly these characteristics that give these descriptions of form their value in architecture. But this same value makes them less than appropriate for describing sculptural forms from a structural perspective. The historical connotations and architectural and engineering associations of words like *beam* or *column* are simply overwhelming.

Fields other than architecture and engineering have also dealt with structure and its descriptions, but in a different way. A traditional and still valuable way of coming to understand the issue of structure is through a study of the living forms. It is common to think, for example, of the skeleton that supports our own bodies as an exemplar of what constitutes a "structure." Indeed, the imagery of the skeleton has even been transferred to other fields such as architecture, where descriptions typified by the term "skeleton frame" are often used to describe the structures of objects such as early skyscrapers. This association of "skeletons" with "structures" is quite curious. It is obvious from seeing real human and animal skeletons propped up in one way or another that a skeleton alone cannot support itself, much less anything else. A skeleton from a living form is hardly a true structure in its own right.

Drawings by Leonardo da Vinci give a glimpse of the true reality of the human structure, which is one of the most marvelous and complex structures that we can ever hope to encounter (fig. 2.2). As the drawings suggest, the bones of a skeleton are only one component of the structure of a human body. Ligaments, muscles, and other body elements are equally important in its functioning and support. But even defining the structure as a set of bones, ligaments, and muscles is not enough. We must further specify a precise spatial *arrangement* and set of relations or connections among these elements before the idea of a structure can be crystallized. The importance of the spatial arrangements of the components of an object to its holistic functioning as a structure is conceptually obvious. What is much less obvious is a precise definition of what arrangements actually make viable structural forms and what arrangements do not; this subject will occupy much of the remainder of this book.

There are many different *types* of relations or connections possible. One might get an idea of the possibilities by looking at how elements of a body join to one another, and at the types of movements (rotations or translations) that each type of joint allows. The shoulder and hip joints are ball and socket joints that allow almost complete rotational freedom. Much more restricted in rotational freedom are simple hinge joints, such as the elbow joint that connects the humerus and the ulna, or the first and second joints of the phalanges in the hand. Other more complicated joints allowing other types of movements exist as well. There are

2.1
The classical language of architectural elements is reflected in Malcolm Cochran's *Dream of Arcadia,* made of the salvaged remains of a building.

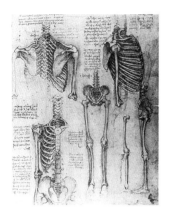

The human skeleton

Shoulder and arms

2.2
The structure of the human body, from the notebooks of Leonardo da Vinci.

gliding joints, for example, between the carpal bones of the wrist and between the tarsal bones of the ankle; during movement the surfaces simply slide across each other. The resulting assembly of jointed bones forms part of an extremely complex kinematic chain of *rigid* elements (bones) in which certain movements are possible, others not. As a simple kinematic chain the skeleton is not self-supporting, nor can it provide the motive power for actual movement. The latter functions are provided by muscles and ligaments, elements that are primarily *flexible* in character. Some muscles expand or contract to provide motive power, while other elements provide simple ties or linkages. Fewer attached muscles or ligaments are needed to control the movements of two members connected by a simple hinged joint than are needed for those connected by a ball and socket. The pattern of muscles and ligaments within a body must have an arrangement in space that is related to the spatial arrangement of the bones in the skeleton *and* to the linked spatial arrangement of the different types of joints connecting individual bones. The final assembly is at last something that can be called a structure.

The specific type of structure found in the human body and other vertebrate forms stands in unique contrast to types found in many other living forms, particularly in that it is primarily internal in character. The overall body type is characterized, in very general terms, as having a soft exterior with all rigid elements internal to the overall form. The rigid part of the structure (the skeleton) and allied muscles and ligaments thus informs and gives shape to the exterior, but does not directly create it. Other nonstructural elements (e.g., the stomach) also inform the shape of the exterior. In many other living forms, the role of the structural support system in giving shape to the exterior is much more direct. The crustaceans—lobsters, crabs, etc.—provide perhaps the best examples of living forms that have *exoskeletons*, typically in the form of hard shells. The hard shell houses the soft body components. Typically these exoskeletons come in the form of surfaces, as opposed to the interior network of elements forming the structure of a human body (many of which are linear in character). These surface-forming structures serve a much different role in the living organism than do the interior framed structure of the human body and have evolved in completely different force environments—such as under the sea.

Where does this discussion of the structure of living forms lead with respect to definitions of structure? Are there any common principles or ideas that are discipline-independent, so that something more general may be said about the idea of structure in connection with sculpture and other fields? One central idea is that a structure may exist as a holistic object (the exoskeleton of a crab), or, alternatively, as connected component elements (bones, muscles, and ligaments in the human body, or beams, columns, and trusses in a building). In the latter case, particularly, these components must be arranged in special spatial order for the group of elements to form a structure. A second idea is the importance of the way these elements are connected or related one to another. Like the human body, building construction includes various specific types of joints (fixed joints, pinned joints, rollers, etc.).

Other useful comparisons can be made. There are indeed some general similarities between the hard shell of a crustacean such as a crab and a dome of the type that sits atop many great buildings, such as the Pantheon in Rome. Likewise the cross sections of some bones bear a startling resemblance to the cross sections of the columns in some buildings. Ligaments are seemingly akin to the cables found in many bridges. Looking more closely at the nature of the forces that are felt within elements of this type, one finds even closer relationships. Ligaments and cables are both subjected to forces that tend to pull the elements apart (tension forces), while columns and some bones are subjected to forces that compress them. When the forces acting on them are similar, the physical nature of the elements also tends to be similar. While analogies of this type can easily be carried too far, some surprising commonalities do seem to exist despite the different vocabularies used to describe them.

One might well expect that such commonalities might find some expression in sculpture as well. Since a language is needed before we can proceed, an informal one will be adopted that on the one hand reflects principles and commonalities of the type noted, and on the other hand freely adopts descriptive words and phrases from other disciplines as needed.

Simple Classifications

The discussion in the last section suggests several possible bases for a language for dealing with structure in sculpture. One basis is a description of a sculpture's kinetic state. A second is some sort of system of geometric description of the shape of the form and the distribution of its mass. A third is a consideration of the intrinsic qualities of the materials of which forms are made. A fourth basis is common precepts and principles that have a structural connotation. As will be seen, a combination of these ideas seems most useful for the purposes of this book. Thus, descriptors might evolve such as "linear rigid forms that balance and move in space."

The first basis addresses the intended kinetic state of a sculpture and is an obvious basis for classification. Does the sculpture have a static or a dynamic quality, is it intended to remain at rest or to move? Historically most sculpture has been static (in the mechanical sense). Recently more and more sculptures have had parts that are intended to move or to reflect in some other way ideas of time and motion. Driving forces come either from natural sources (wind), or from created sources (mechanical, electrical, chemical, etc.). Motions may be simple rotations, complex vibrations, or even more abstract representations of time and motion.

The second basis deals with the general geometry and mass distribution of the work. A classic geometric approach is elusive at best for describing whole sculptures, given the wide range of forms they can assume and the aggregated nature of many works. Still, it can be useful, particularly in describing shapes of constituent elements of larger works. A general distinction between line-forming and surface-forming shapes, for example, is often appropriate. These two main divisions can be further categorized into linear and curved shapes for line-forming structures, and into planar, singly curved, and doubly curved shapes for surface-forming structures. Common and precise geometrical descriptors (spheres, cones, etc.) are sometimes useful. Mass distribution is usually directly associated with the overall geometry of an object but is occasionally more subtle. Certainly distinctions between hollow and solid volumes are important.

For the third basis, concerned with the character of materials, a very general but useful distinction can be made with reference to a material's rigidity or flexibility. A flexible structure, such as a chain, a draped cable, or a ligament, typically undergoes a shape change with each change in the external loading condition present. By contrast, a rigid structure such as a bone or a beam does not undergo appreciable changes in shape with changes in the external loading condition. The specific materials used—steel, bronze—can also be a basis for classification.

The fourth of our bases addresses broad principles that have a structural connotation, such as the principles of balance and of triangulation. This approach often interrelates with the purely geometrical approach noted above, but more is implied. A geometry that can be easily described may not easily translate into a viable structure. It is in this connection that concepts like balance and triangulation become important, as do the types of connections between elements. The phrase "frame action," for example, which will be encountered later, generally refers to a form of stability imparted by the use of special joint connectivity wherein adjacent members are rigidly affixed to one another.

At a more discrete level, the nature of the force state present in an element might also be used as a basis for description (e.g., a member in tension, compression, or bending). This is typically appropriate only for discrete constituent parts of larger assemblies.

These bases for thinking about the physical nature of objects may not be completely comprehensive or precise, but together they are useful in providing a fairly simple way of describing many structures. Thus surface-forming structures may be planar, singly curved, or doubly curved, and made of either rigid or flexible materials. The dome of the Hagia Sophia in Istanbul and the exoskeleton shell remains of a sea animal might both be thought of as structures made of rigid materials that are surface-forming in character, in this case doubly curved convex surfaces. Analogous structures can be found in the field of sculpture. *Pool Balls* by Claes Oldenburg, for example, can be similarly described (fig. 2.3).

An airship and the membrane of the embryo of a common squid can also be thought of as similarly surface-forming in character, but in this case composed of flexible materials. *Air Package* by Christo is similarly made of flexible materials shaped into a doubly curved surface.

Rigid or flexible line-forming members may be used individually or arranged into some larger pattern. Larger config-

urations are usually referred to as *frameworks*. A specific way of arranging these members is to triangulate them. The triangulation imparts great strength and stiffness to the overall configuration. In subsequent chapters the act of arranging individual elements into triangulated patterns will be found to be one of the most fundamental ways of making a sculpture stable under virtually any type of loading condition. Such arrangements are evident in many diverse places, such as internally within the bones of a common pigeon or in enormous supporting structures in architecture. Similar arrangements appear in sculpture as well. Triangulated rigid elements appear in Siah Armajani's *Skyway Bridge*. Other framework patterns not based on triangles are used as well. Sometimes these patterns require special joint connections to ensure their stability, in which case they are often called *rigid frameworks*.

Individual curved line-forming members that are rigid include the arch forms, while their flexible counterparts include suspended cables of the type exemplified in Christo's *Valley Curtain* (see chapter 10). Flexible line-forming elements also can be aggregated to form larger surface forms. Alternatively, net structures that are surface-forming may be made of cable or rope elements.

In specific fields, such as architecture or engineering, component names are often assigned on the basis of a combination of rigidity and geometrical characteristics. A *beam*, for example, is commonly thought of as a rigid linear element that spans horizontally. But these disciplines also consider the type of force state present in the element. A beam, for example, is subjected to a bowing or bending tendency by the loads it carries. Works by Richard Serra, David Smith, and others frequently employ elements of this type. A *column* is a rigid linear element that is commonly thought of as transmitting compressive forces only. Kenneth Snelson's *X Column* (fig. 9.6) provides an example of an analogous form in sculpture. It is especially interesting in that the overall form (rigid under vertical applied loads) is actually made up of shorter members, many of which are flexible cables. Several subcategories of the more general class of framework structures have also become so common that they have assumed their own names. In architecture and engineering, for example, patterns of triangulated elements are widely used and are referred to as *trusses*.

Planar forms having rectilinear arrangements are often called *frame* structures. *Geodesic* structures have particular

Rigid Frameworks

Tree branch

Rigid steel connection

Sol LeWitt, *Five Modular Units*

Triangulated Frameworks

Pigeon bone (wing)

Kallman and McKinnell, Phillips Exeter Academy

Siah Armajani, *Skyway Bridge*

  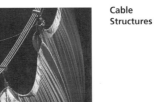

Rigid Surface Structures

Polinices duplicatus

Hagia Sophia, Istanbul

Claes Oldenburg, *Pool Balls*

Rigid Structures

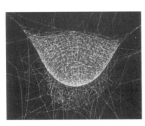 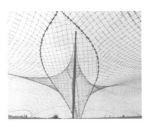  

Cable Structures

Web of *Zygiella x-notata*

Golden Gate Bridge, San Francisco

Christo, *Valley Curtain*

 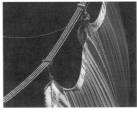 

Stretched–Net Structures

Prolinyphia marginate snare

Frei Otto, net structure

Eva Hesse, *Vertiginous Detour*

Flexible Structures

Membrane Structures

Embryos of the squid

U.S. Navy blimp

Christo, *Air Package*

2.3
Common types of rigid and flexible structures.

geometries and are made by using particular geometric arrangements of members of a particular type (compressive struts and tension cables). *Tensegrity* structures use both compressive struts and tension cables, but are additionally arranged so that the compressive struts do not touch one another while the tension elements are continuous. *Needle Tower* by Kenneth Snelson is an exploration of this type of structure (fig. 2.4).

Assigning specific names like beam, column, or truss may serve the needs of the architectural and engineering disciplines very well, but the full vocabulary developed for these fields does not seem particularly useful in connection with sculpture. Rather, I will adopt a more general language that uses terms like "triangulated patterns." Some words and names are valuable, others are not. What is needed will be used. More important than the names, which may describe forms that are visually different, are some pervasive concepts that apply to the notion of structure in any field. These concepts will be the focus of later chapters.

Connections: Movements and Restraints

The language of structures involves specific terms that describe how parts of a sculpture are attached either to one another or to the ground. The idea of movement is crucial to an understanding of connection types. In structural terms, connections either allow or restrain certain types of movements between attached members. The function of a connection, for example, might be to completely affix one member to another so that relative movements are impossible between them; or it might be to connect one member to another in a way that allows certain specified linear or rotational movements to occur. The choice of which type to use depends on the larger structural concept. In many structures, specified movements are highly desirable. The human body provides many good examples. A shoulder joint allows rotations of several different kinds to occur between a human's arm and body. In many other cases, however, completely restraining movements is desirable. A flagpole would simply topple over if the base connection did not prevent the flagpole from rotating about its foundation. Interchanging connection types in these two examples would be disastrous for both structures.

Movements are typically described as either *translational* or *rotational*. A linear movement in a particular direction, such as sliding, is translational. A spinning or twirling about some axis is a rotational movement. One way of characterizing connection types is in relation to the specific translational or rotational movements they either allow or restrain. Several primary attachment types can be identified: *fixed* or rigid connections completely prevent either rotational or translational movements from developing; *pinned* or axle-like connections allow attached members to rotate around an axis or a point (but do not allow translational movements); and *sliding* or roller connections allow some sort of translational movement in one direction but not in others and typically allow rotations to occur as well. Other more complex types exist as well. The connection at the base of a flagpole would be described as a fixed connection, while the elbow joint is a good example of a pinned connection. Sliding joints are often found in the form of expansion joints in long bridges, which allow temperature expansions and contractions to occur freely.

Shingu's *Gift of the Wind* (fig. 2.5) illustrates several common connections. The connection between the upper assembly and the lower vertical support allows the upper structure to rotate freely in the horizontal plane, and is thus a pinned connection. This particular pinned connection allows rotations to occur only about one axis; there are other types of pinned connections—notably the ball and socket—that allow rotations to occur about more than one axis. Using a ball and socket joint here, however, would result in the upper complex tilting unpredictably and often undesirably. A fully fixed connection is evident at the base of the work.

A more rigorous way of looking at connection types is to explore how many movement possibilities (commonly called *degrees of freedom*) are allowed by a particular connection. All possible movements can be described in terms of three orthogonal axes (corresponding to the typical *x*, *y*, and *z* reference axes of geometry). Any linear movement can be described in terms of translations along these axes. Any revolution or rotation can be described in terms of rotations about these same axes. Together, these movement possibilities provide a total of six degrees of freedom. The connection at the top of the vertical shaft in Shingu's *Gift of the Wind* has one degree of freedom, since the joint allows

2.4
Kenneth Snelson, *Needle Tower.*

2.5
Common types of connections, illustrated in Shingu's *Gift of the Wind.* Pinned connections allow rotational movements to occur; rigid or fixed connections prevent any movements from occurring between adjacent members. In the case of *Gift of the Wind,* the fixed base connection prevents the whole structure from overturning, while the pinned joints allow free rotations to occur.

Susumu Shingu, *Gift of the Wind*

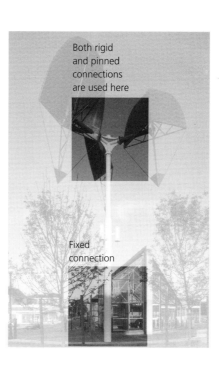

Both rigid and pinned connections are used here

Fixed connection

The upper assembly rotates around the central shaft, while the sails rotate around the projecting arms.

The whole top assembly rotates around the central shaft

See Chapter 7 for a further discussion of *Gift of the Wind*

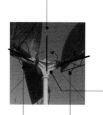

The sails rotate around horizontal shafts

Rigid joint: steel brace maintains a fixed angle between vertical and horizontal parts of the rotating shaft

Fixed connection completely prevents any rotations between the base of the shaft and the foundation and stabilizes the sculpture

Pinned connections allow rotations to occur. The rigid or fixed connections prevent elements from rotating with respect to one another.

rotations to occur around one axis only, and all translational movements are restrained. The fixed base connection has no degrees of freedom since all movements are restrained.

An element that could be moved in any direction or rotated about any axis would have six degrees of freedom. There are only very few examples of connections that actually have six degrees of freedom. Perhaps the cow's jaw is as close as anything. This assembly allows an incredible diversity in translatory and rotational movements, all the better to chew the cud. There are many implications of the number and nature of degrees of freedom present in a connection. Having too many pinned connections, for example, might result in a structure with so many rotational possibilities that it would be inherently unstable and unable to support itself, much less an applied load. Four simple rigid members arranged in a square and connected at endpoints with pinned joints is an obvious example. On the other hand, three simple members arranged in a triangular form with pinned joints (as found in many common truss bridges) is a stable configuration. It is not the nature of the joints alone that determines whether a structural configuration is stable or not.

The careful placement of joints allowing many forms of movement can enable the resulting structure to have great kinematic flexibility. The kinematic virtuosity of the human body is unthinkable without the presence of many different types of joints that allow many different types of movements. The skeleton is an incredible complex of rigid members connected at their ends by a variety of different joint types, the whole complex rendered a viable structure by the attached tendons and muscles. The hip and shoulder joints are forms of ball and socket connections. An index finger joint, by contrast, is a form of simpler pinned joint that allows rotations about only one axis. The different types of joint must be very carefully arranged so that needed movement possibilities can indeed be obtained. Evolution has taken care of this for us in our bodies. In designed structures, kinematic possibilities must be carefully thought through not only to assure that desired or expected movements occur, but also to assure that the configuration is not inadvertently made structurally unstable.

2.6
Christo, *Running Fence.*

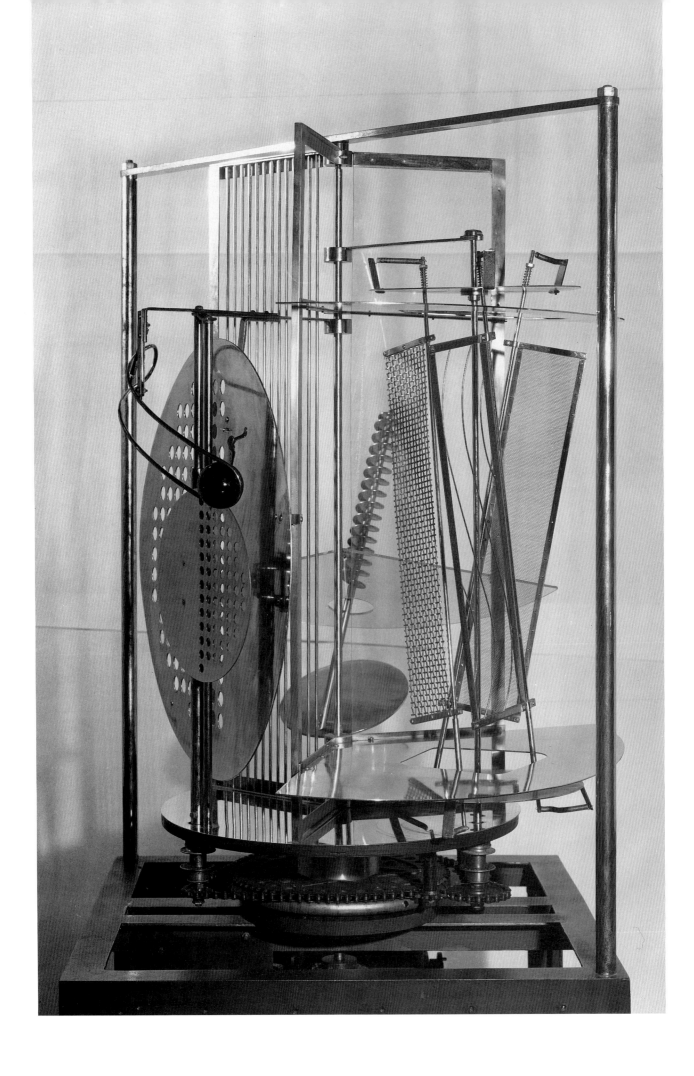

3 Phenomena and Issues

Types of Structural Failure

László Moholy-Nagy's *Light Space Modulator* (fig. 3.1) was first shown in Paris in 1930. This was never intended to be a work of structure but rather a pioneering exploration of light and motion machines, and as such it set a precedent for many subsequent mechanized kinetic sculptures. Moholy-Nagy apparently regarded the sculpture as both a constructivist sculpture in its own right and a sculpture dealing with light in motion. Reflections on the ever-changing configuration rotated by an electrical motor caused what he called an "architecture of light." What makes a brief examination of this work relevant to this text is that after its first showing in 1930, the appearance of the sculpture underwent a significant change. The metal frame that is now a prominent part of the work was added around 1937 to correct a technical problem.

   The sculpture was at the time of its construction, and remains, a fragile structure. Given its mechanical complexity, it was not unreasonably prone to mechanical failure. The machine was designed and built by Moholy-Nagy with the aid of Otto Ball, a skilled mechanic, and Istvan Sebok, a young architect working in Walter Gropius's Berlin office and the theater department of the AEG (the large German electrical company). The metal frame was almost certainly added to stabilize the cantilevered central vertical shaft. The eccentric motions of the moving parts undoubtedly produced off-balance forces that eventually led to various kinds of wobbling and bending in this critical shaft, which in turn would tend to cause the moving parts to malfunction. The external structure that was added to stabilize the shaft is what is commonly called a rigid frame. The frame itself gains its stability from the rigid connections that were devised to connect the verticals to the base structure and to the horizontal crosspiece. (Connections of this type give frame structures their rigidity and ability to resist laterally acting forces, preventing the angular changes between horizontal and vertical pieces that would otherwise produce lateral racking and severe deformations in such structures.) This

3.0
László Moholy-Nagy, *Light Space Modulator.*

frame structure in turn provides a point of support for the central shaft, transforming it from a problematic cantilever structure, naturally prone to the development of large deflections at its free end, to a far more rigid structural element supported at either end. While some deformations can still occur in the shaft due to off-balance loadings, they are quite small in comparison to those that would be developed in a cantilevered element. The frame structure is still present on the sculpture, which is now housed in the Busch-Reisinger Museum at Harvard University. The sculpture has been renovated on several occasions.

The example of *Light Space Modulator* illustrates how seemingly viable sculptures can fail to provide an adequate level of structural integrity or strength. It also illustrates how far more visually complex forms can be broadly characterized in simpler terms (the original cantilevered central shaft of *Light Space Modulator*); and how the addition of a simple new element may transform the whole sculpture into a radically different type (with the addition of the frame, the central shaft is no longer cantilevered). Finally, it reminds us that structural considerations are not limited to obvious form considerations, or even fairly obvious force considerations, but also involve many subtle and complex phenomena dealing with deformations of elemental parts of a work and their consequent effect on the whole work.

An understanding of how a whole sculpture or any of its elemental parts can fail can yield valuable insights into how to prevent this.[1] There are several fundamental ways in which failure can occur. A sculpture can overturn, collapse, deform, or break apart (fig. 3.2). The forces causing overturning or collapse can come from the environment (e.g., wind) or from the self-weight of the form itself. These same loadings also produce internal forces that stress the material used and may cause it to fail or deform. The potential consequences of failure may be minor—on the order of nuisance issues—or disastrous and even life-threatening if the sculpture is large. Problems can become evident immediately during the construction of the sculpture, or can be an indirect consequence of some longer-term phenomenon, such as corrosion in metals, that may cause members to slowly weaken and eventually fail.

Overturning, Sliding, Twisting

One general set of concerns deals with the overall stability of a work. As a whole unit, a sculpture might overturn, slide, or twist about its base when subjected to forces (such as wind) that act in the horizontal direction. Sculptures that are relatively tall with respect to their bases are particularly sensitive to overturning effects caused by wind forces. The taller and broader the upper portions of a sculpture, the greater are the overturning effects caused by wind forces. Forces induced by earthquakes tend to cause similar overturning or sliding actions, but their magnitudes are more critically dependent on the weight of the structure (the heavier the structure, the higher are the earthquake forces induced in it).

Overturning need not be caused only by horizontally acting forces. A work might simply be out of balance under its own self-weight and overturn. In large outdoor sculptures, this kind of overturning can be induced by uneven snow loads.

The use of heavy base pedestals is a traditional way to prevent overturning or sliding. In large sculptures, a heavy "pedestal" can be buried in the ground in the form of a concrete footing. Various forms of tie-downs affixing the base of a sculpture to the ground serve similar stability functions (occasionally large sculptures are tied to piles driven into the ground). Broadly increasing the width of the sculpture at its base is another technique particularly useful for preventing overturning. Projections, or "keys" that extend downward into the ground from the base, are excellent for preventing sliding.

Relational Stability

Another set of concerns is particularly relevant to sculptures made up of discrete pieces. If the parts of a sculpture are not properly arranged in space or interconnected, a whole assembly can inadvertently collapse. Collapses of this type invariably involve large relative movements within the structure itself, with large angular changes between adjacent members.

Simply because an assembly looks stable in a drawing does not mean the real artifact is necessarily so. In some special cases, assemblies might be internally stable under one loading condition and unstable under another. An assembly might stand up under its own self-weight but fall

3.1
Moholy-Nagy's *Light Space Modulator* was originally built without the surrounding frame and was prone to mechanical failure. The added frame stabilized the center shaft and improved the functioning of the piece.

The original sculpture did not have the external frame. During operation, the wobbling of the central shaft caused the mechanism to malfunction (deformations shown are conjectural).

The surrounding rigid frame structure was added later to stabilize the top of the central shaft and prevent its wobbling.

Rigid connection at top of frame

Rigid connection at bottom of frame

1
The term "inherent vice" is often used by conservators to describe intrinsically faulty design or fabrication, including the use of incompatible materials, in the original construction of an art object. Such features lead to later deterioration or faulty performance of the object even in the absence of unusual external damaging forces or actions. Note that this formulation as stated includes design and fabrication issues that go beyond issues related exclusively to material properties.

over (or rack) when subject to a mild wind force. In general, horizontally acting wind or earthquake forces are particular culprits in the potential collapse of a structural assembly.

There are several basic mechanisms for making an assembly internally stable. One involves the careful positioning of members so that the frameworks so formed are inherently rigid and nondeformable (the use of triangulation is particularly important in this regard). A second technique involves the use of carefully placed rigid planes. A third technique relies on making the actual connections between adjacent elements sufficiently rigid that large angular changes are prevented from occurring. Mechanisms of this type must be placed in both in-plane and out-of-plane directions for stability.

Members and Connections
There are many issues that hinge around the strength of individual elements of a sculpture. It is obvious that if part of

3.2
Typical structural problems.

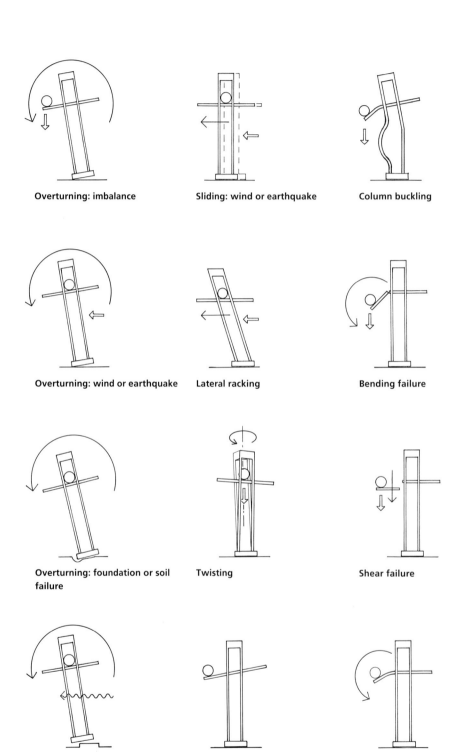

Overturning: imbalance

Sliding: wind or earthquake

Column buckling

Overturning: wind or earthquake

Lateral racking

Bending failure

Overturning: foundation or soil failure

Twisting

Shear failure

Overturning: vibration-induced movements

Connection failure

Excessive deflections

3.3
Typical responses to structural problems.

Common Failure Modes

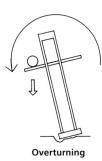

Overturning

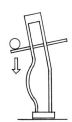

Racking/twisting

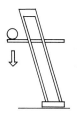

Member or connection failure

Common Design Responses

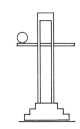

Heavy pedestal with extended base

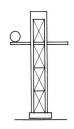

Cross bracing

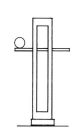

Increased member sizes

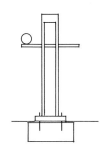

Heavy spread footing

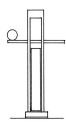

Shear walls

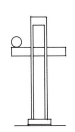

Increased member sizes

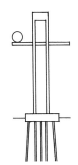

Tie-down piles (for large sculptures)

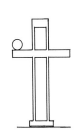

Frame action through connection rigidity

Stiffened connections

a sculpture is made too small, it might bend, crush, badly deform, or pull apart completely. The type of failure likely to develop in a member critically depends on the type of forces experienced by the member and the nature of the material used to make it. Here it is useful to distinguish among basic force states—*tension, compression,* and *bending.* Forces that act along the length of a member and cause it to pull apart are called tension forces. Compression forces also act along the length of a member but tend to cause it to crush. Bending forces act transversely to the long axis of a member and tend to cause it to bow and eventually snap apart.[2] Associated with each of these force states are internal stresses within the fabric of the material itself.

Members in tension can be quite strong, as exemplified by the widespread use of small-diameter cables in bridge construction and other applications. Short members in compression can also be quite strong, since it takes a large force to actually crush something. As compression members become longer and slenderer, however, their load-carrying capacity decreases quite rapidly. The phenomenon of buckling begins to occur, in which the member quite suddenly snaps out from beneath the load. This is an extremely dangerous form of failure since there is no prior visual warning of impending collapse.

Bending is a frequently occurring force state. The common beam in a building is subjected to bending forces. The internal stresses associated with bending can be quite high, and structural members have limited capabilities for carrying loads under a bending action. Long members can be quite susceptible to failure in bending even if the applied transverse loadings seem relatively small. Increasing the depth of the member in the direction of the applied loading helps stiffen the member and prevent bending failures.

In many situations, a member might be strong enough to carry the applied loads without actually breaking apart, but is nonetheless still unacceptable because of the way it sags or droops. Members in bending are particularly prone to excessive deformations of this type. In large structures, the sizes of many members are often determined primarily on the basis of controlling undesirable deformations.

In addition to the phenomena discussed above, there are many other types of possible failure modes, e.g., bearing or torsion, that will be considered in subsequent chapters.

Other Issues

Also relevant to this discussion are related questions as to when a failure might occur. Some failures can occur more or less instantaneously upon installation of a work—a sculpture that is fundamentally out of balance under its own self-weight will tend to overturn from the moment it is put in place. An excessively stressed bolt may shear apart as soon as the weight of a supported part of a sculpture comes to bear on it. More or less instantaneous failures of this type are often associated with the self-weight of the sculpture, less often with external environmental loads (assuming, of course, that a sculpture is not installed during the height of a wind storm or similar event). These failures may be devastating to the sculptor and client, but are at least more likely to occur during the construction or erection of a work than not—when only experienced and presumably wary designers and builders are present.

Other failures may be caused by normal environmental conditions—typical wind, rain, snow, and other phenomena, including the use of the sculpture (people sitting on part of a sculpture). Surely a sculpture must be designed not to fail or deform excessively under these normal conditions. On the other hand, a sculpture may work quite well under normal conditions and fail during a particularly extreme environmental or contextual event—exceptionally high wind forces or earthquake forces might cause a sculpture to overturn. The precise time of such events cannot be exactly predicted. There is, however, a general appreciation of the recurrent nature of such exceptional events and it may be assumed that they can be expected to occur periodically. A sculpture intended to be permanent would need to be designed with these periodic events in mind. Anticipation of such events is reflected to a reasoned extent in building codes.[3] For wind and earthquake force, it is possible to predict (within limits) the actual probability that an exceptional loading will occur that exceeds design values and is likely to cause failure. The following section will discuss these issues in greater detail.

Some failures are progressive in nature, in that they increase in severity over time. A small crack might develop in a weld, for example, that is not initially troublesome. With time, however, the crack might continue to open up until the structural integrity of the connection is destroyed. A sculpture that is subjected to vibrations (e.g., due to proximity of train tracks) and begins to "walk off" its base may finally fall off its base and overturn. The time frame associated with progressive failures may be short or very long, depending on the phenomenon. Some materials (e.g., plastics) are particularly sensitive to the "creep" phenomenon (time-dependent deformations). Deformations upon the installation of a work might be small, but may increase markedly over time due to this phenomenon.

Types of Loading Conditions

Two types of loadings are of concern—those that stem from the self-weight of the object being designed, and those that stem from the environmental context in which the object is to be placed.

The self-weight of an object, often called its *dead weight*, is that associated directly with the amount, distribution, type, and unit weight of the material in the object. The importance of the dead weight depends on the general size of the object. In small sculptures, the self-weight of the object can be virtually negligible. In large sculptures, it can be a major design consideration. Large structures have collapsed under their own dead weight.

The forces that a sculpture experiences as a consequence of its placement in a specific environmental context are typically more complex and harder to predict than dead loads. A sculpture placed in an open garden will be subjected to a whole range of forces associated with the effects of wind, earthquakes , and snow. People walking or sitting on a large piece also create loadings on the structure. Collectively, loads of this type are called *live loads*. Live loads differ from dead loads not only in their sources but also in the fact that they may or may not be present at a given time.

Forces induced on objects by wind are among the more important of live loads. A sculpture in the path of wind causes the wind to be deflected, or in some cases almost stopped. As a consequence, the kinetic energy of the wind is transformed into the potential energy of either pressure or suction on the object. Depending on the shape of the object, these pressures and suctions can act in virtually any direction, but for typical upright sculptures they are predominantly horizontal. Wind forces are thus often characterized as *lateral forces*. The lateral forces induced by wind tend to

2
Strictly speaking, bending is not a unique force state but is actually a composite force state made up of both tension and compression forces that act within the same cross section (see chapter 9).

3
As noted in appendix 2, design wind velocities are often based on a 50-year mean recurrence interval. Wind velocities greatly in excess of these values may also occur, but only within a certain projected probability range and with a much longer recurrence interval (e.g., 200 years).

cause upright forms to overturn, a phenomenon discussed in more detail in chapter 5. Preventing this overturning is a major structural design objective.

Under certain circumstances, wind effects can also generate complex and sometimes disastrous movements in structures. Wind can blow in a steady-state or buffeting way. Depending on the characteristics of both the wind and the structure, either type of wind can cause a structure to begin moving back and forth. These movements can be relatively slow—a swaying to and fro—or extremely rapid. Highly destructive forces can be induced by these motions. Cable or membrane structures are particularly sensitive to these effects, although wind-induced vibrations can occur in rigid structures as well. These effects will be discussed in more detail in chapter 10.

Another important type of live loading that must be considered is that induced by earthquakes. Earthquakes are vibratory phenomena associated with shock movements in the earth's crust. These movements have complex sources but often result from sudden slippages between the tectonic plates that make up the earth's crust. The shock associated with these slippages is propagated in the form of waves that are manifest at the earth's surface in the form of complex vibratory movements. A particular point on the ground might be accelerated and displaced in both horizontal and vertical directions, with the horizontal movements typically predominating. Occasionally these vibratory movements can actually cause ground surfaces to rupture. These movements can be as short-lived as a few seconds or can last much longer.

Earthquakes induce forces in a structure that are primarily horizontally acting (although other types of forces exist as well). As the ground shakes beneath a mass, the inertial tendency of the mass of the form is to remain at rest initially. These forces tend to cause a structure to overturn. It is difficult to predict the magnitudes of the forces induced by earthquakes, let alone their precise effects on a complicated form; of crucial importance, however, is that the magnitudes of the forces induced are dependent on the relative weight or mass of the structure (since the forces involved are inertial in character). The heavier a piece of sculpture is, the greater would be the forces induced in it due to an earthquake.

Loading conditions are discussed in greater detail in appendix 2. The specific effects of earthquake movements on sculpture are explored in depth in chapter 5.

Forces and Stresses

A *force* is characterized in terms of its magnitude and its direction (since direction is important, the term *vector* is often used in conjunction with the description of forces). Equally important is the line of action of a force, or where it acts on the structure. Forces can cause a structure not only to slide but also to rotate or twist about some point. The tendency of a force to cause a rotation or twisting is called a *moment*. These concepts are of great importance in a structural context and will be dealt with extensively in the following chapter.

One useful way of describing forces is to distinguish between *externally applied* and *reactive* forces and moments.[4] Wind acting against a large exposed face is an external force having a magnitude dependent on the velocity of the wind and the size and shape of the sculpture. The forces developed at connection points in response to external forces of this type are called reactive forces. They are reactive in the sense that their magnitudes are in some way directly related to the magnitude of the externally applied force. When there is no external force, there are no reactive forces consequently developed. For a structure to be stable, the complete set of externally applied and reactive forces that act on it must be in *equilibrium*, that is, the actions they produce on the structure must be equal and opposite so that the sculpture does not translate or rotate. These points will be addressed in detail in the following chapter.

To conceptualize how a sculpture experiences the forces described, the applied and reactive forces can both be thought of as external forces. The reactive forces balance the action of applied forces. The complete system of applied and reactive forces acting on a piece, in turn, not only causes a structure to translate or rotate as a whole, but also causes internal forces and associated internal stresses and deformations to be developed within the material fabric of the sculpture.

The forces of tension, compression, or bending generated internally in the members of a structure are resisted by the materiality of the members themselves. These internal forces produce what are called "stresses" within the material fabric. *Stress* is a measure of the internal force intensity per unit area of the member. The magnitude and distribution of the stresses in a sculpture are critically dependent on the nature of the internal force present (tension, compression, bending). In a simple tension member, for example, the stress present is uniform throughout the member. Quantitatively, the magnitude of the stress present is nothing more than the magnitude of the internal force present divided by the cross-sectional area of the member. In other cases, such as beams subjected to bending, stresses are nonuniformly distributed in the member and much more difficult to predict quantitatively. In general, the larger the applied forces on a sculpture of a given size, the larger will be the corresponding stresses developed internally in the structure. Increases in the area of material used within the structure to carry these forces will typically decrease the stress level present within the member for a given force. The actual configuration of the member, however, is a critically important variable affecting how stresses actually change with increases or decreases in dimensions.

The concept of stress allows a concise measurement of the ability of a member to carry a given set of loadings. Surely there are certain minimum size requirements that must be met if the member is not to fail as a consequence of the internal forces present. Larger members could be provided that would work at least as well, but they could be so much larger than needed as to be excessive. Sculptures with high stress levels present within them may be problematic or even dangerous with respect to material failure or distortion. Those with low stress levels are normally safe, but they may have members far larger than the minimum required. (This certainly does not mean that larger-than-minimum members should not be used; the question is rather one of control and knowledge of what is happening within the work.) Exact predictions of the stresses within a sculpture, however, are difficult and will be discussed in more detail subsequent chapters.

Material Properties

Intimate knowledge of the characteristics of materials has long been appreciated as fundamentally important in the creation of sculpture. In working with materials and shaping objects, a sculptor will undoubtedly perceive many qualities that are intrinsically important not only to the shaping of the object but to its structural properties as well, such as

4
In this particular context, the self-weight of a sculpture is usually considered as an applied load. Reactive forces are developed at the interface between the sculpture and the ground.

strength, ductility or brittleness, and other qualities. This section will address some of these properties not so much from the point of view of how they affect the making or shaping of an object, but rather of how these properties are formally defined in relation to structural analysis and design issues.

In the previous section, it was observed that the magnitudes of the internal stresses created in structural members are generally dependent on the magnitude and placement of the applied load and the size and configuration of the resisting structural element. Whether or not a specific member is capable of carrying a particular stress of a given magnitude is dependent on the strength properties of the material comprising this member. Thus a tension force in a member might induce an actual internal stress level of a certain value. A steel member might be able to carry this particular stress level with ease without exhibiting any visual form of distress (e.g., pulling apart), while a plastic member subjected to the same stress level might rapidly pull apart and even break into separate pieces. Different materials have different inherent abilities to resist applied stresses. Some fail at low applied stress levels, others can carry very high applied stress levels.

The relative ability of a material to carry an applied stress of a certain magnitude is determined experimentally. Specimens of different materials of known dimensions are placed in testing machines that subject them to known tension or compression forces. The force at which a specimen breaks (physically pulls apart or crushes, depending on whether the applied force is tensile or compressive) is measured. The actual stress level in the specimen that corresponds to the failure point is then calculated. This stress level—typically called the *failure stress*—is normally a constant for the particular material tested. Failure stress levels for many different materials have already been determined and tabulated in a number of different sources. Depending on the material, stress values associated with phenomena other than actual physical separation or complete crushing are often recorded. Steel, for example, begins very rapidly elongating (a phenomenon called yielding) somewhat before physical separation actually occurs. This stress level—called the *yield stress*—corresponds to the end of the useful strength of the material.

Whether or not a part of a structure actually fails when subjected to some known external force (which in turn develops internal stress of predictable magnitude) depends on whether this applied stress level is less than or greater than the experimentally determined failure or yield stress level for the material used. Obviously if the real stress present is significantly below the failure stress level, then the material is in no danger of failing. If the real stress level and failure stress levels are quite close, failure is imminent. In later chapters that deal more explicitly with the sizes and shapes of structural members, it will be seen that the real stress level allowed to exist in a member is arbitrarily limited to some fractional part of the failure stress level— designated the *allowable stress* level—to ensure the safety of the member.

Another highly important structural characteristic of materials is the way a material deforms under loading. In some materials, such as steel, the deformations present in the material are initially directly related to the magnitude of the stress level present. As the stress level in a simple steel member in tension is increased, for example, the member elongates proportionally to the applied load. Materials exhibiting such properties are said to be *elastic*. In a material such as steel, these elongations are initially virtually impossible to see by eye, but they are nonetheless present. The term *strain* is formally used to describe these deformations. Strain refers to the extent to which a unit length of the material is elongated or compressed as a consequence of the stresses present (which are in turn induced by the action of the external loading).[5] In steel, once the stress level reaches the yield stress, the material rapidly pulls apart before physically separating. This pulling apart is visually evident. This behavior makes steel particularly useful as a structural material. Under expected loads structural deformations are quite small. If loads unexpectedly increase beyond anticipated levels, the material still has a lot of reserve strength. Importantly, visible deformations would begin appearing in the material before it actually physically ruptured, thus providing a visible warning of impending collapse. This characteristic of steel makes it very useful in large structures where public safety is an issue. Materials exhibiting these characteristics are called *ductile* materials.

Other materials exhibit different characteristics under loadings. Aluminum can have similar strengths to steel in both tension and compression and is relatively ductile, but it generally tends to deform more under the same stress level.

Cast iron has a relatively high ultimate strength in compression but has little ability to resist appreciable tension stresses. Tension stresses can cause cracks to develop rapidly and without any prior sign of material distresses. Concrete has a much lower ultimate strength than steel but is an extremely versatile material. Concrete has a reasonable ability to carry compressive stresses but is unable to resist tension stresses. When concrete is subjected to tension stresses, it simply cracks rapidly. Reinforcing steel is often introduced into concrete to improve its ability to carry tension forces. When a reinforced concrete member is subjected to tension forces, the concrete cracks and the steel comes into play to carry the tension forces that are present. Reinforced concrete beams are common in building and bridge construction.

Both cast iron and plain concrete are often described as *brittle* materials since they can quickly fail without any prior visual warning, such as a pulling apart of the material. Extreme care must be taken with materials of this type, since the sudden failures can be extremely dangerous. Materials such as bronze or copper can be either brittle or ductile, depending on their exact makeup.

Other Technical Issues

The discussion thus far has focused only on the structural aspects of sculpture. There are also important technical issues that are nonstructural in character. It is useful to review some of these issues as a way of understanding how they differ from structural issues. To engineering professionals, there is a distinct difference between structural and nonstructural design issues. To others, however, there is sometimes a tendency to lump all "technical" considerations into the same category and call them "structural issues." The phenomena involved, however, may be quite different.

Nonstructural technical issues often center on the normal objective of assuring that a sculpture retains its intended appearance and/or functionality over time, or, frequently, that it ages as intended. Material properties are particularly important here, including general durability, weathering characteristics, sensitivity to airborne or waterborne pollutants, staining characteristics, scratch resistance, and so forth.

Some of these phenomena involve an actual change in the characteristics of the surface of the material (e.g., a

5
The term "strain" thus means something very precise in an engineering context, i.e., deformation per unit length. Thus common usage of the term (such as "the beam is subjected to great strain") may not be correct for the phenomenon the speaker intends to convey, unless the reference is actually to deformations. "High stresses are developed in the beam" might be better usage in normal situations.

change in color) that may or may not be desirable. Copper surfaces, for example, naturally change color over time—a phenomenon that is commonly anticipated and that is usually considered desirable. Many brightly colored materials or surface treatments, however, may simply fade over time when exposed to sunlight.

In some cases, the surface of a material may be physically eroded, flaked, or blistered. Some airborne and waterborne pollutants acting on some materials cause a form of erosion to occur; this is a common and well-documented problem with older carved stonework. In many stones, freeze-thaw cycles can cause surfaces to flake off (water gets into microscopic cracks and freezes; the associated expansion of the freezing water causes the crack to open up further—a process that can be repeated many times until the surface spalls off).

Staining, scratching, and similar surface actions are of obvious importance in maintaining the appearance of a work. Scratches or stains may be caused either by natural phenomena or by vandals. Some materials are naturally more susceptible to these actions than others. Soft, porous materials with rough surfaces are particularly vulnerable, but even hard materials are not immune. For example, Corten is a hard steel deliberately intended to rust in an exterior environment. It is known to be particularly sensitive to graffiti. The surface is directly affected, and common removal techniques invariably leave visible markings (subsequent rusting characteristics, hence colors, are affected—the new rusting is not identical to the original).

Earthwork sculptures are vulnerable to many different actions. Water and wind erosion can obviously occur. Phenomena such as soil compaction or consolidation over time can alter original surface shapes. Shaping some soils into exceptionally sharp slopes can cause a form of slumping to occur.

In sculptures with moving elements (e.g., rotating arms), movement mechanisms can jam over time due to normal wear on bearings in connections. In simpler mechanisms, corrosion can inhibit free movement. A number of other reasons for jamming might exist as well. Forces on a rotating axle, for example, might cause the axle to deform slightly, which would cause it to jam.

These and many other technical issues are of great importance in the design of sculptures. In many works, they are far more significant than purely structural issues. Their consequence is typically some change in the visual appearance and/or functionality of a work over time—a change that is often highly undesirable to the sculptor, the client, or the general public. On the other hand, their consequences are rarely in any way life-threatening, whereas the failure of a large sculpture in a public setting due to structural reasons may well be life-threatening.

Standards for Performance

In this book it is argued explicitly and implicitly that positive benefits to sculpture can accrue through attempts to improve the technical performance of sculptures of any scale—this subject is an easy and happy one to discuss. A thornier question is whether formal assurance of engineering viability (either by the sculptor directly or by a collaborative team with the necessary expertise) should actually be mandated—a question always sure to elicit vociferous debate. Such is already the case in several public art programs. Are there circumstances when an external controlling agency might actually require some sort of formal engineering review of a work, and have the authority to mandate changes in the event of noncompliance with perceived standards? What standards exist in the first place, if any? What are the nature of these controlling agencies, and what powers might they have?

As a prelude, it is useful to review several very broad societal issues, particularly the distinction between the public and private good and the relative right of society to pursue its own well-being. Over the course of time, consensus has been reached on some points vis-à-vis the concept of the public good as a decision-making criterion, particularly with regard to health and safety issues. Other applications of the concept, however, are extremely controversial, as when the concept is muddled with value issues or with taste issues (as in the unfortunate controversy surrounding Richard Serra's *Tilted Arc* in New York City). It is nonetheless useful to view the discussion from this perspective as a way of getting a handle on a difficult subject.

On the issue of threats to physical safety, consensus generally exists that it is not an artist's prerogative to create and put in a public setting any work that poses a threat to anyone's health or safety. Any formal or legal requirement that sculpture give assurance of its engineering viability is frequently predicated on this consensus. In architecture and building construction, the power of society to regulate those aspects of the construction of buildings that might potentially pose threats to life and/or safety is well established. Certain safety and health standards expressed in instruments such as building codes must be met. Ultimately, the requirement to meet these standards is enforceable through the police power of the state. These codes pertain even if the building is not solely in a public setting; a common house built for strictly private use still must meet the applicable standards. A basic societal assumption is that no one has the axiomatic right to harm himself or herself. A more pragmatic reason is that private property invariably changes hands. This position has implications for large-scale sculpture as well. Any sculpture, even one in a purely private setting, is not beyond societal consideration.

Building codes themselves define loading conditions (live loadings, wind and earthquake loadings), allowable stresses for different materials and for different components, deflection limitations, fire hazard limitations and control, stair and railing requirements, ventilation and lighting requirements, and a host of other practices intended to assure that the public health and safety is not endangered, and that minimum practices for what is felt to be good construction are maintained.[6]

In many instances, particularly where there is not a long tradition of public sculpture, codes of this type are automatically considered the primary device for assuring that a large-scale sculpture does not pose a threat to life or safety. How to apply building codes to sculpture, however, is often less than clear. Many provisions are confusing at best when directed toward large sculptures. Yet they are often the only organized sources of potentially applicable standards available. Engineers accustomed to working with loading conditions and serviceability criteria used in building design, for example, frequently find that such familiar measures are of doubtful applicability to large-scale sculptures, but there is typically nothing better to use. Building code and other public officials often find it similarly difficult to assess final proposals for large-scale sculptures from the viewpoint of carrying out their mandated responsibility to assure that public safety hazards are not posed by the work. The field

6
While most provisions are health- and safety-oriented, it should be noted that there are occasionally more troublesome ones that are less objective and may relate to trade practices.

of structures is not an exact science by any means. Consequently the technical design and installation of large-scale sculptures relies heavily on the professional judgment of the individuals and public officials involved. This situation must be respected for what it is, given the current lack of alternatives.

Controversies about the applicability of a code to a particular project often arise when there is disagreement either as to whether or not a potential failure might pose a threat to health or safety at all, or as to the degree to which the threat of failure is present. Not all of the kinds of structural performance difficulties discussed earlier are necessarily life threatening. Large sculptures susceptible to overturning due to either their own imbalance or wind or earthquake forces clearly pose a hazard, as do large pieces that might break off. Sliding may pose a hazard in some cases. Deformations, however, are particularly hard to evaluate. Deflections or warpings in a large piece may ultimately prove to be very important, since they may signify the beginning of a progressive failure that might eventually become life threatening. Alternatively, deformations may prove to be of no real importance, since large deformations can occur without the basic structural integrity of a work being altered (witness the common diving board). Whether or not a potential failure poses a threat must usually be decided on a case by case basis. The normal process for assessing this threat in large sculptures would entail a detailed engineering analysis using design criteria in adherence with local building codes. Often wind tunnel or other tests on models may be required to provide loading data for these analyses.

The actual making and setting in place of some large works may reveal unanticipated imbalances or weaknesses, which is in turn a kind of useful pretesting for common loading conditions. The successful structural performance of a work during fabrication and installation, however, is rarely sufficient to satisfy safety concerns or meet requirements of regulatory agencies, since extreme loading conditions that the work may experience during its lifetime are not reflected (e.g., hurricanes, earthquakes). Full-scale pretesting could be used to meet the requirements of regulatory agencies as long as the loading conditions used reflect extreme cases designated in applicable codes. An elaborate testing program is usually required (see the discussion on the Watts Towers in chapter 15).

In addition to these structural issues, it is important to recall that there are many nonstructural technical issues as well, of great importance in the design of sculptures, that do not lie within the domain of the building code. These issues normally hinge not on public safety but on whether a sculpture remains durable and retains its functionality and intended appearance over time. Sponsoring agencies, concerned with the value they are getting for their money, may reasonably consider these phenomena quite important and may pose performance expectations. For a small piece placed in a public setting, for example, the need for secure installations capable of preventing the theft of the work is normally quite important. In the Arts on the Line project in Massachusetts, one artist whose work was fabricated by a foundry chose to do her own installation of several small pieces. All were relatively loosely fixed and could be easily broken off from the mounting screws used to attach them in place. Three of her sculptures were stolen within a week.[7] Matters of this kind are of undoubted importance to sculptors, to sponsoring agencies, and eventually to the public. As they do not deal with safety and health issues, they are not the domain of instruments like building codes. Other more appropriate instruments and agreements between sponsors and sculptors have been developed in some major public art programs to deal with issues of this type.

The overriding principle appears to be that the degree of control exerted by society should be proportional to the potential impact of a sculpture's failure on society.

3.4
Anthony Caro, *Monsoon Drift.*

7
Upon installation, the artist had
been advised by the client that
the attachments were unsatisfactory. Since she carried no
insurance covering this kind of
event, the artist had to replace
the stolen pieces at her own
expense. ("Arts on the Line:
A Public Art Handbook,"
Massachusetts Bay Transit
Authority, Boston, 1987, p. 35.)

Alexander Calder, *Deux Disques.*

Basic Principles of Balance and Structural Stability

2

4 Force, Moment, and Equilibrium

Fundamental concepts of force and equilibrium provide useful tools for describing the structural behavior of a sculpture subjected to a loading. At a certain level of understanding, the concepts and terms to be discussed are undoubtedly familiar to all. Notions of something being "in balance" or "out of balance" are commonplace. The idea of something "collapsing" also summons up clear images. But what, exactly, is meant by terms like "balance" and "collapse" in the first place? Is it possible to predict a priori if a sculpture assembled from parts in a certain way will or will not collapse? The following five chapters will slowly build up a theory for understanding the nature of forces and how they affect a structure.

The act of analyzing a sculpture from a structural point of view involves several steps after the overall form of the work has been first developed. The first is to determine the self-weights and environmental loads present, as discussed in the previous chapter. The next step is to determine what effect these self-weights and external loadings actually produce on a specific form.

In general, the forces that act on forms tend to cause the overall structure to translate or rotate. The potential magnitude of these translational and rotational effects is first determined through a study of the basic *equilibrium* of the object. The equilibrium of an object depends on the type and location of the applied forces as well as the geometry and mass distribution of the form itself. A study of the equilibrium of an object also entails a study of the characteristics of forces. Forces causing translation and rotation affect the equilibrium of a structure and induce internal forces within it. If a structure cannot resist the translational and rotational effects caused by applied forces, it can slide or disastrously overturn. Basic principles of equilibrium are used to predict the *stability* of an object as well as to lay the groundwork for understanding how these applied forces affect the design of specific structures.

The static equilibrium of an object clearly depends on the nature and geometry of both the applied forces and the structure itself. Less obviously, it also depends on the way in

4.0
Edgar Degas, *Dancer Putting on Her Stocking.*

which the structure is connected to the ground and on the way specific parts of the structure are interconnected one to another. The last part of this chapter will address how connections affect structural behavior.

Forces and Moments

The study of the equilibrium of an object first demands an understanding of the basic concepts of *forces* and *moments*. In a highly abstract sense, a force is a directed interaction between objects that has the effect of causing a change in the shape or motion of both. This rather abstract definition is valuable since it implies that a force has both magnitude and direction. A force need not act just downward but can act in any direction. Indeed, an appreciation of this fact was one of the great breakthroughs of fledgling science in the period between the twelfth and seventeenth centuries. Once force was conceived in directional terms (often called *vectorial* terms), a whole host of individuals that included Galileo and Newton addressed a problem area known as the *resolution* and *composition* of forces. Can a series of forces acting on a single object be replaced by a single larger one? Or can a single force be broken down or decomposed into several individual forces acting in different directions? Positive answers to these questions slowly emerged. Forces came to be graphically represented as arrows having a specified direction and a length that corresponded to the magnitude of the force. Newton formulated a proposition that has since been known as the *parallelogram law*. Briefly, this proposition maintains that when the lines of action of two forces cross, there is a single force—called the *resultant*— that is exactly equivalent to these two forces; the resultant can be represented by the diagonal of the parallelogram formed by using the two force vectors as sides of the parallelogram. Conversely, the two forces may be considered as *components* of the single larger force. The force systems are interchangeable. If the magnitudes of the two forces are known, as well as the angles involved, the magnitude of the resultant force can be determined by simple principles of trigonometry. Alternatively, the force system can be drawn to scale and its resultant simply measured.

The idea that single forces can be considered in terms of components, or vice versa, is an extremely powerful one, since it gives us a way of conceptualizing how a force affects an object. For example, assume that someone was pushing on the Apollo bronze in the three ways shown in figure 4.1. The first force (the self-weight of the bronze) acts vertically downward, the second acts horizontally, and the third acts diagonally downward and to the left. The first vertical force clearly tends to push the statue downward into the ground. (The ground in turn exerts an equal and opposite reactive upward force on the statue, so that the statue remains stationary.) The second force tends to cause it to overturn but does not push it into the ground at all. The third diagonal force tends to do a bit of both. For this third force, thinking in terms of force components provides a way of characterizing these different tendencies. The single inclined force can be interchanged with an equivalent set of two component forces that act in the horizontal and vertical directions, respectively. It is then evident that it is the horizontal component of the original force that contributes to the overturning of the statue while the vertical component of the inclined force tends to push the statue downward against the ground. Note that if the angle of the single inclined force were changed so that it acted more horizontally, then the magnitudes of the two components would change as well. The numerical magnitudes of different components could be easily determined by simple considerations involving the magnitude and geometry of the inclined force.[1] Conversely, several individual forces that act on a sculpture can be mathematically combined into a single resultant force.[2]

A force acting on an object tends to cause it to translate in the direction of the force. But it can also cause an object to rotate about a fixed point. The tendency of a force to cause an object to rotate about a point is called a *moment*. The moment of a force is proportional to the magnitude of the force and the perpendicular distance from the force's line of action to the point about which the object rotates. This distance is often called the *moment arm* of the force.[3] For the Apollo bronze, there is an obvious overturning tendency associated with the rotational effect of the horizontally applied force acting a distance h above a point of rotation at the base of the statue. Note that if the distance h is very large (which is possible if the sculpture is very tall), the overturning tendency could be large even if the applied force is quite small (the converse is true as well). The same moment

1

When an orthogonal reference system is used, the components of a single inclined force F are usually described as F_x and F_y (forces in the horizontal and vertical direction, respectively). The horizontal component F_x of the original force F tends to cause the bronze to overturn, while the vertical component F_y tends to push it downward. The numerical values of F_x and F_y can be determined by trigonometry. Thus: $F_x = F \cos\phi$ and $F_y = F \sin\phi$, where ϕ is the angle formed by the original force F and the x-axis. Components of an inclined force may actually be found on any set of axes, not just an orthogonal x and y system, but the algebraic manipulations then become quite complex.

2

The numerical process for determining the resultant of several forces is fundamentally the inverse of that for determining components. In the prior example, assume that forces F_x and F_y are known and we want to know the value of the single equivalent force F. Since the components are orthogonal, the angle formed by the resultant force F can be found by $\phi = \tan^{-1}(F_x/F_y)$. The magnitude of the force is then given by $F = F_x/\cos\phi$ or $F = F_y/\sin\phi$. The process is more involved when multiple forces are present.

3

Expressions for moments are usually written in the form $M = F \times d$, where M is a symbol for the rotational effect of a force (the "moment"), F represents the force, and d represents the moment arm of the force (the perpendicular distance from the line of action of the force to the point of rotation).

Equilibrium diagram of sculpture: equal and opposite forces exist at the interface between the sculpture and the ground

Vertical force (weight = W)

Reaction = W (equal and opposite to applied force)

Horizontal force F

"Moment" of force F about point O: $M_o = F \times d$

Inclined force F

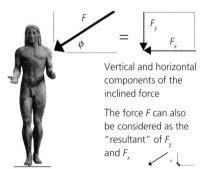

Vertical and horizontal components of the inclined force

The force F can also be considered as the "resultant" of F_y and F_x

4.1
A single force is the equivalent of a pair of component forces (the single force is described as the *resultant* of the two component forces). A force may also cause a structure to rotate about a point. The magnitude of this rotational tendency is called the *moment* of the force.

can be produced by a small force with a large moment arm or a large force with a small moment arm.

In the case of the inclined force in figure 4.1, the moment of the force about the rotation point is the product of the force times the perpendicular distance from the rotation point to the inclined line of action of the force. Considerations as to whether or not the sculpture would actually overturn under the action of this applied moment are discussed in the following chapter.

Equilibrium

The idea of moment can also be explored in relation to the concept of balance. If there is only a single force acting on an object about a point, then the object will surely rotate. On the other hand, any object can be in a state of *natural balance* under the action of the forces acting on it. It is easy to imagine or devise a situation where a number of forces act on an object and where the net sum of their combined rotational effects about a point is zero. Any naturally balancing object represents this situation. A whole class of sculptures rely on the concept of natural balance as part of their fundamental expression. Virtually any of Calder's suspended sculptures would provide such an example. In the part of Calder's *Mobile* shown in figure 4.2, the weight of the ring produces a rotational tendency (or moment) that acts in a counterclockwise sense with respect to the vertical plane we are facing in the drawing.[4] If the horizontal arm of the sculpture is not to initially twist in space, the weight of the fish on the other side of the point of suspension must produce a balancing rotational moment that is equal in magnitude, and opposite in rotational sense, to that produced by the ring. Thus the fish produces a moment that acts in the clockwise direction. When the moments produced by these two forces are indeed exactly equal, the horizontal arm is in exact balance and the whole structure is said to be in a state of *rotational equilibrium,* like a carefully balanced seesaw. In the Calder example, the weights on either side of the balance point need not be the same—but rather the *moments* of the two weights (as defined by the products of their respective forces times distances from the balance point) must be the same. It is evident that the ring weighs more than the fish, since it is located closer to the point of sus-

pension than the fish. For the rotational tendency of the heavier ring to be exactly the same as that of the lighter fish, it is necessary that the ring have a smaller moment arm than that of the fish. Note that when a sculpture of this type is being created, the designer cannot a priori and arbitrarily decide on both weights and distances and expect that a natural state of balance will occur (this would indeed be fortuitous), but must accept what rotational balance considerations dictate. Also note that the sum of the downward-acting weight of the fish and ring must be balanced by an upward-acting reactive force of equal magnitude and opposite sense—in this case the tension force developed in the supporting wire.

This example brings into focus two general principles of equilibrium. The first is that of *translatory equilibrium*. When the resultant force acting on a sculpture is not zero, the sculpture tends to be moved (translated) in the direction of the resultant force. For an object to be in *translatory equilibrium* (for it not to move in the direction of the force), the net translatory effect of all forces acting on the object must be zero—which is another way of saying that the sum of all forces acting on a sculpture in any specified direction must total zero. This is an important condition of equilibrium, since normally sculptures are not meant to inadvertently slide or move up or down. The second equilibrium condition of importance is that of *rotational equilibrium,* as demonstrated by the balancing of the ring and the fish. This condition requires that the net rotational effect (i.e., rotational moments) of all forces acting on a sculpture must be zero. If the sum of all rotational moments is not equal to zero, then the sculpture will be rotated (spun) by the action of the forces. Again, this is a situation that is normally not wanted in typical static sculptures.

Center of Gravity

Fundamental to an understanding of weight and balance is the idea that any form has a point at which the form's entire distributed mass can be considered concentrated without affecting the basic balance or stability of the object. This point is called the *center of gravity* of the object.[5] Many investigators have studied the location of the center of gravity in human forms and in other shapes. In human forms, it tends to be located in the pelvic area, as illustrated by Auguste Rodin's *Study for Jean d'Aire* in figure 4.3.

The location of the center of gravity of many common volumetric objects is intuitively obvious. The center of gravity of a solid sphere, for example, is located at its exact geometric center. The same is true for a solid cube. In more complex forms, the center of gravity is typically located where the concentration of mass is the greatest. In a solid pyramidal shape, for example, the center of gravity is located nearer the base than the apex since this is where most of the mass is located (the exact point is at one-third of the height as measured up from the base).

For forms that cannot be easily characterized in terms of geometric volumes, an alternative way of visualizing the location of the center of gravity is useful. The location of the center of gravity of a shape can be considered as the single point about which the entire object can be freely balanced. A rectilinear bar, for example, could be suspended in a perfectly balanced way from a single string if the point of connection is exactly at the midpoint of the bar. The center of gravity of more complex shapes can be similarly imagined. When the shape is essentially planar, one can imagine balancing it on a knife's edge. This would locate one axis that would pass through the object's center of gravity; turning the shape and balancing it again would establish another axis passing through the center of gravity. Where the two axes cross would define the exact location of the center of gravity of the shape.

Another way of determining where the center of gravity of an object is located is to suspend the object from any single point. The center of gravity of the object must lie directly *below* that point. If an object is suspended, in turn, from several points and vertical lines drawn through the point of suspension, then the intersection point of the lines will locate the center of gravity.

Applied and Reactive Forces

The forces and moments that act on an object can be divided into two primary types: *applied* and *reactive*. Applied forces are those that act directly on an object, such as wind or snow. Reactive forces are those generated by the action of one object on another, and hence typically occur at points

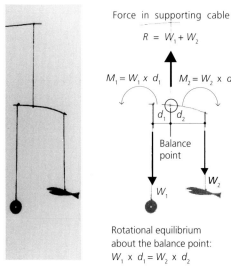

$$R = W_1 + W_2$$

Force in supporting cable

$$M_1 = W_1 \times d_1 \qquad M_2 = W_2 \times d_2$$

$d_1 \quad d_2$

Balance point

W_1

W_2

Rotational equilibrium about the balance point:
$$W_1 \times d_1 = W_2 \times d_2$$

Alexander Calder,
Mobile

4.2
Any structure is in a state of translational and rotational equilibrium under the full set of applied and reactive forces acting upon it.

4
The moment of the ring about the point of suspension is given by $M_1 = W_1 \times d_1$, where W_1 is the weight of the ring and d_1 is its moment arm. The moment of the fish about the point of suspension is given by $M_2 = W_2 \times d_2$, where W_2 is the weight of the fish and d_2 is its moment arm. The arm is in balance (rotational equilibrium exists) when $W_1 \times d_1 = W_2 \times d_2$.

5
The term *center of mass* is perhaps a better descriptor of this same point. Although strictly speaking there are some differences between the concepts of center of gravity and center of mass, the term center of gravity will be used here.

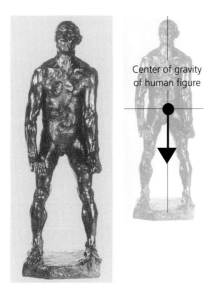

Center of gravity
of human figure

Auguste Rodin,
Study for Jean d'Aire

4.3
**The center of gravity of a structure
is that point at which the entire
mass may be considered to be concentrated. The center of gravity of
a live human figure is in the pelvic
area.**

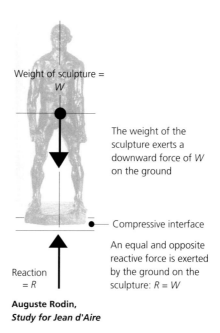

Weight of sculpture =
W

The weight of the
sculpture exerts a
downward force of *W*
on the ground

Compressive interface

An equal and opposite
reactive force is exerted
Reaction   by the ground on the
= *R*   sculpture: *R = W*

Auguste Rodin,
Study for Jean d'Aire

4.4
**An equilibrium diagram shows
the full set of applied and reactive forces acting on a structure.**

6
A formal expression for the
equilibrium is given by $R - W$
$= 0$, where W represents the
weight of the statue and R is
the reactive force that exists
at the interface between the
statue and its pedestal. Obviously, $R = W$ in this simple case.

of support or connections in a structure. The existence of
reactive forces follows from Newton's third law, which generally states that to every action there is an equal and opposite reaction. If one member produces a force on another,
the second always exerts on the first a force that is equal in
magnitude, opposite in direction, and has the same line of
action. In Rodin's *Study for Jean d'Aire,* the weight of the
statue produces a force on the pedestal; the pedestal exerts
an equal and opposite reactive force on the bottom of the
statue (see fig. 4.4). The pedestal produces downward forces
on the ground. The ground in turn exerts forces on the
pedestal that are equal and opposite in sense.

Diagrams of this type, which show the complete system
of applied and reactive forces acting on an object, are called
equilibrium diagrams, or sometimes *free-body diagrams.* The
complete system of applied and reactive forces acting on an
object must be in translatory and rotational equilibrium. In
the simple case of *Study for Jean d'Aire*, the reaction that
exists at the interface between the statue and the pedestal
must equal the weight of the statue.[6]

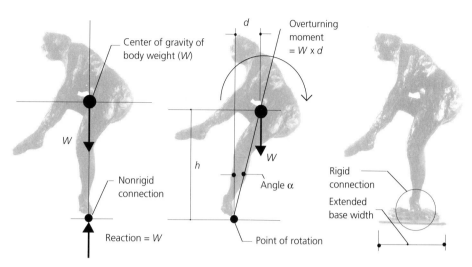

Edgar Degas, *Dancer Putting on Her Stocking*

In a live dancer, the center of gravity of the body weight would necessarily lie directly above the supporting foot.

The higher the center of gravity off the ground, the greater is the potential instability of a real dancer when slightly tilted (as *h* increases, so does *d* and hence the overturning moment *M*).

In a sculpture, the rigid connection of the foot to the wide base provides stability.

4.5
The center of gravity of a *live* figure standing on one leg is always located directly above the point where the foot touches the ground. Otherwise, an off-balance rotational moment would cause the figure to topple. The higher the center of gravity, the more likely is overturning if a slight tilting occurs (this principle is broadly applicable).

A simple equilibrium diagram was also drawn for Calder's *Mobile* in figure 4.2. Not only was the structure shown in rotational balance, but the two suspended weights *applied* to the structure caused an equal and opposite *reactive* force to be developed in the suspension cable (in this case, an internal tension force).

Body Posture and Sculptural Representations of Human Figures

Basic Stability

To further elaborate upon basic issues of force and balance, it is interesting to look at human posture. Living figures cannot be rigidly affixed to a ground plane, so they must be in careful balance. Examining postures thus sheds light on how balance is obtained under an object's self-weight. More generally, it helps clarify balance similarities and differences between *real* or live figures and *sculptural representations* of figures.

Consider the stability of Edgar Degas's *Dancer Putting on Her Stocking* (fig. 4.5) and assume for a moment that it represents a living dancer. Also assume that the distributed mass of the dancer can be considered concentrated as a sin-

7

In terms of the relation presented in note 3, d would equal zero when the forces are collinear. Hence $M = W \times d = 0$. Thus, there would be no tendency for a live dancer to overturn.

8

If W is the weight of the tilted *Dancer*, and d is the distance between vertical lines passing through the center of gravity and the support point, then the magnitude of the overturning moment M is given by $M = W \times d$.

gle force at its center of gravity. This work is useful to examine first since the sculptor obviously intended it to convey visually a sense of precarious balance. A rather large mass having a complicated shape exists over a small base support. The center of gravity of the dancer must therefore be located directly above the supporting foot. This causes the equivalent force representing the entire body weight to be collinear, or on the same line, with the reactive force that must exist between the body and the ground. Since these two forces are equal, opposite in sense, *and* collinear, they tend to produce no sort of rotational moment that would tend to cause the dancer to topple over.[7] Any other location of the center of gravity would produce a rotational moment about the point of support that would tend to cause the dancer to topple over. If the *Dancer* were tilted, the magnitude of the overturning effect, or overturning moment, would be directly proportional to the product of the weight of the sculpture multiplied by the extent to which the center of gravity was dislocated from above the base (i.e., the "moment arm" of the weight about the point of rotation).[8]

A similar condition exists for *Dancer Looking at the Sole of Her Right Foot* (fig. 4.6). If the dancer were alive, to maintain equilibrium the body distribution of mass associated with the exact positions of the various body elements would again have to be such that the resultant location of the center of gravity of the whole dancer was directly above the supporting foot. To put it another way, the rotational moments (force times distance) of the body parts on either side of the foot have to equal each other exactly, otherwise an off-balance moment would exist that would tend to cause the dancer to topple.

The conditions for stability in a live dancer are thus quite restrictive, and a real dancer would have constantly to make minor body movements or shifts (e.g., moving an arm or a leg) to maintain her center of gravity directly over her foot. Other means of maintaining equilibrium are necessary in a sculpture of bronze. In *Dancer Putting on Her Stocking*, the dimensions of the base of the sculpture are greatly increased in size (and the foot rigidly attached to this base) so that the vertical axis passing through the center of gravity has a much greater base area to pass through (in comparison to the limited dimensions of a single foot). The fact that the foot is rigidly attached to the base—surely not the case in a live dancer—is a necessary element in actually utilizing

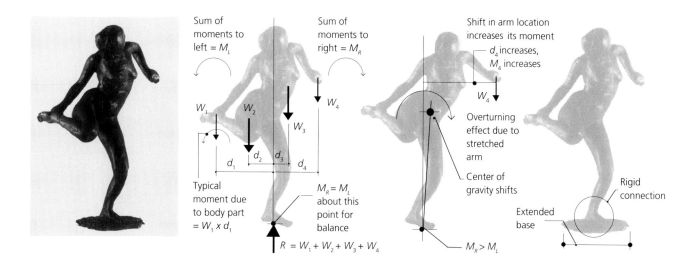

Edgar Degas, *Dancer Looking at the Sole of Her Right Foot*

Balanced dancer: the rotational moments about the foot caused by body parts on either side must always be equal in a live dancer standing on one foot.

A sudden shifting of an arm would change its moment and could lead to toppling of the dancer (unless other body parts change position as well).

In a sculpture, the rigid connection and base width provide stability.

4.6
In a live figure, the extended parts of the body on either side of the foot are subtly manipulated through body movements so that the overturning effects they produce about the foot exactly balance each other. (This is equivalent to saying that the center of gravity of the entire body weight remains above the foot.) In sculptural representations of the human form, the normal fixing of the foot to a wider base allows more variation in the configurations achievable and/or a capability of carrying a wider range of loading types.

the full base width for stability. This is what renders the sculpture stable in lieu of the ability to make minor body adjustments.

The vertical height of the center of gravity of either of Degas's dancers has been estimated to lie somewhere in the pelvic region. The absolute height of the center of gravity is an important stability determinant. Again consider a real dancer. The higher her center of gravity is in relation to the point of support, the more susceptible she is to overturning. The reason for this can be seen in figure 4.5. A high center of gravity means that any small off-center vertical movement of the body results in a relatively large rotational moment or overturning tendency about the point of support (i.e., the "moment arm" associated with overturning becomes large). On the other hand, lowering the center of gravity decreases the rotational moment tendency and thus contributes to the stability of the dancer.

The exact configuration of the various limbs of any live dancer strongly affects the location of the center of gravity of the dancer considered as a whole. This principle is evident in *Siva as Lord of the Dance* (fig. 4.7). Undoubtedly, it would be a real advantage to have four arms and four hands to maintain the exquisite balanced postures so often depicted in Indian sculpture. The added minor weights of the items

Siva carries help make subtle hand movements have a greater impact on the moment adjustments thus produced. The minor nuances possible in adjusting the location of the center of gravity are remarkable.

The addition of a large external load on a real figure would invariably necessitate a drastic readjustment of body posture to accommodate the new loading and still remain in balance. This principle is very eloquently expressed in Koben's *Guardian with Lantern*, a truly remarkable study of body posture. The center diagram in figure 4.8 demonstrates how the Guardian is in equilibrium under the action of its own body weight and that of the heavy lantern. Since the major part of the load is located more over the Guardian's left leg (to the right in the photograph) than the other leg, there is a greater reactive force developed under the left leg than the right. This in turn implies that a larger compressive force exists in the left leg than in the right. The right leg becomes as much a movable balancing force to adjust equilibrium as a primary load carrier. The muscular tension shown in the sculpture reflects these differing functions.

If the Guardian were alive, it is interesting to consider whether an upright posture of the type illustrated in the diagram at right would be possible. Assuming that the lantern

4.7
Siva as Lord of the Dance. Siva engaged in the dance of the universe tramples on the dwarf of illusion, while holding the drum of creation in the upper right hand and the fire of destruction in the left. If Siva were alive, the presence of additional arms and hands would be an undoubted asset in achieving the minor balance movements so essential to the dance.

Siva as Lord of the Dance

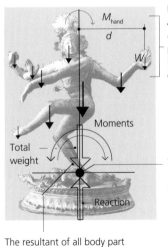

Minor changes in *d* alter the moment $(M_{hand} = W \times d)$ produced by the hand weight *W* (typical)

M_{hand}

d

W

Moments

Total weight

The sum of all moments about the foot must equal zero

Reaction

The resultant of all body part weights must lie above the foot

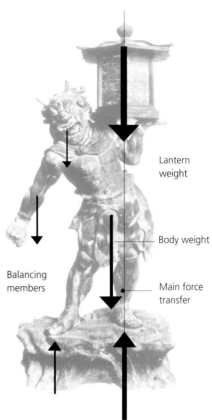

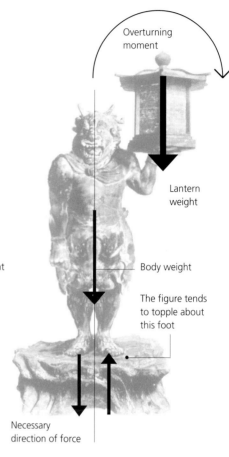

Koben, *Guardian with Lantern.* The body stance shown is normal when the weight carried is heavy.

The posture shown locates the heavy lantern weight directly over his left leg (which experiences a large compressive force). The remainder of the body is poised to provide rapid stability adjustments. Little force is developed in his right leg, a fact suggested by the shape and muscle tenseness.

This improbable stance and muscle shaping implies equal compressive reactions under the feet, which is impossible if the lantern weight is large. The reaction at his right foot would have to act downward for the Guardian not to overturn — an impossibility if the Guardian were alive.

4.8
Koben's *Guardian with Lantern* correctly represents the body posture necessary to support a very heavy load. The posture shown to the right is incompatible with a heavy lantern, since the latter could produce an overturning effect. The posture on the right is appropriate only if the lantern's weight is small.

is extremely heavy, for the upright posture to work the reaction under the right leg of the Guardian would have to be such as to hold the leg down—not possible, since only compressive interface forces can exist with living forms that walk over surfaces. It would indeed be theoretically feasible to make a material sculpture that looked like that shown in this diagram, since a rigid base attachment could be used to tie the right leg down. The suggested posture, however, would look quite silly and unconvincing. Only if the lantern were of paper and quite light would the posture be possible (as if the Guardian were actually a rather unique waiter carrying a tray of drinks), which is quite contrary to the sense portrayed by the original sculpture.

On Moments

While the idea of moment has been explored from several perspectives in this chapter, a final example is useful to convey a real sense of what a moment actually *feels* like. This sense can be gained by simply holding a weight in the hand of an outstretched arm and feeling what happens in the arm. The sense of overturning is directly related to the moment of the weight carried. The heavier the weight, or the more the arm is outstretched, the greater is the moment and the sense of overturning. As the moment becomes greater, so do the forces developed in the muscles of the arm that provide a *resistance* to the overturning moment. It is the latter phenomenon that the individual actually feels internally. In the case shown in figure 4.9, the weight produces a moment about the elbow equal to the magnitude of the weight times its distance from the elbow.[9] This is an *applied* moment. In order to keep the weight in place, the biceps muscles and bone assembly must resist this rotational moment. The way this resistance is provided is through a force developed in the biceps muscle that acts over the very small distance (or "moment arm") from the point of rotation to the muscle attachment point, thus producing a *reactive* or *resisting* moment.[10] The forces developed in the biceps are what an individual actually feels. If the weight is not to rotate about the elbow, then the applied rotational moment of the weight at the end of the arm must be balanced by a resisting moment developed by the force in the muscle acting over the distance from the point of muscle attachment to the elbow joint. The net effect of the two opposite rotational tendencies must equal zero (the applied

Hercules

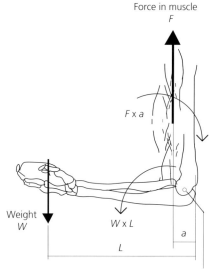

A weight produces an applied rotational moment about the elbow. In a live figure, a force is developed in the muscle that produces an equilibrating moment that is equal and opposite in sense: $W \times L = F \times a$.

4.9
Hercules (gilt bronze). In a live human structure, an external or applied moment is counteracted by an internal moment generated by a force developed in the muscle that acts over the distance between the rotation point and the muscle attachment.

9

If the weight is represented by *W*, and the distance of the weight from the elbow (point of rotation) as *L*, then the rotational moment of the weight about the elbow is given by $M = W \times L$. The heavier the weight, or the longer the arm, the greater will be the overturning moment that has to be resisted by the muscles of the arm. The weight of the arm itself is ignored in this example.

10

This resistance provided by the biceps muscles is given by $M = F \times a$, where *F* is the force developed in the muscle and *a* is its moment arm.

11

For the arm to be in equilibrium, $F \times a$ must exactly equal $W \times L$, or $F \times a = W \times L$. One can then calculate the magnitude of the force in the muscle, $F = (W \times L)/a$. Note that since *a* is very small and both *W* and *L* are large, *F* must be extremely large relative to *W*.

and resisting moments must exactly equal each other). The internal distance between the muscle attachment and the elbow joint is quite small, so the force developed in the muscle must be quite large to balance the applied moment generated from the weight acting over the whole length of the arm.[11] Since biological considerations indicate that muscles develop forces via a contraction mode, the muscle must bulge outward to develop the necessary force. A representation of bulging muscles caused by this effect is apparent in *Hercules*. Instead of simply reacting to forces, muscles may exert forces as well (a contraction associated with muscle bulging causes a force to be developed).

Obviously, the bronze making up the muscle of *Hercules* feels no such force, since sculptural representations do not behave structurally in the same way as live human figures. The projecting arm acts like a simple cantilever beam and alone resists the applied moment via the development of an internal resisting bending moment in the bronze itself, which in turn produces tension and compression stresses in the projecting arm (see chapter 7). The forces developed in the biceps in the *Hercules* sculpture, of course, are also radically different from those in a real muscle, and this member does not serve an analogous role in carrying the projecting weight.

Figure 4.10 further emphasizes the differences between the forces developed in sculptural representations of human forms and those described above for living forms. In the marble *Apollo*, the weight of the arm without the robe would cause bending moments to develop in it, which in turn could lead to the development of high tension stresses along the top surface of the arm and compression stresses along the lower surface (see chapter 7). Marble is weaker in tension, so the arm is highly susceptible to breaking off. The robe, however, provides a stabilizing function by acting as a compressive strut, keeping bending (and hence tension stresses) from developing in the arm. Thus both the arm and the robe behave quite differently from their real counterparts (try to imagine a real robe in compression!). Devices like the robe and stump shown in figure 4.10 were frequently used by sculptors in marble to strengthen projecting parts.

Apollo Belvedere **(Roman copy in marble of lost Hellenistic bronze)**

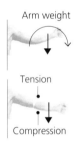

Without the robe, the arm is in bending and tends to crack off.

The robe serves as a supporting compression strut preventing the arm from bending and cracking.

4.10
Sculptures representing human figures carry loads quite differently from live figures. In *Apollo*, bending stresses are developed that cause the marble, which breaks quite easily when subjected to tension, to crack (see chapters 9 and 18). The original bronze did not have the robe and stump, but bronze can carry high bending stresses without failure. The robe and stump were added to make the copy possible in marble.

5.0
Isamu Noguchi, *Strange Bird.*

5 Stability and Balance: Point, Distributed Point, and Base Attachment Sculptures

Basic Stability Issues

Implicit in any work is the need for overall stability in the environmental context in which the sculpture is placed. A small piece should not fall over simply because the work itself is out of balance or because of an inadvertent touch on the part of a viewer or a wayward gust of wind through an open door. A larger piece in an indoor setting must not overturn in the event someone leans against it. An exterior work might well have to be anchored to prevent its being blown over in a windstorm, or, in some localities, a hurricane. The question of how to assure the stability of an object can be an extremely sophisticated one and will occupy many of the following pages.

This chapter will consider two aspects of basic stability. The first has to do with whether an object will fall over because its own weight distribution is somehow out of balance. The second deals with the overturning and sliding effects caused by horizontally acting wind or earthquake forces. A final aspect of basic stability, dealing with possible failures associated with inadequate bracing patterns or poor connections between elemental parts of a work, will be addressed in chapter 8.

There are really only several fundamental mechanisms for preventing an upright piece from overturning as a whole unit—and then there are endless variants of each. One approach relies primarily on the self-weight of the object in relation to its overall mass distribution and shaping. The relation between the center of gravity of the sculpture and its support will be shown to be extremely important in this context. Sculptures of this type are self-standing and can be picked up and moved at will. A second approach for relatively monolithic works relies on the physical anchoring of the work to something else, typically the ground. Obviously, these sculptures cannot be easily moved.

These basic techniques for assuring the stability of an object are illustrated in figure 5.1. For sculptures that simply rest on the supporting surface (those at left in this figure), stability can be accomplished by the use of a heavy base or pedestal, or by using some sort of distributed point support system that is often integral to the sculpture itself. For sculptures rigidly attached to the supporting surface (at right in the figure), there are a number of methods, largely dependent on the type of supporting surface.

While this chapter will focus on the physical stability of sculptures, it should not be forgotten that many other issues arise as part of or in response to meeting stability requirements. The historical heavy base or pedestal, for example, has served other functions than simple physical stability: especially as a visual transition and mediator between the sculpture itself and the surrounding world, often reflecting an architectonic character that stands in marked contrast to the representational figures above. An important consequence of moves toward sculptures with distributed point supports and/or base attachments has been the disappearance of the pedestal and the introduction of new ways of relating the sculpture to its context. Conversely, the desire to dispense with the pedestal has commonly called into play the use of a series of distributed point supports to impart stability.

In addition, the *imagery* of stability imparted by different techniques—such as adding mass near the base of an object and/or widening its base to prevent its overturning—is quite important in many sculptures. William Tucker deals with imagery of this sort in *Early Modern Sculpture*, arguing that Auguste Rodin's more convincing figures are those built up from the feet where relatively large masses exist that are coterminous with the ground.[1] Tucker refers to *The Burghers of Calais* as among the more striking examples of Rodin's "feeling for gravity" (as Tucker describes this type of imagery). His *Nude Balzac Study C* also illustrates coterminous masses of this type. The act of placing a large mass low to the ground actually does contribute to the physical stability of the object, in addition to its obvious visual value in imparting an image of stability.

Sculptures with Single Point Supports

Stability under Self-Weight:
The Function of Heavy Base Pedestals
In the last chapter it was argued that the crucial determinant of stability for a figure under its self-weight is that of the location of its center of gravity in relation to the sup-

[1]
William Tucker, *Early Modern Sculpture: Rodin, Degas, Matisse, Brancusi, Picasso, Gonzales* (New York: Oxford University Press, 1974), p. 146.

5.1
**Basic techniques for assuring the
stability (resistance to overturning and sliding) of a sculpture.**

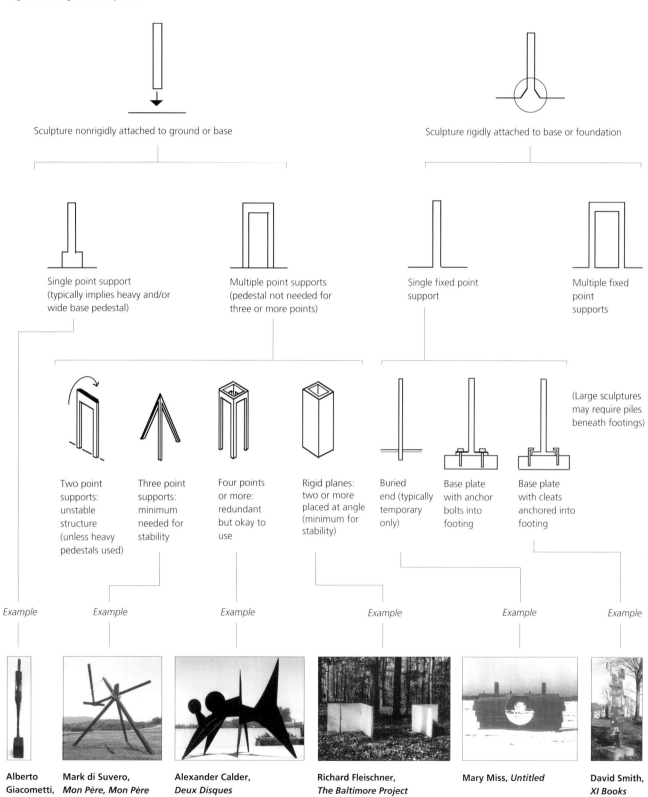

Sculpture nonrigidly attached to ground or base

Sculpture rigidly attached to base or foundation

Single point support
(typically implies heavy and/or
wide base pedestal)

Multiple point supports
(pedestal not needed for
three or more points)

Single fixed point
support

Multiple fixed
point
supports

(Large sculptures
may require piles
beneath footings)

Two point
supports:
unstable
structure
(unless heavy
pedestals used)

Three point
supports:
minimum
needed for
stability

Four points
or more:
redundant
but okay to
use

Rigid planes:
two or more
placed at angle
(minimum for
stability)

Buried
end (typically
temporary
only)

Base plate
with anchor
bolts into
footing

Base plate
with cleats
anchored into
footing

Example *Example* *Example* *Example* *Example* *Example*

**Alberto
Giacometti,
Tall Figure**

**Mark di Suvero,
Mon Père, Mon Père**

**Alexander Calder,
Deux Disques**

**Richard Fleischner,
The Baltimore Project**

Mary Miss, Untitled

**David Smith,
XI Books
III Apples**

porting base. If the center of gravity of a piece is located such that a vertical axis passing through it also passes through the base support of the piece so that no rotational effect is produced, then the object is essentially stable whether or not the base is attached to the surface. The higher the center of gravity of the mass above the base, the more likely the sculpture is to overturn if slightly tilted out of alignment. The more a sculpture projects outward over a small base, the more likely it is to overturn. These propensities are evident in David Smith's *Australia* (fig. 5.2). Sculptures with lowered centers of gravity, and those with wide bases, are much less likely to overturn under their own self-weights.

The importance of lowering the center of gravity is reflected in Rodin's *Nude Balzac Study C* (fig. 5.3). This sculpture conveys an almost overpowering sense of stability. The actual physical stability of the object (its resistance to overturning) is enhanced by the overall triangular shape of the work associated with both the spreading of the legs, which increases the base support width, and the filling in of matter between the legs, which tends to lower the center of gravity of the whole figure far below that normal in a live human figure. It is difficult to imagine the line passing through the center of gravity of the form falling outside of the base support; consequently, the form is extremely resistant to overturning.

The importance of a heavy base underneath a sculpture for the stability of the whole under its self-weight can be seen with reference to Giacometti's *Tall Figure* (fig. 5.4). The base of this work is clearly heavy; thus the center of gravity of the whole assemblage is quite low and consequently the structure is probably quite stable. Nonetheless, assume that the sculpture is tilted out of alignment and then released: will it right itself or fall over?

The stability of the tilted object can be viewed in terms of the rotational effects of the weights. For small tilts, both the weight of the base and the weight of the figure would act to the left of the rotation point in the diagram, causing restoring moments that would tend to right the sculpture when it was released. If the tilt were greater, so that the center of gravity of the upper figure began to project beyond the rotation point at the edge of the base, the weight of the upper piece could cause an overturning rotational effect about the right edge while the base pedestal weight would

5.2
David Smith, *Australia*.
Sculptures with high centers of gravity and parts that project over a narrow base are inherently sensitive to imbalances and possible overturning.

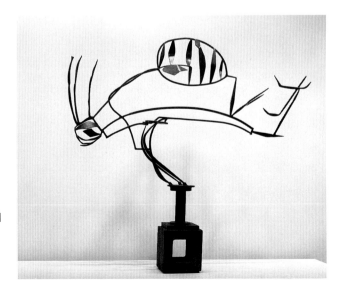

Auguste Rodin,
Nude Balzac Study C

Filled mass and
base lower the
center of gravity
of the sculpture

Extended base
width

5.3
The actual and visual sense of
stability in Rodin's *Nude Balzac*
***Study* C is enhanced by the fill-**
ing of the mass between the legs
and the extended base width.

2
Assume that a force *F* acts at
a height *h* above the ground.
When the horizontal force
begins pushing against the
sculpture, it produces a rotational moment of $M_a = F \times h$
about the rotation point that
tends to cause the whole sculpture to overturn. The weight of
the sculpture produces a balancing moment about the rotation
point of a maximum value of
$M_a = W \times d$, where *d* is one-half
the pedestal width. If $W \times d$ is
greater than $F \times h$, then the
sculpture will not overturn. If *W*
$\times d$ just equals $F \times h$, then the
work is precariously balanced.
If $W \times d$ is less than $F \times h$, the
sculpture will overturn.
Increasing either *d* or *W* clearly
increases the resistance of the
sculpture to overturning.

continue to provide a restoring moment. These rotational
tendencies would occur about the right edge of the pedestal
base. All moment arms would consequently be measured
from this edge. The initial balancing moment of the base, for
example, is given by the weight of the base multiplied by its
moment arm (one-half the pedestal base width in this case).
If the moment tending to restore the sculpture from its tilted
position is greater than that tending to topple it, then the
sculpture will right itself.

Notice that the heavier the base is made, the more likely
it is that the balancing moment will exceed the overturning
moment at a given degree of tilting. The stability of the
object could also be increased by increasing the width of
the base of the structure, thereby increasing the balancing
moment available to resist overturning.

A slightly different view of the function of a heavy base is
that it lowers the center of gravity of the whole piece. The
heavier the base of the object in relation to the upper part,
the closer the center of gravity of the whole figure is to the
base. The consequent lowering of the overall center of gravity tends to improve stability.

Stability under Laterally Acting Forces
The problem of stability for a point-supported piece that is
not rigidly attached to the base surface is made more difficult if it is placed in a context where it is subject to large
forces that act primarily in a horizontal direction, such as
winds. In some parts of the world earthquakes are common
as well. Forces from earthquakes are induced in objects primarily in the horizontal direction. Forces of this type inherently cause overturning effects in any typical vertically
oriented object. In larger works, overturning due to laterally
acting loads can be life threatening.

Common sense suggests that the resistance to overturning can be increased by manipulating the size and weight of
the base. The wider and heavier the base is made, the less
likely it is that a work will topple over when subjected to
forces impinging on the upper part of the structure from the
side. These principles can be examined by looking again at
Giacometti's *Tall Figure* (fig. 5.5). Assume that the figure is
subjected to a horizontal force that acts at a certain height
above the ground (perhaps wind blowing against it).[2] When
the horizontal force begins pushing against the figure, it
produces a rotational moment on the sculpture that tends

to cause the whole to overturn (by tipping about an edge of its base). The magnitude of the rotational moment tending to cause overturning is the product of the applied force times the distance of the force from the point of rotation (i.e., the moment arm of the force).

As the overturning begins, however, the weight of the sculpture tends to keep the sculpture from overturning. The total weight of the sculpture (base plus the upper part) produces a balancing moment that is opposite in sense to the moment tending to cause overturning. The maximum value of this balancing or righting moment is equal to the product of the weight of the structure times its distance to the point of rotation (one-half the base width in this case). The magnitude of the balancing moment thus depends directly on the weight of the structure and the width of the base. So long as the magnitude of the balancing moment available to resist overturning exceeds the applied moment, the sculpture will not overturn. If the applied overturning moment just equals the balancing moment available, then the work is precariously balanced. If the balancing moment available is less than the applied moment, the sculpture will tend to overturn. The design factors that help contribute to resisting overturning are the weight of the sculpture and its pedestal, and the width of its base. Generally, the greater the total weight of the sculpture, the greater the moment available to resist overturning, confirming the intuitively obvious notion that making something heavier will help prevent it from overturning.

The distribution of weight is also important. If overturning actually begins and the sculpture starts tipping over dramatically (as in the diagram at right in figure 5.5), the weight of the upper part of the sculpture actually begins contributing to the overturning effect initially caused by the horizontal load, instead of resisting it. Once this occurs, the sculpture will surely overturn. Note that the base weight remains effective in attempting to resist overturning until the sculpture is almost on its side. Hence if more of the weight were placed in the pedestal rather than at a higher location, the sculpture would become more stable.

Not only is the weight of the pedestal important, but its dimensions as well. Even if the pedestal weight were maintained constant, increased resistance to overturning could be obtained simply by increasing the base dimensions of the pedestal (since the balancing moment available is directly

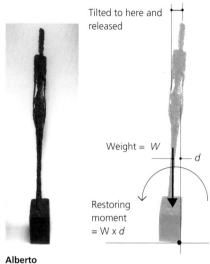

Tilted to here and released

Weight = W

d

Restoring moment = $W \times d$

Alberto Giacometti, *Tall Figure*

5.4
If Alberto Giacometti's *Tall Figure* **were accidentally tilted out of alignment a limited amount and then released, the base weight would provide a balancing moment that would restore the structure to its original position. The wider and heavier the base, the more it serves to stabilize the structure. The upper body weight could cause either a balancing or overturning moment, depending on the amount of tilting.**

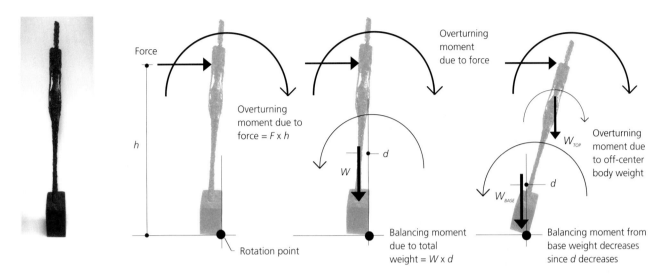

Force

h

Overturning
moment due to
force = F x h

Rotation point

Overturning
moment
due to force

W

d

Balancing moment
due to total
weight = W x d

Overturning
moment due to
to off-center
body weight

W_{TOP}

W_{BASE}

d

Balancing moment from
base weight decreases
since d decreases

Alberto Giacometti,
Tall Figure

**Any applied horizontal force
tends to cause the work to
overturn.**

**The overturning tendency is
balanced by a moment developed
by the total weight of the
sculpture that tends to right the
sculpture if the overturning
tendency is small
(F x h < W x d)**

**If the overturning force is large,
the work begins to topple
unstoppably (the self-weight of
the sculpture contributes to the
overturning).**

**5.5
Base pedestals also serve to keep
a sculpture from overturning
when subjected to a laterally acting force (wind, an earthquake,
or a person pushing against
it) by developing a resisting
moment that tends to stabilize
the structure.**

dependent on the dimensions of the base). It is also easy to
see that if the pedestal were somehow directly affixed to the
base plane, say by anchor bolts connecting the pedestal to
an underground concrete pad, it would be relatively easy to
prevent overturning. As the sculpture tended to overturn,
the rotation would pull against the anchor bolts, putting
one or more of them in tension. This tension force would in
turn hold the sculpture in place.

In the above it has been assumed that the laterally acting
force continues to act against the sculpture once it is
applied. In many instances the horizontal force will be
quickly applied and then quickly released. This might be the
case, for example, when someone knocks up against the
sculpture. If the load is applied quickly and then released,
then even if the sculpture has started overturning it might
return to its normal position because of the restoring
moment provided by the base weight (if it is not knocked
too far over) or even swing past its normal position because
of inertial effects. Thus the sculpture would tend to rock
back and forth after the load is released. Dynamic loadings
of this type are much more difficult to treat analytically since
the speed and duration of the applied load and other factors
become important. In normal cases where unusual dynamic

loads are not expected, the simpler type of analysis shown above is perfectly adequate.

Sculptures with Distributed Point Supports

Stability under Self-Weight
Freestanding sculptures with multiple support points rarely have weighted pedestals at the support points, since the geometry of the arrangement is more important than sheer weight in maintaining stability. Obviously the number of support points is critical. A minimum of three is necessary for the structure to remain upright. Two support points represent an unstable situation (the structure would tend to tip over laterally). Four or more support points are certainly possible but involve a certain redundancy. An implication of this redundancy can be seen in the stability of a three-legged stool as opposed to a four-legged table. A three-legged structure always has all three support points resting evenly on the base plane. There is no wiggle or rocking present even if the legs are not quite the same length or the stool plane is warped. A four-legged table, however, is often susceptible to rocking if all four legs are not exactly the same length or the supporting floor surface is not perfectly planar. Visually, a table with four legs might suggest that all four legs equally share in carrying the weight of the table. The reality, however, is that if rocking is present not all four legs are carrying an equal portion of the weight. This rocking indicates that one of the legs is actually redundant—a table could be made with three carefully placed legs. By contrast, no one leg could be removed from the three-legged stool without the entire structure collapsing. Consequently all bear against the base plane. If more than four legs were present in the table, the difficulty of making them all equally bear on the supporting base plane would increase.

A fundamental reason that two-legged assemblies are clearly unstable is that two supports inherently define a line, and that a lateral or transverse overturning can occur about a line. Virtually any force (external or self-weight) that is not directed exactly through the line will cause overturning to occur. It also follows that to obtain equilibrium using three point supports, these three points must *not* lie on the same line. In fact, they are most desirably situated when they describe a triangle with the vertices as removed from one

another as possible (e.g., a simple equilateral triangle). The closer the points come to being on the same straight line, the higher are the forces developed at these points and the more unstable the structure tends to become.

Many of the same stability principles developed in the previous sections apply here as well. Noguchi's *Strange Bird* provides an example (fig. 5.6). If the center of gravity of the weight lies above the triangle formed by the support points, the downward-acting weight will cause upward vertical reactions to be developed at each of the three support points. A compressive force exists at the interface between each support point and the ground, and therefore it is not necessary that each leg be somehow tied down (and thus capable of resisting tension forces).

As long as the center of gravity of the weight lies above the midpoint of the area defined by the support triangle, the sculpture is stable and will not overturn. Stability does not necessarily mean that all of the reactive forces have the same numerical magnitudes; this would occur only if the center of gravity of the force were exactly centered over the supporting triangle. If the shape of the upper mass caused the center of gravity to be outside the triangle formed by the support points, then the sculpture would tend to overturn. The mass of *Strange Bird*, to be sure, lies over the triangle. But if it were reshaped so that the center of gravity of the body of the bird lay outside the support triangle, as illustrated in the second diagram in figure 5.6, then the mass would tend to produce a rotational moment about an axis formed by two of the legs that would cause the bird to overturn. If the center of gravity of the mass were directly above the rotational axis, there would be no overturning tendency, but the bird would be in a very precarious state of balance (often called neutral equilibrium).

Obviously, the stability of the bird against overturning under its own weight can be enhanced by several means. One is to make sure the center of gravity is exactly centered over the supporting triangle. Others are to widen the absolute dimensions of the supporting triangle (this would allow more flexibility in the placement of the center of gravity of the mass) and to keep the supports as equidistant from one another as possible (to preclude three points lying on the same line).

Finally, the stability of a point-supported object under its own self-weight can be dramatically increased by affixing the

5.6
Sculptures on three distributed point supports are stable when the weight of the sculpture produces only compressive reactions. Imbalances that lead to tension reactions may create instabilities if the points are not affixed to the ground surface.

Three point
supports

Isamu Noguchi, *Strange Bird*

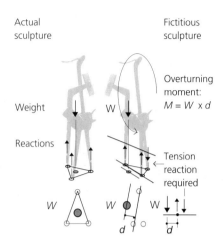

Actual
sculpture

Fictitious
sculpture

Weight

Reactions

Overturning
moment:
$M = W \times d$

Tension
reaction
required

W W W

Since the center of gravity lies within the triangle formed by the support, the sculpture is stable. If it were outside the support triangle, the sculpture would tend to overturn as illustrated in the fictitious modification at right (unless the legs were tied down).

point supports to the base plane so that tension reactions can be developed. If the ground connections were tied down so as to prevent the uplifting of the support point associated with overturning, then the sculpture would remain stable under a much wider variety of massing and lower support configurations (leg spacings).

Stability under Laterally Acting Forces
In the case of *Strange Bird*, laterally acting forces might tend to overturn the sculpture about an axis formed by two of the point supports. If the sculpture is not tied down, all that would resist overturning would be the weight of the work itself, which provides a balancing moment to resist overturning effects. The balancing moment available to resist overturning is the weight of the sculpture acting over its center of gravity times the perpendicular distance (in plan) from the center of gravity to the rotational axis. When either the weight or the base dimensions are small, the balancing moment is consequently small and the sculpture is prone to overturning under light winds.

If the same sculpture were tied onto its supporting surface via connecting bolts, then the work would be much more stable. If the wind force were sufficiently large to overcome the balancing moment available through the self-weight of the sculpture, then a tension force would begin developing in one of the base attachment bolts. The tension force would produce yet another resisting moment (the tension force times its moment arm from the rotational axis) that would prevent overturning. Indeed, the sculpture could never overturn as long as the bolt held.

Structures with Base Attachments

As is evident from preceding discussions, structures with either single point supports or distributed point supports can usefully be attached to the base plane or ground via anchor bolts or other devices. Base attachments can prevent a sculpture from toppling over due to the eccentricity of its own dead weight or the action of a laterally acting load (e.g., wind, earthquakes, pushes). Sculptures so attached can afford to rely less on either high dead weights or widely separated point supports as a basis for achieving stability. The disadvantages, however, are obvious. Sculptures relying on base attachments for stability cannot be easily moved, nor can they be installed just anywhere. Installing base attachments on sculptures placed inside buildings, for example, often requires penetrating the floor surface so that attachments to the underlying building structure can be made. This might be possible in some cases where the work is to remain permanently, but is obviously undesirable in many other cases.

The actual mechanism for a base attachment depends primarily on the type and size of sculpture involved and on the nature of the supporting base plane. Several approaches are noted in figure 5.1. For large works, on common loose soil, the ends of tall totem-pole-like sculptures, for example, can be simply buried in the ground. (Bear in mind that wood sculptures would tend to rot away at the base after a while.) If rock ledge is present at the surface, holes could be drilled in the rock and expansion anchor bolts could be inserted for tie-down attachment points. Alternatively, a large hole could be dug and filled with concrete to provide a large footing. Anchor bolts could be cast into the concrete and ends left protruding for eventual connections to the sculpture itself.

A related approach for small sculptures is to attach the base of a sculpture to a concrete footing using bent L-shaped anchors or cleats. This option is not unlike the direct use of a heavy base or pedestal, but in this case the footing is below grade and not visually part of the sculpture. David

Smith's *XI Books III Apples* uses an approach of this type. The base attachments to the footing must develop a resisting moment that is equal and opposite to the applied moment associated with the overturning action of a lateral load. This resisting moment is developed by the moment formed by a tension reaction on one edge of the base and a compression reaction on the other edge. Clearly, in order for the cleats on one edge of the base to develop a tension reaction, they must be designed to prevent uplifting tendencies. The simple devices shown in figure 5.7 do this admirably. Wide separation in the specific points of connection is always desirable. There is a possibility that when small concrete footings are used, the whole assembly (sculpture plus concrete base) could overturn. In this respect these assemblies behave exactly like sculptures that rely on heavy bases for stability. Since concrete footings are often built into the ground, however, they can be made quite large and heavy without influencing the visual appearance of the work. Consequently, the possibility of the whole assembly overturning can be made quite remote.

Older stone statues may also be tied down to bases using cleats. These works, however, are often quite delicate, and care must be used so that the cleats neither mar the surface of the work (padding usually helps) nor induce localized cracking by being tied down too tightly.

When large sculptures have widely spaced point supports, as with Calder's *Two Disks* (illustrated in figure 5.1), the potential for overturning is considerably reduced. Sliding induced by earthquake movements remains a possibility. Hence, it is always good practice to affix the legs in a positive way to footings. Usually this is relatively easy to do.

Special Lateral Loading Problems: Earthquakes

Earthquake effects can cause sculptures to overturn or slide. Consider a simple work on a pedestal. Ground motions associated with earthquakes act primarily laterally, with a highly complex back and forth movement (see chapter 3 and appendix 2). The accelerations associated with these movements are particularly troublesome. In a sense, the ground underneath an upright statue will tend to move laterally out from under the statue. As ground accelerations begin, the statue itself would initially tend to remain in its

David Smith, *XI Books III Apples*

5.7
Directly attaching the base of a sculpture to a footing can completely stabilize small sculptures. Wind forces would cause both tension and compression reactions to develop. Cleats spaced far apart work better than closely spaced ones.

The cleats provide the necessary tie-downs to prevent the sculpture from overturning.

5.8
David Smith's *Voltron XX* is stabilized through a direct base
attachment.

5.9
Earthquake motions subject
sculptures to sliding and overturning effects. Positive attachments to bases reduce the
potential for sliding or overturning. Earthquake motions may
also induce bending that can
cause failure in stone sculptures
because of their inherent inabil-
ity to carry the tension forces
involved.

original position through the natural inertial tendency of an
object at rest to remain at rest. The consequence is that the
statue would tend to topple over or just slide off its base,
almost as if the pedestal were suddenly pulled from beneath
the statue. Figure 5.9 illustrates this behavior.

If toppling or sliding does not occur during the initial
ground accelerations, then an even more complex set of
forces and movements begins to occur in the structure. As
the ground moves, the mass of the object is ultimately set in
motion. Once in motion, the inertial tendency of the mass is
then to remain in motion in the direction first taken. Soon
the mass of the structure might be moving in one direction
while the ground might suddenly start reversing its direction. Now it is as if the statue were being pulled in one direction and the pedestal beneath it jerked in the opposite
direction. Again the statue could topple over or slide. If the
statue is adequately attached to the pedestal and does not
topple or slide at this point, then the mass will eventually

**Statue in front of the cathedral of
Palermo, Sicily**

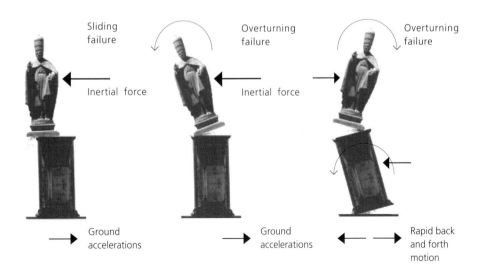

Sliding
failure

Inertial force

Ground
accelerations

Overturning
failure

Inertial force

Ground
accelerations

Overturning
failure

Rapid back
and forth
motion

**Lateral ground motions
associated with earthquakes
cause inertial forces to develop
that are dependent on the weight
of the structure. Sliding failures
can occur.**

**The lateral ground motions can
also cause a sculpture to overturn.
The magnitude of the overturning
effect depends on the weight of
the sculpture and its height above
the ground.**

**Back and forth ground motions
can cause different parts of the
sculpture to move in different
directions. Overturning or
cracking of elements can
consequently occur.**

reverse direction and try to follow the reversed ground motions. But these ground motions are probably ready to change direction again. Eventually the ground is rapidly moving beneath the structure in one pattern and the structure is moving about above it in a different to and fro pattern.

In addition to creating forces that tend to topple the mass or slide it off its footing, such movements cause severe stresses to develop within the statue, stresses that can cause bending failures. Stone is particularly sensitive to failure through the tension stresses associated with bending (see chapter 9) and could easily crack apart. Metallic statues are less likely to break apart because of the material's inherent ability to carry tension, but they are still quite susceptible to overturning.

While the ground motions associated with earthquakes are usually predominantly lateral in character, some up and down movements can also occur. These up and down accelerations can cause inertial forces and associated bending to develop in long outstretched members. A projecting arm of a statue could potentially crack off due to the effects of these vertical ground motions. It is easy to imagine, for example, that the outstretched arm of a marble *Hercules* (see figure 4.10) without the stiffening robe could easily break off as shown.

The magnitudes of the earthquake-induced forces associated with such sliding, toppling, and bending failures are dependent on the character of the earthquake movements, notably the magnitudes of the ground accelerations, and on the mass (or weight) of the sculpture itself. The heavier the sculpture, the greater the forces induced within it. (This observation generally follows from Newton's observation of the relation between force, mass, and acceleration, i.e., $F = ma$.) The magnitude of the overturning tendency present also depends on the height of the center of mass above the rotation point. The taller the statue, the higher the center of mass, and the greater the tendency to overturn.

Since earthquake forces are mass-dependent, effects are largely negligible in small light pieces—although the vibratory effects might still tend to cause them to walk off of their settings. Fairly minor tie-downs can prevent this. In large and massive sculptures, however, earthquake forces can be very large and must be consciously considered in the design of the object and its foundations. Positive tie-downs

that fix the base of a sculpture to a ground foundation designed not to overturn or slide itself are usually necessary. Various forms of base plates and anchor bolt systems are possible in large newly designed structures, and frequently can be directly integrated into the design of the work. For intermediate-sized works, various cleat systems attached in turn to larger footings can be used.

When the sculptural material is stone, positive tie-downs are more difficult but still possible. For new works, a number of technologies exist for connecting stone to other materials (such as a concrete foundation) via the use of drilled holes and expansion anchor bolts.

The treatment of existing works in a museum or gallery context is a highly complex topic and beyond the scope of this book. It may be noted, however, that tie-down techniques are still applicable and most prevalent. Again, various forms of cleat systems are possible. When earthquake motions occur, however, severe localized stresses could develop around the region of a cleat, which could result in cracking or other forms of failure. It must also be remembered that surfaces can potentially be badly marred when working with delicate stonework and other sensitive materials. Soft padding systems help.

An innovative technique for mitigating the effects of earthquakes that is gaining in currency is the use of what are called *base isolation* devices. First explored in the context of building design in earthquake-prone areas, these devices are conceptually quite simple and elegant. Base isolation devices are special connections that are designed to allow the ground to move more or less freely beneath a structure. A simple conceptual model is illustrated in figure 5.10 as a set of rollers beneath the mass of the object. The rollers would allow the ground to move freely beneath the object. The object would remain more or less in its initial position due to its inertial tendency to remain at rest. Overturning tendencies are minimized or eliminated, as are stresses within the object itself. Turning this conceptual model into a viable device, however, requires careful detailing. The base connection, for example, must still serve the purpose of stabilizing the object with respect to normal impact or wind forces (the roller system as diagrammed here certainly does not accomplish this end). In an earthquake, the upper mass would still tend to move somewhat, and the extent of this movement must be limited by some sort of constraint sys-

The sculpture tends to remain at rest due to inertial tendencies.

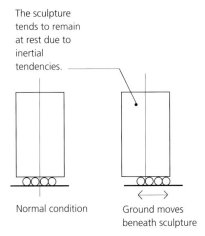

Normal condition   Ground moves beneath sculpture

Basic concept

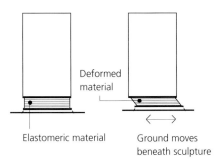

Deformed material

Elastomeric material   Ground moves beneath sculpture

One type of base isolation device

5.10
An innovative way of mitigating the effects of laterally acting earthquake ground movements is through the use of base isolation devices that allow the ground to move more or less freely beneath the mass of the sculpture. Several different designs for base isolation devices are possible.

tem. These same movements of the upper object could cause detrimental pounding against the constraint system, and some sort of system for damping out these movements is desirable.

Largely in connection with building design, various types of realistic base isolation devices have been designed. Constrained and damped roller systems are possible but complex. Another approach shown in figure 5.10 is to use specially designed elastomeric materials that easily deform in the lateral direction, thereby allowing some ground move- ment beneath the upper structure. These material deforma- tions can also positively absorb energy associated with the earthquake movements and damp out oscillations. In very heavy objects with a single point support, imbalances in the upper load distribution could cause uneven distortions of the compressed material, with potential tilting resulting. This potential tilting is less of a problem when the structure has multiple base supports. Ideally, for lateral forces, the mate- rial should be somewhat stiffer with respect to deformations in the vertical direction to mitigate this potential tilting. On the other hand, some flexibility is desirable in the vertical direction because of the possible vertical components of the earthquake ground accelerations and the need to mitigate these effects. Identifying or designing materials with appro- priate stiffness levels is a major difficulty in this approach to base isolation. These and other approaches developed largely for buildings have applicability as well in mitigating the effects of earthquakes on sculptures.

6.0
Alexander Calder, *Mobile.*

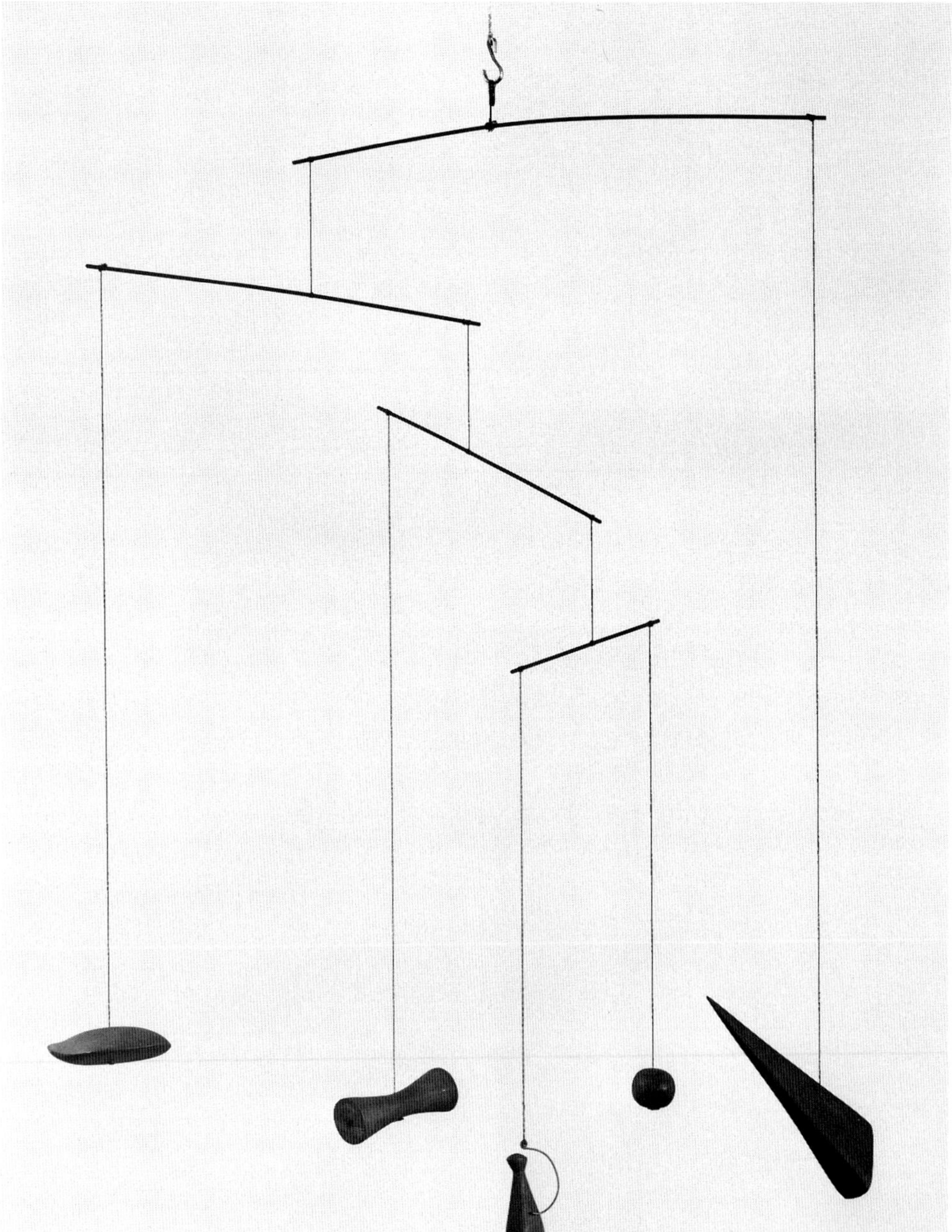

6 Sculptures with Balancing Elements: Real and Illusory Balance

The subtitle for this chapter comes from a passage in William Tucker's book *Early Modern Sculpture* in which he discusses Degas's sculpture in terms of "the hard-won equilibrium of volume, surface and silhouette."[1] He goes on to deal further with the *imagery* of balance in Degas's sculptures, but he also notes the potential dependence of some of Degas's forms on the *real* balancing of some of the initial armatures of modeling wax, tallow, and pieces of cork.

The previous chapters have focused on the basic stability of different types of sculptures. This chapter explores more complex balance principles. It deals first with forms that are the direct outgrowth of the real balancing of objects. Calder's mobiles and other similar works surely mean to convey a sense of balance as well as actually be in a state of balance. Next addressed are the technical implications of creating objects that may visually imply a sense of balance but not actually be physically functioning in the way that is visually suggested. Barnett Newman's *Broken Obelisk* (fig. 1.1) is perhaps one of the most elegant of sculptures of this type. Such works seek to reflect states of balance that are at once conceptually possible yet highly improbable. Hence they have intriguing characteristics.

Real Balance

Balanced Elements with Lowered Centers of Gravity
An important balance principle is illustrated by Calder's Acrobats (fig. 6.1). The upper acrobat seems not to be connected in any really substantial way to the head of the lower acrobat. What then keeps the upper acrobat in place? Why does it not rotate and slip off the head of the lower acrobat? Is it simply a case of a not too obvious connection providing stability? Yet virtually any observer simply knows that the upper acrobat is not going to slip off the head of the lower, and that this perception does not depend on "hidden connections" or the like.

The physical and visual stability of the upper figure can be explained in terms of its center of gravity. A careful exami-

1
Tucker, *Early Modern Sculpture*, p. 152.

nation of the distorted proportions of the upper acrobat indicates that its center of gravity must lie somewhere *beneath* the hip area (instead of in the pelvic area as is more normally the case in a realistically proportioned figure). This lowering of the center of gravity is caused by the increased mass of the extended legs relative to the reduced mass of the upper body. In *Acrobats*, the center of gravity of the acrobat is actually now located *below* its point of support. Since the center of gravity represents that point at which the entire mass of the figure may be considered as concentrated into a point, it follows that the upper acrobat cannot topple over in the same way the Degas's *Dancer Looking at the Sole of Her Right Foot* (fig. 4.6) could. In order for toppling to occur, the center of gravity would have to lie *above* the point of support. In Degas's *Dancer*, for example, tilting the statue would cause it to topple because of the overturning moment induced by the eccentric location of the center of gravity in the tilting figure.

In *Acrobats*, tilting the upper acrobat would not cause it to overturn even if there were no connection at all between the two figures. Rather the tilting would actually cause a form of *restoring* moment to develop, which would in turn cause the upper acrobat to resume its original upright position. If the upper acrobat were not rigidly connected at all (but simply pinned in place with some sort of axle), tilting it and releasing it would only cause it to rock back and forth. Thus the upper acrobat is inherently stable. In actuality, it is lightly connected to the head of the lower acrobat, but the connection need not be substantial and is necessary only for handling purposes as well as to keep the potentially detracting rocking from occurring. The same principle is eloquently demonstrated in Kenneth Snelson's *First Study for Moving Sculpture* (fig. 6.2).

In situations where the mass of the sculpture is distributed throughout the sculpture, it is often difficult to imagine where to consider the weight concentrated. Sculptures of this type may be treated by considering the masses of different parts of a work to be concentrated at their respective centers of gravity. Calder's *Shark and Whale* (fig. 6.3) illustrates this approach. The shark is clearly in balance about the nose of the whale. In order to consider rotational balance more precisely, however, it is necessary to identify the weight and location of the center of gravity of *each portion* of the shark on the left and right hand sides of the point of

Alexander Calder, *Acrobats*

6.1
Since the center of gravity of the upper figure lies below its balance point, the upper figure is inherently stable and resistant to overturning. In Calder's *Acrobats*, the upper figure is actually rigidly attached to the head below it. Live acrobats having these same proportions would be stable without being attached.

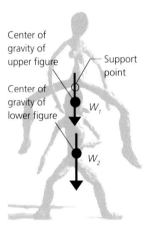

Center of gravity of upper figure — Support point
Center of gravity of lower figure — W_1
W_2

The center of gravity of the upper figure is directly below its point of support. The figure is thus inherently stable.

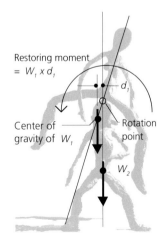

Restoring moment = $W_1 \times d_1$
d_1
Center of gravity of W_1 — Rotation point
W_2

If the upper figure were accidentally tilted, the figure would tend to right itself rather than continue to overturn because of the restoring moment present.

support. The weight of each side would then be considered concentrated at its respective center of gravity. The dimensions of the mass suggest that the centers of gravity of the two portions are about at the points indicated in the diagram, with the slimmer proportions of the mass to the right suggesting that its center of gravity is further removed from the support point than is the case with the mass to the left. For the shark to be in equilibrium, the rotational effect produced by the weight of the part of the shark to the left acting over its moment arm must be the same as the weight of the part of the shark to the right acting over its moment arm.[2]

The shark is delicately balanced. The stability principle is similar to that for *Acrobats* and *First Study for Moving Sculpture*. The convex shape of the shark means that its center of gravity lies below the center point of support. This means that it is very difficult to overturn the curved element; it has a great degree of inherent stability. If the shark were imagined as exactly straight, rotational balance might possibly still exist, but it is doubtful if it would ever easily sit exactly horizontally. Any very minor error in locating the center balance point would cause the shark to remain permanently tipped in one position (the tipping would cause minor changes in the two moment arm lengths, which would in turn reestablish rotational equilibrium). With the center of gravity below the point of support, the shark will always seek to maintain its initial position. The lowering of the center of gravity thus stabilizes the shark both physically and visually. In reality, the shark and the whale are attached.

Achieving stability by distributing the mass of an object such that the resultant center of gravity lies below the point of support is actually a fairly common technique. A tightrope walker in a circus who uses a long curved balance pole is essentially achieving balance by the same mechanism—the downward curve of the heavy pole lowers the center of gravity of the whole mass (walker plus pole). If the curved pole is long enough, the center of gravity is actually below the point of support provided by the wire, and consequently the walker is quite stable.

Complex Balanced Elements with Simple Point Forces
A number of sculptures derive their essence from the actual physical balancing of forms, notably Alexander Calder's mobiles. Figure 4.2 illustrated a simple example of a single

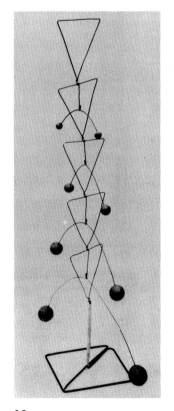

6.2
In Kenneth Snelson's *First Study for Moving Sculpture*, physical and visual stability rely on the center of gravity of each pair of weights lying below their suspension points.

2
With respect to figure 6.3, rotational equilibrium demands that $W_1 \times d_1 = W_2 \times d_2$. For the shark to be in equilibrium, it follows that W_1 is larger than W_2 since d_2 is smaller than d_1. The reaction (R) that exists at the point of contact between the shark and the whale has a magnitude $R = W_1 + W_2$, which is in turn simply equal to the weight W of the whale ($W = R$). Note that rotational moments could be summed about any point on the whale and the net effect would still have to be zero.

6.3

The rotational effects of parts of a structure around a point are considered by establishing the center of gravity of each of the parts. The upper figure is stable because the center of gravity of the whole is beneath its suspension point.

Alexander Calder, *Shark and Whale*

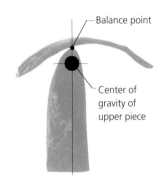

The center of gravity of the total weight of the upper piece is below the balance point for stability.

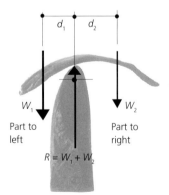

The distributed masses to the left and right of the support point may be considered as concentrated loads for a rotational equilibrium analysis: $W_1 \times d_1 = W_2 \times d_2$.

arm of one of his mobiles; this section will look at more complicated examples in greater depth.

One of Calder's works, now at the Hirshhorn Museum Sculpture Garden, consists of four arms in a state of physical balance (fig. 6.4). Knowing nothing more about the sculpture, we can still infer some things simply by looking at the points of balance of each of the horizontal arms. Consider arm *A* of the assembly. The fin on the left produces a counterclockwise rotational tendency (or moment) about its support point equal to the magnitude of the force multiplied by the perpendicular distance to the line of action of the force (its moment arm). The total weight of the suspended assembly on the right (arms *B*, *C*, and *D*) similarly produces a clockwise rotational tendency about the suspension point. For arm *A* not to spin (for the subassembly to be in rotational equilibrium), the counterclockwise moment produced by the weight at left must exactly equal the clockwise moment produced by the suspended arms to the right. Inspection reveals that the distance between the left weight and its point of support is less than that of the the suspended weights to the right. It follows that the weight of the fin to the left must be somewhat greater than the combined weights of suspended arms *B*, *C*, and *D*. (Recall that a large force acting over a small distance can yield the same rotational effect as a smaller force acting over a larger distance.)

The rotational equilibrium of each of the other arms can be similarly studied. At the lowest level of the suspension hierarchy, arm *D* is in rotational equilibrum about its support point. The upward reactive force developed at its support point equals the weight of the whole arm assembly. This same force acts downward on arm *C*. Note that the force is shown on the diagram at the point of connection as acting equally but in an opposite direction on the two arms. This force is internal in nature. Decomposing it into two equal and opposite forces follows from Newton's third law. The equilibrium of arm *C* then results from a careful balancing of added weights at either end and the judicious adjustment of their respective moment arms. The upward force developed at the suspension point of arm *C* is equal to the sum of all the downward forces present in arms *C* and *D*. This same force then becomes a force acting downward at the end of arm *B*, which is in turn balanced by a carefully located weight at its other end. Arm *A* is treated as discussed above.

Each arm is in rotational
equilibrium about its support
point.

6.4
Each arm in this mobile is in a
state of balance. The forces in
the tension members suspending
an arm exert downward forces
on the arm above.

Alexander Calder, *Mobile-Stabile*

The various operations above could be done numerically to ascertain exact weights and their locations. Mathematically, one would start with arm *D* at the lowest level of the hierarchy and work upward (since the exact weights needed for balancing any typical assembly depend in turn on the forces exerted on it from the assemblies below, and these are not known until the balance requirements of the lower assemblies are determined). Conceptually, it is of some interest to note that these steps in analyzing the balances and interrelationships of different subassemblies probably reflect the steps used to create the mobile in the first place. Subassembly *D* was most likely created first and then attached to assembly *C*, and then the other elements and moment arm lengths were adjusted to balance the whole assembly.

Another of Calder's mobiles, *Small Spider*, illustrates another aspect of balance not especially evident in the previous example. The issue is what effect the curving of the arms supporting the individual masses has on the equilibrium of the form. Consider one of the curved shapes that supports weights *A* and *B* and is in turn suspended from a point. Figure 6.5 shows a diagram of the force system acting on the curved member—a force system that must be in translational and rotational equilibrium. Weight *A* and weight *B* produce equal and opposite rotational moments about the suspension point. In the example previously considered, the moment arm of a force was essentially the same as the linear distance along the member from the point of attachment to the point of suspension. The curved element in this case complicates the issue—what, exactly, is the moment arm of weight *B* with respect to its tendency to produce a rotation about its suspension point? The answer is simple, somewhat surprising, and goes back to the basic definition of a moment—a moment is the product of a force times the perpendicular distance to its line of action. In this case, the distance is measured from *B* along the horizontal to a vertical line dropped through the suspension point.[3] The weight thus produces a clockwise rotational effect or moment about the suspension point. The length along the curve and the exact shape of the supporting rod have nothing whatever to do with the rotational sense or the magnitude of the moment of weight *B* about the suspension point (assuming that the small dead weight of the wire itself is ignored). Thus despite the fact

Alexander Calder, *Small Spider*

Moment arm = perpendicular distance to the line of action of the force

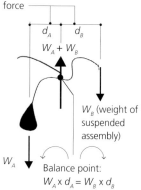

If the self-weight of the curved arm is small, the curved shape does not affect the length of the moment arms.

6.5
In the rotational effects of a load about a point, the shapes of connecting elements play no role (assuming their weights to be negligible).

3
The moment arm of weight B about the suspension point is d_B. The moment of weight B about the suspension point is $W_B \times d_B$. The moment of weight A is $W_A \times d_A$. Overall, $W_B \times d_B = W_A \times d_A$. This expression could be used to vary weights and moment arms to achieve perfect balance.

that the wire is sharply curved, the net rotational effect of weight *B* is the same as if the wire were a simple straight line. The rotational effect of a mass about a point depends only on its weight and absolute location in space.

Determining Reactive Forces
A common objective of an equilibrium study is to determine the sense and magnitudes of any unknown forces that might be developed on or within a structure. For example, consider Ernst Barlach's *Güstrow War Memorial* (fig. 6.6). The *Memorial* is suspended by two cables. One might want to determine the forces that must exist within these two cables, as a quantitative understanding of these forces is a prelude to determining the sizes of the cables necessary to safely support the memorial. This example will be analyzed in some detail to illustrate the type of analysis used in studying the structural behavior of an object.

The weight of the *Memorial* acts downward, causing tension forces to develop in each of the supporting cables. *If the center of gravity of the weight were located exactly between the two supporting cables, then simple symmetry considerations would indicate that the weight would be equally shared between the cables, and that tension forces present in each cable would be identical. Since the shape of the *Memorial* is complex, however, there is little reason to believe that the center of gravity of the weight is located exactly between the two cables. Suppose then that the center of gravity is located somewhat to the right of center (as shown in the diagram in figure 6.6). Tension forces are again developed in the two cables, but in this situation there is no reason to believe that the two cables would equally share the weight of the *Memorial*. Since the weight is concentrated nearest the cable on the right, it can be expected that this cable would carry more of the weight than the cable on the left. Consequently, the tension force in the cable on the right would be greater than that in the cable on the left. The sum of the two cable forces still equals the value of the weight acting downward. This must be the case since the sum of all forces acting in the vertical direction must equal zero from simple equilibrium considerations. The relative magnitudes of the cable forces can be determined by considering the rotational equilibrium of all of the forces and weights acting on the *Memorial*.[4]

Ernst Barlach, *Güstrow War Memorial*

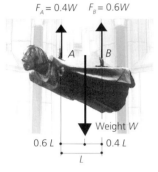

$F_A = 0.4W$ $F_B = 0.6W$

Weight W

$0.6 L$ $0.4 L$

L

Equilibrium diagram showing how the weight of the sculpture develops reactive forces in the supporting ropes. Note that $F_A + F_B = W$.

6.6
In Barlach's *Güstrow War Memorial*, the tension forces developed in the supporting cables provide the necessary reactive forces to keep the sculpture in translational and rotational equilibrium. These same equilibrium considerations may be used to determine the magnitudes of the forces and, ultimately, their required sizes.

4
Assume that the whole weight of the sculpture can be considered equivalent to a force of W that acts at the assumed center of gravity of the shape. W can be estimated or measured by simply weighing the *Memorial*. The forces F_A and F_B in the suspended cables, however, cannot be known a priori. It is naive to expect that they would necessarily be equal one to another. From translatory equilibrium considerations, however, $F_A + F_B = W$. The rotational effects of all the forces acting on the *Memorial* about point A are: $W \times 0.6L - F_B \times L + F_A \times 0 = 0$, or $F_B = 0.6W$. Alternatively, consider rotational effects about point B: $-W \times 0.4L + F_A \times L + F_B \times 0 = 0$, or $F_A = 0.4W$. Note that $F_A + F_B = 0.6W + 0.4W = W$ as expected. (Where moment arms are zero, the force passes through the assumed point of rotation and does not produce any moment about that point. An algebraic sign convention is also used: clockwise rotations here are considered positive and counterclockwise rotations negative. These conventions are not too important here, but are necessary for detailed analyses.)

A different principle is illustrated by Mahonri M. Young's *Man with a Wheelbarrow*, executed in 1915 (fig. 6.7). If the man and the wheelbarrow were actual rather than sculpted, then the wheelbarrow would obviously derive its balance from the support offered by the man's arms. Without this support the wheelbarrow would simply rotate about the forward axle and collapse downward. As a consequence of the support provided, it is equally obvious that large forces are developed in the arms of the man. One could ascertain the magnitude of the forces in the man's arms by studying the equilibrium of the wheelbarrow. The wheelbarrow is supported at its front end by the wheel and at its back by the man. Thus the wheelbarrow itself must experience forces exerted on it at these two points. The force at the front is reactive in nature and exists at the interface between the wheel and the ground. The force at the rear is also reactive and is located in the man's arms. As yet the directions of these forces (whether upward or downward) are not known, but they can be easily inferred. Since the weight of the load in the wheelbarrow obviously acts downward, it follows that the reactive force acting on the wheelbarrow at the junction of the wheel and the ground, and the force in the man's arms, must act upward. The precise magnitudes of these two reactive forces are as yet unknown, but it is known that their sum equals the downward-acting weight.[5]

The only way to determine the magnitudes of these two reactive forces is through rotational equilibrium considerations. The product of the left reactive force times its distance from the location of the weight at the center of the wheelbarrow balances that of the right reactive force times its comparable moment arm.[6] Instead of considering moment equilibrium about the location of the center weight, any other point could be used. With reference to the axle of the wheel, for example, it is evident that the weight acting downward produces a rotational moment about the axle that acts in a clockwise direction. If no other forces existed than this weight, the wheelbarrow would spin in a clockwise direction about the axle. In actuality, however, forces in the man's arms are developed that create a counterbalancing rotational moment about the axle that acts in the counterclockwise direction. With reference to the axle, the clockwise moment produced by the weight is identically balanced by the counterclockwise moment produced by the forces

6.7

If the man were alive and the wheelbarrow were real, the lines of action of the three forces acting on the wheelbarrow would necessarily meet at a point for the structure to be in equilibrium. Note how the slope under the wheel causes the force through it to be inclined. The man's arm is aligned with the direction of the force developed at the handle of the wheelbarrow.

Mahonri M. Young, *Man with a Wheelbarrow*

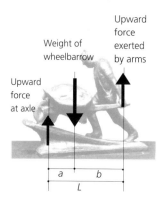

Simplified diagram of the forces acting on the wheelbarrow (imagined as a real situation)

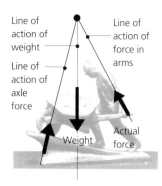

The lines of action of the three forces meet at a point.

developed in the man's arms.[7] Knowledge of these relationships can then directly lead to an exact determination of the forces in the man's arms, as well as of the reactive force under the front wheel.[8]

Actually, a careful observer would note, from the directions of the man's arms and the fact that the wheelbarrow is being pushed uphill slightly, that the assumption of vertical directions for the reactive forces at the wheelbarrow and in the man's arms is not quite right. Rather they are more likely to have the slightly inclined directions shown in the diagram at bottom. The force transmitted through a wheel is always perpendicular to the surface it rests upon (no matter what degree of incline is present). The forces in the man's arms must be aligned with their actual directions. It can be demonstrated that these inclinations do not affect the basic force and rotational equilibrium arguments made above very much, but they do convey a much clearer sense of what is actually happening in a real-world equivalent of the sculpture. The force at the wheel has a horizontal component acting to the right; therefore the man must exert a force to the left for the wheelbarrow to be in equilibrium in the horizontal direction. As long as the ground is inclined, the man's arms must therefore be at an angle. Otherwise the wheelbarrow would roll back down the hill. If the ground were horizontal, the reactive force at the wheel would act vertically and the man would not have to lean to hold up his end of the wheelbarrow.

This diagram also demonstrates an interesting property of forces acting on an object. If there are only three forces acting on an object, the lines of action of these three forces must meet at a single point if the object is to be in translatory and rotational equilibrium. This is a fundamental principle of force analysis that is given a strong visual manifestation by *Man with a Wheelbarrow*. The man's body stance is aligned with the direction of the inclined force necessary for equilibrium that acts through his body.

The observation that the lines of action of any three forces acting on an object must meet at a single point is not generalizable to more forces than three.[9] For more than three forces, it can only be observed that the net translatory and rotational effects of the applied and reactive force system must be zero. For a simpler case where only two forces act on an object, it is possible to stipulate that these two

5

If W represents the wheelbarrow weight, R_A the upward component of the reactive force to the left, and R_B the upward component of the reactive force to the right, then considerations of translatory equilibrium require that $R_A + R_B - W = 0$ or $R_A + R_B = W$.

6

If the location of the load is used as a reference center, it follows that $R_A \times a = R_B \times b$. Since W passes through the reference center, its moment arm is zero and it does not enter into the equation.

7

If the axle of the wheel is used as a reference center, $W \times a - R_B \times L = 0$. Hence, $R_B = (W \times a)/L$. Since R_A acts through the reference center, its moment arm is zero and it does not enter into the equation.

8

From moment considerations, $R_B = (W \times a)/L$. If W, a, and L are known, R_B can be determined. R_A can then be found from noting that $R_A + R_B = W$.

9

Even in the case of three forces acting on a body, the case shown earlier where the three forces are parallel would seemingly belie the truth of this statement. The validity of the point is retained, however, by noting the common proposition that parallel forces can be considered to meet at a point indefinitely far away.

forces must be equal in magnitude, opposite in sense, and have collinear lines of action.

Illusory Balance

Two pieces provide examples of the technical issues involved in creating a sculpture that relies on the concept of implied balance. Barnett Newman's *Broken Obelisk* was executed in 1967 in steel (fig. 6.8). The piece consists of a pyramid of four isosceles triangles, with an upside-down obelisk with broken top seemingly balancing on the apex of the pyramid. The drama of the piece relies on the apex-to-apex meeting of the two forms coming as close to an infinitesimal point as physically possible. Indeed, a basic tenet of the piece is that the meeting *be* a point. Closely related to this idea is that of maintaining the profiles of the two pointed forms as extensions of one another in common planes—a reality not possible unless the apex-to-apex meeting is actually a perfect point. Yet these ideals are potentially compromised by structural concerns on the one hand and technological issues on the other. In a marvelously ambiguous way, the idea of the piece contradicts physical reality, which demands that the two forms meet in anything but a perfect point.

While the visual gestalt of the sculpture hinges around an image of a balanced object—with an implied preoccupation with vertically acting gravity forces—the real structural issue at hand is that of how to prevent laterally acting wind or earthquake forces from overturning the upper obelisk. Since no other device is present to provide the necessary resistance to these overturning moments, it follows that the juncture *cannot* actually be a true point connection in the sense discussed in chapter 2. By its very nature, any true point connection would allow three degrees of rotational freedom. This is exactly what cannot be allowed happen in the obelisk. Rotational freedoms would allow the upper part of the obelisk to fall over in the event of any minor lateral force. There are always some minor forces present, such as wind. So there must be some rigid device that prevents rotational freedom at the apex-to-apex point.

Resistance at the apex-to-apex meeting point was provided by cutting off the very tip of each form and inserting a steel collar and pipe that allow the two forms to be screwed together. Since the upper obelisk is relatively small, laterally

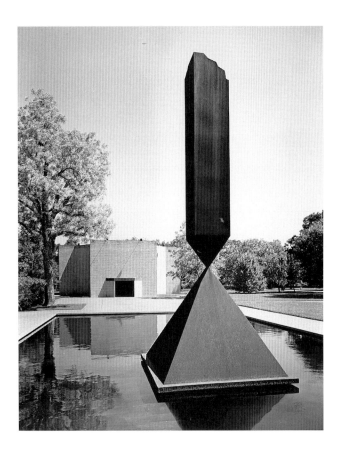

6.8
The seemingly improbable configuration of Newman's *Broken Obelisk*, with its suggestive reminiscence of stone, is possible only because of the capability of the small steel interface between the two masses to resist the high bending stresses developed there.

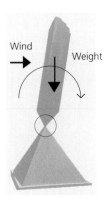

Detail of the junction that provides the necessary stability

Compression stresses due to dead weight

Bending stresses are developed in junction to resist overturning tendency due to wind (compression = *c*, tension = *t*).

Combined stresses developed at junction

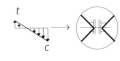

6.9
Menashe Kadishman,
Suspended. **This work also**
demonstrates how modern
technology (in the form of weld-
ing) can render the improbable
possible.

acting forces are not excessively large. Consequently, the connection could be made relatively small and not particularly noticeable. The success of the approach is clearly dependent on the scale of the objects themselves. Had the size of the sculpture been significantly increased, structural demands for rigidity at the apex-to-apex meeting would have been even more dramatically increased because of general scale effects (see chapter 20): the force and the required sizes of members in bending do not increase linearly with increases in size, but increase more quickly.

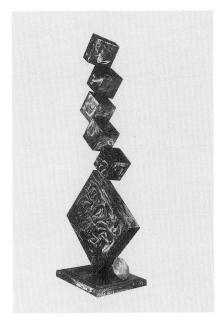

David Smith, *Cubi I*

The circular piece helps stabilize the whole form. Without it only the base weld would provide resistance to overturning.

6.10
Often minor elements play an important role in stabilizing seemingly improbable configurations. Such is the case with the small circular piece at the foot of the large blocks in Smith's *Cubi I*.

This effect might have led to a requirement for different relative proportions at the point of connection, to the extent that it might have appeared even less as a point and more as an obvious connector. The intent to have the profiles of the pointed forms appear in the same planes would also be compromised by a nonlinear increase in the relative size of the member. The piece as executed is about as large as it could be without scale effects causing the important "point" to become visually large.

Finally, it should be noted that *Broken Obelisk* takes fine advantage of the rather incredible strength and stiffness of steel. The whole form would have been very difficult to execute at this scale using other common materials, and, of course, virtually impossible using the stone materials that formed the original pyramids and obelisks that provided the antecedent images and references for the work.

Cubi I was created by David Smith in 1963 using stainless steel (fig. 6.10). Six stacked rectilinear volumes are welded to one another, with the lowest meeting a base along a corner edge. As with *Broken Obelisk*, a serious technical concern with the overturning effects of lateral forces naturally arises because of the base connection, which is expressed as a point connection about one axis. In this instance, the problem is quite elegantly handled in a completely different manner from that used in the previous example. Stability is provided by another element—the circular form at the base—that seems to be almost casually placed. The circular form typically serves in compression as a type of prop or strut to maintain the stability of the larger assembly. But under some lateral loading conditions, this same element may serve in tension as a sort of tie-down. Overall, then, the larger assembly is attached to the horizontal base plate at two separated points of connection, which in turn create a rigid, moment-resisting connection capable of carrying forces that act laterally. In order for this structural action to be obtained, however, the specific points of contact must be welded to provide continuity. If the circular form were actually simply leaning against the larger form, it would serve no structural function.

The question naturally arises whether the sculptor could have elected not to place the circular form there at all, relying on the weld line at the connection of the larger assembly to the base to provide the necessary resistance to overturning. Most likely in a piece of this size or larger, this alternative would have necessitated some flattening out or blunting of the lower tip of the form to create a longer and more dispersed series of welds. If the sculpture were considerably smaller, it is possible that the single weld line might have proven sufficient.

Robert Bladen's *Untitled* (fig. 6.11) visually seems prone to overturning and derives its essence from this appearance. Actual stability could be provided through any of several means, with a heavy base weight the most appropriate solution since the forms themselves are most likely hollow and do not produce much of an overturning moment. Burying the end of a form into the ground is sensible only on very rare occasions and normally only for temporary works.

Robert Bladen, *Untitled*

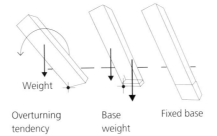

Weight

Overturning
tendency

Base
weight

Fixed base

6.11
The improbable configuration of Robert Bladen's *Untitled* is possible only through the use of special base weights or base connections. For hollow shapes made of a light thin surface material (e.g., plywood), the use of a heavy base weight is the more straightforward technique.

7.0
George Rickey, *Summer III.*

7 Balance and Movement

Many individuals have explored the kinetic potential of sculpture. Duchamp, Calder, Gabo, and Moholy-Nagy were among the pioneers; Duchamp's *Bicycle Wheel*, executed in 1913, remains a classic exemplar of these formative works. George Rickey's *Two Lines—Temporal I*, executed in 1964, provides a more recent example. Within a broad definition of the field, many forms of movement may constitute the basis of a kinetic sculpture. Gabo's remarkable 1920 *Kinetic Construction* uses a vibrating length of vertical flat spring steel accentuated by an electric motor. Mark di Suvero's *Isis* (fig. 7.1) involves balance on a much larger scale, although in this case movement is restricted to a simple occasional swinging.

This chapter looks at two examples of sculptures with nonrigidly attached balanced elements that rotate about one or more axes—one of the more elemental but powerful forms of kinetic sculpture. Some works that rely on this principle, such as Moholy-Nagy's *Light Space Modulator*, are motor driven. Others are meant to respond to some external stimuli, such as a breath of wind, and are allowed to stop at any position when the stimuli are removed. Others, such as Shingu's *Echo of the Waves*, are meant to move during a wind but return to a predetermined position after the wind stops.

Small-scale sculptures of this type are conceptually straightforward explorations of balance principles previously discussed. As works get larger, however, this seemingly simple approach can become extremely complex and difficult to implement.

Elements can obviously be designed to rotate about an axis placed at any orientation, but it is easier to understand underlying principles when axes are placed vertically or horizontally. The fundamental principle is invariably one of balance about an axis. One of the reasons for the problematic performance of Moholy-Nagy's *Light Space Modulator*, for example, was that the various parts of the original sculpture were not precisely in balance around the central shaft, which in turn caused bending to develop in the shaft prior to the subsequent addition of the external frame.

7.1

The steel prow of Mark di Suvero's *Isis* is carefully suspended from a cable and moves when pushed. The weight of the prow is carried primarily by bending in the cantilevered steel beam. The upper cables running from the point of suspension toward the back of the sculpture have little direct structural value.

An excellent example of a much larger balanced sculpture with moving parts was briefly introduced earlier—Shingu's *Gift of the Wind*. It is useful to look at it again (fig. 7.2). There are several rotating parts to it. The three sail-like cups are attached to horizontal axles and can rotate freely under the action of the wind about these axles. The horizontal axles are in turn connected to a central hub that allows free rotation about the vertical shaft. Obviously these elements would not rotate freely and easily if they were not in careful balance to begin with. Also of obvious importance is that the connections have one degree of freedom each and allow only one type of movement (rotational). The complicated movements that one perceives when the sculpture moves in the wind is a consequence of the particular way these quite simple joints are located in space.

In the three-armed part of the sculpture, the dead weight of the sails can be treated as forces acting vertically downward. The three-armed part is in obvious balance about the central shaft. With respect to *any* line in the horizontal plane that is drawn through the shaft, the sum of the rotational moments associated with the vertical forces about this line will be zero if the three-armed assembly is truly balanced. This is a design condition for free balance. In this specific case, the weights of the three sails are identical. For the 120-degree geometry of the figure and with respect to the specific location of the reference axis shown here, the moment arm of the single weight to the right of the rotation axis is exactly twice that of the moment arms of the two weights to the left of the axis. This means that the rotational moment about the axis of the single force to the right is exactly balanced by the moments of the two forces on the other side of the axis (or the net moment of all the forces about the axis is zero). The symmetry of forces and angles is not an absolute requirement for balancing a three-armed assembly about a central point, but it surely makes designing the assembly easier. If the arms were not 120 degrees apart, moment arm distances would change, and there would have to be a consequent change in the relative weights of the sails to continue to maintain balance.

If this ideal state of balance were *precisely* realized, the central hub connection would not have to be an axle at all but could even be a ball and socket type of joint. Such a joint, with its three degrees of freedom, would allow tipping of the upper assembly if the forces acting on it were ever out of balance. But loadings and environmental forces acting on the assembly are *not* precise. Some minor imbalance will inevitably develop in the applied forces. Thus unless the choice is made to allow the three-armed assembly tilt liberally about the central support (which would in turn make the design of the attached rotating sails very dubious), a ball and socket type of joint should not be used. Using a joint with only one degree of freedom will keep the three-armed assembly in the horizontal plane while allowing it to rotate about the vertical axis. Any imbalanced loading, however, will tend to cause forces to be exerted against the vertical shaft. These forces would tend to jam the hub against the shaft and bend the shaft.

Consequently, the shaft must be carefully designed to be able to carry the bending involved, and special roller bearings must be used to prevent the jamming effect from binding the three-armed assembly. The following chapter will generally address the issue of bending in structural elements. There it will be seen that bending forces tend to produce a bowing or curvature in the element, involving compressive stresses on one face of the element and tension stresses on the other face. The element must be designed to carry these stresses without distress to the material. The bowing or curvature associated with bending, if it becomes excessive, can be quite troublesome since deformations of this type cause the roller bearings to jam or otherwise work poorly. The design of the roller bearings (and their surrounding encasement) in *Gift of the Wind* will not be addressed in detail, but it should be noted that this assembly is an exceedingly complex design in its own right. Further analysis might indicate, for example, that wind forces could have a tendency to spin the assembly too quickly. A bearing assembly and wing configuration that slowed the movement to a controlled rate would then need to be designed. Depending on the type of bearing assembly selected, an oil feed mechanism might also be needed to ensure the proper long-term functioning of the bearings (as was the case with *Gift of the Wind*). Obviously, more attention has to be paid to considerations of this type in large sculptures in public settings than would be the case in smaller ones in protected environments.

It is reasonable to assume that design complexities in large-scale sculptures increase with increasingly complex

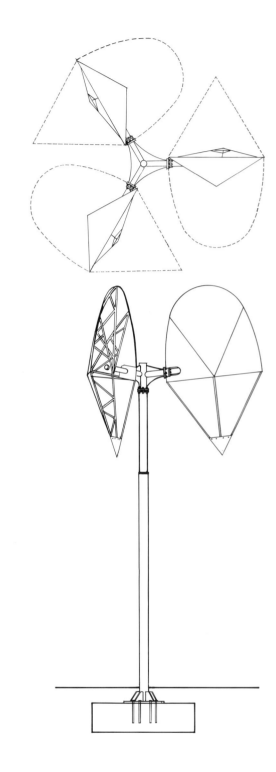

Susumu Shingu, *Gift of the Wind*, plan and elevation: including base connection anchor-bolted to below-grade reinforced concrete foundation.

7.2
Gift of the Wind has a balanced assembly that rotates as a whole unit about a central vertical shaft. The sail elements attached to the upper assembly rotate around horizontal shafts.

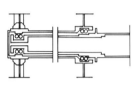

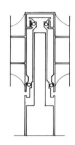

Section through rotating connection on arm

Section through rotating connection on central shaft

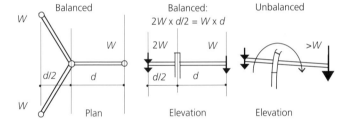

Loads are balanced about the central shaft: an unbalanced loading may cause bending and jamming of the rotation bearings.

Susumu Shingu, *Gift of the Wind*, plan and elevation: including base connection anchor-bolted to below-grade reinforced concrete foundation

rotational motions. Another of Shingu's works, *Echo of the Waves* (introduced in chapter 1), provides a useful example (fig. 7.3). As with *Gift of the Wind*, the upper part of the sculpture rotates about a central vertical shaft and, consequently, the whole assembly must be in a basic state of balance about the shaft. Each of the projecting arms must be in a state of balance about its horizontal axle as well. The complexities of the rotational motions due to wind and related uncertainties about the resultant forces developed in the structure necessitated a number of detailed technical studies. The studies had several aims: to make sure that the main elements (e.g., the mast) were indeed adequately designed from a structural perspective; to make sure that the rotating elements did indeed sensitively rotate under light winds as desired (and not just sit there); and, conversely, to make sure that the rotating elements would turn in an anticipated and controlled way even during high winds (and not rotate uncontrollably, producing dangerously high forces that could destroy the structure and endanger the public).

Early in the project, consultants recommended actual wind tests, even if such tests only roughly modeled the actual installation. Eventually a specialized engineering research team analyzed the loading conditions on the structure (e.g., wind, self-weight, ice) via the use of a sophisticated computer-based structural analysis program. Winds coming from any angle were considered. Many different positions of the wings were also studied. Wings were considered as crude airfoil shapes that become unbalanced about a pivot axis. Analyses were made in terms of aerodynamic response of flat plates with different camber ratios. Estimates were made of the number of times the assemblies were likely to rotate for a series of different wind velocities (e.g., 10,000 cycles for an 80 mph wind). A primary design loading condition assumed that the clean dead weight of the structure was always present with these different wind speeds and associated rotational cycles. Other design conditions assumed the presence of other types of loads. One condition assumed that there was an additional loading of an inch and a half of ice over all sides and surfaces of the sculpture. (Since such events were expected to occur infrequently, in these cases design velocities and assumed rotational cycles were lowered.) The forces were assumed to be distributed over the structure. Several cases were

7.3
Echo of the Waves has a quite complex movement. The upper assembly rotates and the attached forms also undulate in the wind. The structure was designed for a variety of wind speeds, rotational cycles, and positions.

Susumu Shingu, *Echo of the Waves,* section through upper rotating assembly

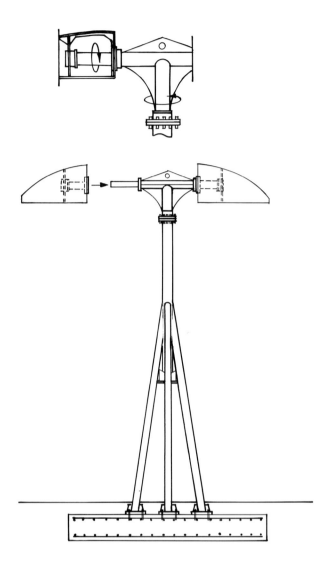

considered for the wing positions (see fig. 7.3). Maximum member stresses were subsequently calculated, along with fatigue effects.

As a consequence of these studies, a number of design changes were recommended. The original design restrained some rotations. After the analyses, the design was changed to allow more rotations, since projections for doing so indicated improved performance. Limits were imposed on the size of the structure, because size increases would result in larger centrifugal forces. It was also discovered that the wings as designed would attain high rotational velocities and high centrifugal accelerations. In order to reduce accompanying forces, modification of the aerodynamic sur-

faces was required. Given the need to maintain the basic appearance of the sculpture and not reduce its desired movement sensitivity to wind, the recommended changes included slightly changing the location of some axes (moving them forward) to reduce high instantaneous accelerations, changing the slope on the tail fin of the front wing, adding perpendicular surfaces to the main wing tail, and modifying the wing trusses. Thus, some areas originally meant to be open truss work became boxed in by surfaces. All of these changes were approved by Shingu, who in turn suggested further modifications.

The research team also found Shingu's original requirements for the sculpture to be somewhat in conflict. He

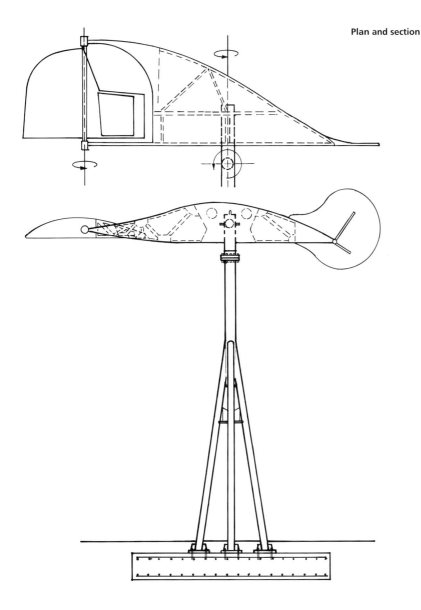

Plan and section

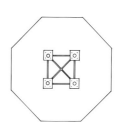

Base connections and reinforced concrete foundation

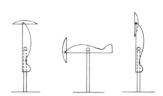

Possible positions of rotating elements (assumed during design stages)

wanted it to be responsive to light winds but to return to a horizontal position in the case of no wind. This condition is quite difficult to achieve, given the realities of friction in the bearings and other factors. By slightly adjusting the center of gravity of the upper assemblies and careful design of the bearings, a suitable compromise was reached so that the structure would normally come to rest more or less horizontally but still begin to move when relatively low winds were present.

Eventually the research team attached strain gages (experimental devices for monitoring actual deformations in a member, hence allowing the actual stresses present to be estimated) in the structure as finally erected. Initial evaluations indicated no unforeseen effects.

Without investigations of the type described and without implementation of the suggested changes, it is entirely possible that the work would either not have rotated at all under winds as envisioned, or rotated uncontrollably and hence dangerously. It should be noted that even now the reliability of the design is predicated on its continuing to function as anticipated during the analyses. Maintenance is thus essential to keep the bearings operating freely so that rotations occur as anticipated.

8.0
David Von Schlegell, *Untitled.*

8 Relational Stability

The discussion of the overall stability of different works has thus far assumed that the sculptures themselves rotate or slide like big rigid units. There has been no implication that the constituent pieces of a sculpture might form an unstable assembly simply by virtue of the way they are positioned or connected to one another. There are many situations, however, where a sculpture might collapse for these very reasons. This situation most often arises in connection with horizontally acting loads, although vertical loadings may cause instability as well. Configurations of elements can also be made that might stand up under normal gravity loads but collapse internally because of lateral forces associated with wind or earthquake effects.

Consider simple horizontal members resting on relatively light vertical members, but nonrigidly attached to them (fig. 8.1, top left). If carefully placed, a vertical load could be applied to the horizontal beam and the overall assembly could support it. On the other hand, it is obvious that any type of significant horizontally acting force would cause racking deformations of the type shown in figure 8.1 to develop. Clearly, the structure has no capacity to resist the applied forces, nor does it have any mechanism that would tend to restore the initial shape of the structure if the applied horizontal force were removed. The structure would collapse, almost instantaneously, under the applied load. Notice that the collapse would have to be accompanied by large changes in the angles between constituent parts of the structure. A type of parallelogramming occurs. Such a pattern of members is often called a *collapse mechanism* because of its inherent instability. Vertical or horizontal loads can also cause a structure to twist and form a slightly different type of collapse mechanism, also accompanied by large changes in the angles between adjacent members.

There are really only a few fundamental ways of converting a collapse mechanism of the type shown into a stable configuration. These methods include the use of dead weight, diagonally placed members, stiffening planes, and rigid joints between members (fig. 8.1, middle and bottom). These approaches are not mutually exclusive, and more than

8.1
Assemblies of elements may be internally unstable and tend to collapse due to racking or twisting actions. Several alternative means for ensuring internal stability are illustrated (facing page).

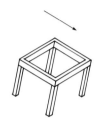

Racking

Twisting

Overturning

Common Types of Stability Failures

one might be found in a single work. Since stability must be achieved in all directions, it is not uncommon for one approach to be used in one direction and a different one to be used in an orthogonal direction.

Dead weight. One traditional method of preventing collapse is through the weight and proportioning of the verticals themselves. If these elements are heavy enough and have sufficiently wide bases, they resist overturning for the same reasons discussed in chapter 5 in connection with base pedestals. This approach is obviously limited and imposes severe restrictions on the form of the work itself due to its dependence on mass.

Diagonal bracing. The use of diagonal members is a time-honored and accepted way to achieve relational stability between members. If the diagonals are properly placed, a structure cannot undergo the internal parallelogramming or angular change accompanying collapse without a dramatic change in the length of the diagonal members, which could be prevented if the diagonals were designed to be adequately large to take the forces involved.

Mark di Suvero's *Mon Père, Mon Père* (fig. 8.2) achieves stability through the careful diagonal placement of its massive steel members. Stability is achieved in all directions because of the tripod nature of the arrangements. Many of di Suvero's works rely on this approach (e.g., *Are Years What?*). Siah Armajani's *Limit Bridge 3* (fig. 8.3) explores the visual sense of stability imparted by the use of repeating patterns of diagonal members. Diagonals are used in both the long and short directions of the work, since rigidity must be achieved in more than one plane for an overall work to be stable. *Limit Bridge 3* uses stiff members to form the necessary diagonals. Stiff members are well able to prevent the parallelogramming associated with collapse. The tall vertical structure of *Mirror Way* by Mary Miss (fig. 8.4), installed in the Fogg Art Museum at Harvard University in 1980, elegantly derives its lateral stability from the diagonally placed members that run from one vertical to another.

The large rectangular form in David Von Schlegell's *Untitled* (1969), located in the Hirshhorn Museum and Sculpture Garden, uses a subtle approach to diagonal bracing as a way of achieving stability. Here flexible cables rather than rigid members form the diagonal pieces. Cable elements are suitable for carrying tension forces only; they tend to buckle or collapse under the action of any compres-

Massive elements with wide
bases

Bracing

Shear walls

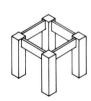

Rigid frames

Cross bracing

Walls

Common Means of Imparting
Stability

8.2
Mon Père, Mon Père by Mark
di Suvero illustrates one of
the most direct of all stability
approaches—the simple triangulated form.

8.3
Siah Armajani's *Limit Bridge 3*
recalls through suggestion the
importance of triangulation as a
way of ensuring relational stability in familiar large-scale engineering structures.

8.4
Extensive patterns of rigid cross
bracing render the tall section
of *Mirror Way* by Mary Miss
quite stable.

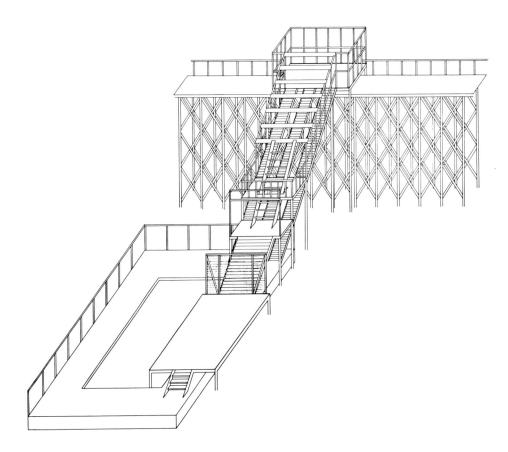

sive force. Given this sensitive directionality to load-carrying capability, can a cable always be used as a diagonal in lieu of a rigid member to achieve stability? If the cable were always subjected to tension forces, then the answer is yes. But in many cases, there are applied loading patterns that may tend to cause compression to develop in the cable, causing it to buckle and collapse and hence to collapse the whole sculpture. This means that using cables to stabilize structures typically requires extremely careful attention to how the flexible elements are located in space. *Untitled* is stabilized through the use of a crossed cable system in the form of a large X (fig. 8.5). Where the application of a load from the left would tend to cause the rectangle to parallelogram, locating a cable between the lower left and upper right corners would stabilize the form by preventing the two points from drawing apart. Since its role would be to keep the two points from drawing apart, tension forces would naturally develop within it. In this example, the forces would

be minor and a cable of virtually any size could carry them. But if the load suddenly came from the right rather than the left (as wind loads may surely do), then the cable that was in tension is now subject to compressive tendencies (since these same corners would tend to draw together, any member placed between the two points would be subjected to a compressive force). A cable is inherently incapable of carrying compression and would buckle uselessly out of the way. It follows that a single cable is never adequate alone as a stabilization device. A solution is obviously to use two cables in the form of a cross. When the structure deforms to the right, tension develops in one cable and stabilizes the structure, while the other cable goes limp and serves no function. When the structure deforms to the left, a reverse situation exists. Hence the X configuration is of critical importance.

Note that this shape is necessitated only by the use of cables. A single rigid member capable of carrying either compression or tension would serve equally well in stabiliz-

David Von Schlegell, *Untitled*

Box tends to collapse via a parallelogramming action

Adding a cross cable in tension stabilizes the box by preventing parallelogramming

A reverse loading will cause the cable to go into compression and buckle

Another cable in tension will again stabilize the structure

With crossed diagonal cables, one cable is always active in stabilizing the structure

8.5
Triangulation may be achieved through the use of carefully positioned cables. Because cables cannot carry compressive forces, it is usually necessary to use a pair of crossed cables to stabilize a form.

ing the structure. Crossed rigid diagonals may be used, but one or the other is actually redundant.

Shear planes (walls). Another technique to assure relational stability is to incorporate rigid surfaces into the structural assembly. Walls are inherently rigid with respect to forces that act parallel to their surfaces, but not with respect to forces that act in the perpendicular direction. If the surface is rigid enough, it would be sufficient to prevent parallelogramming and eventual collapse. These surfaces are often called *shear planes* or diaphragms to characterize their structural role. This approach is quite elegantly reflected in Richard Serra's *House of Cards (One Ton Prop)* and *Wright's Triangle* (fig. 8.6). These works clearly suggest the stability that is obtainable through the use of stiff planar elements.

Stability can be achieved with fewer than four planes if these are carefully arranged so that generous angles exist between the planes. A single plane is clearly useless, since it would fall over laterally. (Richard Serra often uses one *surface*, as in *Tilted Arc*, but the surface is curved in plan. This gives the structure stability about an overturning line in much the same way that any structure with multiple supports achieves its stability about a line; see chapter 5.) Two planes can work if the planes are directly attached to one another, as in Richard Fleischner's *The Baltimore Project* (fig. 5.1). Three planes can easily be made to work, as Serra's *Wright's Triangle* illustrates. The use of three planes suggests the essence of stability obtained through controlling the geometry of the sculpture.

Frame action. A final technique is to make a rigid joint between members so that their angular relationship remains unchanged under any loading, thus preventing the large angular changes between members that are associated with collapse. A typical table, for example, is a stable structure because there is a rigid joint between each leg and the table top. The knee brace found in many building structures, including old barns, also serves to assure stability by preventing angle changes between vertical and horizontal members. Structures that use rigid joints to achieve stability are called *rigid frames*. David Von Schlegell's *Untitled* series (fig. 8.7) are rigid frame structures. Mark di Suvero's *Blue Arch for Matisse* (fig. 8.8) relies on frame action for part of its stability, but with the frame itself subsumed in the work. The tilted central U-shaped figure provides stability along one axis of the structure and unquestionably can be de-

8.6
These two sculptures by Richard Serra illustrate how rigid planes may be arranged to form internally stable arrangements. *Wright's Triangle* and *House of Cards* rely on the overall self-bracing nature of the geometry of the structural planes for stability; hence the plates may be quite thin.

Richard Serra, *House of Cards (One Ton Prop)*

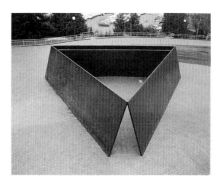

Richard Serra, *Wright's Triangle*

8.7
David Von Schlegell, *Untitled*.
This series of structures in alu-
minum and stainless steel relies
on rigid-frame action for stabil-
ity. Relational stability between
elements is obtained by rigidly
joining vertical and horizontal
elements to one another. The
rigid joints themselves prevent
the angular changes associated
with collapse. No diagonals are
needed when rigid-frame action
of this type is obtained.

scribed as a rigid frame structure (the bracing diagonals pro-vide stability in the other direction). *Veiled Landscape* by Mary Miss (fig. 11.1) eloquently suggests the essence of a rigid frame structure. Due to the small scale of the work, joint rigidity is achieved through simple tightened connec-tions. Use of rigid frame action to achieve stability is com-mon in many of Sol LeWitt's works as well.

Historically, the term "rigid frame" and its identification as a unique type of structure derive from the field of build-ing structures. In this context, a frame is a pristinely simple arrangement of beams and columns rigidly connected to one another, typically in an orthogonal arrangement of verti-cal columns and horizontal beams and with a complete absence of triangulated arrangements anywhere within the larger configuration. This form of structure evolved during the latter part of the nineteenth century when high-rise buildings first began their skyward reach in cities such as Chicago and, to a lesser extent, New York. Distinctions were subsequently drawn between the structure itself and the enclosing skin of the building. Rigid frame structures con-tributed to the conceptual development of separating skele-ton and skin, and in turn evolved from it. The development of the frame as a structural device was also inextricably linked with the development and use of steel, and later rein-forced concrete, because of the need to make rigid connec-tions between members—a straightforward task with newer materials such as steel but exceedingly difficult in timber and virtually impossible in stone. Chapter 11 explores rigid frameworks in greater detail.

8.8
Mark di Suvero, *Blue Arch for Matisse*. This structure gains its stability in one direction through the incorporation of a rigid frame.

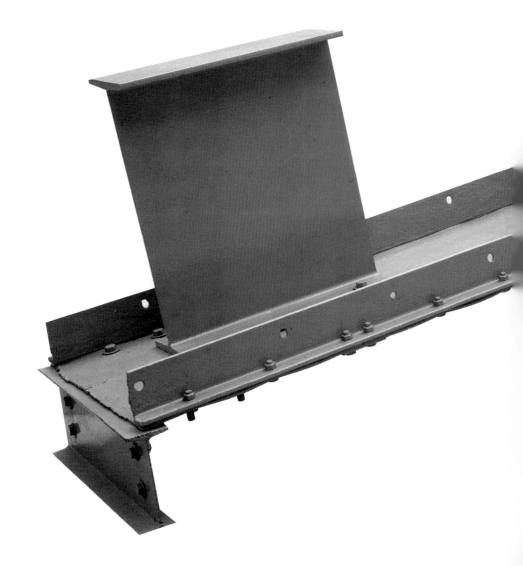

Anthony Caro, *Midday*.

Shapes and Elements

3

9.0
Eva Hesse, *Vertiginous Detour.*

9 Linear Members in Tension, Compression, and Bending

The chapters in part 3 examine the structural behavior of what might be described as the building blocks of more complex structures. These elements may or may not form complete structures in their own right. Many are more normally constituent parts of larger and more involved forms. Included are linear and curved members in tension, compression, and bending, as well as frameworks, plates, shells, and membranes. Connections are addressed as well.

This chapter will initially explore the structural behavior of members in tension, compression, and bending. More generally, however, the discussion will also suggest why certain forms have the shapes they have. Anthony Caro's *Homage to David Smith* (fig. 9.1), for example, uses parts of several common steel beams originally manufactured for use in architectural or engineering structures. The cross section of these members is in the shape of an I, a shape that gives rise to the common term I-*beam*. This powerful shape automatically brings with it a strong image of its origins in engineering. Yet few sculptors or observers really understand *why* the shape exists in the first place. Is it random, or did a hard-nosed structural engineer merely think it winsome? Hardly. There are strong conceptual reasons for this shape. It reflects a specific way of distributing material in a cross section that is particularly efficient when the member is subjected to forces that tend to bend it. That this same shape finds itself used in the sculptures of artists like di Suvero or Caro is not without interest.

The force states of tension, compression, and bending were briefly introduced in chapter 3. A *member in tension* is a linear element that carries forces acting outwardly at its ends and along the length of the member. Tensile forces and related tension stresses are consequently developed internally in the member. If the member is made out of a material that can carry *only* tensile forces and not compressive forces, it is often referred to as a "cable" for convenience. Since a cable or similar element (such as a thin rod or a chain) can carry tension forces only, any tendency of an external force to bend or compress it will result in the member collapsing or radically changing its shape.

9.1
Anthony Caro, *Homage to David Smith.*

A *member in compression* is a linear element that carries forces at its ends that act inwardly and again along the length of the member, thus developing internal compressive forces and related compressive stresses in the member. Such elements are sometimes said to be *axially* loaded. When placed vertically, compression members are often called "columns," although "strut" is occasionally used as well. The term "column" commonly connotes a member able to carry compressive forces only—such as might be the case with a column made of stacked stones. More generally, however, elements of this type made of material such as steel can normally carry both tension and compression forces.

A *member in bending* is subjected to a bowing action by loads. A linear element that typically carries loads placed perpendicularly to its long axis is subject to bending. When placed horizontally, such elements are often called "beams." But a member placed vertically and subjected to lateral forces might also carry loads by a bending action, as is the case of a common flagpole in a windstorm. Whether the members are horizontal or vertical, their condition under transverse-acting forces is radically different from that of axially loaded cables or columns.

Also important to the discussion will be ideas relating to both the *strength* and *stiffness* of structural members—that is, their ability to carry loads without excessive distortions or failure. In chapter 3, the concept of strength was considered primarily in relation to material types. Here the primary concern will be strength and stiffness in relation to the size and shape of the cross section of a member, and also in relation to any variations in shape that might be present along the length of a member.

To understand concepts of strength and stiffness, it is necessary to describe different properties of member cross sections. One may need to decide whether it is structurally better to use a round, a rectilinear, a triangular, or some other shape as the basic form of long linear elements. If a member is compressed by the action of a load, for example, is it better to use an open hollow tube (a pipe) or a solid round rod? To understand choices of this type, it is necessary to understand relations between the size and configuration of a shape and resultant stiffnesses and strengths. For any element other than simple tension members, "area" alone will be seen not to be a sufficient descriptor of cross-sectional configurations when structural phenomena are considered. What is really needed is to be able to describe both the amount and distribution of material in a cross section with respect to some specified reference axis.

Two important geometric properties of shapes are commonly used. One is the *centroid* of a shape. The centroid of a shape is that singular point on which it can be imagined that the whole shape would exactly balance if the figure were imagined to be cut out of a flat thin sheet. The centroid of a circle is clearly its center point. In a rectangular section the centroid lies at the point of symmetry of the shape where the axes cross. But where is the centroid for a triangular shape? This is not as obvious, but it can be shown to be located one-third of the way from the base to the top of a triangle. The centroid for an L-shaped figure can be shown to lie outside the figure itself—it is at a point between the two legs that depends on the relative dimensions of the legs themselves. The centroid is that singular point that somehow represents the "point of balance" of a geometric figure; it thus has value and interest far beyond its structural applications. It is obviously comparable to the center of gravity of an object. A second and much more complex shape descriptor bears the highly unlikely name of the *moment of inertia* of the section. This quantity describes both the *amount* and *distribution* of material in a figure about a specified axis. A property of the figure, it can be used as a measure of the stiffness of a cross section. This measure will be discussed subsequently.

Linear Members in Tension

Members in tension are found in many sculptures. An obvious example is Eva Hesse's *Vertiginous Detour* (fig. 9.2; 1966). Taut rope or cable elements are not only efficient tension-carrying structures in their own right but are also visibly symbolic of a more abstract concept of tension as a perceptual or experiential state.

The structural behavior of a member subjected to a given tension force is remarkably easy to understand (the problem is often more of identifying what force is present to begin with). Once the applied forces are understood, the required sizes of tension members may be easily determined. A tension force pulling on a member causes tension stresses to

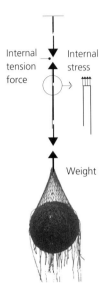

Eva Hesse, *Vertiginous Detour*

Tension stress in rope = force/area.

9.2
The supporting rope in this eloquent work is subjected to a simple tension force and related tension stresses. Stress is a measure of internal force intensity per unit area of material. In a simple tension member, the stresses are uniformly distributed.

1
In the case of steel rods, for example, the allowable stress level $f_{allowable}$ is known to be 24,000 lbs/in2. Thus the required area for a steel rod in tension that carries a force P of 6,000 pounds is as follows: $A_{required} = P/f_{allowable} = 6,000$ lbs/ (24,000 lbs/in2) = 0.25 in2. A half-inch by half-inch square rod would work.

develop within it. The magnitude of the actual internal tension stress in a member is obtained by dividing the force present by the cross-sectional area of the member: *stress = force/area*. If this force intensity per unit area is greater than the material can withstand, the material will fail by pulling apart. The member can be designed to be safe for a given load by limiting the actual stress level developed in a member to a value less than or equal to some *allowable stress level* known to be appropriate for the material used (see chapter 19). Actual stresses can be limited either by somehow reducing the force in question or by increasing the cross-sectional area of the member. If the load is fixed, the needed cross-sectional area for a safe tension member is obtained by dividing the load present by the allowable stress level for the material. This is an easy process if the forces are known because allowable stress values have been experimentally determined and tabulated for different materials.[1]

This formulation implies that the stresses are uniformly equal along the length of a member, and are uniformly distributed across any cross-sectional face. The implications of this are important. The load-carrying capacity of a member in tension is *not* dependent on its length, nor is it dependent on the arrangement of material in a cross section. (This assumes, of course, that the material is homogeneous and does not have "weak spots.") Tension members can be made almost as long as wished without negatively affecting their load-carrying capacity. Nor does it make any significant difference if the member used is square or round in cross section. Only the cross-sectional area and type of material are of primary importance. These are the characteristics that make tension members so incredibly versatile and efficient.

The sizing processes described above say nothing of how to use tension members effectively or to determine forces within them in more complex situations. This is often best done through examples. Tension members are quite evident in Christo's *Running Fence* (1972–1976; fig. 9.3). This work was 18 feet in height and extended some 24½ miles in Sonoma and Marin counties, California. The cable supporting the curtain along its top is certainly in tension. The periodically placed masts are in compression. The masts in turn are held vertically upright by pairs of guy cables. If it is assumed that a mast is placed vertically and the stabilizing cables are very lightly snugged against it, the mast will surely remain upright in the absence of wind. When a horizontal wind force blows the curtain, the draped cable

Christo, *Running Fence*

9.3
Christo's *Running Fence* is a careful assemblage of elements in tension and elements in compression. The suspended curtain directly induces compressive forces in the supporting columns. When wind acts against the curtain, tension forces are generated in the stabilizing cables. These tension forces induce additional compressive forces in the columns. Pretensioning the cables to "snug them up" would generate additional compressive forces in the column as well.

2
If F is the horizontal force at the top of the mast caused by the wind and T is the force in the guy cable, then rotational moment equilibrium about the base of the pin-connected mast demands that $T\cos\phi \times h = F \times h$, or $T\cos\phi = F$, or $T = F/\cos\phi$, where h is the height of the mast and ϕ is the angle the guy cable makes with respect to the horizontal.

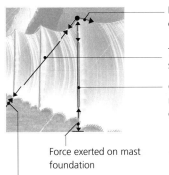

Force from wind acting on curtain

Tension force is developed in stabilizing cable

Compression force is developed in mast from downward components of cable forces

Force exerted on mast foundation

Force exerted on ground connection by cable

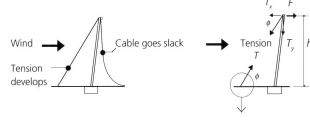

Wind

Tension develops

Cable goes slack

Tension is developed in one stabilizing cable while the other buckles harmlessly out of the way (when the wind blows from the other direction, the cables reverse roles).

T_x F

ϕ

Tension T

T_y h

ϕ

The vertical component of the tension force developed in the cable causes a compressive force to develop in the supporting mast.

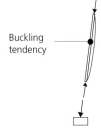

Buckling tendency

Force developed on mast footings

The mast must be large enough to carry the compressive forces present without buckling.

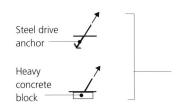

Steel drive anchor

Heavy concrete block

Possible alternative methods for resisting the uplift forces from the stabilizing cable

Wind blowing against the curtains causes forces in the cables to develop, which in turn cause forces on the mast.

Construction of the fence

supporting the curtain will transfer a horizontal force component to the top of the adjacent masts and tend to cause them to overturn, a tendency resisted by the stabilizing cables. In a mast, there would be a natural tendency for one of the stabilizing cables to pick up the applied horizontal force caused by the wind and the other to go slack (the direction of the force tends to cause it to be in compression, which it cannot withstand, so it simply tends to buckle out of the way). Equilibrium considerations then demand that (for the pin-connected mast to be stable) the horizontal component of the force in the stabilizing cable be equal to that of the applied force.[2] This horizontal component would imply a larger inclined force in the guy cable itself. The magnitude of this force would depend on the angle of the stabilizing cable. If the cable were very nearly vertical, then the consequent forces in it would have to become extremely large to produce the required horizontal component. If the angle were more generous and the cable more inclined, as indeed is the case in *Running Fence*, then the force induced in the cable would decrease. Obviously the force induced in the cable needs to be resisted by a ground connection (either a buried ground anchor of some type or a concrete pad). If a concrete pad were used, its weight would have to be more than the upward-acting component of the force in the guy cable or it would simply be lifted out of place.

This discussion assumes lightly snugged guy cables. A difficulty with this approach, however, is that the slackening caused by wind effects is generally undesirable. Repeated back and forth wind forces would cause the whole assembly to loosen up. Masts would begin to lean one way or another. To prevent this loosening up, both guy cables in such arrangements are often pretensioned via turnbuckles or some other device. The consequence of this pretensioning is that wind forces do not cause one of the attached cables to go slack. The pretensioning force is simply reduced somewhat by the action of the wind. If the pretensioning force is high enough to begin with, then the cable remains in tension. Pretensioning of this type can be quite effective. It does complicate, however, exact determinations of the force states present within the members, and actually increases the compressive forces present in the masts. In larger structures, engineers can calculate required pretensioning forces with accuracy.

Linear Members in Compression

Buckling

In Christo's *Running Fence*, the supporting masts are in compression due to the minor weight of the attached curtains and the large forces induced by wind loads. The additional pretensioning of the stabilizing guy cables may induce even greater compressive forces in the masts, as would tension induced by applied wind loads. If inadequately designed, compression members of this type are potentially subject to a disastrous form of failure called buckling.

The general structural behavior of members in compression is far more complex than that of members in tension. To appreciate these differences it is useful to look first at possible failure modes. The material in a short member can be overstressed in compression and fail by simply crushing—the compressive counterpart to a material pulling apart in tension. Here there is no surprise. On the other hand, a very long, slender member subject to compressive forces will not fail at all by crushing, but by a unique phenomenon called *buckling*. Buckling is a type of failure associated with a sudden loss in member stiffness and hence ability to carry load. It is a form of geometric instability. Buckling can occur at relatively low stress levels. A member that has buckled can carry no more load, but it does not necessarily initially entail an actual physical rupture of the material. Pushing on the ends of a thin plastic ruler induces a buckling failure. In this situation the member can carry no more load, but the member itself still retains its physical integrity. Continuing to push on the ruler will eventually cause it to snap—this is a secondary failure associated with bending that is of little interest here because the structural value of the member ceased when the member initially buckled. The sensitivity of a long member to buckling is critically important in the shaping of compressive elements. Long members in compression need to be larger in cross section than do short ones even if the applied loading is the same.

The longer and slenderer a member is in compression, the more susceptible it is to failure by buckling. For a given cross-sectional size and shape, the sensitivity of a member to buckling increases quickly with increasing lengths, longer columns being much less capable of carrying external loadings than shorter ones (load-carrying capacities vary inversely with the square of the column length). There is thus nothing structurally good about the buckling phenomenon. It is always associated with a reduction in the load-carrying capability of a member. The sensitivity of buckling to the length of a member does suggest that shorter members are always preferred to longer ones if it is desired to carry compressive loads efficiently. For similar cross sections, short columns that are associated with a crushing type of failure always have a higher load-carrying capability than longer ones that are susceptible to buckling.

Cross Sections

The shape of the cross section involved also obviously affects the magnitude of the load required to buckle a member. In the case of purely symmetrical sections, such as circles or squares, it is obvious that the larger the cross-sectional size of the member, the greater is its load-carrying capability for a given column length. But for a given cross-sectional area, the load-carrying capacity of a column can be increased by distributing the area about the axis of the member in specific ways. The more the material is located away from the central axis, the stiffer will be the resultant cross section. This increased stiffness in turn makes the whole column more resistant to buckling and capable of carrying higher loads. For a given cross-sectional area, for example, a pipe is able to carry higher loads than a comparable solid round section; a square tube is better than a square rod. A section can be made even more resistant to buckling by the use of individual linear elements widely separated about a central axis but still periodically connected. The latticed members of older truss bridges and other large structures reveal a design attitude of this type in the shaping of compression elements. Structural engineers have ways of characterizing the stiffness, and hence resistance to buckling, of different kinds of configurations through the use of a measure called the *moment of inertia*. Although it is not important to do so here, quantitative values for this measure can be readily determined for different cross-sectional shapes.

Other member shaping issues are important as well. A member that has a completely symmetrical cross-sectional shape, e.g., round or square, does not have a preferred "direction" of buckling. In a case like this, the member has

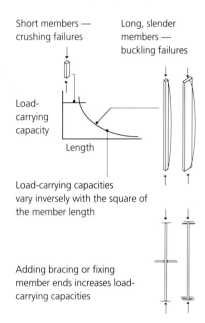

Short members — crushing failures

Long, slender members — buckling failures

Load-carrying capacity

Length

Load-carrying capacities vary inversely with the square of the member length

Adding bracing or fixing member ends increases load-carrying capacities

9.4
The load-carrying capacity of a compression member is strongly influenced by its length and cross-sectional proportions. Short members that fail by crushing can carry high loads. By contrast, long, slender members often fail at quite low stress levels by buckling. Members that fail by buckling cannot carry substantial loads.

equal stiffness in all directions, so there is nothing that causes the buckling shape to snap in any particular direction. But other cross-sectional configurations, such as rectangular sections, have different stiffnesses in different directions. A member with an asymmetrical cross section will always tend to buckle in a direction associated with its least rigidity. A member with a rectangular cross section, for example, always tends to buckle in a direction parallel to the short dimension of the member. Another way of saying this is that the member buckles about its weak axis. A common plastic ruler, for example, always buckles about its weak axis. Note that the same ruler could conceivably buckle in a perpendicular direction (about its strong axis), but it is highly unlikely to do so since a much larger load would be required —one that would far exceed that required to buckle it about its weak axis. In general, the presence of a weak axis means that the member is particularly susceptible to buckling about this axis.

In some sculptures, a distinction should be drawn between what might be called the "structural" section (that which carries loads) and the more inclusive shape. Brancusi's *Endless Column* (fig. 9.5), executed in 1937 at Tirgu Jiu in Romania, illustrates this. Prior to the work at Tirgu Jiu, Brancusi carved many versions of *Endless Column* in wood. A plaster study model about ten feet high was made in direct preparation for the larger work. The *Endless Column* at Tirgu Jiu was made of cast iron and steel. Working with a Romanian engineer, Stefan Georgescu-Gorjan, Brancusi carved a wooden form for the repeated elements, which were subsequently fabricated in cast iron. A tall steel column, square in cross section, was erected over a five-meter cube of concrete, and the individual cast iron elements were threaded over the internal steel column. Ultimately, the assembled column was covered with a coat of sprayed brass. The work thus relies on a heavy, extended base for stability, and on the rigidity of the *internal* steel column for its structural integrity. The shaped repeated elements contribute nothing to the structural essence of the work, but obviously provide its visual essence. In 1968 the column was reported as standing a few degrees off the vertical (presumably due to differential soil settlement underneath the column).[3]

Constantin Brancusi,
Endless Column

9.5
Brancusi's *Endless Column* carries only its own weight and those forces associated with wind or earthquake loadings. Shaped castings were threaded over a rigid central spine that provided the necessary resistance to buckling and bending. The spine was cantilevered from a large spread footing beneath the sculpture.

3
Geist, *Brancusi*, p. 123.

Threading the shaped castings over the rigid spine.

Bracing

The sensitivity of a member to buckling can be reduced significantly by the use of *bracing*. Bracing a member is holding in place one or more points along its length, usually by framing other members into these points in a perpendicular direction. The effect of bracing is to reduce the effective length of the column, transforming it from a single long column to the equivalent of a series of short columns, and thus reduce its susceptibility to buckling.

Bracing is particularly useful in situations where the column member itself is asymmetrical, such as one with a rectangular cross section. The load-carrying capacity of a slender rectangular member can be more or less equalized (so that it is equally likely to buckle in either direction) by careful placing of bracing in one plane and not the other, thus shortening the effective length of the member with respect to buckling about its weak axis. Obviously, the number of brace points required has something to do with the relative proportions of the original cross section. A single midheight brace point is all that is needed for a rectangular section having a 1:2 proportion. But a flatter section would require more brace points. A rectangular section having a 1:5 proportion, for example, would require four brace points. The bracing itself can be supplied in a number of different ways. It can be external to the work itself, or an integral part of it. Bracing is very effective, but its use can be misunderstood. Consider a compressively loaded round member with bracing in a single plane. Since the member is initially equally likely to buckle in any direction by virtue of its symmetrical cross section, the bracing serves no structural function. The member would simply buckle in the out-of-plane direction at the same load as if the bracing were not present at all.

Another factor that affects the load-carrying capacity of a column is the way it is connected to other elements. A member that is very simply connected so that its ends tend to rotate freely as buckling occurs has a lower load-carrying capacity than a similar member that is rigidly connected to its neighbors. The difference can be significant. A member rigidly connected at both ends can carry four times the load without buckling of a comparable one with simply connected ends.

Stress and Euler's Formulation

Both long and short members subjected to compressive forces develop stresses that can be determined in a manner similar to that described for tension stresses, i.e., the stress level present equals the load divided by the cross-sectional area. But in the case of a long member, the magnitude of the stress level at which failure (via buckling) actually occurs is much lower than the comparable failure value (via crushing) for a short member having an identical cross-sectional shape and area. In quantitatively evaluating the safety of a member in compression, it is not possible to use an "allowable stress" value that is a function of material type alone. Rather, more complex measures must be used that depend on the slenderness of the member in addition to the material type.

Quantitative expressions do exist that take into account all of the variables qualitatively discussed above for predicting the load required to buckle a member. Leonhard Euler formulated a now classic derivation for the buckling load of a column as far back as 1744 in St. Petersburg. This mathematician working in czarist Russia was exploring what was then the newly developed calculus and solved the problem partly by way of an example how this mathematics could actually be used.

This more complex formulation of the buckling problem is used by structural engineers calculating the buckling loads of important structural members.[4] Although rarely necessary in the design of small sculptures, it remains important for communicating with engineers in the design of large works. More conceptually, Euler's expression clearly shows how the buckling load of a column depends on the following physical parameters: the inverse of the square of the length of the member; a measure of the stiffness properties of the member as related to the material used; and a measure of the stiffness properties of the member as related to the amount and distribution of material present in the cross section. Euler's examination of the column buckling problem showed, for example, that if the length of a compression member is doubled, then its load-carrying capacity is reduced by a factor of four (alternatively, if the length of the member is halved, its capacity is increased by a factor of four). Increasing its length by a factor of four reduces its capacity by a factor of sixteen, and so forth. Euler's formulation also showed that both the amount *and* distribution of

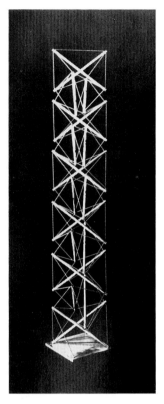

9.6
Kenneth Snelson, *X Column*. This column is a form of tensegrity structure (see chapter 11).

4
The formal expression for Euler's critical buckling load for a pinended column is $P = \pi EI/L^2$, where L is the length of the column, E is the modulus of elasticity of the material used (see chapter 19), and I is the moment of inertia of the cross section. See Daniel Schodek, *Structures*, 2d ed. (Englewood Cliffs: Prentice Hall, 1992), chapter 7, for further details.

material in a cross section affect the load-carrying capacity of a compressively loaded member. As with the example of buckling in a plastic ruler, common experience verifies that this is so. Euler's formulation quantifies these ideas by introducing a stiffness measure (called the *moment of inertia*) for the shape of the cross section about each axis. (As previously noted, the more a given amount of material in a cross section is moved away from the center point of the column, the greater is its stiffness and hence resistance to buckling.) The same formulation introduces a stiffness measure for the material used, called its *modulus of elasticity* (this measure is discussed extensively in chapter 19).

Linear Members in Bending

Bending Stresses
Bending is an everyday phenomenon. A common beam in a house is subject to bending as people walk across it. Structural members are extremely sensitive to stresses induced by bending. It is trivially easy, for example, to snap a piece of chalk by bending it. But it is surprisingly difficult to either pull it apart or crush it by hand. This sensitivity to bending stresses usually means that members that are subject to bending must be made relatively larger than members that are subject to only tension or only compression. From a structural point of view, subjecting a member to bending is one of the worst things that can be done to it, since relatively small bending forces induce high stresses in the members being bent. Consequently, members that must be designed to carry bending are frequently much larger than their counterparts carrying either tension only or compression only.

A member that is subjected to a bending action by the presence of loads acting transversely to its long axis naturally bows into a curved shape. As a consequence of this bowing, one face of the member is stretched and the other is compressed. Stresses are naturally developed in any material as a consequence of its being stretched or compressed. *Tension stresses* thus naturally develop along the face of the member that is stretched, while *compression stresses* are developed along the other face. Thus, tension and compression stresses exist within the same cross section. Taken together they are called *bending stresses*. In a common building beam carrying a downward load, compressive stresses are developed in the upper region of the beam and tension stresses in the lower region. The magnitude of these stresses depends on several factors, including the magnitude of the bending tendency that causes the bowing to develop in the member, and the amount and distribution of material in the cross-sectional shape of the member itself.

It is obvious that a member that is too small can be over-stressed in bending and fail by the pulling apart of material along the face being stretched or by the crushing of material along the face being compressed. The fact that at the same cross section a member is potentially being pulled apart and crushed at the same time must mean something both interesting and unusual about the types of stresses within the cross section. For example, it is evident that if tension and compression stresses exist continuously in the same cross section there is some region of zero stress as the force state makes a transition from tension to compression.

If a portion of the common beam is examined in greater detail (fig. 9.7), it is evident that bowing must be associated with certain types of deformations (or *strains*) in the member itself. Indeed, the top part of the member must physically compress the most and the lower part physically elongate the most. The fibers of the member just below the top surface compress as well, but not to the same extent as those on the upper face. An investigation of the geometry of the bowed section reveals that these deformations vary linearly from the top to the bottom surface, passing through a point at the middle of the section where no deformations at all are occurring. In a linearly elastic material, such as steel, stress levels are directly proportional to strain levels. Consequently the stress distribution across the face of the cross section looks like that shown in figure 9.7. Thus there is a plane of zero stress within the shape, a somewhat surprising and not immediately obvious fact. This plane is sometimes called the *neutral axis* of the member and is of some importance to structural designers.

There are significant implications of this remarkable stress distribution for the behavior and proportioning of objects in bending. One is that the material nearest the outer faces of the member does most of the work in carrying loads by bending. In a typical rectangular beam the outer faces are highly stressed, but those interior parts of the member near the neutral axis (or region of zero stress) are much more lightly stressed. Hence this would be a good place to put a hole through a loaded member if one had to do so.

There are quantitative relations between member cross-sectional shapes, linear dimensions, and the pattern of the applied loading. These formulations are fairly complex and are discussed elsewhere.[5] These formulations indicate that the actual magnitudes of the bending stresses developed in a member depend on the magnitude of the bending action present at a cross section (which is in turn dependent on the overall geometry of the beam and the loading present) and a measure related to the amount and distribution of material in the cross section of the member about a specified axis (see below). Stress magnitudes are quite sensitive to the shape and absolute dimensions of the cross section. Doubling the depth of a rectangular beam, for example, decreases the maximum bending stresses present by a factor of four, and vice versa. Doubling its width decreases stresses by a factor of two. Making rectangular members deeper thus tends to decrease the stresses developed more dramatically than making members wider.

Member Cross-Sectional Shapes

The influence of member shape in cross section is fundamental to an understanding of members in bending and worth exploring in detail. As an example, consider the common diving board. Surely the fact that it is rectangular is important—a square cross section simply would not provide the same springing quality. So it is easy to predict that the "shape" of a cross section must somehow be important. A moment's thought indicates that something needs to be said also about the orientation of the rectangle in space. The deep side of the board could be organized either horizontally or vertically. Obviously diving boards are typically placed with the deep dimension horizontal (and the least dimension of the board vertical) so that the necessary springing quality can be obtained. It is somewhat difficult to imagine (to say the least) springing off of a rectangular member with its deep dimension placed vertically—its rigidity would simply be too great. But in a common beam in house construction, carpenters go to great pains to place the deep sides of beams vertically, not horizontally. Why? Here the carpenters want the rigidity associated with placing the deep dimension vertically. Few people would appreciate

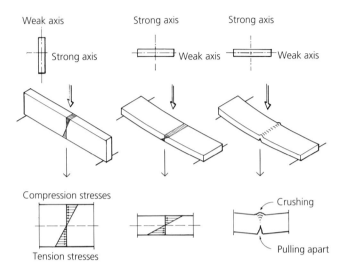

9.7

Members in bending. The bowing action caused by a transversely applied loading leads to this development of bending stresses in a member. Bending stresses consist of both tension and compression stresses at the same cross section. These stresses have their maximum values at the outer faces of the member. Large member sizes are usually required to prevent failures due to excessive bending stresses.

5
A general expression for bending stresses takes the form $f = My/I$, where M is a measure of the bending developed at a section, I is the moment of inertia of the member (a measure of stiffness), and y locates the point in the beam under consideration. Virtually any basic textbook dealing with structural analysis and design describes the origin and use of measures of this type in great detail (see, for example, Schodek, *Structures,* chapter 5).

6
For a common rectangular beam, the moment of inertia is given by $I = bd^3/12$, where b is the beam width and d is the beam depth (see Schodek, *Structures,* chapter 5).

the springing quality that would result from a "diving board orientation" of beams in their own floors.

A very general shape descriptor such as "rectangle" is inadequate for describing structural issues in the above examples. Even if the area of a member is maintained constant, surely its structural behavior changes as the relative proportions of the rectangle change. For a given cross-sectional area the diving board can be made wider and thinner than before. Doing so might well increase its springing quality up to a point, after which it might begin drooping so much under its own weight as to be useless. It is also reasonable to surmise that its strength would be affected as well. It is not without reason that beams in buildings are often designed to be relatively deep with respect to their width. Hence, it is necessary to be able to say something about the shape other than that it is "rectangular." What is important is the exact proportionality and size of the member about an axis in relation to the direction of the loading and associated bending action.

In these examples the need for reference axes proves important. In the diving board example, the implied reference axes of importance are simply horizontal and vertical. The direction of the applied load (the diver) acts vertically, so a vertical and horizontal reference axis makes sense, as it also does in the house beam example. (If the applied force acted in some odd direction, such as diagonally, it might be necessary to consider some other reference axes to describe the best placement of the resisting member in space.) For rectangular sections, a useful approach is to define reference axes that are orthogonal with respect to the beam section and intersect at the shape's centroid (fig. 9.7). In the house beam example, the beam bends or bows in the direction of the vertically acting loads, or, equivalently, it bows *about* the *x*-axis (as if the latter were indeed a physical axle that the beam was literally bent around). In this example, the beam has its greatest rigidity (stiffness and/or resistance to deformation) about its *x*-axis, and its least rigidity about its *y*-axis. Alternatively, one could call the *x*-axis the "strong axis" of this beam and the *y*-axis its "weak axis."

A difficulty arises when it comes to describing in quantitative terms the amount and distribution of the material in these cross sections with respect to the specified reference axes. This may seem easy, but it is not. In more advanced books on structural design, relatively complex ways are pre-

sented for dealing with this issue. A specific measure, the moment of inertia, can be derived by considering how far different parts of the area of the figure are located from the axes and using a form of weighted summation. The details of this measure are not important except to an engineer charged with exactly sizing a beam to carry a precise load.[6]

What is important is that the resulting formulations suggest that the stiffness of a member depends on several parameters, with the depth of the section relative to the direction of the applied load being most important. They also suggest that the stiffness of a member (resistance to deformations) does not linearly increase (or decrease) with linear changes in the dimensions of a member. Exactly doubling the cross-sectional dimensions of a rectangular beam does not just double its stiffness, it increases it by a factor of sixteen. The converse is also true—reducing all dimensions by a factor of two reduces member stiffnesses by a factor of sixteen. These examples suggest the importance of dealing with the dimensions of shapes in a very careful way when structural applications are considered.

Member Shaping Attitudes

The fact that bending stresses vary from a maximum at the outer fibers of a member to zero at its middle suggests that if a designer wanted to *position* material within a cross section where it would be the most effective in carrying loads by bending, then most material should be located near the outer faces of the member (where the stresses are naturally the greatest) and least near the neutral axis (where the stresses are the lowest). This line of thinking has been traditionally used in other structural fields in attempts to make the most economical use of materials in carrying a given load by bending. The common steel I-beam, more correctly called a steel wide-flange beam, has been one result. The I-shape tends to place large amounts of material near the outer faces of the beam where the bending stresses are naturally the highest. Reduced amounts are placed in the web near the neutral axis of the member where bending stresses are lower. Efficient use is thus made of material.

The shapes of common steel beams have been adopted for use in many sculptures, such as those by Anthony Caro. Caro's *Midday* (fig. 9.8) prominently features a steel wide-flange section. In this case, however, the wide-flange section is a referent only. It is supported along its length and cannot

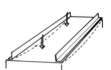

Simple wide-flange beam in bending

The wide-flange
beam shape is not
in bending

The flat structure
is in bending

9.8
**The common steel wide-flange
shape has been specially devised
to carry bending stresses efficiently by concentrating material
where bending stresses are the
highest. The short steel wide-
flange so prominent in Anthony
Caro's *Midday* may be highly
evocative of its engineering origin, but in this sculpture it is not
actually subjected to the kinds
of bending action that led to
the shaping of the form in the
first place.**

possibly be in an actual state of bending. Interestingly, another part of the sculpture—the supporting plate—*is* in a high state of bending. The attached steel angles on either edge serve a highly important stiffening function and carry most of the bending induced in the member by the weights of the other elements installed on the plate.

Other shapes work this way as well. A box beam, for example, has a separated double vertical web rather than the single web of the steel wide-flange member, but again the principle is to move material to the outer faces of the member where the bending stresses are the highest. Box sections have long been used in engineering structures. Robert Stephenson's remarkable Britannia Bridge completed in England in 1850 is an early example. In sculpture, David Smith is well known for his extensive use of hollow open steel sections. His *Cubi X* and *Cubi XXIII* make extensive use of box sections as a way of carrying the bending induced in the members by their own self-weights.

Wide-flange beams and box beams are efficient structural shapes for use in bending. Virtually any other shape can be used as well, however, if the efficient use of material is not considered important and loads are relatively low: for example, solid circular shapes, hollow pipes, L-shaped sections, and so forth. In general, shapes that concentrate material near the neutral axis (such as a solid circular shape) are less structurally attractive than those that move material away from the neutral axis.

Shapes that concentrate material in the compression zone of the member and reduce the material in the tension zone (such as T-shaped sections) can certainly be used, but for members made of homogeneous materials such as steel these shapes are not particularly efficient since very high stresses are developed on one face and low stresses on the other. T-shapes can, however, be potentially quite efficient when the material used is intrinsically less able to carry tension forces than compressive forces (e.g., cast iron, concrete).

Lateral Buckling

Previous discussions suggest that, as a general principle, it is always structurally preferable to orient the deepest dimension of a rectangular member in the direction of the load, so that the bending takes place about the strong axis of the member, and that the deeper a rectangular shape is made

with respect to its width, the stronger is the member with respect to bending. While generally true, however, taking this idea to its extreme would yield members of cardboard-like proportions (very thin but extremely deep). If this is done another type of possible failure becomes important—that of the *lateral buckling* of the part of the member subjected to internal compression forces. In much the same way that a long column subjected to compression forces can buckle via a type of geometric instability associated with a lack of rigidity, so can a thin part of a member buckle in bending. This complex phenomenon is illustrated in figure 9.9. The top part of this very thin member is in compression and the lower part in tension. Buckling begins when the top part moves quickly in an out-of-plane or lateral direction. This phenomenon can occur instantaneously and result in a total collapse of the member.

Lateral buckling can be prevented by a few simple means. One is to somehow brace the part susceptible to buckling with cross members. Another is to change the proportions of the member itself, making it wider and less deep and thus increasing its out-of-plane stiffness, which would in turn increase its resistance to lateral buckling. Members with width-to-depth ratios of say 1:3 or 1:4 rarely buckle laterally even if heavily loaded. Any technique for increasing the out-of-plane stiffness of the member could work equally well. In a steel plate structure, for example, longitudinal stiffening ribs can be welded lengthwise to the member.

Distribution of Bending Moments in a Member

The emphasis of the discussion of bending thus far has been on what is happening at a particular location in a member. But the magnitude of the bending tendencies present in a member are typically not constant throughout the length of a member, and this variation gives rise to other design issues and opportunities. First note that the following factors affect the overall distribution of bending in a structure: the type, location, and magnitudes of the loads present, and the length of the member and how it is supported.

In Calder's *Southern Cross* (fig. 9.10), a typical arm of the mobile is subjected to three forces—one at each end and an upward reactive force at its middle. The portion of the arm to the right (or left) of the center suspension point where the reactive force exists is a simple cantilevered member. Consider one of the cantilevered members carrying a load

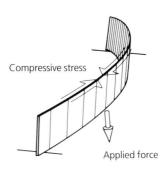

9.9
Thin members subjected to bending may prematurely fail by lateral buckling—a sudden transverse snapping out of the part of the member subjected to compressive stresses.

Compressive stress

Applied force

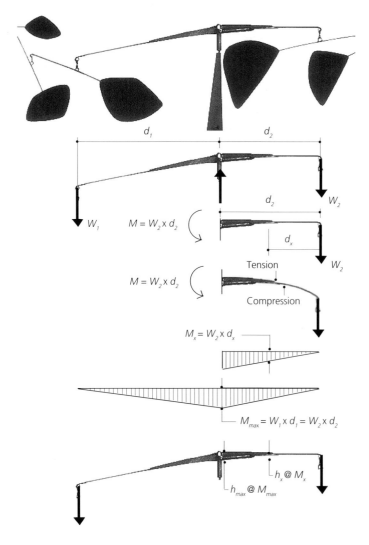

Alexander Calder, *Southern Cross*

The central arm is balanced over the center support: $W_1 \times d_1 = W_2 \times d_2$.

Bending is developed in each arm. The maximum bending occurs at the base of each cantilevered section.

The bending present causes tension stresses to be developed along the upper surface and compression stresses along the lower surface of each arm.

The magnitude of the bending moment present (and hence the stresses) at any point along the length of the beam may be graphically depicted by the use of bending moment diagrams.

The depth (h) of the structure is largest where the bending moment diagram indicates that maximum bending moments are present. The depth of the structure generally decreases with decreasing bending moments.

at its end. Tension stresses are developed along the upper surface of the member and compression along the lower surface. If the member were to break by bending, the failure would surely occur at its support (in this case, the point of suspension) as far away from the load as possible. The magnitude of the bending effect tending to cause failure at the support is derived by multiplying the force (load) present by the distance over which it acts—the "moment" of the force.[7] Since it is this value that tends to cause the beam to bend, it is commonly called the *bending moment*. Note that the same bending effect, or bending moment, at the support can be caused by a small load supported by a member with a long length or by a very large load acting over a much shorter length. In each case the product of the load times the length could be the same, hence the bending tendency at the support could be the same as well. Structural designers who work with beams prefer to use the concept of the bending moment rather than just load or length because it reflects the simultaneous interaction of these two parameters and yields a single measure of the bending tendency present in a member at a particular location.

Obviously the magnitude of the bending tendency in this cantilevered member is not constant along its length. The deflected shape of the structure appears to show that the bending tendency has a maximum value at the support and decreases away from the support. This can be seen visually by observing that the beam is locally bent or bowed more at the support than at the extremities. The degree of curvature present at any point is directly proportional to the magnitude of the bending tendency, or bending moment, present at that same point. If the curvature varies, so does the bending moment present.

This variation in the magnitude of the bending present along the length of the member can be determined quite easily for this simple example. The bending moment at any point equals the force times the distance from the point of the force's action to the point being considered.[8] It is possible to draw a simple diagram or graph, called a *bending moment diagram*, showing how the bending moment varies along the length of the member. The ordinate of the graph at a point represents the magnitude of the bending moment at that point. A glance at the diagrams in figure 9.10 shows that the bending moment varies linearly from zero under the load to a maximum value at the support.[9]

9.10
The amount of bending induced in a transversely loaded member varies along the length of the member, depending on exactly how the structure is loaded and its geometry. The size of a structure may be varied along its length to reflect this variation in bending.

[7]
In a cantilever beam of length L and carrying a load P, the maximum bending moment present is given by $M = P \times L$, or, in the case of the right branch of *Southern Cross*, $M = P \times d_2$.

[8]
The bending moment M_x at a point a distance d_x from the load equals $W_2 \times d_x$. If d_x equals d_2, then $M = W_2 \times d_2$ at the support as before. But if d_x equals zero (a point directly beneath the load), then the bending moment there is zero ($M = 0$).

[9]
A bending moment diagram for a common building beam (i.e., a member supported at either end, with a single downward-acting load in between) would resemble an inverted version of the diagram for an arm of a Calder mobile. When a diagram is placed on top of a line it means that the member is bent concavely. When it is placed beneath a line it means that the member is bowed in a convex direction.

Since the required size of a member to carry bending depends directly on the magnitude of the bending moment present at a point, it follows that in a cantilever beam the member can be quite small toward the end of the member under the load, where the bending moment nears zero, and has to have its maximum dimension at the support, where the bending moment is greatest. A uniform member, sized for the maximum bending moment present at the support, could be used (it would simply be oversized elsewhere); or the member could vary in size in response to the varying magnitudes of the bending actually present at different points. In the latter case the member itself is shaped to reflect the variation in bending moments present. This is partly done in the portion of the arm of *Southern Cross* illustrated. Varying a member's size along its length is a common shaping attitude for a cantilevered member in bending. Certainly this shaping attitude is clearly illustrated in many of Calder's works.

It was quite easy to determine the variation in the bending present in this simple example. More complex structures with more complex loading conditions are naturally much harder to deal with. Structures carrying uniformly distributed loads along their lengths typically have moment diagrams that vary parabolically rather than linearly. One way of qualitatively ascertaining how the magnitude of the bending tendency varies along a member's length is to visualize the way the member deforms or deflects under the action of the applied loads. Where the curvature of the deformed shape is greatest, it can be expected that the bending moments present are similarly large. Where the curvature is almost flat, small bending moments can be expected. These deformations are often difficult to visualize and it is occasionally useful to experimentally determine them. (This can sometimes be done simply by loading a flexible plastic ruler in the same general way the actual member is loaded and watching it bend.) Note that reversals of curvature are possible.

In large sculptures in public settings, it might well be necessary to deal with more complex loading and support conditions in quantitative ways so that the minimum safe dimensions of members can be determined in an exact way. This is typically a task for a structural engineer. There are several ways of quantitatively determining the bending moments present in a structure. Due to the complexities of either the structure or the loading condition, the bending

moment diagrams that result often have radically different shapes than those associated with the simple cantilever beam discussed earlier. Other diagrams can be drawn for related structural phenomena, such as the shearing forces that are developed within structures as a consequence of the action of the external loadings. These forces tend to cause parts of the structure to slip with respect to one another (shear forces act tangentially to the face of a section). Engineers invariably draw diagrams for shear forces and bending moments as a way of recording the results of their analyses, and in turn use these diagrams as a basis for quantitatively determining the required sizes of structures to carry the bending present.[10] As such these diagrams become an important, if often esoteric, form of communication.

Composite Members (Reinforced Concrete)
Many members are not made of single materials but use two or more in the same cross section to carry internal forces. Generally, forces are shared between adjacent materials, with the stronger and stiffer material taking the greater portion of the forces present.

Reinforced concrete is a common composite material. Concrete carries compression well but cracks easily when subjected to tension. In common bending, tension stresses do develop that would crack a plain concrete member and cause it to collapse. Consequently, steel in the form of rods is introduced in zones where tension is likely to develop. As bending develops, the concrete in the tension zone cracks. The cracks are intercepted, however, by the reinforcing steel. Tension forces are in turn developed in the steel. In bending, the amount of reinforcing steel needed depends directly on the magnitude of the internal bending moment present. The higher the bending, the more steel is needed. If the internal bending moment drops off along the length of a member, so may the amount of reinforcing steel used. Calculating the exact amount of steel required is difficult and beyond the scope of this book, but relatively little is commonly needed (say the equivalent of around 2.5 percent of the total cross-sectional area of the member). Steel is commonly placed near the face of a member to minimize the forces developed within it.

Care must be taken so that potential cracks from *any* anticipated loading condition are taken into account via the appropriate placement of reinforcing steel to intercept the

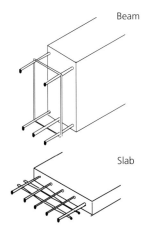

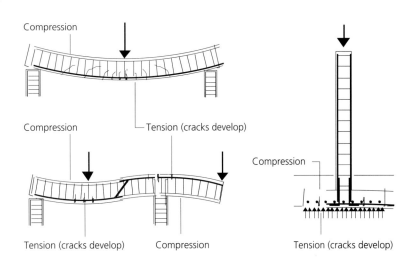

9.11
Reinforced concrete members in bending. Plain concrete cracks easily when subjected to bending with its associated tension stresses. Reinforcing steel must be placed where cracks are likely to develop. The amount of longitudinal steel necessary depends on the degree of bending anticipated. Steel is frequently placed on both faces of a member when forces are likely to come from any of several different directions. Shorter transverse steel elements (normally called "stirrups") are used to intercept cracks caused by shear forces.

cracks. This often means that it is desirable to place steel on both faces of a member when loading conditions are uncertain (fig. 9.11).

Shear stresses also lead to cracking in concrete members. In beam elements, the common U-shaped steel "stirrups" that are periodically placed throughout the length of the member intercept shear-induced cracks.

In lightly loaded slabs a mesh of welded wire fabric is often used for reinforcing. Even if loads are negligible, it is invariably wise to incorporate some kind of mesh or rod reinforcing to prevent cracks from shrinkage or expansion in the concrete from occurring.

Large structures may necessitate the use of prestressing or post-tensioning. In prestressing, a cable-like member is stretched (and tensioned) via a jacking system before casting. Concrete is subsequently cast around the tensioned member, allowed to cure, and the tensioning apparatus is removed. As the tensioned cable tends to return to its original state, it causes compressive stresses to be developed in the surrounding concrete. These compressive stresses then offset the tension stresses that would develop in the member as a consequence of an applied loading. Cracking is thus reduced, and members may be made smaller.

Post-tensioning is similar in end result, but the process is different. A cable is placed inside a conduit. Concrete is cast around the conduit and allowed to cure. The cable is then secured on one end and the other end is jacked to stress the cable. Once the cable is sufficiently stressed to develop the

10
Any basic textbook on structural design discusses the concept of shear and moment diagrams at length (see Schodek, *Structures*, chapter 2).

desired compression in the concrete, the cable ends are secured and the conduit pumped full of grout to assure permanent bonding.

Both prestressing and post-tensioning are common in building and civil works but rare in sculptures since the small scale of the latter rarely demand these kind of approaches.

Combined Stresses

It has been seen that forces directed along the length of a member normally produce either tension or compression stresses, while transversely acting or off-center loads normally produce bending stresses. In many cases, however, the action of the applied loads is such that both axial tension or compression stresses and bending stresses are developed at the same time.

A situation of this type was illustrated with *Broken Obelisk* (fig. 6.8). The junction between the two masses is subject to a complex force state. The large upper weight acts downward and tends to produce compressive stresses in the junction piece. Wind or earthquake forces cause the upper mass to tend to bend over, causing bending stresses to develop in the same junction piece. What the junction piece actually feels, however, is a combination of these stress states as they interact with one another. The compressive stresses caused by the downward action of the load combine with the compressive part of the bending stresses caused by the lateral loads to produce very high compressive stresses on one face of the junction piece. On the other face, the compressive stresses caused by the downward load tend to be negated by the tension stresses associated with the bending action.

Combined stresses of this type make the affected member more apt to fail than if subjected to either stress state alone. Consequently, members subjected to combined stresses need to be made larger than their simpler counterparts or made of stronger materials.

10.0
Christo, *Valley Curtain.*

10 Curved Members: Arches and Cables

Suspended Cables

Shapes

Curved members are widely used in sculptural applications, though most uses function compositionally rather than structurally. When used structurally, curved members have special characteristics that distinguish them from their linear counterparts. This chapter reviews the simple suspended cable and the arch.

A simple draped cable is beautifully illustrative of a curved member in tension. Examples of the draped cable as a structural device abound in many fields—witness the many suspension bridges throughout the world—but are curiously infrequent in sculptural applications. Christo's *Valley Curtain* (1971–1972), which spanned an entire valley in Rifle, Colorado, provides a dramatic exception (fig. 10.1). The work stretched 1,250 feet and was 185 to 365 feet in height. The curtain used 200,000 square feet of nylon polymide and 110,000 pounds of steel cables. The enormous thrusts developed at either end were carried by foundations tied into the surrounding bedrock. The curtain was periodically tied into concrete foundations placed along the bottom of the curtain.

Cable structures are by definition flexible. This means that the geometry of the structure is directly dependent on the type of load present and shapes itself to it. If the loading condition changes, so does the shape of the structure. This characteristic stands in marked contrast to the rigid elements largely discussed thus far, which do not exhibit large changes in the geometry of the structure as a consequence of the loading present.

The specific shape of the curve assumed by a simple cable or chain suspended between two points is responsive to the weight of the chain itself, which is uniformly distributed along its length. The resulting curve—called a *catenary*—is not circular in shape but parabolic. If an extremely heavy point load is applied to the same cable structure at its midpoint, the cable dramatically changes shape into a V as a consequence of the new loading. Adding another load would cause a new shape change.

Forces exerted by cable on
foundation anchor

Reaction force
provided by
foundation anchor

Cable

Maximum force developed in cable

Minimum force developed in cable

Christo, *Valley Curtain*

Cable loads and forces

The cable exerts an inward and
downward force on the anchor,
which provides an equal and
opposite resisting reaction force.

**The curtain edges are specially
reinforced to distribute
concentrated forces into the
fabric without tearing.**

**End foundation anchor (tied into
surrounding rock)**

10.1
Christo's remarkable *Valley
Curtain* **is an excellent example of
a suspended cable structure. The
forces developed at the ends of
this long-span structure were
quite high, and massive foundations tied back into the surrounding rock were required to
sustain them.**

In Christo's *Valley Curtain*, the shape that the cable
assumes is dominated by the concentrated loads associated
with attaching the curtain at discrete points. If the curtain
had been attached more frequently, then the cable would
have assumed more of a continuous curve. If the point loads
on the cable weighed different amounts, then the cable
would have tended to sag more under the heavier loads
than under the lighter ones. There is a direct relation
between the sag amounts present and the magnitudes and
locations of the loads. This is an important point, since it
implies that a designer may not dictate the shape the cable
assumes a priori. The cable will do what it wants to do, and
will respond in a way related to the magnitude and distribution of the loads rather than to the whim of a designer.
What a designer can do, if the particular shape is important,
is to vary the magnitudes and locations of the loads until the
cable assumes the desired shape. This can be done experimentally, as would be the most reasonable approach in
most small-scale sculptural contexts. Alternatively, there
are analytical methods for accomplishing the same end for

large-scale sculptures where experimental approaches are not feasible.[1]

Sometimes the exact shape is less important than controlling the absolute magnitude of the largest sag present. If this is the case, it is possible to vary the length of the cable to achieve exactly the desired maximum sag. In this case, however, the sag under other points cannot be exactly controlled. Along these same lines, it is interesting to note that if the length of the cable were allowed to vary (but with the loads held constant), the gross overall geometrical characteristics of the cable would not be altered even though the absolute depths of the sags would indeed change. Figure 10.3 shows the deflected shapes of a number of different cables of varying lengths, with the loading held constant. In each case the numerical *ratio* of the different sag distances remains the same. Thus there is a *family* of cable shapes associated with a particular external loading condition.

Forces

In a cable subjected to a loading, tension forces are obviously developed within the cable itself. These forces are clearly dependent on the magnitude and locations of the loads present, but they are also dependent on the relative degree of sag present in the cable. The *deeper* the absolute sag of a cable (the more it is draped) for a given loading condition, the *smaller* the tension forces developed internally in the cable. Conversely, a more tightly stretched cable develops very high internal tension forces for the same external load. In the examples shown, the largest internal forces are typically developed in the end cable segments rather than in those toward midspan (fig. 10.2). If the angles of the cable segments are not identical, then the resulting internal forces in the cable segments are also not equal.

The tension forces developed in a suspended cable exert, in turn, forces on the end connections that typically pull inward and downward. In large structures, these forces can be enormously high and difficult to resist. Obviously, abutments must be provided that do not slide inward or downward when subjected to the cable thrusts. The inwardly directed force component is particularly serious. In Christo's *Valley Curtain*, extremely large concrete elements were placed at cable ends (fig. 10.1). These concrete elements were in turn tied back into surrounding bedrock by a large

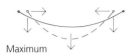

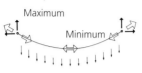

Cable forces

Force exerted by cable on supporting foundation

10.2
Suspended cables: cable forces exert inward and downward forces on supports where equal and opposite reactive forces are developed. The maximum internal force in the cable is developed at either end. The cable force is smallest at midspan.

1
This is again typically a task for a structural engineer, even though the methods are not particularly difficult. See, for example, chapter 4 in Schodek, *Structures*.

number of prestressed restraining cables. The restraining cables distributed the primary cable thrusts into the bedrock. A typical element was 1³/₈ inches in diameter and 40 feet long. The design and installation of these devices was among the more costly and difficult issues of the entire enterprise.

In smaller structures, smaller foundations can be used, but even so they invariably remain a primary design element. Alternatively, the inwardly directed component of the cable forces can be resisted by a large compression member placed between the cable ends. Foundations would then need to be designed to carry only downward forces. Some building and bridge structures have adopted this approach.

Once cable forces are known, the minimum size of the cable can be determined in the same manner as for simpler tension elements (see chapter 9). Wound cables of high-strength wire are often used. The small cable structures typically found in sculptural contexts are rarely problematic, due to the inherent strength of common cables. Determining the forces present in larger cable structures typically requires the help of a structural engineer.

Wind Effects

A particularly troublesome aspect of cables that are simply hung between two points is their sensitivity to wind effects. Winds can induce unusual loading conditions on curved shapes, including uplift or suctional forces. These suctional forces can cause a light cable structure to rise and fall rapidly and generally undergo dramatic shape changes. These effects can be amplified when the wind itself has an undulating nature to it. In the worst event, a simply draped cable can very rapidly vibrate, or flutter. This fluttering action can be very destructive for the cable, its supports, and anything connected to it.

In certain rare circumstances, the natural period of vibration of the cable can be the same as that of an undulating wind and a phenomenon called *resonance* can occur. The cable begins wildly swinging in a completely uncontrollable way when resonance occurs. Failure follows shortly afterward. Many suspension bridges have failed because of this phenomenon—one well-known instance was the destruction of the Tacoma Narrows Bridge in Washington, which was captured on film. The bridge deck began a severe undulating and twisting motion under a moderate but consistent wind until it collapsed into the Narrows.

Preventing such effects can be difficult. In some instances, the addition of simple dead weight is adequate. Various kinds of restraining cables can be used to help stabilize lighter surfaces. Alternatively, pretensioned systems can be used as described below. In a sculptural context, the need for some aggressive prevention of flutter or related effects depends largely on the size, context, and temporality of the work. A small temporary installation may need nothing as long as public safety is not threatened and the ultimate longevity of the work is of no concern. The contrary is true for large permanent works. It is of interest in this context that *Valley Curtain* was not conceived as a permanent installation.

Special Forms: Pretensioned Systems

A whole host of cable forms may be generated by combining cable elements that are pretensioned in some way with rigid elements capable of carrying compression. For the class of long curved cables discussed here, two alternatives are shown in figure 10.4. A pair of cables is separated by series of struts. A jacking force is applied to the ends of the cables during installation. In one variant, high tension forces are developed in the pair of cables and compressive forces are developed in the struts. A remarkably stiff system results that can be particularly resistant to the wind effects discussed above. Any applied transverse loadings, however, tend to cause compressive forces to develop in the upper cable and increased tension forces in the lower cable. As long as there is sufficient pretensioning in the upper cable to offset the compression tendencies so that all cables remain in tension, the system will remain stiff. Obviously the pretensioning must be maintained by supplementary elements (masts, tie-back cables, etc.) and, ideally, it should be adjustable over time.

A variant approach is to pretension separately the upper and lower cables, which in turn causes tension to develop in the connecting struts. Applied transverse loads tend to cause the pretensioning in the lower cable to decrease and the tension in the upper cable to increase. Also highly resistant to wind effects, this approach demands a host of supplementary elements to make it work.

Although shown here as simple planar forms, either of these approaches can be more flexibly used in either radial or gridlike geometries.

Many other pretensioned cable approaches are possible as well, particularly when incorporated with triangulated or other repeating geometries. Kenneth Snelson's *X Column* provides a good example (fig. 9.6).

Arches

Basic Actions

With origins dating back to antiquity, the arch is one of the most recognizable structural forms in the world. Variants are found in so many buildings and bridges throughout the world that the shape has often been used as a symbol of the concept of structure or engineering. Yet the use of the arch is curiously infrequent in sculptural applications, except as an icon.

Arches can be very efficient structures. If properly used and shaped, a steel arch can be designed with a much smaller cross section than a beam to carry an external loading over a given span. Arches are also far stiffer than beams and consequently do not tend to droop or sag as much.

The familiar shape of an arch is no accident. Ancient builders found that if wedge-shaped blocks were arranged in a certain way the resulting configuration could be used to span large openings (a perennial problem in early stone or masonry construction). Indeed, it was even found that mortar was not particularly necessary to maintain the shape of the configuration. The wedging action itself seemed adequate. Even the wedging action was found not strictly necessary if the overall geometry of the arch was carefully controlled and no off-balance loadings were present. It was also appreciated that the stability of an arch was vastly increased if it were not made freestanding but embedded in a wall. Freestanding arches of slender proportions proved very prone to failure because of off-balance loading caused by winds, earthquakes, and settling of foundations.

In an arch subjected to a uniformly distributed load acting downward, the forces developed internally in the structure are all compressive. Bending is typically not present because the curved shape of the structure channels loads to the ground in a direct way. In any arched shape, whether

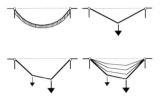

10.3
A freely deforming cable is always in tension. The shape assumed depends on the type of loading present. For a particular loading condition, a family of geometrically similar forms is possible. Forces in cables with shallow sags are higher than those with deeper sags.

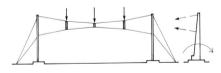

The main cables are in tension and the struts are in compression.

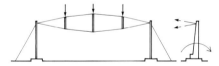

The main cables and struts are in tension.

10.4
Double cable systems: special forms of cable structures may be obtained by pretensioning. These structures are inherently resistant to wind-induced flutter. The pretensioning causes large forces to be developed in supporting members.

made of masonry or of a continuous material, the applied loading tends to cause the arch to flatten out. As the arch tends to flatten, it exerts horizontally acting forces at its bases along with the vertically acting ones normally associated with a downward loading. These are actually components of the same inclined force. The horizontal thrusts must be contained by some type of abutment system or absorbed by a tie-rod connecting the two end points of the arch (the tie-rod is consequently in tension since it tends to prevent the ends from drawing apart). A masonry arch would flatten out and collapse completely if these thrusts were not contained. A rigid arch would flatten out and begin carrying loads much like a curved beam, and hence would not be terribly efficient as a structural device, or it would simply fail in bending. Menashe Kadishman's *Segments* (fig. 10.6) is an example of this kind of structure. It has the classic arch form but actually carries loads by bending rather than arch action, since its ends are unrestrained.

The material from which an arch is made is very important. When bending is present in masonry arches, typically because of off-balance loadings, the resulting stresses often lead to collapse (the tension stresses associated with bending cause mortared joints to crack and eventually pull apart completely). Early builders did find, however, that arch members made of iron or steel could be made much more slender than their masonry counterparts and carry off-balance loadings much better. This was attributable to the ability of an iron or steel member to resist the bending stresses that are generated in arches by off-balance loading conditions—something simple masonry members are unable to do. Consequently, arches made out of materials able to resist bending stresses (steel, aluminum, etc.) can be made much slenderer than those made of masonry.

Geometries and Forces

A good way to look at arches is to imagine them as inverted cables. A simple flexible cable suspended between two points will naturally sag into a parabolic shape; tension forces are naturally developed within it. Imagine this cable to be somehow "frozen" (changed into a rigid structure) and then inverted and subjected to the same external loading. If only pure tension forces were developed in the original suspended form, the inverted form would naturally carry

10.5
Andy Goldsworthy, *Arch*.
Compressive forces must exist between adjacent stones for this structure to be stable.

10.6
Menashe Kadishman, *Segments*.
This structure is shaped like
the familiar arch but does not
behave like one structurally since
the ends are not restrained.
Rather it is more like a curved
beam. Under a vertical loading
the structure would tend to flatten out and bending stresses
would develop. The work has
enough stiffness so that this flattening does not occur.

Structures in tension

Corresponding structures in compression: appropriate shapes for loading conditions shown

Structures in bending: inappropriate shapes used for loading conditions shown

10.7
Exactly inverting the shape assumed by a freely deforming cable yields an analogous form that is always in a state of compression for the same loading. There is only one funicular shape for a given loading condition. Using a shape derived on the basis of one loading to support another causes undesirable bending to develop.

only compressive forces. Seen in this way, the simple draped cable and upright arch are mirror images of one another. Sometimes they are both called *funicular* structures.

Looking at the arch as an inversion of a cable implies that its best shape for carrying uniformly distributed loads (including its own self-weight) is parabolic, not circular. If large point loads are considered, on the other hand, it is evident that the compressive counterpart to the suspended cable is made up of linear rather than curved elements (assuming the self-weight of the structure is negligible compared to the magnitude of the point loads). Thus the ideal shape of an "arch" carrying two point loads might not be curved in the traditional manner at all (fig. 10.7, center right). Such a shape would still not be subjected to bending and would carry forces by comparatively efficient axial compression. These are indeed unique structures!

It follows that there is one, and only one, funicular shape for a given external loading condition. If a structure is not configured to have the funicular shape for a particular loading, then bending is developed within the structure (fig. 10.7, bottom). It can be shown that the relative magnitude of the bending tendency present is directly proportional to the amount of the deviation between the line of the actual structure and the corresponding funicular line. If the two lines coincide, no bending moments are present. Such is the case of a cable or a precisely shaped arch. Obviously this is not the case in a structure such as a linear beam, which has high bending moments within it. Even in cases where an arch is precisely shaped for a particular loading condition, say that of its own self-weight, an off-balance additional load would tend to induce bending in the structure because of the new funicular line associated with that loading.

Possible bending in a small arch is not troublesome if the member is made of a continuous material, such as steel, and has a sufficiently large cross section to carry the bending (the cross section would have to be much larger, of course, than in the case where only compression was present). If the member is made of masonry, however, the bending would lead to collapse as previously described. Arches made of steel or similar materials are consequently much more versatile than those made of masonry. Every effort, however, should be made to minimize these bending tendencies by shaping the structure as precisely as possible for the expected loading.

With these observations as a background, it is useful to briefly reconsider the circular masonry arch. The funicular line for the distributed loading present is surely not circular but some parabolic shape. The funicular line and the line of the structure are surely not exactly coincident, so some bending must be present. So why do circular masonry arches work? The answer lies in the large sizes of the masonry blocks themselves. If the blocks are made large enough, the structure can contain the funicular line within its dimensions (since the circular and parabolic lines are reasonably close together). This means that the structure still works largely in compression. Embedding the circular form in a wall adds further resistance to bending by preventing the arch from deforming freely. Hence circular forms can be made to work if their dimensions are large enough.

In closing, it should be emphasized that the internal forces within an arch are not necessarily constant. Arches are *not* "constant force" structures. In a simple parabolic arch, it can be shown that the maximum internal force present is greatest at the springing of the arch and least at its crown. If desired, the size of the cross section used could be designed to reflect this distribution of forces (recall the shape of the gigantic gateway arch in St. Louis). In compressive structures carrying point loads, it can be expected that the internal forces present differ in each segment of the structure, with the largest again typically being at the supports.

11 Frameworks

⌐ ‑ ‑ ‑ ‑ ‑ ‑ ‑ ‑ ‑ ‑ ‑ ‑ ┐

Types of Frameworks

The framework is among the most persuasive of all structural devices. Frameworks are open interconnected assemblies of (typically) linear elements, arranged in a systematic way and capable of supporting different loadings without overall changes occurring in the geometry of the structure. *Veiled Landscape* by Mary Miss (fig. 11.1), erected in Lake Placid, New York, in 1979, provides one example of a framework. Usually most of the constituent parts of a framework are made of rigid elements, capable of carrying a variety of different internal force states (tension, compression, bending) without appreciable deformations or changes in shape. In some geometries, special members, such as cables, that are capable of carrying only tensile forces may be used as well.

The overall geometry of a framework governs its behavior as a structural device and places requirements on the nature of the connections between individual elements. A basic distinction is between *triangulated* assemblies of elements and those ordered in some other way. *Skyway Bridge*, executed in 1980 by Siah Armajani, illustrates a framework based on one form of triangulated pattern (fig. 11.2). Triangulated assemblies form a special subclass of open frameworks having remarkable strength properties. These assemblies derive their fundamental strength and rigidity from the geometry of the structure more than from how specific elements are connected. Indeed, elements in a triangulated framework can be pinned together in a very simple way. The forces induced in members in triangulated forms are by and large only those of tension or compression. Adverse bending effects are typically not present or are only marginally important. Members can be designed to be relatively slender.

By contrast, *Veiled Landscape* and Sol LeWitt's *Five Modular Units* (figs. 2.3 and 11.11) represent a more general class of framework that involves no triangulation. Often called *rigid frameworks*, open frameworks of this type are structurally stable only if many, if not all, of the constituent

11.0
Nicolas Schoffer,
Spatiodynamique.

11.1
Mary Miss, *Veiled Landscape*.
The idea of a rigid framework is
eloquently conveyed in this outdoor work.

pieces are rigidly connected one to another by specially constructed rigid joints that prevent angular changes from occurring between attached members. Great freedom is obtained in gaining stability through rigid joint connections, for there is no need to triangulate the position of members at all, but there are drawbacks. With some materials, making the required rigid joints is easy. Steel elements, for example, can easily be rigidly joined to one another by simple welding. But with other materials, such as wood, making rigid joints is far more difficult. Members in a rigid frame structure are also subject to bending as well as tension or compression. This necessitates that they be made larger than their counterparts in triangulated frameworks. Still, in many cases (especially in smaller works), these drawbacks are not particularly important and rigid frame approaches can easily be utilized.

Both triangulated and rigid frameworks provide stability. Triangulated structures will probably always occupy a warm spot in the hearts of purist structural designers because they derive their stability from the conscious placement of members in space according to rules that can be intellectually derived and they are invariably visually responsive to the kinds of loadings present. Nor do they rely at all on the potentially hidden connections of rigid frameworks. Rigid frameworks, however, always offer greater ease and flexibility of member placement than is possible in triangulated frameworks, and can thus potentially respond to a broader set of design intents. The strength of the modern welded connection is such, for example, that the desire to "defy gravity" or make a structure appear to "float" can be approximated—but of course never actually met—via rigid frameworks with welded joints.

Triangulated Frameworks

General Principles

An assembly of individual linear rigid elements arranged in a triangle or combination of triangles forms a framework that is inherently stable under *any* loading condition—a characteristic that stands in marked contrast to other geometric patterns of assembly (fig. 11.3). If a single triangle of rigid members is a stable form, it follows that *any* assembly of triangles also creates a larger structural form that is

11.2
Siah Armajani, *Skyway Bridge*.
This structure illustrates a triangulated framework. Such frameworks are particularly rigid and capable of carrying high loads using small member sizes.

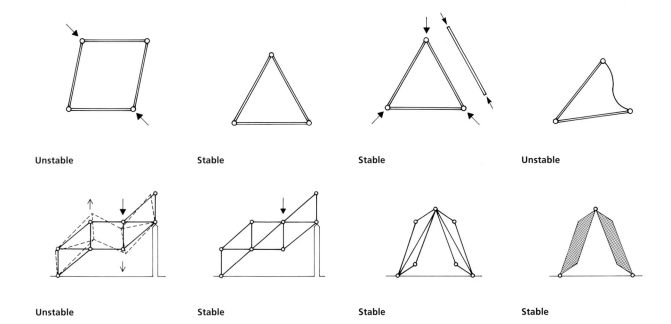

Unstable   Stable   Stable   Unstable

Unstable   Stable   Stable   Stable

11.3
When members are pin-connected (nonrigidly joined to one another), triangulated configurations must be used.

inherently rigid and stable. This principle underlies the usefulness of the triangulation as a fundamental structural device. Since it is the triangulation that is important, the connections between members can be made very simply. Often members are simply connected at a single point via a bolt or weld. These joints can transmit axial forces of tension and compression, but not any type of bending or rotational forces. Specific members are consequently in a state of either pure tension or pure compression, either of which is preferable to the adverse force state of bending. Members can consequently be made quite slender. The careful positioning of material in space in this way yields structures of great stiffness with the use of little material. It must be emphasized, however, that the presence of a single nontriangulated shape in a structure of this type could lead to a collapse of the whole (fig. 11.3, bottom left).

In architecture and engineering, the principle of triangulation has long been applied in structures called *trusses*. Trusses are the workhorses of many common structures (bridges, roofs) found in our cities and landscapes. They normally serve a role similar to that of beams in that they are frequently used as horizontal spanning elements. Siah Armajani has celebrated the power of these common structures in his series of "bridges." His early works closely mime their vernacular progenitors, while later ones are more reflective. While often primarily reveries on time and passage, several in the series nonetheless hint at the quality of the structures themselves.

The fundamental structural virtue of triangulation need not be associated so literally with the familiar truss. Susumu Shingu's use of triangulated networks of rigid members in *Path of the Wind* (fig. 11.4) is both an intrinsic part of the design ethic of the work and an effective structural method for carrying the large laterally acting wind and earthquake forces that might act on the tower. The cross bracing described in chapter 8 also involves triangulating elements, as does the bracing in the supporting framework for the enormous Statue of Liberty (see chapter 15).

Another of Shingu's sculptures, *Gift of the Wind*, shows the use of triangulated rigid members as a way of increasing the overall stiffness of a component part of a sculpture (fig. 11.5). The large wind-catching surfaces are stiffened by the triangulated members framing into them. Note that the triangulation itself occurs in three orthogonal planes. This assures that each of the surfaces is indeed fully stabilized. The actual members of the framework are relatively small in cross section: triangulating rigid elements is among the most efficient of all basic structural approaches.

Can a triangulation pattern incorporate nonrigid or *flexible* members, such as cables or chains, and still be stable? As figures 11.3 and 11.6 illustrate, the answer is a highly qualified yes. Stability in this case depends on the nature of the force state induced in the form by the action of the applied load. Where this internal force state is that of tension, then either a rigid or a flexible member may be used. If the force state is that of compression, then a rigid member *must* be used for the form to be a stable one (a flexible member subjected to this type of force would simply buckle out of the way and cause the structure to collapse). Thus, before flexible members are used in triangulated frameworks, something must be known about what types of forces will be induced in specific members by the external loading—a subject that will be addressed in the following section.

Triangulated frameworks work best structurally when any large concentrated loads or weights that the structure might be expected to carry are applied at a nodal point (a joint) rather than at some odd point along the length of one of the members. This allows the external weight to be carried down to the foundations of the structure in a highly efficient manner involving the development in individual framework members of internal tension or compression forces

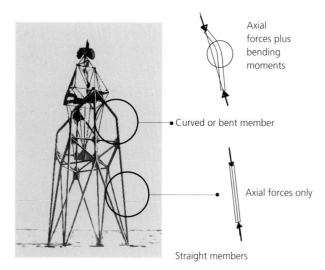

Axial forces plus bending moments

Curved or bent member

Axial forces only

Straight members

Susumu Shingu, *Path of the Wind*

11.4
Susumu Shingu, *Path of the Wind*. When straight members are used in triangulated forms, as is the case in the familiar truss, only tension or compression forces are developed in the members. When a member is curved, detrimental bending may be present that must be taken into account in sizing the member.

Tension or compression forces are developed in straight members of a truss. Bending additionally develops when members are curved.

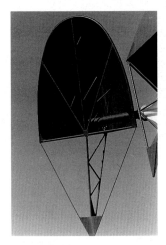

11.5
Triangulated elements stiffen the sails of Shingu's *Gift of the Wind.*

only. Loads or weights can be applied along the length of a member, but doing so would cause localized bending stresses to be developed in the member. Accommodating these stresses would in turn generally necessitate an increase in member sizes. This can certainly be done in smaller structures. The slender proportions often associated with members in a triangulated framework made of steel, however, are associated with external weights applied at nodes rather than along member lengths.

Normally the individual members in a triangulated network are simply connected to one another via a pin of some type, but they may also be rigidly connected, typically with welded joints. When joints are pin-connected, framework members are in a state of either pure tension or pure compression. When members are rigidly connected, some marginal increase in strength and overall resistance to deflections results. But this increase is associated with the development of additional bending stresses in individual members, which in turn may dictate some level of increase in member size. Normally, there is no significant structural advantage to be gained by using rigid joints in comparison to simpler pinned connections if members are triangulated.

Individual members in triangulated frameworks are typically straight elements and work best when shaped this way. Nonetheless, members need not always be linear, as is evident in Shingu's *Path of the Wind*. Bending stresses beyond those that might normally be present are induced in specific members by the act of curving them. This, in turn, might dictate some increase in required member size. For relatively small works this issue is generally inconsequential. But as the size of a work increases, the use of curved members can become increasingly difficult. Still, note that *Path of the Wind* is a fairly large structure with member sizes that are fairly small in cross section. The positive benefits of the general strategy of triangulation outweigh the negative aspects of using curved members in this example.

11.6
Cables may be used in triangulated configurations so long as they are not subjected to compression forces. When subjected to compression, they buckle out of the way and the whole configuration may collapse.

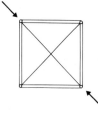

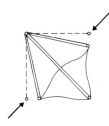

Stability and Force Distributions
in Triangulated Frameworks

In most triangulated frameworks, a simple visual inspection will tell whether or not the specific pattern of members is indeed triangulated in a way that results in a stable structure. Certainly the appearance of nontriangular shapes in a bar pattern is a sure sign that a dangerous condition could exist. Only one nontriangulated form in an otherwise acceptable bar pattern will lead to failure. Occasionally, however, some seemingly nontriangular forms are nonetheless stable. In the final two diagrams of figure 11.3, the central space is not a pure triangle but the structure is nonetheless stable because of the exact way members are placed. The group of triangles on either side form rigid clusters and, in a sense, can be thought of as single bars from the base to the apex—which would then make the overall form a simple stable triangle.

As an aid in ascertaining the stability of simple planar triangulated configurations, a simple relation between the number of members and the number of vertices (or joints) in a stable structure can be determined. A single triangle has three bars ($n = 3$) and three vertices ($V = 3$). Adding a single new vertex beyond the original three requires the addition of two new bars or members. Hence the total number of members (n) in a truss having a number of vertices (V) is given by the following: $n = 3 + 2(V - 3)$. This expression can be rewritten more simply as $n = 2V - 3$. In the sixth diagram of figure 11.3, $V = 8$ so n must equal 13 [$n = 2(8) - 3 = 13$]. The structure has exactly this number of members, so it is stable. In the fifth diagram, $V = 8$ so n must again equal 13. But the truss has only 12 members: this structure forms a collapse mechanism and is dangerous. The formula $n = 2V - 3$ is not foolproof, particularly when cables are used, but it is a useful aid in determining whether a complex bar pattern is indeed a stable configuration. In the seventh diagram of figure 11.3, for example, it is quite difficult to ascertain if the truss is truly stable. Using our formula, $V = 7$, so n must be 11. Since 11 bars are actually provided (the ground connecting the two base points is considered a member since it must carry forces), the truss is most likely stable.

The process used to arrive at the expression for the number of free movements present in a pin-connected planar structure can be repeated for three-dimensional aggregations. A simple tetrahedron is known to be a stable structure. Three bars are required to form each additional new node added to this basic form. There are six bars to begin with and new bars are added at the rate of three for each node beyond the original four. Thus for a form composed of tetrahedral shapes, $n = 6 + 3(V - 4) = 3V - 6$.

If a bar network is stable, and if the individual members of a triangulated framework are simply connected (for example, pinned), the effect of an external load on a triangulated framework is to produce a state of either pure tension or pure compression in the individual members of the assembly. Whether or not a specific member is in tension, compression, or even has no force in it at all depends on the pattern of the triangles and on the placement and direction of the external loads. The nature and magnitude of the force in each member would, in turn, be a determinant of its minimum size. Members that are always in a state of tension under all reasonable external loading conditions can even be made out of cable-like elements that can carry only tensile forces.

One simple way of determining the sense of the force in a particular member is to visualize the probable deformed shape of the structure as it would develop if the member were removed. The sense of the force in the member can then be determined on the basis of its role in preventing the deformation visualized. For example, consider member BF in the simple truss form shown at left in figure 11.7. If this member were to be removed, the truss would begin collapsing as illustrated—that is, points B and F would draw further apart. This means that the role of member BF is to prevent this drawing apart. Consequently, BF must be being pulled upon and be in a state of tension. If a member were placed between A and C its role would be to prevent these points from drawing closer together—hence it would be in a state of compression.

The technique of removing members and assessing the resultant deformed shape is a valuable way of intuitively understanding how structures of this type behave, but it is quite tricky to use in complex triangulation patterns and obviously says nothing of the magnitude of the forces developed. Another technique for qualitatively understanding the forces developed in a triangulated framework is based on a consideration of the equilibrium of the different vertices as they are acted upon by both external loads and internal forces in adjoining bar members. This method conceptualizes a triangulated framework as composed of a set of

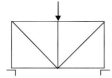

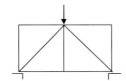

In a triangulated configuration, the orientation of a member affects the type of force developed within it.

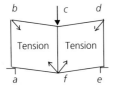

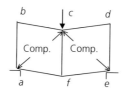

A member placed between *b* and *f* keeps these points from pulling apart, and hence is in tension. A member between *a* and *c* keeps these points from closing in on one another, and hence is in compression.

11.7
The nature of the forces in some simple triangulated patterns can be inferred by visualizing the deformed shape the structure would assume if the members of interest were removed.

1
Many books discuss more advanced analytical procedures of this type (see, for example, Schodek, *Structures*, chapter 4). There are also a number of computer programs for determining force states in member networks, based on these more advanced analytical procedures.

members and a set of points that represent the connections. It might be good to envision the attached members as either compressed springs (members in a state of compression) or stretched rubber bands (members in tension). Thus any particular joint is subject to a set of pushes by the springs or pulls by the rubber bands. The joint must be in equilibrium under this set of pushes and pulls (and not tend to slide or rotate in any direction).

In figure 11.8, for example, the downward-acting external load at B causes upward-acting reactive forces to develop at A and C. The applied force in AB must push on vertex A, and thus must be compressive in nature. If AB pushes on vertex A, however, it tends to slide it to the left because of the horizontal component of the force in AB. Thus a tension force must be developed in member AC. This force would tend to keep vertex A from sliding to the left by pulling on it to the right. The same line of reasoning can be applied to vertex C. The downward force at B is balanced by the upward-acting vertical components of the two internal forces in AB and BC. The horizontal components of these forces are equal and opposite to each other. Knowledge of these relations could be used to predict the magnitudes of the internal forces in the three members, though actually doing so is beyond the scope of this book.

A similar line of thinking can be applied to three-dimensional triangulated structures. Alexander Calder's *Calderberry Bush* (fig. 11.9), executed in 1932, utilizes a simple three-dimensional bar structure—in this case a simple tetrahedral form—as its base and support for the suspended mobile. The mobile obviously causes a point load *P* acting downward. The accompanying diagram illustrates the forces developed in each of the members of the form by considering in turn the equilibrium of each of the vertices. Thus the load *P* at the apex generates compressive forces in the sloped members, which are shown acting upward to balance the downward load *P*. These members in turn induce tension forces in the base members.

Forces can often be inferred by looking at the overall deformed shape of a structure. The cantilevers in Panamarenko's *General Spinaxis* (fig. 11.10) undoubtedly have tension in the top members and compression in the bottom members when the loads act downward because of the general behavior of a cantilever member (see chapter 9). Reversing the loads would reverse these force states.

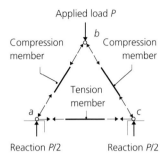

Applied load *P*

Compression member

Compression member

Tension member

a

b

c

Reaction *P*/2

Reaction *P*/2

11.8
Forces can be inferred by noting that each node must be in translational equilibrium in both the vertical and the horizontal direction. Forces may be envisioned as pushing or pulling on a node. The net effect of these pushes and pulls at a node must be zero. Members are either in tension or compression (no detrimental bending is present).

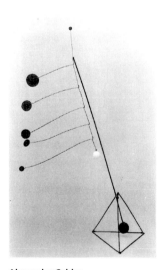

Alexander Calder,
Calderberry Bush

11.9
Three-dimensional triangulated configurations are quite rigid. Members are in tension and compression (no bending is present). Each node is in translational equilibrium.

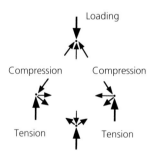

Loading

Compression

Compression

Tension

Tension

Only tension or compression forces are developed in the supporting tetrahedron.

When actual magnitudes of forces in specific members are needed—for either planar or three-dimensional member networks—the same general approaches described above can be repeated using actual numerical values.[1] Usually exact determinations of force states in complicated member networks require the assistance of trained structural engineers.

Rigid Frames (Nontriangulated Systems)

Sol LeWitt's *Five Modular Units* (fig. 11.11) is a frame structure that does not rely on triangulation for its rigidity. The connections in structures of this type *must* be rigid rather than pinned for the forms to be structurally viable. The function of these rigid joints must be to prevent angular changes from occurring between attached members, which would lead to a parallelogramming, and hence collapse, of the structure when it is subjected to a lateral force such as from someone pushing on it (fig. 11.12). One of LeWitt's cubes could potentially fail by one of two means—one or more joints could fail or one or more of the members could fail. If joints failed, they might no longer be able to maintain the original 90-degree angles between attached members, and revert to pinlike joints. The structure would collapse by parallelogramming. Alternatively, the joints could remain viable, but the members themselves might not be able to withstand the bending induced in them. Bending is highest near the ends of the members, so failure would still most likely be near the end joints. Failure of a single member would again lead to an overall collapse.

The use of rigid joints to achieve stability is very common and need not assume the extreme form of *Five Modular Units*. Neither is it a difficult approach when structures are small in scale. Alberto Giacometti's *The Palace at 4 A.M.* (fig. 11.13), executed in 1932–1933, is composed of a great many rigid frameworks. The external forces that come into play on an open framework such as this would undoubtedly be fairly small, and thus slender members can be used that rely on rigid connections at their ends. Max Bill's *Thirty Similar Triangles* (fig. 11.14) shows the flexibility of rigid frameworks. Many other sculptures illustrated in this book derive their basic stability from rigid connections.

Most of the clearest examples of rigid frame structures in sculpture are of fairly recent vintage. This is not surprising,

Panamarenko, *General Spinaxis*

Wing support (a cantilevered truss)

Tension forces

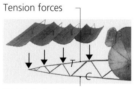

Compression forces

Member forces associated with
the static self-weight of the wing

Compression forces

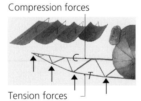

Tension forces

Member forces associated
with uplifts

11.10
**The forces in a simple triangu-
lated member are quite sensitive
to the directions of the applied
loads. Cantilevers carrying
downward-acting loads have
tension forces developed in
upper members and compression forces in lower members.
Forces in the diagonals
alternate between tension
and compression.**

11.11
Sol LeWitt, *Five Modular Units*.
This structure illustrates the
essential characteristics of a rigid
frame structure.

Pinned connections

Rigid connections

11.12
A pin-connected nontriangulated
framework could collapse. The
same configuration made with
rigid joints between members
would be stable. Rigid frame
structures undergo complex
bending actions when subjected
to loadings.

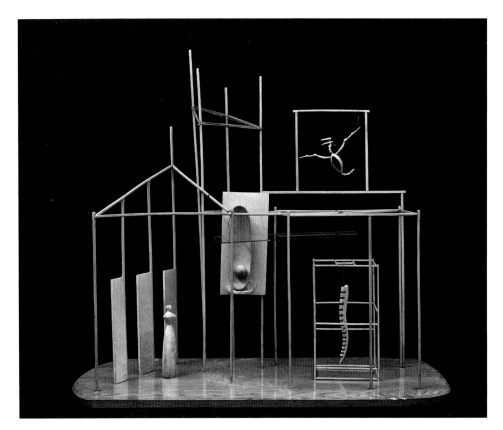

11.13
Alberto Giacometti, *Palace at 4 A.M.* Several small-scale rigid frame structures are evident in this work.

11.14
Max Bill, *Construction with Thirty Similar Elements.* Rigid frame structures can be quite versatile in their shape-forming capabilities as long as applied loadings are small.

since the idea is closely linked to that of assemblage rather than representation. The rigid frame as a conceptually understood structural device is of recent origin as well. The dependence on modern technology (e.g., welding) is also obvious.

Frameworks Based on Repeating Geometries

Patterns that are built of repeating elements are among the most pervasive in both art and nature. In nature repeated patterns are found in both plant and animal forms: the famous radiolarian skeletons from the nineteenth-century *Challenger* explorations, for example, which led to changed perceptions of the evolution of life on earth, or the familiar honeycomb. Many widely used structural frameworks have their underlying rationale in a pattern of repeated geometric forms as well. So far we have looked at triangulated and rigid frame structures without regard to larger pattern; but the larger patterns can involve repeated geometric forms that have interesting characteristics in themselves.

Plato provided one of the first systematic attempts to describe and inventory geometric shapes. He developed five solids that are the only convex polyhedra bounded by identical regular polygonal faces (i.e., with all vertices identical). These five solids—the tetrahedron, the octahedron, the hexahedron, the icosahedron, and dodecahedron—were used by Plato both in his studies of forms in nature and in his studies of cosmology. Four of the forms were identified with the four elements. The cube (a hexahedron) represented earth; the tetrahedron, fire; the octahedron, air; and the icosahedron, water. The dodecahedron became the symbol for the the shape enclosing the universe.

These forms have faces made of regular polygons. A *polygon* is any closed shape made of a finite set of line segments joined end to end. The forms are described in terms of their *edges* (sides) and *vertices* (corners). If the polygon is equilateral and equiangular, a *regular polygon* is formed. A polygon has *bilateral symmetry* (or mirror symmetry) when one side is a reflection of the other about a common line bisecting the polygon. A *plane tesselation* is an extendable set of polygons fitting together to cover a surface (like a mosaic), so that every side of each polygon belongs also to one other polygon.[2] Within this general category, a *regular tesselation* is a pattern built of congruent regular polygons,

so that each vertex of the tesselation is alike. Only three polygons—square, hexagon, and triangle—can generate regular tesselations (fig. 11.15). A *semiregular tesselation* requires that all polygons be regular and vertices congruent, but allows the use of more than one type of polygon. Eight semiregular plane tesselations exist, formed by various combinations of squares, triangles, hexagons, octagons, and dodecagons. Tesselations can be used to divide a plane uniformly with polygons having either no symmetry or only bilateral symmetry, although many involve one form or another of *rotational* symmetry. The rotational symmetry of a figure is determined by counting the number of times the figure repeats itself in one turn about an axis. Only four kinds of rotational symmetry (two-, three-, four-, and six-fold) are possible in the uniform subdivision of space. By relaxing some of these constraints, such as allowing the use of nonregular polygons, many other tesselation patterns can be developed. Recently there have been further insights into this field by mathematicians and physicists such as Roger Penrose who have explored new tiling patterns based on shapes that fit together in an orderly way but are not perfectly repetitive. The idea of "fractiles" is also relevant here. While easily graspable conceptually, their properties of self-similarity are more readily explorable in a computer context.

An important relation between the number of edges and vertices in an arrangement of polygons is given by the expression $P + V = E + 1$. The number of polygons (P) present plus the number of vertices (V) is equal to the number of edges (E) plus one. The simplest example is of a single triangle having one face ($P = 1$), three vertices ($V = 3$), and three edges ($E = 3$); or $1 + 3 = 3 + 1$. The relationship generally extends, however, to any finite but arbitrary sample of an infinite plane tesselation. This relationship among components in a tesselation is a variant of Euler's more general formulation for polyhedra, discussed below.

The idea of a reciprocal or *dual* network is important to an understanding of repeated patterns. A dual network is formed by joining the center of each polygon in a tesselation to the centers of all neighboring polygons through the shared edges. The dual network always forms a second set of polygons having the same number of edges as there are edges meeting within the vertex it encloses. Thus a tesselation of regular triangles is a dual to a tesselation of regular hexagons (fig. 11.15).

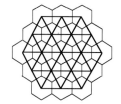

Regular: hexagon

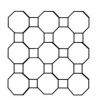

Semiregular: octagon and square

Semiregular: hexagon and triangle

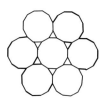

Semiregular: dodecagon and triangle

11.15
Common regular and semiregular tessellations of a plane. A dual network is also shown for the first figure.

2
H. S. M. Coxeter, *Regular Polytopes*, 2d ed. (New York: Macmillan, 1963).

3
This topic is admirably addressed, for example, in Peter Pearce and Susan Pearce, *Polyhedra Primer* (New York: Van Nostrand Reinhold, 1978).

A *polyhedron* is a three-dimensional volume formed by a finite set of connected plane polygons that form a closed figure. Each side of every polygon is shared with one other polygon. These polygons meet at vertices in groups of three or more. A *regular polyhedron* is one having all faces of identical (congruent) regular polygons, and all vertices equivalent (i.e., one of Plato's five solids). Polyhedra and their duals can be discussed in many of the same terms as their planar counterparts. Plato's tetrahedron has four faces; the hexahedron, six; the octahedron, eight; the dodecahedron, twelve; and the icosahedron, twenty. There are also thirteen semiregular polyhedra—usually called the *Archimedean polyhedra* since they are believed to have been described by Archimedes. Five of these semiregular polyhedra are obtained by *truncating* (cutting off) vertices—and thus creating new faces—on each of the five basic solids. In addition to the regular and semiregular polyhedra, there are many more polyhedra whose faces are composed entirely of regular polygons, but which do not have congruent vertices. A *stellated* polyhedron is formed by extending in the same plan each face of a convex polyhedron until the faces intersect to form a new volume. A boundless set of *prisms* are formed by two congruent and parallel polygonal faces that are then joined by a set of parallelograms. *Antiprisms* occur when the faces are connected by a set of triangles. A *parallelopiped* is a prism whose bases and sides are parallelograms. The *dual* of a polyhedron is created by joining a point that is perpendicular above the center of each face of a polyhedron to similar points above adjacent faces. The dual of a tetrahedron, for example, is simply another tetrahedron; while the cube and octahedron are dual to each other, as are the dodecahedron and the icosahedron.

Leonhard Euler developed a general theorem for polyhedra relating the number of polygonal faces (P) to the number of vertices (V) and the number of edges (E): $P + V = E + 2$. A tetrahedron, for example, has four faces ($P = 4$), four vertices ($V = 4$), and six edges ($E = 6$); thus, $4 + 4 = 6 + 2$.

In filling space with polyhedral forms (the three-dimensional counterpart to tesselating a plane), only certain ones of the many shapes available will pack together to fill completely all space. This complex topic requires an initial look at the basic symmetry classes of polyhedra, and specifically at the different axes of symmetry in different forms.[3] Within

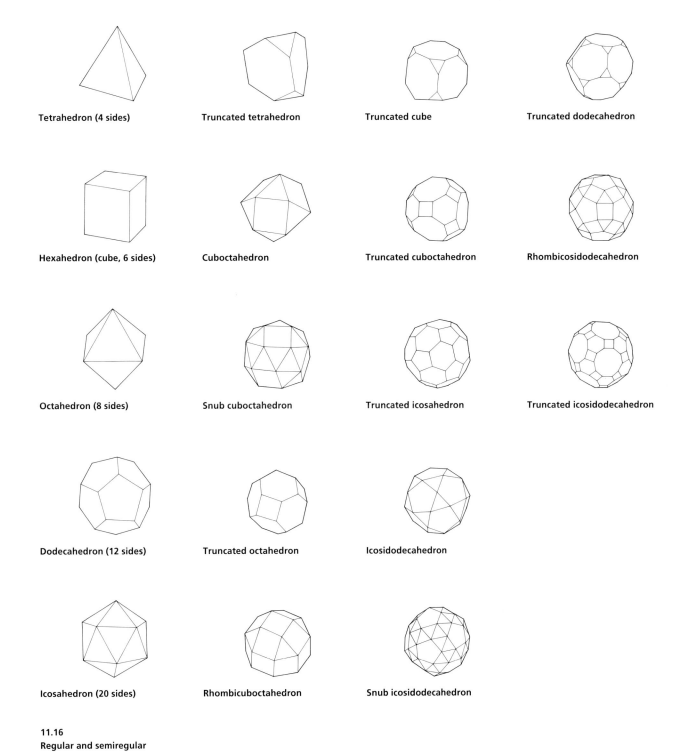

Tetrahedron (4 sides)

Truncated tetrahedron

Truncated cube

Truncated dodecahedron

Hexahedron (cube, 6 sides)

Cuboctahedron

Truncated cuboctahedron

Rhombicosidodecahedron

Octahedron (8 sides)

Snub cuboctahedron

Truncated icosahedron

Truncated icosidodecahedron

Dodecahedron (12 sides)

Truncated octahedron

Icosidodecahedron

Icosahedron (20 sides)

Rhombicuboctahedron

Snub icosidodecahedron

11.16
Regular and semiregular
polyhedra.

the boundless class of three-dimensional figures known as parallelopipeds, there are several fundamental symmetry classes—cubic, tetragonal, orthorhombic, monoclinic, trigonal, triclinic, and hexagonal—that are commonly used in fields such as crystallography. These classes rely upon different combinations of twofold, threefold, fourfold, sixfold, and no rotational symmetry. The cube is the most symmetric of polyhedra and has no less than thirteen axes of symmetry. The cubic class is therefore the most useful of the space-filling classes. The hexagonal class has seven axes of symmetry; the tetragonal, five axes; the orthorhombic, three axes; the trigonal, one axis; the monoclinic, one axis; and the triclinic, none. Lattices of unit cells can be made representing each of these symmetry classes.

Among regular polyhedra, the cube is the only universal space filler. Among the Archimedean solids and the family of prisms and antiprisms, the truncated octahedron, the hexagonal prism, and the triangular prism are all space fillers. Of the thirteen Archimedean duals, only the rhombic dodecahedron will fill all space.

The complementarity of adjacent dihedral angles (a dihedral angle is the angle formed between the planes of two adjacent polygons) is as important as axes of symmetry in considering space-filling polyhedra. In a space-filling aggregation of polyhedra, the dihedral angles formed by the meeting of polygonal faces along a common edge must total 360 degrees.

While the number of regular and semiregular polyhedra that can be used alone to fill space completely is limited, the simultaneous use of different regular and semiregular polyhedra within the same volume allows new packing arrangements. A combination of tetrahedra and octahedra, for example, can fill space completely. Obviously, this approach requires that different polyhedra must have parallel faces in common. But a number of Platonic and Archimedean figures still become possible for use in combination as space fillers. If requirements are further relaxed, including that vertices be congruent (identical), then there is a boundless number of different combinations possible.

New research by physicists has resulted in especially interesting new forms. Quasicrystals have been devised that are made up of three-dimensional shapes that fit together in an orderly but not perfectly repetitive way. Some units have even been devised with five-way symmetry. This research is often done in connection with understanding the internal make-up of materials.

Geometrical Preoccupations and Network Stability

A fascination with repetitive patterns has formed the basis for the work of a great many sculptors. Sol LeWitt's *13/11* (fig. 20.1), a cubic lattice, is an extreme example. Polyhedral forms can be made directly into structural forms in one of two fundamental ways: by making an open bar network in which placement of the rigid bars coincides with the "edges" of the polyhedra of interest; or by making surfaces (typically of rigid material) in the shapes of the faces and joining their edges. Each approach has different structural implications. This discussion will focus on bar networks.

Consider a simple tetrahedral form made by using bars along each edge and connected at the nodes (fig. 11.18). It is evident by inspection that the form is quite stable under any loading from any direction, since it is composed essentially of triangular figures. In complex aggregations, however, it is useful to have a way of predicting the internal consistency of the aggregation by looking at the number of bars (edges) in relation to the number of nodes (vertices) and faces. Note that if Euler's expression is rearranged ($E = P + V - 2$), it can be used as a general predictor of whether the actual physical construction has the requisite number of bars and nodes. For a simple tetrahedron, $E = 4 + 4 - 2 = 6$. Thus, the structure *must* have a minimum of six bars in it to make the tetrahedral form. Note, however, that using Euler's theorem in connection with arbitrarily chosen polyhedra only predicts a numerical relationship between faces, edges, and vertices and does not necessarily predict structural stability under all possible loadings. LeWitt's *Five Modular Units* undoubtedly meets Euler's criterion but is certainly not a stable structure unless each of the nodes has been made into a rigid or "moment-resisting" joint (as discussed earlier). If the joints were simple pinned connections, the sculpture would lack rigidity.

Stellated polyhedra

Dual

Dual

Prism

Antiprism

11.17
Stellations and prisms.

11.18
Typical rigid three-dimensional bar networks.

4
Note that this formulation is similar in spirit to Euler's theorem for relating components in planar tesselations, $P + V = E + 3$, but relates members and nodes more directly and does not "count" the number of polygons formed. This is sensible in bar networks, since polygons are, after all, formed only by building node-member networks.

A more useful formulation can generally be derived from considering characteristics of structures known a priori to be rigid, such as networks of planar triangulated figures. The expression discussed earlier for a rigid planar structure utilizing only pinned connections ($n = 2V - 3$, where n is the number of members required to connect a number of nodes V)[4] can be rearranged as $0 = 2V - n - 3$, or more generally $m = 2V - n - 3$. The quantity m on the left is sometimes referred to as the number of possible *free* or *unconstrained movements* present in the structure (the number of different kinds of collapse movements that can be formed) as a function of its member completeness.[5] A structure with $m = 0$ generally has exactly the minimum number of members needed to assure completeness and, normally, stability; hence parts do not tend to collapse or freely move in an unconstrained way with respect to one another. A simple triangle has three members ($n = 3$) and three nodes ($V = 3$), so $m = 2(3) - 3 - 3 = 0$; there are no freely occurring movements in the structure and it is a stable shape. A planar pin-connected four-member network with four nodes (e.g., a square) has one free movement possibility, since $m = 2(4) - 4 - 3 = 1$; it is thus not a rigid structure since it can move in one mode (parallelogramming). Only by changing the joint from a pinned to a rigid connection, or adding one bar diagonally, could the assembly be made rigid. (With the added bar, $n = 5$ and so $m = 2(4) - 5 - 3 = 0$.)

These evaluations assume that each bar can carry either tension or compression forces as needed. Substituting a cable (capable of carrying only tension and not compression) would cause the triangular structure (with $m = 0$) to be non-rigid, capable of forming a collapse mechanism under some specific loading conditions (although it could be rigid under other conditions).

High values of m generally mean that many movement modes are possible (rotations, translations). Values of m less than zero generally mean that the structure has more members than is minimally necessary for rigidity. A planar square shape with two crossed diagonals is such a figure: $m = 2(4) - 6 - 3 = -1$. One bar could be removed from this configuration and the resultant assembly would still form a rigid or stable assembly. Structures of this type are said to be redundant.

More generally, the number of free movement possibilities present in a three-dimensional network based on polyhedral forms can be found from the stability expression derived previously: $n = 3V - 6$; or $m = 3V - n - 6$. As before, if $m = 0$, a pin-connected structure is rigid, and if $m = -1$ it has more than the minimum number of bars for stability. A simple cubic shape, for example, is clearly shown by this approach to have many movement possibilities if it is pin-connected: $V = 8$, $n = 12$, and $m = 3(8) - 12 - 6 = 6$. Parts of a simple cube can thus potentially rotate or translate in six different ways (fig. 11.19). Hence, LeWitt's *Five Modular Units* would obviously not be stable as a pin-connected form. It has been made into a rigid form by making the joints into the special moment-resisting connections discussed earlier.

Expressions of this type are useful but not foolproof, and it is easy to think up specific configurations of nodes and bars that give a proper "count" for rigidity but are actually not rigid. Some forms can be only partly rigid. Rigidity problems particularly arise when shapes are composed of bar elements that are parallel to one another. It is best to remember that the expressions are derived from a consideration of simple tesselations of triangles and/or tetrahedra, and that applying results to other shapes is dubious at best.

The process of finding force states in members of structures with complex geometries (e.g., three-dimensional triangulation patterns) is the same as described previously for simpler triangulated member networks, but obviously more computationally elaborate; such tasks lie fundamentally with engineers.

Tensegrity Structures

The lure of trying to develop unique geometric frameworks (sometimes as a way of exploring space) has led many to an infatuation with what have come to be called "tensegrity" structures. Kenneth Snelson is well known for his works using this type of construction. His *Needle Tower* at the Hirshhorn Museum and Sculpture Garden provides a good example (fig. 2.4). Snelson's *Free Ride Home* provides another example, though one not based on a repetitive geometry. In an essay on Snelson, Howard K. Fox argues that Fuller credited Snelson with the "invention of a new structural principle."[6]

Snelson was a student at Black Mountain College in the summer of 1948 when Buckminster Fuller gave a series of talks on geometry. Afterward Snelson began experimenting with different small sculptures using threads, wire, and so forth. From an initial series of explorations concerned with the balance of successive modular elements, he soon developed a simple form involving rigid plywood X shapes suspended in space by means of tension elements only. On seeing photographs of the models sent to him by Snelson, Fuller commented in a 1949 letter: "in my public lectures I tell of your original demonstration of discontinuous-pressure-(compression) and continuous tension structural advantage. … If you had demonstrated this structure to an art audience it would not have rung the bell that it rang in me, who had been seeking this structure in Energetic Geometry."[7] Snelson

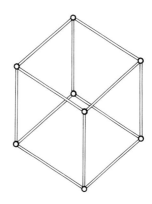

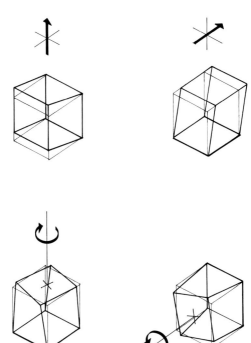

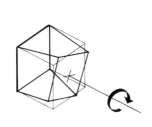

11.19
Possible deformation modes in
a cube made of pin-connected
members.

5
For readers with an engineering background, it may be useful to note that the term *m* is sometimes called degree of freedom. But its use here differs from that associated with typical matrix displacement methods of structural analysis. As used, the term has its origins in the mathematics related to polyhedra.

6
Douglas Schultz and Howard Fox, *Kenneth Snelson* (Buffalo, N.Y.: Albright-Knox Art Gallery, 1981), p. 11.

notes that in a subsequent meeting Fuller commented about the plywood piece that it was "a solution to a puzzle (or problem) which he had been looking for some years."[8] Later Fuller came up with his own variations that appeared in his numerous publications and lectures. Other variations soon came from many students making experimental models in the heady atmosphere of the time. Snelson renewed his inventive explorations some years later.

The word "tensegrity" is apparently a combination of "tension" and "integrity," suggesting a continuity of tension members. In this view, tensegrity structures are those structures consisting of continuous tension elements and (presumably) discontinuous compression elements. The tension elements are almost invariably thin steel wires or cables. The compression elements are typically short, rod-like elements, but there is no requirement that this be so; on some occasions the forces generated in the compression members are so large that big, built-up members have the character of a mast. The arrangement of the tension and compression elements is such that any nodal point is in a state of equilibrium.

It is instructive to look at Kenneth Snelson's *Cantilever* (fig. 11.20) and to take it at face value as a literal projecting structure. *Cantilever* is made up of short rigid elements and longer flexible cables. Presumably the assembly was made on the ground and lifted into place—a common process for this type of structure. Each of the cables in the assembly was probably pretensioned before the whole assembly was lifted. These initial built-in tensioning forces serve to maintain the shape of the assembly after it is put in place. If the cables are truly continuous, the pretensioning forces existing in each of the cables *prior* to lifting are more or less similar. The built-in tensioning forces in turn produce compressive forces in the short rigid members. The magnitudes of the compressive forces depend on, but are not the same as, the magnitudes of the initial tensioning forces in the cables. The magnitudes of the forces developed in each of the rigid members are probably roughly comparable to one another prior to lifting. In a structurally ideal scenario, it might be hoped that the lengths of the compression members would be such that they are at the transition point between short and long column behavior (chapter 9), so that the length of the member is maximized while counterproductive buckling tendencies are prevented (this principle,

however, is not at all necessary to the definition of a tensegrity structure).

The natural deformation tendency of any cantilevered member is such that a tension field generally develops along the upper face of the member and a compression field along the lower face. These same general tendencies would occur in a cantilevered tensegrity structure but are less clear in their effect because of the built-in pretensioning forces. Assume for a moment, however, that the pretensioning forces did not exist. The natural deformation tendency of the drooping cantilever under its own dead weight would be such that compressive forces would tend to develop in the cables along the lower zone of the structure. Obviously this is untenable. The cables would buckle inward on themselves and the whole structure would collapse, unless the whole assembly were remarkably organized internally so that tension is transmitted to them via other elements. Pretensioning is a very useful way of overcoming the compression tendencies in the lower cables. The amount of pretensioning is critical. Pretensioning forces must be larger than the compressive forces that tend to develop in the lower cables of the cantilever, so that when these begin to occur there is a net residual tension present. The initial pretensioning force in the lower cables would thus be reduced by an amount equal to the value of the compressive force that tends to develop. By a similar token, the pretensioning forces in the upper cables would be increased by an amount equal to the value of the added tension forces that tend to develop as a consequence of the cantilevering. In chapter 9 it was observed that the tension and compression fields associated with a cantilever are not constant but vary along its length, with forces highest at the base of the cantilever and reducing toward the free end. Thus the upper and lower cables would be affected differently along the length of the member (net residual tension forces would vary). The changes in the tensioning in the upper and lower cables induced by the cantilevering action would in turn cause changes in the forces in the attached rigid elements.

All of these induced variations in the tension and compression forces may cause some shape changes. While a pretensioned structure of this general type on the ground might have a pristinely straight center line, the force variations may cause it to sag and/or warp peculiarly when it is actually put in place. Sometimes these sagging and warping

Kenneth Snelson, *Cantilever*

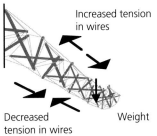

Increased tension in wires

Decreased tension in wires

Weight

In a cantilevered structure, tension normally develops along the top surface and compression along the bottom surface. These same tendencies affect the final tension in structures with prestressed cables.

11.20
This structure illustrates what are often called tensegrity structures. These structures have continuous tension elements (cables) and discontinuous compression elements (struts) and normally rely on pretensioning for their stability.

Kenneth Snelson, *Free Ride Home*

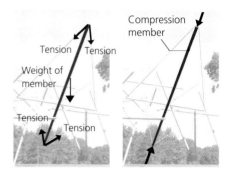

The cables are pretensioned and maintain the placement of rigid members. The pretensioning forces induce large compressive forces in rigid members, which are in turn potentially subject to buckling.

11.21
Every element in a stable structure is always in translational and rotational equilibrium under the set of internal and external forces acting upon it. A typical compressive strut in the sculpture shown here is held in place by pretensioned cables. If the cables all had the same initial pretensioning, the weight and rotational tendencies of the mast would further increase tensions in some cables and decrease those in others.

effects can be mitigated by adjusting the tension in the cables *after* the structure is put in place. Thus the tensioning in the cables along the upper face can be artificially increased even more, causing the projecting cantilever to bend upward (even to the extent of going past the level axis). But such adjustments are quite tricky. Sags and warps are simply not uncommon in long tensegrity structures. A nice characteristic of Snelson's *Cantilever* is the casual acceptance of strange warps, making them into a positive design feature.

Snelson's *Free Ride Home* (fig. 11.21) behaves quite differently from *Cantilever*, as its geometry and support conditions are different. Certainly the rigid members are long enough to be potentially subject to buckling (not that this is particularly likely in this case, but from a structural viewpoint it is usually preferable to avoid long columns). Support conditions tend to cause compressive forces in different places than was the case with *Cantilever*. Warping and deformations again occur, but are less obvious due to the more compact geometry. One way of analyzing the behavior of a tensegrity structure of this type is based on an equilibrium analysis of the tension and compression forces acting on each of the nodes of the structure. Each node must be in a state of equilibrium. An analysis of this type can be complex due to the large number of nodes and complex geometries involved, and usually involves computer formulations developed by engineers.

Several general observations can be drawn from the above examples. One is that while *Cantilever* may have started out as something like a constant tension/compression structure, it surely changes character when it is actually put in place and its own self-weight and environmental loads cause new forces to develop within the structure. Another is that the initial tensioning of the structure is highly critical. These structures must be highly tensioned to overcome any compressive forces that might tend to develop. These high tensions in turn imply high design forces for rigid compression elements. Thus member forces are necessarily made artificially higher than those that might exist in a simpler nonpretensioned structure. While this consequence is rarely troublesome in small works, it can have difficult ramifications in larger-size constructions. It is also extremely difficult to keep structures of this type from warping or otherwise deforming.

From a theoretical perspective, a potentially useful definition of a tensegrity structure can be obtained by considering the formulations for the number of free movement possibilities m present in a network. As was noted, a pure tension element such as a cable can not be simply substituted for a bar and the configuration still be stable under all loading conditions. Thus if $m = 0$, cables cannot be used except under carefully controlled circumstances. If $m = -1$, then the structure can be said to be "overbraced by one" and is normally stable. This specific definition of "overbraced by one" has been used as a definition of tensegrity (the term *hyperstatic* has also been used in this context). If a structure is overbraced, then it is probable that one or more cable elements *can* be used effectively if intelligently placed. (In these definitions, reference is to a basic unit; thus "overbracing by one" does not mean that only one cable may be used in an entire structure.) Qualifications should be added. Based on the simple method presented above for determining the number of free movement possibilities present, one can dream up configurations of bar-cable structures with $m = -1$ that are not stable (but are still "tensegrity" structures according to previous definitions). These circumstances are of theoretical interest but are practically rare. Values higher than $m = -1$ are possible, but extreme redundancy can occur that is not in the spirit of this type of structure.

A definition of tensegrity structures based on redundancies and degrees of movement could be much more useful than the vague tension-integrity notion that is currently common. A tensegrity structure may be defined as a rigid structure made of discrete rods in compression and continuous cables in tension in which each constituent unit has one degree of member redundancy (i.e., a unit is overbraced by one).

In closing it should be emphasized that while the idea of tensegrity in structures is undoubtedly fascinating, the real structural value underlying this approach is far from clear. A tensegrity sculpture may be a wonderful spatial exploration, but this does not necessarily mean it has any special structural virtues. This general point will be explored in more detail in connection with broader issues raised in chapter 20.

11.22
Kenneth Snelson, *Easy K.*

12 Plates and Shells

Many sculptures are based on the use of relatively thin flat or curved surface-forming elements that are made of stiff materials such as steel, aluminum, or plastic of one type or another. Structures of this type are well represented in nature by the hard exoskeletons of crustaceans such as crabs, the hard external shells surrounding soft nonstructural interior parts. Rigid planar forms, flat or folded, are usually described as *plates*, while various forms of singly and doubly curved surface forms are often called *shells*.

Much of Anthony Caro's work relies on the use of flat steel plates cut into different shapes and connected to other elements. The concave element in *Sun Feast* (fig. 12.1) is the end of a boiler and illustrates a hard-surface shell form. Richard Serra's *House of Cards (One Ton Prop)* (fig. 8.6) is another sculpture made of flat plate elements. Often plate or shell elements are used in conjunction with frameworks to create a more complex configuration.

The structural behavior of plate or shell configurations differs quite radically from that of the frameworks of linear elements described in the previous chapter. Forces are distributed throughout the whole fabric of these forms. Properly shaped plate and shell structures can exhibit remarkable strength and stiffness. The specific geometry of these surface forms is of particular importance with respect to their load-carrying capabilities. A piece of paper is a form of plate structure that is remarkably useless as a structural device when it is used as a single planar surface. When carefully *folded*, however, resulting shapes can be both stiff and strong—as witnessed by many of the products of the Japanese art of origami. The common egg is a structure that gains its strength from its special curved geometry. An egg is remarkably resistant to inwardly directed uniformly applied forces. But what determines the strength and stiffness of a surface form is not just the fact that the surface is curved, but rather the precise *relationship* between the exact geometry of a form and the loading conditions it is expected to carry. The egg cracks quite easily when the loading is changed from a uniform one to a concentrated one (as when an egg is tapped against the edge of a table).

12.0
Alexander Calder, *The Arch.*

Flat Plates

Planar shapes made of a rigid material, such as steel, are frequently used in sculpture. For small works, the inherent strength and stiffness of flat plates of this type are usually adequate for most applications, and little needs to be said about them here. As the linear dimensions of a plate increase relative to its thickness, however, and the plate becomes proportionally thinner, the ability of the shape to maintain its own geometry—much less carry external loads—decreases. This is an important concept. The flexibility of an everyday item such as a thin sheet of cardboard is well known. One might think that this flexibility is associated with *just* the thickness and type of material used. A comparably dimensioned small flat plate of steel, with the thickness of a thumb, would surely not be similarly flexible. But if the linear dimensions of the steel plate increase dramatically while the thickness is held constant (creating a plate with a very high length-to-thickness ratio), then even the steel plate *can* be extremely flexible. The steel plates used to make water tower tanks or similar structures are actually quite flexible. Thus the *relative* dimensions of a plate structure are more important determinants of a plate's stiffness than are its absolute dimensions.

The load-carrying capacity of a flat plate also depends on the orientation of the plate relative to the direction of the applied forces. Large flat plates are least capable of carrying forces that tend to compress them along their length, a loading that can lead to disastrous buckling of the plate (fig. 12.2). Nor can a plate easily carry loads that act in an out-of-plane direction, a situation in which the plate can bend rather easily (fig. 12.3). But a plate can relatively easily carry tension forces that tend to elongate the plate. Relatively small plates can also carry various types of shearing forces that act parallel to the plane of the structure, but larger plates do not perform very well under this loading and can exhibit a local form of buckling.

Flat thin plates are least satisfactory when they are subjected to compressive forces. Common forms of failure associated with compressive forces are either crushing or buckling. In most sculptural applications, small flat pieces are unlikely to crush due to the relatively small loads involved (unless the sculpture is a very large outdoor work of building-like dimensions). With particularly thin plates,

12.1
Anthony Caro, *Sun Feast*. The steel boiler end used in this sculpture is a form of doubly curved shell structure. Flat plate elements are also used.

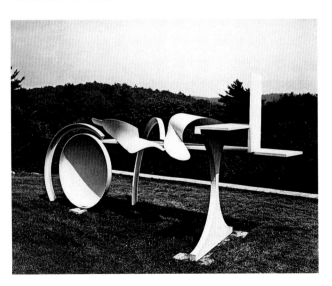

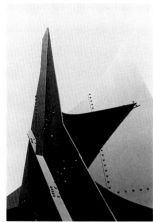

Buckling in a thin plate

Use of stiffeners

Localized buckling

12.2
Alexander Calder, *The Big Sail*. Thin plate elements are prone to failure by out-of-plane buckling at low stress levels. Using orthogonally placed stiffening plates significantly increases load-carrying capabilities for the whole plate structure. Nonetheless, undesirable local buckling may still occur in individual plate elements—a failure that may be prevented by increasing plate thicknesses or by using frequently placed stiffeners.

however, buckling can be a problem in sculptures of any size. As discussed in chapter 7 with respect to columns, the general phenomenon of buckling is a type of geometric instability associated with any slender form subjected to compressive loads. It is a mode of failure associated with inadequate out-of-plane stiffness, and not initially with actual material rupture. Buckling failures can occur in plates at relatively low stress levels where there is no question of the material itself actually pulling apart or crushing. Only *after* buckling has occurred in a plate does material failure occur, and this is a secondary effect due to the massive deformations typically associated with a buckled shape. In Calder's *The Big Sail*, it is evident that there are indeed compressive forces developed in each of the plate elements that meet the ground. Figure 12.2 illustrates a hypothetical buckling failure of the type that could occur in such a plate element. A failure of this type could result from the plate's simply being too thin to carry the compressive forces involved (clearly this is not the case with this work).

There are several ways of preventing buckling failures in thin plates. All have to do with increasing the out-of-plane stiffnesses of plates. One obvious way is to increase uniformly the overall thickness of the plate. Another is to increase the out-of-plane stiffness of the plate locally by adding one or more ribs. In this event, the additional ribs are best placed so that their maximum depths are orthogonal to the plate to be stiffened. The use of ribs to provide local stiffening to a plate susceptible to buckling is evident in *The Big Sail*. The plates that meet the ground are particularly vulnerable to buckling because of their role in picking up the

12.3
Thin, flat plates bend easily when subjected to transversely applied loadings. Folding a plate increases its resistance to bending. If in addition to folding the plate the edges are also restrained, the load-carrying capabilities become extremely high (the folded plates would behave like arches in the transverse direction). When edges are unrestrained, the form tends to flatten out. The topmost joint *must* be rigid in this case.

large reaction forces that exist at the base of the structure and distributing these forces into the remainder of the structure. These reactive forces become internal forces within the vertical plates, which could cause buckling.

In large flat plates, it might be necessary to create a pattern of closely spaced ribs attached to the surface. This in effect subdivides the large plate into a series of smaller ones that are inherently resistant to buckling. Obviously the degree of stiffness imparted to the whole plate depends upon both the nature of the ribs and their spacing. If ribs are spaced far apart, the portions of the plate between the ribs can become flexible as before.

Not all ribs serve structural functions. A rib is evident in Anthony Caro's *Sculpture 2* (fig. 12.4), executed in 1960. Diagonally placed on the large plate shown in the upper right, this thin rib does indeed add stiffness to the larger plate. In this case, however, the forces that exist in the plate are probably not significant to begin with and there is little likelihood of its buckling. Hence the added stiffness imparted by the diagonal rib is of marginal importance from a structural point of view; presumably it answers a compositional concern. Nonetheless it would still implicitly serve a technical function—that of maintaining the planarity of the large plate over time (since such plates can slowly warp out of shape due to temperature, creep, and other effects). The same is true for several of the ribs in the upper part of Calder's *The Big Sail*.

Folded and Curved Plates

Yet another way to increase the out-of-plane stiffness of a large thin plate is to change the geometry of the plate itself. A plate that has been folded or curved in some way is much more resistant to buckling than a simple planar one. Corrugated roofing of galvanized sheet steel or fiberglass provides a common example of a deformed plate. Without the corrugations the sheets themselves can hardly be picked up due to their flexibility. With the corrugations they become stiff elements capable of carrying appreciable loads. The specific geometry of the corrugations—a continuous undulating curve, a running W, or other shapes—is of secondary importance. But the deeper the corrugations or deformations, the greater is the stiffness imparted to the plate.

12.4
Anthony Caro, *Sculpture 2*. The diagonal rib in this work does indeed stiffen the larger flat plate, but the plate thickness itself would probably be adequate since applied forces are negligibly small.

12.5
Ellsworth Kelly, *Untitled*. This sculpture is composed of two plates that have been rigidly connected along one edge and derives its stability from a simple form of rigid frame action. Both plates are unrestrained at their bases and are subjected to bending from their self-weight and the vertical reactions. Stresses, however, remain within the range acceptable for steel.

The deformations need not be as fully continuous as in the case of corrugations. Rather folds or bends can be used to periodically subdivide a large planar sheet. As a consequence, the surface itself is far stronger and stiffer than it would be if simply used as a planar element. Between the folds a plate may still be planar, but its flexibility has been reduced because the plate folds effectively reduce the linear dimensions of the plate—changing it back into a smaller, and hence stiffer, plate.

A fold in a plate can be interpreted as providing an equivalent stiffening function to a rib. In the case of a fold, however, the stiffening is provided by the in-plane orientation of one plate acting against the out-of-plane orientation of the adjacent and potentially flexible plate. As with a plate stiffened by ribs, if folds in a plate are widely spaced, then the plate between is more flexible than if the folds are closely spaced.

In some materials, particularly steel, it is relatively easy to roll sheets into simple curved forms. David Smith's *Zig IV*

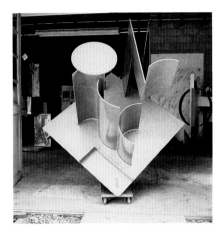

12.6
David Smith, *Zig IV*. Curving plates increases their strength and stiffness. The curved plate in the middle of *Zig IV* is extremely stiff and would be capable of carrying high forces.

(fig. 12.6) illustrates the use of sheets curved into parts of cylinders. Clearly these elements have great stiffness, as is visually suggested by the placement of the horizontal circular form on top of them. In the case of *Zig IV* the plates are used vertically and are inherently stiff in this direction and resistant to buckling, a phenomenon that could easily occur if the plates were simply flat elements. There is no loading of significance on *Zig IV*, but the curved sections would be quite capable of carrying high loads if necessary.

The same folded or curved shapes can also be used horizontally, resembling an extended arch; in this configuration they would also have great stiffness and resistance to vertical loads, particularly *if* the ends of the plates were rigidly connected to the base of the sculpture. These connections would restrain the curved plates from flexing easily, as would occur if the ends of the plates were allowed to slide over the horizontal surface. If this sliding were allowed to occur, the curved plate would not really be any stiffer than a flat plate loaded transversely to its surface.

The degree of stiffness present in a curved plate depends directly on its curvature. The term "curvature" refers to the rate of change per unit length of arc. A flat sheet has zero curvature, while a small circle has a high degree of curvature. Note that low curvature is associated with large radii of bending, while high curvatures are associated with low radii of bending. A large flat plate gently bent into a form with a low degree of curvature (a large radius) is stiffer than an equivalent planar plate, but not appreciably so. Rolling the same plate into a form having a sharp curvature (a small radius) will result in a shape that is appreciably stiffer than before. A form of this latter type is certainly better able to carry the type of in-plane compressive forces that tend to cause buckling in large flat plates. In Smith's *Zig IV*, for example, the resistance of the vertical forms to buckling is appreciable because of the sharp curvature present in the plates. These forms are also more resistant to out-of-plane forces that tend to cause bending or excessive sagging in large thin plates.

If the idea of increasing stiffness by sharpening curvatures is carried to an extreme, the curved plate becomes a pipe column—a structure known to have appreciable stiffness and load-carrying capacity.

Shells

Shell structures typically have more complex three-dimensional surface shapes than do the plate structures discussed above. The boiler end used in Caro's *Sun Feast* is curved not in one direction only but doubly. Associated with the double curvature are significant structural advantages, particularly increased surface stiffness relative to flat plates. This double curvature characterizes many shell forms.

Fundamental to the structural behavior of shells is their geometry. Here it is useful to distinguish first between a singly curved surface, such as a portion of a cylindrical shape or a cone, and a doubly curved surface, such as a portion of a sphere or a part of a hyperbolic paraboloid. Singly curved surfaces have the property of being *developable*, that is, the complex three-dimensional surface form can be cut out of a flat sheet of material and bent into its final shape without the necessity of distorting the material beyond a few basic cuts. Doubly curved surfaces are *nondevelopable*. Surfaces of this type cannot be exactly created by any amount of cutting and rearranging of flat sheets. In order to create a nondevelopable surface from a flat sheet, it is necessary to deform or distort the material itself in some way. A sphere, for example, cannot be made directly out of a flat sheet. Alternatively, a sphere or other doubly curved surface cannot be completely "flattened out" into a perfectly flat sheet no matter how one cuts up the shape. This issue is acute and difficult when one attempts to make doubly curved surfaces out of steel. Such forms can be pressed, but this is a major operation. When the sculptural material is concrete or some other moldable material, the issue becomes rather how to make the formwork (fig. 12.7).

Doubly curved plates normally have even greater structural value than their more simply curved counterparts. The double curvature imparts a measure of stiffness to thin plates that makes such forms intrinsically resistant to both buckling and bending. The continuously varying curvature in both directions means that the tangent surface plane at any particular spot is bounded by other parts of the surface that have an out-of-plane direction to them, which contributes to the stability of the point in question. In terms of the discussion in the previous section, it is as if the plate were gently folded in a continuous fashion and in a multidirectional way.

Doubly curved shell surfaces with low curvatures are, however, potentially subject to a type of buckling failure not unlike that already described for flat plates. The exact mode of buckling differs depending on the specific geometry of the surface. A significant portion of a spherical surface, for example, can virtually pop inward. This type of buckling failure can be easily demonstrated with a ping-pong ball: sharply pressing inwardly can cause a large part of the surface to cave in. The caving in is a later manifestation of the initial loss of rigidity and buckling of the surface. In other geometries the failure mode might differ. Some geometries are more resistant to phenomena such as pop-through buckling than are others.

The nature of the external loading condition strongly impacts the structural behavior of a shell form. The nature of a shell as a form of continuous surface makes such elements particularly suitable as structural forms when the external loading also takes the form of a continuous or distributed force. This is normally the case with either the self-weight of the shell or common environmental loads such as wind. A spherical shell, for example, performs quite well under loadings of this type.

The normal self-weight of a shell and environmental loads present cause internal forces to develop. In a simple hemispherical shell, compressive forces develop in the shell surface in the meridional direction from the apex to the base. In addition, hoop forces develop in the shell surface in the circumferential or latitudinal direction that are compressive near the apex of the shell but turn into tensile forces near the base of the shell. Normally these forces that act within the surface of the shell are fairly small. The forces in the meridional direction, however, also cause outwardly directed thrusts to develop at the base of the shell; in big structures these thrusts are relatively large and must normally be resisted or contained either by a series of surrounding buttresses (as seen in the Hagia Sophia in fig. 2.3) or by a continuous ring structure around the bottom edge of the shell.

Most shell structures with continuously varying surfaces are ill-suited to carrying large concentrated forces that can be characterized as point loads. Loads of this type might result from affixing a large weight to a specific point on a shell, or by running another structural member, e.g., a compressively loaded column, directly into the surface of the shell. Loads like this cause high localized stresses to develop

Claes Oldenburg, *Pool Balls*

A plaster model was first made and then a mold. The reinforcing steel for the final casting is evident in the mold being lifted.

**12.7
Oldenburg's great balls of reinforced concrete are shell structures.**

and particularly lead to pop-through buckling failures. (A finger caving in a ping-pong ball similarly suggests the application of a point force.) The particular problem is that large concentrated forces of this type typically have correspondingly large force components that act in an out-of-plane direction, and which are sufficiently large to overcome the natural stiffness provided in the out-of-plane direction by the curving plate. While distributed forces, e.g., wind, may act similarly, their out-of-plane components are much smaller per unit surface area and can be handled by the inherent stiffness of the curving shell surface. Thus concentrated loads that act in an out-of-plane direction on shell surfaces should be avoided whenever possible.

The degree of stiffness of a doubly curved shape and its consequent resistance to any type of buckling or bending depends on the thickness of the plate relative to the sharpness of the curvature present. For the same plate thickness, a sharply curved surface (one with a small radius) is inherently stiffer than a surface with a gentle or nearly flat curvature (one with a large radius), which is almost as susceptible to buckling or bending as its planar counterpart. As the degree of curvature increases, out-of-plane stiffness increases as does the form's resistance to buckling and bending. Obviously the plate thickness relative to the curvature is also important. A sharply curved thin plate may be as susceptible to pop-through buckling or bending as a thicker plate that is more gently curved.

If the susceptibility of a thin curved surface to pop-through buckling cannot be handled by plate thickness and degree of curvature alone, it is always possible to use stiffening ribs as well. These ribs would ideally be placed so that their maximum depths are orthogonal to the surface of the shell. Obviously this is easier said than done when the shell has complex curvatures, but it might well be possible in some situations. Many of the same principles for using ribs that were discussed before apply, notably using regularly spaced patterns to limit the dimensions of unbraced portions of the shell's surface. The use of ribs is particularly advisable when the shell surface is subjeced to large concentrated forces. Obviously the best location for a rib, or pair of crossed ribs, is directly beneath the concentrated loading.

Reticulated Plates and Shells

The discussion thus far has assumed that the plate and shell forms are made of continuous surfaces (e.g., fiberglass, steel, or reinforced concrete surfaces). Structures that have generally similar geometries and consequent structural properties in the larger sense can be made by assembling small rodlike elements into the same shapes. A spherical shape, for example, can be made by dividing the surface into regular or semiregular polygonal flat surface forms and placing rigid elements on the edges of these forms. The now-familiar geodesic dome is a structure of this type. The common planar space frame used in many building applications provides an example of aggregating small tetrahedrons made of rigid elements into a large, planar structure. Structures of this type are sometimes called "bar networks."

The overall structural behavior of structures of this type can be generally characterized as being similar to comparable structures with continuous surfaces. Measures already discussed, such as relative curvatures, are of like importance in reticulated structures as in continuous structures. A large sphere with a low degree of surface curvature, for example, is as susceptible to dangerous pop-through buckling as is a continuous surface (and potentially even more so). The obvious difference is that the internal forces in continuous surface structures are distributed throughout the surface while in bar network structures they are concentrated in the bars themselves. It is more or less as if a bar in a given location replaces the function of the surface, and the forces previously in the surface are concentrated in the bar. Consequently, forces in bars can be quite high and, in large structures, members can be susceptible to buckling when forces are compressive. In small-scale structures, buckling is not a problem.

It should be noted that reticulated bar networks of this type have no mysterious properties that make them extraordinary structures (despite the mythology propagated by later Fuller proponents). A large geodesic sphere, for example, does work quite well, but the bars do not experience equal force states, nor are they all in compression. As noted in the discussion of polyhedral shapes in chapter 11, it is also evident that neither can member lengths all be identical (subtle variations occur). Large structures of low curvature are sensitive to snap-through buckling and other phenomena not part of the rhetoric of geodesic structures. When properly used, they are good structures, but a sphere can be subdivided in many other ways and the result be just as structurally effective.

13 Membranes

A *membrane* is a thin flexible surface structure that carries loads through the development of tension stresses. Inflated forms, stretched-skin structures, and tents all use membranes as surfaces. As in flexible cable structures, the shape that a membrane structure assumes is dependent on external factors, such as the way it is loaded or supported. Membranes can be supported by internal pressurization or by externally applied jacking forces. The common soap bubble is a membrane supported by internal pressurization. A soap bubble is subjected to radially directed internal pressures and thus assumes a spherical shape, except where it intersects with other bubbles.

Several of the inflated sculptures of Christo, such as *5,600 Cubic Meter Package* (fig. 13.1), are supported by internal pressurization. Works of this type are typically called *pneumatic* structures. By contrast, membranes that are pulled along their edges or in some other way assume radically different shapes (e.g., the stretched skins of many tent structures). The membranes are stretched into a predefined shape by attached cables that are in turn tightened with turnbuckles (or by some similar technique). Structures of this latter type usually involve other elements, such as columns or masts, in addition to the surface-forming membrane.

The flexibility of membrane surfaces makes them especially sensitive to failure by folding and to the aerodynamic effects of wind. Folding is typically caused by forces that tend to put the membrane into a state of compression. Aerodynamic effects associated with wind tend to cause membranes to vibrate rapidly back and forth, or flutter, until they tear apart (see the discussion on this point in chapter 10). These adverse effects may be prevented by stabilizing the membrane using either internal pressurization or an external jacking force. Stabilization through either of these methods is achieved as a consequence of the development of internal tension stresses induced in the fabric of the membrane (the membrane is said to be "prestressed") that mitigate the effects of the forces developed in the membrane by environmental loads. Even stabilized membranes, however, are sensitive to tearing failures that tend to be produced by point forces.

13.0
Christo, *5,600 Cubic Meter Package.*

Christo, *5,600 Cubic Meter Package*

Surrounding cables maintain the shape of the package.

The rigid network of members at the base cradles the bottom of the inflated column form without inducing point forces that would tend to cause the membrane to puncture.

13.1
Wind blowing on Christo's massive inflated membrane causes both bowing in the sculpture and tension forces to develop in the stabilizing guy cables. Both of these actions tend to cause compression to develop on one face of the membrane. Folding and potential instability could possibly result. Initial inflation pressures and subsequent additional continuous inflation pressures must be high enough to create sufficient tension in the membrane to offset these tendencies.

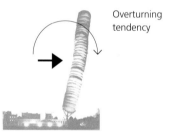

Overturning tendency

The sculpture would easily overturn due to wind forces if not stabilized by the surrounding guy cables.

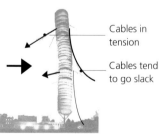

Cables in tension

Cables tend to go slack

Cables on one side go into tension to stabilize the structure. Those on the other side tend to buckle harmlessly out of the way.

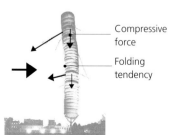

Compressive force

Folding tendency

Both the bowing induced by wind forces and the downward components of the tension forces developed in the stabilizing guy cables tend to cause one face of the membrane to go into compression and fold.

Pneumatic Structures

By and large, most pneumatic sculptures are *air-inflated* rather than *air-supported* structures. (Air, it should be emphasized, is only one of many media that can be used in connection with pneumatic structures. Other gases or even liquids could be used as well.) Air-inflated structures have enclosing membranes containing pressurized air that are fully continuous and are typically shaped into a predetermined form. Typically no one actually goes inside the form itself. The automobile inner tube is a common example of an air-inflated structure. Air-supported structures, by contrast, typically consist of single membranes enclosing functionally useful spaces on the ground. Edges of the membrane are sealed. These structures are commonly used for buildings, as is witnessed by the hundreds of them used to cover tennis courts, tracks, and other large spaces.

In either case, the internal pressurization must be high enough to overcome any compressive stresses in the membrane that might tend to develop as a consequence of the action of the externally applied loads. Consider the example of a cantilevered air-inflated tube. Under the action of a wind load, the structure would naturally be subjected to bending. As described in chapter 9, the bending action would normally tend to induce bending stresses that consist of both tension and compression stresses acting at the same cross section. One face of the member would normally be in tension and the other face in compression. These same stresses tend to develop whether the cantilevered structure is a solid tube, a hollow stiff tube, or an inflated membrane. In the solid and hollow tube examples, the inherent stiffness of the material carries the compression and tension stresses induced by the bending action. In a membrane structure, however, these same stresses would tend to cause the fabric to fold or otherwise collapse. But if the membrane were inflated internally to such an extent that tension stresses were induced in the fabric that were *larger* than the potential compression stresses, then the fabric would remain in a state of tension, and hence not fold. The two stress states tend to cancel each other out. In a lightly inflated structure, the tension stresses present may not be large enough to overshadow the compressive tendencies, and a fold would develop. In a highly inflated structure, the tension induced would be so large as to overshadow completely the com-

pressive stress tendencies and the fabric would remain tautly stretched.

But increasing the pressure of inflation obviously entails its own problems. The tension present in the membranes is increased and might possibly require using thicker or specially reinforced fabrics. These same forces make seams and other connections more difficult. Due to natural leakage it is also difficult to maintain high pressures. For these reasons it is usually best to inflate structures only to the extent needed to carry the applied loads without folds developing. Such pressures are actually not very high. Even very large structures use relatively low internal pressurization, and some minor folding is often tolerated. With respect to large structures, the image of a lightly inflated air bag is more appropriate than that of a small highly pressurized balloon or inner tube. The need to maintain initial pressures over time is similarly important, since pressure changes due to leakage and temperature change invariably occur (see the discussion on Christo's *5,600 Cubic Meter Package* below).

An important advantage of the relatively low pressurization commonly needed is that resultant inflated forms are not terribly sensitive to punctures (accidental or vandal-induced). Air will indeed leak out in the event of a puncture and the structure will deflate, but not necessarily in the form of an explosion. There is actually quite an important distinction between highly pressurized and lightly pressurized structures in this regard. In a highly pressurized structure, such as a small balloon, a puncture will cause a flaw to develop in the fabric of the material that propagates throughout the structure almost instantaneously. The rate of tear propagation is critically dependent on the the amount of energy stored in the skin as a consequence of its being stretched. All of this stored energy goes into propagating the crack. Consequently, a balloon seems to explode when a pin is stuck into it. In a structure with a less stressed skin, a puncture still tends to cause a tear to propagate, but there is less stored energy in the skin to drive the tear forward. Hence the tear develops more slowly or not at all. Thus the structure does not explode but rather deflates. This is the situation that would be present in a work such as Christo's *5,600 Cubic Meter Package* (1967–1968), a work that could be characterized as a low-energy system. High-energy systems are far more dangerous.

13.2
5,600 Cubic Meter Package
during inflation, before
elevation.

Other features of *5,600 Cubic Meter Package* are also of interest here. The work itself was enormous, with a height of 280 feet, a diameter of 33 feet, and a weight of 14,000 pounds. It used 22,000 square feet of fabric and 12,000 feet of ropes. The cylindrical shape of the inflated membrane was maintained by a series of cables surrounding the membrane. Obviously, in the absence of these shape-sustaining cables, the membrane would have tended to assume a much more bulged shape because of the nature of the internal pressurization that was present. In smaller structures, actual cables need not be used; internal threads or diaphragms of one type or another are often used in lieu of surrounding constraining elements.

The base of Christo's structure was a specially designed cradle. A structural function of this cradle was clearly to allow the membrane to assume a natural shape while at the same time transferring the large base reactive force into the structure in a distributed way. A less generously dimensioned cradle might have tended to cause a punch-through type of failure.

The tower's enormous height obviously tended to cause it to fall over or be pushed over by the wind. The guy cables attached to the upper part clearly served the function of preventing this overturning. Depending on the direction of the wind, one set of cables would go into tension and absorb the horizontal force of the wind, while the set on the opposite side would slacken somewhat (assuming that they were not pretensioned). The downward components of the cable forces would lead to additional compressive stresses in the membrane that had to be overshadowed by the inflation pressure.

The wind acting against the side of the form also caused bending in the membrane due to the large height of the structure. It was much like a beam supported at two points (in this case by cables) and turned vertically. The bending tended to produce compression on the face toward the wind and tension on the opposite face. The compression tendencies produced by the bending were additive to those produced by the downward component of the cable force. Both caused the windward face to tend to fold. Inflation pressures had to be high enough to prevent this folding. The addition of more cables at about midheight also helped reduce this bending tendency.

The inflation pressure in *5,600 Cubic Meter Package* had to be maintained over time to assure its stability. Losses in pressure due to leakage and temperature changes naturally occurred. Inflation pressure was continuously maintained through the use of generators. A special emergency generator was put in place to take over in the event of a power blackout.

Making large inflated shapes work involves a lot of juggling of inflation pressures in relation to support locations and the like. Engineers can calculate required pressures and support locations to a reasonable extent, but these are complex structures that invariably require care and judgment in their execution. Smaller inflated structures are typically much less difficult from an engineering point of view.

Net and Stretched-Skin Structures

Net and stretched-skin structures are quite similar. Both have their shapes maintained through the action of externally applied jacking forces (typically along their edges). Stretched-skin structures are typically made of a tension-resisting fabric while net structures utilize crossed cables to carry the tension forces developed (a nonstressed skin can then be attached to the cable net). The external forces are typically applied along the edges of the net or skin by the action of turnbuckles, hydraulic or mechanical jacks, or some other pulling device. In order to create anything other than a simple flat plane, the stretched skins or nets are pulled around some other object (e.g., a column or beam) to create a volumetric shape that is typically doubly curved. Large forces are developed in these supporting elements, which in turn must be carefully designed.

For membranes that obtain their surface stability by being stretched, it is usually advisable that the membrane be as uniformly loaded as possible. This typically means applying the stressing force all around the edges of the membrane in a uniform way. In very large membrane structures, flat areas are to be generally avoided and sharp curvatures in the surface are generally preferred. Flat areas tend to be unstable, or flutter, under the undulating action of wind even if they are highly stressed. Increasing the degree of curvature present in a membrane surface also tends to

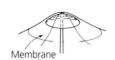

Membrane

Blunted cap

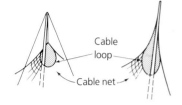

Cable
loop

Cable net

Cable loop. The cable net is tied into the cable loop which is, in turn, tied into the point support.

13.3
Stretched-net structures rely on edge cables and loops to distribute concentrated forces into the mesh and to mediate between different geometries. Blunted caps are sometimes used to distribute point forces in either a net or membrane structure.

increase its resistance to the fluttering effects of wind. Anticlastic surfaces (surfaces convexly curved in one direction and concavely in the other at the same point) are extremely resistant to these wind effects.

From a purely technical vantage point, the choice of whether to adopt a stretched skin or a stretched net approach depends largely on the size of the structure. In small structures, there is rarely any need at all to use a cable net approach. Cable nets are difficult and expensive to make, primarily because of the "nondevelopable" characteristic of typical surface shapes (see chapter 12). This in turn means that the cable net cannot have a uniform grid spacing. Cable nets are, however, capable of carrying very large forces and spanning great distances. In small structures, a surface-forming membrane can be stressed directly as long as the jacking forces do not induce stresses so high as to cause ripping. For intermediate-size structures, specially reinforced fabrics (with built-in threads or small ropes) can be obtained that are capable of carrying tension forces that are quite large.

Geometries

The geometry of the shapes membranes assume is of critical importance to both their structural functioning and their construction. As a consequence of the stabilization of the skin by means of internal pressurization or external jacking forces, membrane structures are rarely composed of flat surfaces and only infrequently of developable surfaces exclusively. Shapes generated by internal pressurization are normally doubly curved, or nondevelopable. Thus common shapes are convex (such as a portion of a common sphere), concave, or warped. Some materials, such as the rubber sheets used in common balloons, are capable of deforming into nondevelopable shapes by virtue of their remarkable extensibility. In larger structures, however, it is often necessary to use stronger materials to withstand the tension stresses developed within the fabric of the material. These materials often come only in flat sheets.

The creation of nondevelopable surfaces (e.g., spherical) from essentially flat sheets requires that surfaces be carefully subdivided into facets that are often of odd shapes. Creation of a simple air-inflated hemisphere, for example, might require that the surface be made up of a series of wedge-shaped flat segments joined along their edges. The segments might be made of any of several varieties of reinforced synthetic fabrics or rubberized canvases. Far more complex geometries are also possible. The discussion on faceted polyhedra in chapter 11 is relevant here. A common spherical shape, for example, can be created using various regular and semiregular polyhedra (witness the common soccer ball).

Stretched-skin structures are also normally fashioned into overall shapes that have double curvatures present within them. Instead of convex shapes (e.g., portions of spheres), however, stretched-skin or cable-net surfaces are more apt to have some sort of anticlastic curvature present. A surface in the shape of a hyperbolic paraboloid is not unusual. Surfaces of this type must again be made by assembling small flat strips into larger forms.

Predicting the exact final shape of a membrane structure can be extremely difficult because of the way final shapes depend on loading and support conditions. This must be done exactly, however, so that the individual segments of the final structure can be cut to fit exactly. If the final shape provided does not correspond to the natural shape associated with the forces and loading conditions present, then troublesome folds will invariably develop. Form finding is often done experimentally. Care must be exercised in this regard, however. In many examples, images of expected final forms have been derived by model studies using nice, ideally extensible materials (such as rubber) that freely deform in any direction. The subsequent making of the real form from materials that are naturally not freely extensible in any direction is fundamentally inconsistent but necessary. Adjustments may well have to be made to fit the reality of the materials used.

Support Conditions

Any flexible membrane surface is especially susceptible to tearing or ripping whenever it is subjected to point or concentrated forces. These point forces may arise from an external loading or be internally generated at a location where the membrane is attached to the ground or where it is attached to other structural elements (e.g., where a stretched skin passes over a column). Membranes work best when they carry continuously distributed rather than concentrated forces.

Edges of membranes are frequently attached to cables as a way of distributing a concentrated force into a membrane. Consider, for example, Christo's *Valley Curtain*, which was suspended from an upper cable at a series of discrete points (fig. 10.1). If the curtain had been merely attached directly at these points, concentrated forces present might have caused it to rip extensively. In the actual structure, a smaller cable system ran between the primary attachment points and the curtain was wrapped around this smaller cable. Thus the curtain felt only continuous support along its edges. The curtain was connected at its base to the ground via a series of similar cable attachments.

The use of cables at the free edge of a membrane as mediating members is a common way of addressing the problem of potential ripping due to the presence of large point forces. Similar devices have found their use in pneumatic structures, where the issue is typically how to tie the inflated structure to the ground.

When stretched-skin structures pass over pointed elements, such as columns, the potential for tear-through failures is particularly high. Again cables can be used as mediating elements, typically with cable loops or eyelets. Alternatively, the tip of the pointed element can be artificially blunted by the use of some sort of distribution cap. The cap is made large enough so that the concentrated forces present in the pointed element are more or less uniformly distributed throughout the membrane that passes over it.

14.0
Mary Miss, *Tempe, AZ.*

14 Connections

The joy, the agony, and the underlying complexity of making connections between two or more objects has occupied individuals who work with materials since humans became toolmakers. Here is the wonderful world of interlocking pieces, of nuts and bolts, of welds and nails. In architecture the importance and beauty of connections has long been appreciated. The interlocking capitals at the tops of columns in early Chinese and Japanese architecture are masterpieces of workmanship (fig. 14.1); their origin was dictated by pragmatic constructional needs, but they have long since evolved to reflect and convey complex religious and cultural values and to possess an inherently artistic content. The importance of connections in other fields (such as furniture making) is scarcely less.

The task of making connections between elements has also long occupied sculptors, but the introduction of assemblages as a primary sculptural construct in this century has given it renewed importance. Without connections, elements cannot be assembled. Yet in many sculptures the connections seem like afterthoughts. There is typically little that stirs emotions in this regard.

The realities of making connections are seemingly straightforward but are filled with subtle complexities. Influencing factors include the structural intent of the connection (types and magnitudes of forces to be transmitted, whether the connection is to be rigid or to allow sliding or rotations to occur), the geometry of the configuration (numbers of members, type and sizes of members, angles of joining), the stiffnesses of the members joined (whether they are rigid or cable-like), and the materials available for use.

Basic Connection Strategies

Two simple linear members can be joined lengthwise, transversely, or at some odd angle. Multiple linear members meeting can involve each of these options. Connection characteristics are invariably dependent on the geometry of the intersection and whether a pinned, rigid, or sliding joint is

14.1
Connections in an ancient Japanese temple.

desired. The strategies noted below can be used to make either pinned or rigid connections. Rigid connections, however, are invariably more complex and difficult to make because of the need for widely separated points of attachment.

Consider the joining of two simple linear members that are to transmit a simple tension force. Most connection forms employ a strategy of either *deforming and interlocking* the two elements, *lapping* them, or *butting* them end to end. In some materials (reinforced concrete and some plastics), *monolithic* joints are possible as well. Two of these connection types, lapping and butting, invariably require the additional use of what might be called *third-element connectors* (bolts, nails, screws, welds). Third-element connectors can be usefully described as point, line, or surface connectors (e.g., bolts, welds, and glue fields, respectively). Point and line connectors (e.g., bolts and welds, respectively) may be either single or multiple.

Deforming and interlocking members lengthwise is among the more elegant ways of connecting two members together. When the material is wood, this strategy almost invariably dictates careful carving, as in the fabulous connections of Japanese and Chinese temple construction. The ancient mortised connection provides another example. When metals are used, pieces can be bent or looped in many elegant ways. In most of these connections, the connected members remain in alignment with one another.

Lapping members lengthwise requires the use of third element connectors. In wood and metal lapped joints are common. Nails, screws, or bolts are usually used to connect wooden pieces; bolts, rivets, or welds are used to connect metal pieces. When loads are light, glue can be used. An obvious issue with the use of the simple lapped joint is that the members connected are no longer in line with one another but are offset.

Butting members often requires the use of some sort of splice or cover plate, which may be made of the same material as the member joined or of some other material. The splice plates lap the butted members. Bolts, screws, rivets, welds, or glue are then used, as with lapped joints. Butt joints allow connected members to line up with one another.

Members that meet transversely can also be connected in these basic ways, as can members that meet at odd angles. Orthogonal transverse connections can be straightforward.

1
For a bolt subjected to a shear force of magnitude P, the shear stress (f_v) developed within the bolt is given by $f_v = P/A$, where A is the bolt's cross-sectional area. Hence, a bolt 1 inch in diameter ($A = \pi d^2/4 = 0.785$ in^2) carrying a 5,000 lb load experiences a shear stress of $f_v = P/A$ = 5,000 lb/0.785 in^2 = 6,369 lbs/in^2. The allowable shear stress F_v of a steel member is given by $F_v = 0.4F_y = 14,400$ lbs/in^2. Since the actual stress is less than the allowable stress in this case, the bolt will not fail in shear. If desired, the minimum required area of the bolt could be found directly: $A = P/F_v$ = 5,000 lb/14,400 lb/in^2 = 0.35 in^2.

2
It is possible to determine the required thickness of a plate by considering the area of the plate in bearing and limiting the stresses developed to an allowable value.

Simple lapping or butting strategies are most common, again involving the use of third-element connectors if the connections are not to slip and forces are to be transmitted from one member to another. When butting approaches are used, the third-element connectors are typically complexly shaped. Deformed and interlocking members are quite possible and elegant, as again demonstrated by Japanese and Chinese construction.

The geometry of the connection may well dictate that one or another strategy be used. Multiple members that meet at a point cannot all be continuous through the connection when materials such as wood or metal are used. One might be continuous through the connection, but others must butt or lap. Frequently, in structures such as space frames, all members are designed to butt into a single third-element connector, which is typically quite a complex member. In the latter case, the joint is almost always characterized as a pinned connection from a structural perspective.

Types of Attachments

Point Attachments
A typical bolt, rivet, screw, or nail is capable of effecting a force transfer between two attached members by two means: through a shear force transfer through the bolt or screw itself, and through frictional forces that might be developed as a consequence of the clamping action of connectors of this type. A typical bolted connection can potentially fail either by shearing apart, by a local crushing of the material in the attached members around the bolt, or by a tearing away of this same material. Consequently, a typical bolt, screw, or nail of a given size can be subjected to only a given amount of force, depending on the size of the connectors, the placement of the connectors in the members being attached, and the thicknesses of the attached pieces. If loads are sufficiently high, multiple bolts may be required to carry the forces involved. This is a common situation in the design of bridges or buildings, and can occur in larger sculptures.

The forces in the attached members are transmitted to one another via the development of shear forces, and, consequently, shear stresses, in the bolt. Shear forces and stresses act transversely to the cross section of a member.

A bolt with a small diameter can be overstressed in shear and fail as illustrated in figure 14.3. For small members, such as bolts, the strength of a member in shear is directly proportional to its cross-sectional area. The same concepts used to size members in tension can be used to size bolts in shear (actual stresses developed by the loadings are kept below the allowable stress of the material in shear).[1] The bolt shown in figure 14.3 is said to be in a state of *single shear* since only one cross section of the bolt is prone to failure. A bolt connecting a single plate sandwiched between a pair of plates would have to shear or slip along two planes rather than one before actually failing. Consequently, such a bolt is said to be in a state of *double shear*. Bolts in double shear are stronger than bolts in single shear since twice the cross-sectional area is available to resist failure.

Bearing failures in the attached members can result from the material being too thin. If the attached members are very thin, the compressive bearing stresses that develop as a bolt bears against an attached member, and transfers forces into it, can be quite high. A local crushing or buckling of the surrounding member can then occur. This kind of bearing failure, common in light-gauge steelwork, can be prevented by making the attached plates thicker and/or by increasing the diameter of the bolts used (both strategies reduce bearing stresses in the attached plates).[2] Using multiple bolts also reduces the chances for bearing stress failures.

Pull-out failures in the attached members can result if bolt holes are placed too near the end of the members. The end material is subjected to shear stresses as the bolt transfers forces into the member; if the end distance is too small, an end plug can simply slide out. Failures of this type, common in wood construction, can be prevented by increasing the distances used from the end of the member to the bolt hole or increasing plate thicknesses (both strategies reduce shearing stresses in the attached plates).

Line Attachments (Welding)
Welding has the remarkable potential of providing a line-forming connection. Welding is the joining of metals by fusion via the application of intense heat. The parent materials can be fused together directly, or metal from a supplementary welding rod can be fused onto the plates being connected. Gas and arc welding are most common.

Common gas welding relies on the high heat of combus-

Mary Miss, *Staged Gates*

Common connection types (nonrigid connections)

Mary Miss, *Tempe, AZ*

Butt weld along edges (rigid joint)

14.2
This set of photographs from the work of Mary Miss illustrates several common connection strategies.

Mary Miss (with T. Williams and B. Tsien), detail of *Telephone Booths:* third-element connectors (rigid joint)

tion (around 6,300° F) of properly proportioned oxygen and acetylene. Different mixtures of these gases are used for common flame cutting. In welding, adjoining metal elements (e.g., steel plates) are heated to melting, a puddle formed, and the torch moved along the joint in a circular motion to allow intermixing of metals. Filler rods are dipped into the puddle to add extra metal. (Residual excesses can be ground off afterward.) Various metals, including steel, copper, brass, aluminum, bronze, and cast iron, can be welded, as well as dissimilar metals (e.g., brass and steel) under certain conditions. When bronze is gas-welded, the metals are not heated to melting but to a lower tinning temperature. Bronze filler rods are invariably used. Stainless steel may also be welded, but this is more difficult. Too much oxygen tends to destroy the chromium base to stainless steel and render it susceptible to corrosion. Special flux must also be used to enable greater control over the molten metal to be maintained. Special filler rods must also be used. Special forms of electric welding (see below) are preferable for use with stainless steel.

Electric arc welding is equally common and relies on the heat in an arc that develops when low-voltage, high-amperage electricity jumps between a gap of air separating an electrode and a base metal. A grounding cable from the power source is attached to the metal to be welded and a second to an insulated electrode that also serves as a coated filler rod. Close proximity to the base metal completes a circuit, causing an arc of intense heat and brightness to form. Nearly opaque eye shields must be worn. Control of gap spacing is difficult. Although requiring practice, arc welding is straightforward and can be quicker than gas welding. A particular problem with arc welding is that exposure of molten metal to oxygen and nitrogen in the atmosphere can lead to difficulties in controlling the weld, embrittlement, and ultimately to loss of corrosion resistance (see chapter 18). The coating on the rod helps mitigate this problem in several ways, including the development of slag by-products covering the weld (which can subsequently be brushed off). Resulting welds are more ductile and less brittle.

Recently developed methods include gas-shielded metal arc welding (MIG) and gas tungsten arc welding (TIG). In these, a more complete shielding of the weld from detrimental exposure to oxygen and nitrogen in the atmosphere occurs via the propulsion of inert argon gas around the torch itself. The arc is also stabilized in the process. Deep penetrating welds are produced. Gas-shielded processes are particularly good for welding stainless steel, since the inert gas prevents exposure of the chromium to atmospheric gases. In the MIG process, currently best used for lighter stock, a continuous-feed wire electrode is used. The process is relatively easy. Gas tungsten welding (TIG) is similar to standard arc welding, but a tungsten rod rather than a flux-coated filler rod is used. The tungsten rod serves as a conductor only, with additional filler rods used. An argon gas shield is also used.

There are many different types of welded joints possible with any welding method. Butt and fillet welds are among the most common. A butt weld joins two members that meet (or butt together) in the same plane. The strength of a butt weld in tension depends on the allowable stress of the weld material in tension times the minimum area of the weld itself. The thickness of the weld is thus quite critical, as is the length of the weld.

A fillet weld joins two lapped members; it is normally triangular in cross section, with one of the legs of the triangle equal to the thickness of one of the joined plates. A weld of this type would normally fail by shearing apart along its length through the diagonal (or throat) of the weld cross section, where the weld has its least thickness. The strength of a weld is proportional to the area of this surface that is subjected to shearing and the unit strength of the weld material itself. Increasing the leg thickness of the cross section of a weld increases its strength, since this in turn increases the area of the weld that resists the shearing action. Lengthening a fillet weld generally increases its load-carrying capability proportionately (doubling the length of the weld doubles its load-carrying capability).

Allowable force per unit length values can be determined for welds of different thicknesses based on a consideration of the geometry of the weld and the allowable stress values for the weld material.[3] These values are quite useful in determining required weld lengths.

Surface Connectors

Gluing is far the most common form of attachment that operates over a large surface area. The strength of a glued joint obviously depends on the type of glue used and the area over which the glue acts. Usually relatively large areas

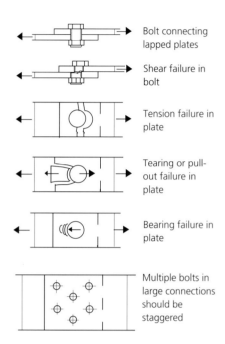

14.3
Common failure modes possible in a simple bolted connection. Most of these failures can be prevented by either increasing the size and thickness of the connected plates or increasing the bolt diameter or number of bolts used.

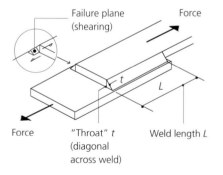

14.4
The strength of a typical fillet weld depends largely on the area of the weld in shear (throat thickness times weld length) and the yield strength of the weld material.

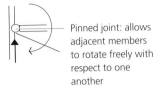

Pinned joint: allows adjacent members to rotate freely with respect to one another

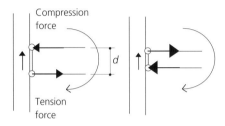

Compression force

d

Tension force

Rigid joint: one member is fixed to another (relative rotations are prevented; forces developed in separated point attachments get larger as d gets smaller)

14.5
Point attachments, such as bolts, may be used to form either pinned connections or rigid connections (by widely separating two attachment points).

3
For a common 45-degree fillet weld, the area subjected to shearing is $A = Lt \sin 45°$, where L is the length of the weld and t is its throat dimension. The load-carrying capability of the weld is $P = AF_v$, where F_v is the allowable stress for the material. If $F_v = 13,600$ lbs/in² (a common value), then $P = 9,600tL$. A ¼-inch-thick (leg) weld 6 inches long could thus carry a force of $P = 9,600(¼)(6) = 14,400$ lbs.

are required to use glue effectively as a structural connector. Pressure setting invariably increases strength.

General Structural Issues

Underlying any specific attachment device must be a conscious consideration of the basic intent of the connection. Often there are few structural constraints in small-scale works other than that the connection somehow affix one member to another and not fall apart. In these cases, members are usually simply tacked to one another via screws, spot welds, or whatever. As the scale of the sculpture increases, however, more attention must be paid to the exact structural intent of a connection.

In larger-scale sculptures it is sometimes structurally preferable to use clearly defined pinned connections that allow members to frame into one another so that the connections do not restrain the free rotation of the attached members (as is the case with trusses), while in other cases it is preferable to use rigid connections that do not allow members to rotate with respect to one another at connections, as is necessary with structures that obtain their lateral stability through frame action. In simplest form, a pinned joint uses a single axle or large bolt as the focal point of the attachment, with attached members allowed to rotate freely about the axle. The upper joint on Shingu's *Gift of the Wind* (see fig. 7.2) is a particularly elaborate pinned connection. *Tempe, AZ* by Mary Miss (fig. 14.2) obtains its stability via the use of rigid joints, in this case welded, and associated frame action.

While rigid connections are often monolithic, rigidity can also be obtained through the use of at least two widely separated point attachments. Free rotation between attached members cannot occur if separated multiple attachment points are used. The specific discrete attachment points can be simple individual bolts or welds. When only two points of attachment are used, forces generated in the individual bolts or welds as a consequence of the joint's structural role can be quite high and are directly dependent on the distance separating them (forces in the bolts or welds decrease as they are more widely separated, and increase when placed close together). In large-scale structures, it may be necessary to determine the exact number of bolts or length of welds necessary, as well as separation distances. This task is fairly complex and typically lies within the domain of a structural engineer.

In some cases, some sort of sliding joint may be necessary or useful. A sculpture incorporating kinetic movement may require the use of some sort of telescoping or sliding connection. There are pragmatic reasons for using sliding connections as well. Large-scale structures are susceptible to forces caused by thermal expansion and contraction. Changing temperatures cause the members to change in length, which in turn normally causes the whole structure to want to expand or contract. These movements are very small (not generally visible to the eye), but it is highly desirable that they be allowed to occur, particularly in very large structures. If the movements are restrained, extremely large forces can build up in structural members that can actually cause failure. In order to allow thermal expansion and contraction to occur freely, especially in very large structures, special roller connections are often used that are specially designed to allow free movement in one or more directions. Face-to-face plates with teflon between them, for example, can work quite well.

Special Structures

4

Christo, *Surrounded Islands.*

15 Large-Scale Sculptures

The issues involved in exceptionally large sculptures are conceptual on the one hand, pragmatic on the other. On a conceptual level, a brief inspection of really large structures will readily suggest that their overall shapes and forms are quite different from small pieces that sit on tabletops. Ideas of scale dependence have already been introduced in chapter 1 and will be investigated more abstractly in chapter 20. To put it briefly, many structural approaches that work on a small scale do not necessarily work on a large scale.

On a pragmatic level, special attention needs to be paid to sculptures of building-size proportions simply because of their potential threats to life and safety in the event of failure. Many issues that are of marginal concern in the design of small-scale structures often become paramount in the design of large ones. A significant difference is the degree of confidence with which the structure must be designed. In smaller-scale structures, the need to control deflections or other deformations rarely governs the sizing and placing of members. In the design of large-scale sculpture, the converse is typically true: the designer needs to be much more in control of the structural action of the sculpture, and, consequently, structural dictates often play a more predominant role in the shaping of the work. The structures of many large-scale works, for example, are frequently designed primarily in response to the lateral loading conditions associated with wind and/or earthquake forces rather than the downward-acting gravity loads that form the common frame of reference for smaller works.

In our current society, really large-scale sculptures are normally designed in conjunction with a structural engineer—an exception is Simon Rodia's *Watts Towers* to be discussed shortly—so that the viability of the structure is indeed assured and it would conform to public safety requirements found in building codes and other regulations. These same large works are also sometimes subject to unusual loading conditions or exhibit unique structural behaviors not always found in small-scale sculptures. Some very tall and slender sculptures, for example, have proven sensitive to complex aerodynamic phenomena associated with wind.

Large-scale sculptures can be usefully grouped into two basic classes. One class consists of sculptures that have internal frameworks or armatures that provide the structure for carrying all applied forces. These internal frameworks are typically not externally visible and are surrounded by skins that may define the final form of the sculpture but are not in themselves primary structural elements. A second class of sculptures consists of those in which the structure and the sculpture itself are one and the same. (Recall the contrast, introduced in chapter 2, between the internalized structures of mammals and the exoskeletons of crustaceans.) In fields such as architecture and engineering, similar distinctions are common. A crucial ingredient in the development of the great multistory buildings in Chicago in the latter part of the nineteenth century, for example, was the conscious separation and internalization of the building structure, or "skeleton," from the enclosure, or "skin," of the building. The structures of most recent bridges, by contrast, typically coincide with the overall form and image of the artifact.

Sculptures with Internal Structures

Frédéric-Auguste Bartholdi's Statue of Liberty provides a classic example of a sculpture with an internal framework (fig. 15.1). The torch arm is created by a projecting framework. The skin is attached periodically to the framework but is not conceived as having a primary structural function in itself. The statue has recently undergone massive restoration. A central issue during the restoration was how to deal with its poorly performing structure. The torch arm, for example, was known to be tilting and twisting in a potentially dangerous manner. To understand the issues involved, the origin of the structure must be reviewed.

Bartholdi is known to have been familiar with G. B. Crespi's 76-foot (23.2-meter) high statue of St. Carlo Borromeo in Arona, Italy. This seventeenth-century statue is made of repoussé copper over an iron armature. He was also familiar with Aimé Millet's statue of Vercingetorix, also built of repoussé copper over an iron armature. The latter was designed by the famous architect and restorationist Eugène-Emmanuel Viollet-le-Duc and was built by the

15.1
The Statue of Liberty. **The statue has an internal structure, a secondary framing system that attaches to bars stiffening the copper skin, and the skin itself.**

The internal iron tower and secondary framing for attaching the skin

The internal banding stiffened the skin and allowed free thermal contraction and expansion to occur.

Successively larger plaster models were used to determine the surface shape.

Molding of the left hand of the statue. Thousands of point by point measurements were needed to increase the scale of the model to the final size.

Wooden templates were made from the final plaster casting. Copper sheets (2.5 mm thick) were formed against the templates with hammers and presses.

The face of the statue and its interior framework

Etablissement Monduit. (This firm was the predecessor of Gaget, Gauthier et Cie, the firm that later built the Statue of Liberty.) Bartholdi, who had studied with Viollet-le-Duc as a young man, asked him to design the structure and the skin attachment system for his proposed colossal sculpture at the entrance to New York harbor. Viollet-le-Duc proposed supporting the 151-foot (46-meter) statue with masonry compartments filled with sand up to the hips. A lighter system of construction would rise above these compartments. He also developed an armature system of iron bars to support and stiffen the copper enclosure (it remains unclear how he proposed attaching the armature system to the masonry). Viollet-le-Duc died, however, in 1879, before construction of the statue could begin.

Bartholdi subsequently approached the engineer Alexandre-Gustave Eiffel for help. Although he was already well known for his bridges, Eiffel's great tower was still in the future. Eiffel immediately proposed a new solution for the structure of the statue—a great central iron tower, not unlike those he had developed in his bridges. A secondary structure reflecting the general form of the statue was then devised as an attachment to the tower. He then developed a system of flat bars or springs to connect the armature system to the secondary structure. This skin attachment system is a remarkable design. It allows the shaped copper skin to move independently with respect to the secondary and primary structure (thus allowing for phenomena such as thermally induced expansions and contractions in the copper), while at the same time transferring gravity and wind forces into these same structures. The exact form of the skin itself was developed by making a series of plaster models of ever-increasing size, a common copper repoussé technique of the time. The construction of these models was a feat in itself. Increasing the scale of one model to another necessitated making thousands and thousands of point by point measurements by hand to define the surface shape of one model and to shape the next.

Eiffel's original design for the primary tower (illustrated in fig. 15.2) is a straightforward framework that gains its stiffness from the triangulation of its members. In addition to downward-acting gravity loads, it was designed for a static wind pressure of 56 lbs/sq ft acting laterally on the face of the statue. The lateral action of the wind produces an overturning effect that is resisted by a special anchorage

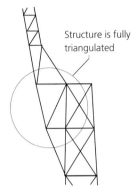

Structure is fully
triangulated

Eiffel's original design, circa 1880

15.2
Gustave Eiffel's original design for the basic structure was never built. A number of structural problems consequently developed, notably sagging and twisting of the torch arm, and the structure was subsequently modified in remedial attempts. It was restored completely in time for the centennial of its initial building.

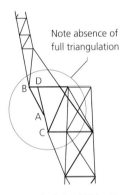

Note absence of
full triangulation

B
D
A
C

Structure as built in 1885 by Gaget, Gauthier et Cie

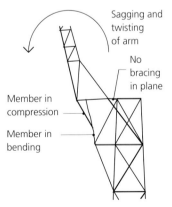

Sagging and
twisting
of arm

No
bracing
in plane

Member in
compression

Member in
bending

Excessive twisting and other deformations occurred in the structure as built.

system in the pedestal, which was designed by the architect Richard Morris Hunt. The anchorage system consists of two sets of crossed beams, called dunnage beams, interconnected by vertical tension bars. Although there is some ambiguity in the design intent, the upper set of beams appears to have been designed to carry downward loads and the lower set to help resist the uplift caused by laterally acting wind forces.

The central structure was not, however, built according to Eiffel's plans. The head was offset by 2 feet (60 cm) and the shoulder by 1.5 feet (46 cm). The framing pattern was changed in a highly unfortunate way. Why these modifications occurred is a matter of speculation, since a fire long ago destroyed many of the relevant documents in the case. It is surely hard to believe that Eiffel had anything to do with the modified structural framing pattern. There is as much a signature present in the framing patterns developed by a brilliant engineer as there is in the brushwork of a great painter; here is no sign of Eiffel's brushwork.

The modified framework that was built soon experienced problems. The torch began twisting and moving excessively. Reasons for these movements are many (fig. 15.2, bottom left). The weight of the torch arm, for example, undoubtedly caused compressive forces to develop in member AB. In a departure from sound design practices discussed in chapter 11, this same member does not frame into a nodal point on the framework but rather frames transversely into the side of member CD. Member CD is therefore subjected to extreme bending and associated high deflections. This would in turn contribute to an overall tilting in the projecting torch. (In Eiffel's original design, there would have been no such effects since the members are all connected at their nodal points.) The eccentricity of the torch arm also caused the whole central structure, and particularly the shoulder connections, to be subjected to a twisting action. Adequate bracing in the horizontal planes at the various levels in the structure could have prevented this twisting, but this bracing was inadequate or nonexistent.

In 1932 the torch arm framing and shoulder connections were altered. Some new bracing was added and other members were reinforced. Note that a new member was added to create a node on member CD where none existed before. The hope was clearly to eliminate bending in this member. The new member EF would be in a state of compression and

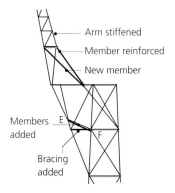

1932 repairs included the addition of stiffening members.

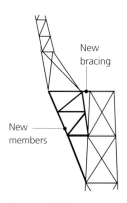

Proposed 1984 replacement scheme

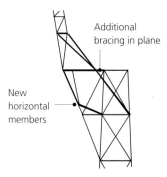

Implemented 1984 repair scheme

1
Rita Robinson, "Saving the Lady," *Civil Engineering*, January 1986, p. 35.

2
Richard Hayden and Thierry Despont, *Restoring the Statue of Liberty* (New York: McGraw-Hill, 1986), p. 45.

help transfer the compressive force in member AB back to a node in the central primary structure.

Even with the 1932 improvements, structural problems persisted. It soon became evident that bracing in the horizontal planes was still inadequate. With the great restoration effort to prepare the statue for its 1986 centennial celebrations, a new look was taken at the structure by several American and French engineering teams. One proposal was to completely replace the shoulder structure with a new configuration that was very similar to that originally proposed by Eiffel. A second proposal was to modify yet again the structure as built.[1] The choice posed a difficult dilemma. While both designs were thought able to yield a safe structure, proponents of one argued for a return to the structural elegance of Eiffel's original design, while proponents of the other argued for preserving the structure as built as a historical record, even if it lacked structural clarity. In the end the latter view prevailed and the original structure was subsequently modified again.

Other concerns raised during the restoration work ranged widely. Many had to do with corrosion caused by the contact of the copper in the skin with the iron in the secondary framework.[2] In the presence of moisture, copper and iron in contact produce an electrolytic reaction that causes corrosion and eventual disintegration in the iron (see chapter 18). Armature elements and connections were subsequently replaced on a large scale. There was also some fear that the constant twisting of the torch arm over the years and movements in the anchorage rods might have caused metal fatigue to develop in the structure. (When a metal is subjected to alternating cycles of high and low stress, premature failure can sometimes result at a fairly low stress level. This phenomenon can be witnessed by bending a paper clip back and forth rapidly until it breaks.) The structure was originally made of puddled iron, which is similar to wrought iron. Tests were made on samples by artificially subjecting them to many stress cycles, with the finding that no problem existed in this regard. Radiographic weld testing on the structure did not disclose any indications of cracks around rivet holes. Eventually the skin and supporting secondary framework were completely renovated, with many of the complex corroded secondary framework pieces having to be completely replaced with new elements made by hand techniques.

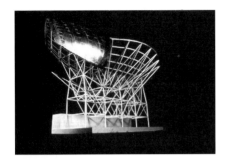

Structural steel framework

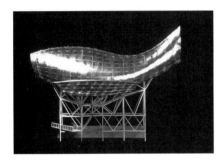

**Frank Gehry, *Villa Olímpica*
(in progress)**

15.3
**Frank Gehry, *Villa Olímpica*. This
35-meter-high fish is a project
for Barcelona, Spain. The final
surface shape for the great
fish was precisely defined and
adjusted using a computer-
based three-dimensional modeling system.**

3
Initial drawings and models
were done at Frank Gehry's
Los Angeles office. Initial computer modeling was done at
the Graduate School of Design
at Harvard University, and
further developed in Frank
Gehry's office.

Sculptures with internal structures and external skins are
still being made. One of the largest sculptures ever to be
made is projected for Barcelona, Spain. Frank Gehry's
monumental fish sculpture that is part of the *Villa Olímpica*
project for Barcelona (fig. 15.3) is anticipated to rise approximately 115 feet (35 meters) high and be approximately 178
feet (54 meters) long. The fish is part of a hotel project for
the Travelstead Group designed by Bruce Graham of SOM,
and is located within the 1992 Olympic Village redevelopment site. The external skin of the fish is to consist of panels
of latticed members. These elements are to attach to a secondary framing system, which in turn attaches to a primary
steel structure. The primary steel structure is to be roughly
configured in the shape of the external skin but not to follow it precisely. The secondary framing system not only provides attachment points for the panels but also provides the
transitional geometry between the carefully modeled surface panels and the more roughly shaped primary steel
structure. The steel structure consists of a series of shaped
structural steel elements supported by a braced steel frame.

A series of drawings and models were first made to establish the general appearance and geometry of the fish. Due to
time constraints, the general shaping of the internal steel primary structure was done prior to the final and exact shaping
of the skin of the fish. A knowledge of the exact shape of
the skin was crucial in deciding on how the latticed skin was
to be designed and attached. The final shaping of the three-
dimensional skin surface was done using a computer-based
three-dimensional modeling system.[3] This allowed the shape
to be manipulated easily and minor kinks and other undesirable features to be worked out of the surface. Further modeling allowed the shapes and positioning of the secondary
framing system to be determined. The complex geometries of
the surface panels were also developed using the computer-
generated surface model. This method of working stands in
interesting contrast to the use of increasing scale models and
point by point measurements necessarily used in the making
of the skin of the *Statue of Liberty*.

External Structures

Unlike the *Statue of Liberty*—in more ways than one—the
Watts Towers built by Simon Rodia have external structures

that coincide with the forms themselves. The remarkable Italian immigrant crafted this well-known fantasy between 1921 and 1954, then gave the structures to a poor neighbor, walked away from them, and never returned. Throughout the years the towers have been a source of both controversy and adoration. Controversy came to a head in 1959 when city building officials condemned the towers and planned to forcibly remove them, declaring them a potential threat to public safety due to the dangers of collapse or overturning (Rodia did not exactly have Eiffel's reputation as an engineer). A series of investigations into the safety of the towers ensued as concerned community advocates rallied to save them. An actual load test culminated the investigations (fig. 15.4).

The west tower is the tallest, standing 99.5 feet. It was built without the use of a ladder or a scaffold. The main structure consists of around 6,000 members. A series of slender vertical columns are encircled by other members. Arched spokes radiate at intervals from a central spine to join the columns. Members were made from a variety of steel sections (T-sections, angles) and pipe. No rivets, bolts, or welds were used. Members were spliced and connected by lapping them and wrapping them with expanded metal mesh or wire, then handpacking the whole with mortar. The 13.5-foot-diameter foundation was only 7 inches wide and extended 14 inches deep below a 2-inch patio. Rodia dug a trench, put in sixteen steel sections (eight T-sections and eight angles, alternating) for the legs of the tower, and poured the whole with concrete. The base was covered with broken concrete and fill, with a 4-inch shell-like cover. The top of the foundation was decorated with his typical embedments.

Prior to load tests in 1959, the towers had already successfully withstood environmental events of the time. In a partially completed state they survived the powerful Long Beach earthquake of 1933. Under a wind or earthquake loading, one of the towers generally behaves like a tall cantilever beam (actually a "cage") subjected to a lateral loading. The base width and tower weight mitigates against overturning. The slender external verticals primarily carry the bending action caused by the wind. The bending induces compression in verticals on one face and tension in those on the opposite face. The tower weight induces compression in all verticals. Some of these members are consequently sub-

jected to high compressive forces on one face when bending and weight-induced forces interact, which in turn could potentially cause buckling due to their slenderness. Buckling resistance is provided via a combined action of the steel members and the surrounding concrete. The maximum unsupported length of the elements between encircling bracing points is only around 6 feet—a feature that also helps reduce buckling tendencies. Nonetheless, the members still have high slenderness ratios. Forces are most likely transmitted from one lapped member to another through the development of bond stresses between the embedded members and the concrete, then through tension in the wire-reinforced concrete (with the wire playing a major role), and then back again via bond stresses to the next member. The central spine probably does relatively little in carrying wind or earthquake loadings, although it and the accompanying spokes undoubtedly add some stiffening to the outer cage elements.

After Rodia left in 1954, the towers fell into disrepair and were vandalized. Decorative elements were smashed or removed; cracks were present in the mortar surrounding steel members. Various stress analyses prepared by city engineers indicated that the structures were unsafe. A demolition order was issued by city officials in 1957. The newly formed Committee for Simon Rodia's Towers sought to save the structures.

A conflict developed between the city and the Committee over the validity of the stress analyses. The structure of the towers is redundant and difficult to analyze. The city analyses made various simplifying assumptions: the first analysis assumed that the steel columns alone carried the forces developed under design loadings; a second and third assumed that varying levels of partial support and combination action were offered by the mortar covering. N. J. Goldstone, an engineer on the Committee and later involved with the Apollo program, made his own calculations and assessments of the safety of the structure based on the lines of a reinforced concrete structure that postulated a more important role for the surrounding mortar and wire. Each of these analytical models yielded different allowable column loadings and hence different degrees of safety for the whole structure.[4] The different results were discussed at open municipal hearings. Due to the complexity and unusual nature of the original structure, there was

The whiffletree system that distributed the applied loads along the tower height via web straps was supported by scaffolding during the testing.

15.4
Simon Rodia built his towers by hand in Los Angeles between 1921 and 1954. The tallest is 99.5 feet high. In 1959, the City of Los Angeles, fearing that the towers were unsafe, condemned them. In a fight to save the towers, engineer N. J. Goldstone analyzed them and argued for their safety. Eventually a load test to ascertain the safety of the towers was agreed upon. A loading was applied that simulated an equivalent to design wind loadings required by the city building code. The tower sustained the required loading and the condemnation order was removed. The towers have since undergone extensive restoration.

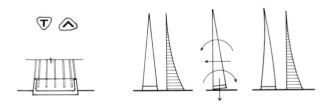

The beams of the whiffletree system were designed to begin yielding at exactly the target load level to protect the tower against accidental overloads. They yielded as planned.

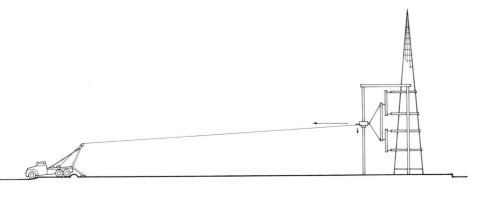

no way of resolving which of the models was most likely to be correct.

Eventually city officials agreed to a test devised by Goldstone. In conjunction with officials, a test on the largest (hence most critical) tower involving the application of a 10,000 pound force acting 33 feet off the ground was devised to be equivalent to a 76 mile per hour wind.[5] The load was applied via a hydraulic jack and a stabilized winch truck. The test called for the repair of all cracks up to 25 feet high, various wire strap stiffeners, and the attachment of a "whiffletree" (a device to distribute a concentrated load equally to different points) via web straps and padding around the tower at heights of 15, 27, 39, and 51 feet. Forces were applied in increments. Various strain gages and transducers measured movements and deformations in the structure during the test. The loading was sustained for a minute (less than the design duration, but still considered acceptable by city officials). Testing was stopped because the whiffletree's main 10-inch beam began yielding.[6] The tower itself showed no sign of distress during the test. From the experimental findings, a force of some 4,000 pounds was determined to exist in one of the base verticals containing an angle without it showing signs of buckling. Obviously the tower did not overturn either.[7] After the conclusion of the test, the city engineer took down the demolition order and handed it to a member of the group organized to save the towers.

After the test, funds were raised for the repair of the towers. They were listed as a historic monument in 1963 and eventually deeded to the state in 1979. Problems persisted over the years with cracking and deterioration of the

Simon Rodia, *Watts Towers*

4
A steel angle alone was estimated to have an allowable load of 1,090 pounds, a combination column 2,120 pounds, and Goldstone's reinforced concrete model 5,725. (See N. J. Goldstone, "Structural Test of Hand-Built Tower." *Experimental Mechanics*, January 1963, p. 8.)

5
Design pressures were 15 psi on the exposed surface area below 60 feet, and 20 psi above 60 feet. A conservative drag coefficient of 1 (for usual building shapes) was used, even though actual coefficients for most tower members are lower.

6
The yielding of the beams was widely reported in a way that described the "failure" of the testing rig as evidence for the high strength of the towers. This is wholly misleading. In actuality, the beam was designed to yield in bending at exactly 10,000 pounds so that an excessive load could not be accidentally applied that might cause the structure to fail at higher than anticipated load levels.

7
A consideration of overturning suggests that the structure need weigh about 50,000 pounds or so to provide a necessary balancing moment: $F \times h = W \times d$; $10,000 \times 33 = W \times (13.5/2)$. A few moments' calculation indicates that the tower and its base easily weigh at least the amount required for stability.

mortar that forms the cover for the steel members, exposing surrounding wire to the effects of rusting and other forms of deterioration. Many long and wide cracks developed. Since the strength of the structural elements depends on a composite action of the base members and surrounding mortar and wire, cracking and deterioration of the latter is extremely troublesome. Loss in continuity and strength can occur due to the effects of the cracking. Consequently, major programs of crack repair, replacement of weakened members and of deteriorated mesh and metal reinforcement, and other forms of maintenance have been instituted.

Claes Oldenburg's *Batcolumn* (1977) in Pittsburgh is a more recent large-scale work that is, in a certain way, surprisingly reminiscent of Rodia's towers in its basic fabric. The lattice steelwork of the *Batcolumn* functions as a huge stiff tube in which the structure defines the exact shape of the object itself (fig. 15.5). The *Batcolumn*—a little over 100 feet high—rests on a concrete footing.

In addition to its vertically acting self-weight, the structure is subjected to wind loadings. *Batcolumn* may be generally considered to be a cantilevered structure that is subjected to bending from the action of horizontally acting wind forces. The steel lattice acts as a type of open tube structure—a form reasonably well suited to carrying bending. The bending action of the wind would tend to induce compressive forces and related stresses on one face of the tube and tensile forces and stresses on the opposite face. The highest bending stresses are developed at the base of the cantilever structure where the bending moments due to the wind forces are the greatest. The self-weight of the structure produces compressive forces throughout the structure. At any given point in the lattice, the forces due to bending and those from the self-weight are additive.

On one face of the *Batcolumn* the compressive forces from the self-weight add to those from the bending action and produce a high final force state. On the opposite face the two tendencies tend to counteract each other. If the wind forces are sufficiently large, it is even possible that the tension forces on a face due to the bending would overshadow the compressive forces due to the self-weight of the structure, with the result that tension might well exist on one face of the *Batcolumn*.[8] The diagonal members inside the form serve stiffening, rather than primary load-carrying, roles.

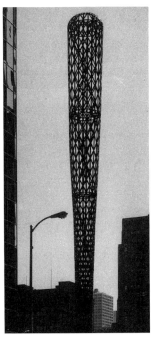 

Claes Oldenburg, *Batcolumn*   **Steel framework**

The steel cage

15.5
Oldenburg's *Batcolumn* gains its stability with respect to lateral forces in much the same way as do the simpler pedestal-based sculptures discussed in chapter 4. The projection at the footing base helps prevent sliding actions.

R. H. Fuchs in his book on Oldenburg discusses the influence of the imagery of the great lattice towers of early battleships, and of the immense John Hancock Building in Chicago, on the *Batcolumn*.[9] It is well known that efficiency in carrying wind forces was a prime consideration in the overall shape determination of these structures. While presumably a similar design goal was of no importance in the *Batcolumn*—given Oldenburg's intent to present a familiar object in an incongruous way—it is still instructive to look at the form he selected in these terms simply as a way of understanding something about tall structures.

As discussed in chapter 9, the distribution of bending moments in a cantilevered structure varies along the length of the member. The bending moments in a uniformly loaded cantilever are maximal at the base of the structure and decrease parabolically to zero at the free tip. The resisting member must consequently have sufficiently large dimensions at its base to carry the bending moment there. Since the bending moments present decrease elsewhere, using the same size section throughout is not particularly efficient (low stress levels would result that do not utilize the full capacity of the material present); it is evident that the resisting member could be tapered in a gradual way from a maximum at its base to virtually nothing at its free end to reflect the decreasing value of the bending moment present. The cross section of the *Batcolumn* is indeed tapered, but obviously in the opposite way since its dimensions are smaller nearest the base of the cantilever, where the bending moments are the highest, and larger near the top where the

Wind or earthquake forces tend to cause the *Batcolumn* to overturn. When the resultant force (combination of lateral + vertical) passes through the base to the right of the rotation point, the structure does not tend to overturn. When it passes to the left of the base, the resultant force produces a net overturning effect.

8
The possible development of tension on one face would not be problematic in the steel *Batcolumn* since steel can carry both tension and compression stress states, but if similar tension conditions existed in a tall masonry structure, cracking and potential collapse could occur.

9
R. H. Fuchs, *Claes Oldenburg: Large-Scale Projects, 1977–1980* (New York: Rizzoli, 1979).

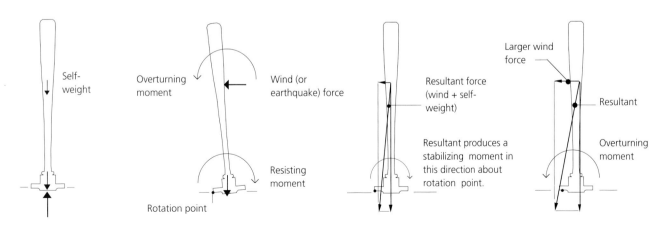

Self-weights and base reaction

Overturning and restoring moments

Resultant passes through base: a stable condition

Resultant passes outside of base: an unstable condition

bending moments are the lowest. If structural efficiency for actual loadings were desired at all, the *Batcolumn* should at least be turned upside down (fig. 15.6)!

Curiously, the same structural effects are present in actual baseball bats when these are held by batters at the narrow end and subject to lateral forces from batted balls at the opposite end. Bats are shaped and held in the way they are to maximize the chance for hitting a ball, not because of structural concerns. This produces maximum bending moments at the point of least structural strength (the handle); hence the tendency of wooden bats to break at this point.

The discussion of the structural shape of the *Batcolumn* raises the intellectual question of the appropriate structural shaping of a form of this type. Surely it should be tapered to reflect the decreasing bending moments along its length. Indeed, the size of the cross section could be continuously adjusted so that the bending stress level present at any point along the length of the member would be the same as at any other point. If this stress level is near the safe capacity of the material, then the material itself is being efficiently used. While the exact nature of the tapering to achieve this end differs for differing loading conditions and types of structures (e.g., truss versus beam), some general observations can be made. For uniformly distributed loading conditions and open framework structures, a parabolic tapering can be very efficient. The Eiffel Tower provides one image of this type of tapering (it is well documented that Eiffel was particularly concerned with efficiently carrying the wind forces that act on the latticework of the tower). If a solid beamlike section is used instead of a framework, a linearly varying section is more likely to result. If the structure is subjected to external point loads rather than uniform loads, open frameworks often assume linearly tapering configurations and solid beamlike sections assume convexly curved parabolic shapes. These shaping issues are discussed in more detail in other sources.[10]

Attention must also be paid to the overall stability of the *Batcolumn* and its resistance to overturning. Figure 15.5 shows a horizontally acting wind or earthquake force on the column. In actuality, the force does not manifest itself on the work as a discrete, concentrated force of the type shown: wind acts in a distributed way against the whole face of the structure. But for preliminary stability considera-

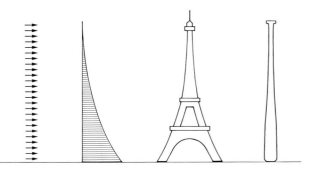

15.6
If structural efficiency were the only criterion, *Batcolumn* would be more sensibly inverted. This would lower its center of gravity and render it more stable. An inverted *Batcolumn* would also have a structural depth variation that would better reflect the bending moment distribution caused by wind forces, as does the great tower by Eiffel.

10
See, for example, Schodek, *Structures*, chapter 6.

tions, it is useful to imagine such a distributed force as being concentrated into a single equivalent load. An engineer would determine an equivalent concentrated force of this type by considering the force intensity of the wind per unit area on different parts of the structure and multiplying the average value by the total exposed surface area. This equivalent force could then be considered as acting at the centroid of the exposed surface area. Determining the magnitude of these forces is not straightforward because of the open lattice. Consequently, building code requirements for wind loadings that might be thought applicable are difficult to apply directly. Wind tunnel tests are often needed in situations of this type. Earthquake loadings would be similarly considered. In the Pittsburgh area, wind forces are generally more of a design problem than earthquake forces because of the relatively low earthquake hazard present. In some other parts of the country, earthquake forces would have to be more carefully considered. Earthquake-induced forces are similarly complicated to analyze in detail. They are inertial in character and depend on the amount and distribution of mass in the structure. For very simplified purposes, earthquake forces can be considered as a single equivalent force acting at the center of mass of the steel structure.

Stability considerations for a large structure with a base weight are essentially the same as those for the smaller pedestal-supported structures discussed in chapter 4. The effect of the horizontal force acting on the structure is to tend to cause it to overturn by rotating as a unit about the edge of the foundation (fig. 15.5). The weight of the structure plus base provides a moment about the foundation edge that tends to resist the overturning moment caused by the wind or earthquake force; the structure will not overturn as long as this resisting moment is greater than the overturning moment. It is also possible to view the stability of the structure in more graphic terms. As previously discussed, any two forces can be combined into a single resultant force. The final diagram in figure 15.5 illustrates a situation in which the wind or earthquake force is quite large and the weight is small. The resultant of these two forces passes to the left of the rotation edge (i.e., outside the base). Since the resultant represents the net of all forces present, it is evident that the force tends to cause a counterclockwise rotation that would overturn the structure and cause complete collapse. Figure 15.5 also illustrates a situation in which the

applied force is small with respect to the weight. In this case the resultant would pass to the right of the rotation edge, and the resultant would produce a clockwise rotation that tends to push the structure into the ground, preventing overturning.

It is obvious that larger wind or earthquake forces produce greater overturning potentials. But also note the importance of the location of the line of action of the applied force with respect to the rotation point. If the structure is very tall, the overturning potential is increased. If the structure is made lower, the tendency to overturn is reduced. Increasing the horizontal dimensions of the footing directly increases the resisting moment available to prevent overturning. Increasing the weight also serves to help stabilize the structure. An easy way to increase the value of the total weight is simply to increase the size of the concrete footing, which forms part of the combined weight. Since these footings are typically below ground, their size and weight can normally be increased as needed without altering the visible proportions of the sculpture. Putting the additional mass low also mitigates earthquake forces, which could be increased if the mass were placed high.

In structures as large as the *Batcolumn* or even larger, it is conceivable that adding stability by continuously increasing the weight and dimensions of the footing might prove impossible. For very large structures of this type, it would then prove necessary to tie the structure into a much more extensive base, perhaps even using piles driven into the ground. If the concrete base were attached to the tops of the piles, the overturning effect of the horizontal force would tend to push down on some piles and pull up on others. If special piles are used that can resist both tension (caused by an upward pulling) and compression, then the upper structure can be rendered stable under virtually any anticipated lateral load.

In the discussions thus far the effect of wind on sculptures has been assumed to be fairly straightforward, with wind effects simplifiable to laterally acting static forces. Actual wind effects are invariably more complicated and can be extremely complex to understand and predict. As wind flows around unusually shaped objects, complex currents can be developed. Some of the air flow might be laminar in nature (smooth-flowing) while in other cases severe and erratic turbulence might be present. The action of water swiftly flowing around rocks in a stream is analogous and may be helpful here. In some instances water might flow smoothly, while behind rocks and in other places complex eddies might form or wild turbulence might exist. The same is generally true for air motion around complex objects. Associated with each of these different movement patterns, and varying with them, are different sets of pressures and suctions on the object within the windstream. In simply shaped objects of small dimensions, the simpler characterization of wind as a static lateral force can be useful. In a gross way the static arrow represents the complex wind action sufficiently well to derive an appropriate structural response. In larger and more complex structures, however, this characterization might be wholly inadequate and even misleading. Similarly, forms that work at a smaller scale may not work at a larger scale.

Richard Lippold's towering piece in Seoul (fig. 15.7) demonstrates how complex dealing with wind forces can be. The sculptor first designed the enormous work to consist of three tapering identical hollow legs, each triangular in cross section and made of aluminum. The three legs were to join as a tripod 60 feet up, then project upward independently the remaining 120 feet. An engineering consultant analyzing the effects of wind forces on the structure soon predicted that the deflections present at the ends of the projecting legs would be extremely large and complex, with bending and twisting occurring. The material was changed from aluminum to mirrored stainless steel to help lessen these deflections (recall that steel is stiffer than aluminum on a unit size basis). Equally importantly, four more connecting struts had to be added above the one at the tripod joint. These struts serve to tie the three projecting legs together, forcing them to behave structurally as a single unit. This in turn mitigates deflection problems as well.

An aerodynamic phenomenon called "vortex shedding" (an undulating pattern of swirls and ebbs) at the corners of the legs of Lippold's work was also a concern, since under certain conditions the associated force might cause resonance and potential failure to occur. The engineers recommended adding strakes (coiled wind spoilers) periodically along the midpoint of the upper third of the structure to guard against such an event. (This approach was rejected, and the engineer filed a disclaimer letter.)

Finally, it is interesting to look at one large-scale work that was never built. The model of Vladimir Tatlin's *Monument to the Third International* has a massive structure externally placed and visually dominant. The model was conceived as a prototype for a real multistory structure. It was to be 400 meters high (1/100,000 of the Earth's meridian)—higher than the Eiffel Tower. The axis tilts 23°27' (the angle of the Earth's axis). The external spiral was to contain glass volumes—a cube, pyramid, cylinder, and hemisphere—that would contain rooms, halls, and offices. Each of the four volumes would rotate at a different rate. The glass cube would turn once a year, the pyramid once a month, the cylinder once a day, and the hemisphere once an hour. The original model was built during an eight-month period in 1920 in Leningrad. Other versions of the model were subsequently built.

As a sculpture and a model, the *Third International* is rightly acclaimed.[11] Tatlin's design attitudes were such that the material-artifactual part of his works was usually moved to the exterior of the forms (in marked contrast to the attitude of another constructivist, Naum Gabo) and made visually manifest. The structural approach used in the *Third International* seems painfully obvious at first. The great spiral is heavily triangulated, a great projecting girder is present, and arches abound. Once past the striking visual imagery of the work, however, the structural rationale is far less clear and can only be surmised. At the risk of great oversimplification, the structure may possibly be interpreted as that of an interior inclined cone (actually somewhat truncated) formed by a series of radially organized inclined smaller members, two independent layers of rolled and stiffened spiral planes that wrap the truncated cones, and a single large inclined composite member or girder (fig. 15.9). Transverse beamlike elements connect the spiral layers and the truncated cone members. A basic "radial unit" with a diagonal in the wrapped plane is formed by the wrapping modules in conjunction with inclined cone elements. Inside this complex are the suspended rotating volumes. The model was made of wood; presumably the large-scale structure was to be in steel.

With respect to gravity loadings, it is unclear how the structure was intended to work. There are several plausible models. One is that the outside sloped cantilever was some-

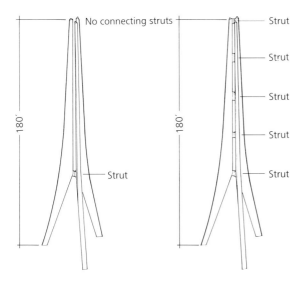

No connecting struts

Strut

Strut

Strut

Strut

Strut

180'

Strut

180'

Strut

Sculpture as originally designed

Sculpture as modified to take into account the aerodynamic effects of high winds

15.7
Tall structures are extremely sensitive to aerodynamic phenomena. Richard Lippold's tower needed to have additional struts added to stiffen the structure.

11
In view of the discussion in chapter 20 on spirals, it might be of interest to note that the *Third International* appears to be not a logarithmic or equiangular spiral, but generally what is often called an Archimedean spiral. While somewhat similar in appearance to a logarithmic spiral, it does not have the character of geometric similarity along its length. Rather it is much more like the spiral obtained when a rope is coiled. Each whorl is of the same width as that which precedes and follows it. With successive whorls, the radius will thus increase in an arithmetic rather than logarithmic progression.

how intended to suspend the rotating volumes directly, with the cone and wrappings serving no role in carrying this enormous load. Technically the idea of the sloped member serving as a gigantic cantilever with a huge load at its terminus is intrinsically dubious, due to the potentially enormous forces and deformations induced in a cantilever of this dimension and the gigantic foundations required at its base to carry the twisting involved. Even if the cantilever were accepted as possible, this model also leaves completely unresolved the role of the cone and wrappings. What role would they serve if the cantilever picks up all the load? The possibility that the great spiral would serve little or no role seems hard to accept, and, if it serves no role, the whole enterprise seems confused and doubtful. A second, contrasting model holds that the volumes were to be suspended from the top of the rigid internal conical form. This proposition is more feasible technically: the basic internal conical form reflects a sound way of carrying an enormous downward-acting point load (the suspended rotating volumes) from its apex, assuming that the inclined members serve as compressive elements. In this model of a stiff interior cone, however, the great sloped member becomes redundant and ambiguous (if the load is carried by the cone, what does the girder do?). The wrapped spirals would also serve little function in carrying this massive point load downward. Possibly some combination of actions is possible. A third model could presumably involve the spirals themselves in carrying the vertical load. It is unclear how they would have the capacity for doing so in the absence of the inner cone. In any case the structure seems to contain some redundancy.

Assuming for a moment that the internal cone is the dominant structural device present, the all-important lateral wind and earthquake loadings in a real multistory structure would presumably also be carried by the conical structure, in this case interacting with the wrapped spirals. Again it can be suspected that the conical structure would do most of the work. The wrapped spirals would aid and stiffen the conical form but would not be the primary load-carrying device. Again the large sloped composite member serves no convincing function in this model.

The notion of massive volumes suspended from the top also poses a rather scary scenario in the event of an earth-

15.8
Tall structures can be effectively made of reinforced concrete. *Five Tower Square* **was executed in Mexico City by Mathias Goeritz in connection with architect Luis Barragán.**

quake. It is obviously necessary to prevent a rather gigantic pendulum action from occurring. The suspended volumes could possibly be tied in laterally to the surrounding cone and spirals to prevent such an action, but the fact that the volumes were intended to revolve clearly complicates such an approach.

The surface structure is necessarily separated from the interior volumes so that the latter can revolve; the volumes would necessarily have to have fundamentally independent structures. These would have to have special structures in their own right with respect to floor loadings and the like. They could possibly be connected to the wrapping structure (cone and spirals) at intervals via some sort of bearing assembly that would allow rotation but still prevent lateral swaying of the suspended volumes. Some measure of lateral support value could possibly be gained from the exterior wrapping in this way. Many other issues (power systems, water systems, plumbing systems, etc.) are obviously problematic in relation to suspended and revolving habitable areas. Problems of horizontal span, circulation, environmental controls, and simple enclosure cannot be ignored in real building volumes, particularly ones that rotate.

In summary, the massive external spiral wrappings that are so visually dominant in the famous model would not have a corresponding degree of structural importance in a real multistory structure constructed on the basis of the model. The actual structural functioning would be quite different, probably with the interior cone doing most of the actual work. In all likelihood, the suspended interior structure would be extremely complex in its own right and would have to have a significant visual presence far beyond what is suggested by the idea of "glass" volumes. To say that these rotating internal volumes are less than convincing in large scale is to understate the issue. Could the design ever actually have been made to work? Possibly, since the capabilities of modern engineering are not to be dismissed lightly, but certainly only at great cost and presumably with significant design changes (which in turn would have a visual impact). The very design intent originally proposed (a wrapped and visually manifest structure enclosing dematerialized volumes) would most likely be highly compromised and the result perhaps satisfying to neither sculptor nor engineer. It may be just as well that the *Third International* remains a proposal rather than an actuality.

Vladimir Tatlin, *Monument to the Third International*

15.9
Vladimir Tatlin's *Monument to the Third International* was partly conceived as a prototype for a real multistory structure. The great spiral was to house rotating glass volumes (a cube, pyramid, cylinder, and hemisphere). When viewed through this narrow lens, the actual functioning of its various elements is ambiguous at best. (Since the original was destroyed, the above interpretation is highly speculative.)

Interlocking spirals

Assumed load application point (two models)

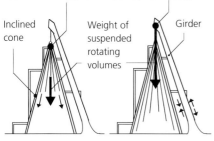

Inclined cone   Weight of suspended rotating volumes   Girder

1. The cone carries the weight by axial compression and stiffens the spirals (girder is redundant)

2. The cantilevered girder carries the weight by bending (cone only stiffens the spirals)

Alternative models for interpreting how the structure would carry the massive vertical loads from the suspended rotating volumes

16 Floating Sculptures

16.0
Christo, *Surrounded Islands*.

There are not very many floating sculptures. Nonetheless, the excitement underlying the very thought of this class of structure necessitates some treatment, however short, in a book of this type.

As a start, sculptures that float can be broadly divided into those that rely on displacement hulls for buoyancy, as is the case in a common boat where the hull actually displaces water to achieve buoyancy, and those that rely more directly on the buoyancy of the material used itself, for which relative unit densities become highly important. These types can be further characterized in terms of the degree to which they are intended to be movable, and the degree to which they are considered temporary rather than permanent works. One clear approach is to render the sculpture boat-like, perhaps even to the extent of using a boat hull to support a traditional objectlike sculpture, in which case the notion of ready movability is included. Flotation in such works is based on the displacement of water by the hull itself, and they are usually subject to the same physical design constraints and issues as are actual boats. Normally such sculptures are not regarded as temporary works. A contrasting approach is to utilize displacement flotation elements that are clearly not intended to be easily movable, in the manner of a harbor buoy. These elements are invariably meant to be moored in place in some way, typically through anchoring cables. The shapes of these kinds of flotation elements are quite different from those of boat hulls. A variant on this theme is the use flotation devices that rely on the buoyancy of the material itself. Examples include interconnected dispersed flotation elements, such as floating oil containment booms or log chains.

Archimedes' principle states that when a body is immersed in a fluid, the buoyancy force that holds the body up equals the weight of the fluid displaced. When a body is freely floating in water, the weight of the body equals the weight of the water displaced. If the weight of the body exceeds the amount of water it displaces, then it sinks. A solid piece of wood floats because its unit density (weight per unit volume) is less than that of water. A solid piece of steel has a higher weight per unit volume than water. Thus, even when submerged, a solid piece of steel cannot displace a greater weight of water than its own weight, hence it sinks. A traditional boat hull derives its buoyancy from the shaping of the hull to displace sufficient water (replacing it, so to speak, with air) so that the weight of the hull is less than the weight of the water displaced. The incorporation of air bubbles or lighter-than-water constituents in any material tends to reduce its weight per unit volume and increase its buoyancy.

Large Floating Forms

One rather remarkable floating sculpture was Christo's *Surrounded Islands* (fig. 16.1). This project was a temporary installation in Biscayne Bay, Miami, Florida; it was in place for only a couple of weeks in 1983. The islands were surrounded by about 6.5 million square feet of pink woven polypropylene fabric. The fabric covered the surface of the water for a distance of about 200 feet from each island into the bay. Technical considerations in this unique project were many. Gigantic sheets had to be cut into complex shapes. Ways had to be found to unfurl the gigantic sheets. Devices had to be found to stabilize the sheets and hold them in place. Eventually a floating fabric was anchored to the islands on one end and supported on its outer edges by floating booms, which were in turn anchored to the bottom of the bay. Complex sheet shapes were sewn together. A series of more or less radial ties further connected the booms to the shore.

Finding a suitable pink material that floated and could hold its color proved difficult. Many available materials were tested and found unsuitable. Test pieces either sank below the surface or were found not to be colorfast in the harsh sun and salt water environment. A West German firm finally agreed to supply a pink polypropylene that met requirements. The polypropylene contained very minute air bubbles that gave the fabric a low density (0.5 grams/cm³) and consequent buoyancy in water. Rolls of fabric were cut into complex shapes appropriate for surrounding the islands (some 72 shapes in all were cut; the largest island required 12 sections to surround it). The giant sections were presewn and laced together, with radial lines under the fabric.

The outer booms were made of octagonally shaped styrofoam (12 inches in diameter and about 100 feet long) cut from square shapes. The booms were found to be highly flexible and susceptible to lifting by wind forces. Consequently, a special "water bag" was devised to encase the booms and prevent them from being lifted. The booms were in turn connected to floats. A large buoyant piece of styrofoam was anchored to the sea bed so that it floated just beneath the mean low water level. It was attached to a smaller white buoy that floated on the surface and was in turn attached to the floating booms. This arrangement allowed the boom flexibility to adjust its position according to wind and tidal movements, while at the same time still anchoring it in place. Small navigation lights warned boaters of the subsurface elements.

Connections to the seafloor were made by special drive anchors. These elements, reminiscent of common toggle bolts, were driven through the soft seabed into underlying limestone. When pulled upon, the end piece of the anchor rotated and provided a resistance to being pulled out. Some 610 of these anchors were used. Some 900 connections on the island end were made using similar devices.

Experiments were made concerning the best way to unfurl the sheets. Eventually the sheets were housed in cocoons on the booms and simply pulled toward the shore. Fortunately, little resistance was encountered in the pulling. On the first day of unfurling, a violent upsurge of wind caught several of the spread but as yet unmoored sections of the fabric and blew them like sails. Workers in the water held down the fabric by lying flat on top of it.

In its final state the fabric floated as one sheet. It reflected the rippling movements of the water beneath it. And then it was completely removed.

Buoyancy and Stability of Floating Vessels

Boat hulls and other floating vessels encapsulate air voids that decrease the average or effective density of the whole, rendering it more buoyant (hence steel may be used for the surface as long as the encapsulated air void is large). Obviously the greater the volume of the hull, the greater is the volume of air encapsulated and the more buoyant the shape. It is easy to calculate the dimensions of a boat hull in

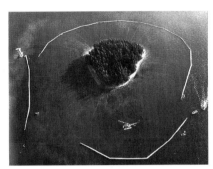

Christo, *Surrounded Islands*

Putting the octagonal booms in place

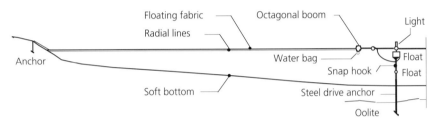

Typical section showing floating fabric and end anchorages

16.1
In *Surrounded Islands*, a number of islands in Biscayne Bay, Florida, were surrounded by Christo and his helpers. A special fabric was identified that both floated and was color-resistant to the effects of the sun and the salt water environment.

relation to the weight of the skin, other parts of the boat, and the loading it carries, such that the total downward weight displaces an amount of water sufficient to maintain buoyancy and reasonable freeboard (the distance between the water line and the deck).

Stability must also be considered in planning the size and shape of hulls. Shapes intended to float upright may turn over on their sides or even capsize completely. Tall structures on narrow hulls, for example, tend to overturn. The reasons for overturning are somewhat more complex than those described earlier for imbalances in land-based sculptures, but the principles are decidedly the same. A hull in the water displaces a volume of water equal to the weight of the whole structure. The center of gravity of the displaced water volume is called the center of buoyancy. Its exact position depends on the shape of the hull itself. For the buoyant object to be in equilibrium, the center of gravity of the weight of the whole object and its contents must lie in the same vertical plane as the center of buoyancy (fig. 16.2). Moving weights around in the object will tend to shift the hull, thus tending to change the shape of the water displaced and tending to shift the location of the center of

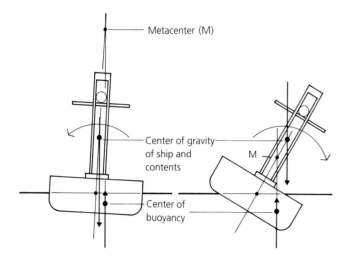

Metacenter (M)

Center of gravity of ship and contents

M

Center of buoyancy

Stable: ship rights itself   **Unstable: ship capsizes**

16.2
This diagram shows the stability principles present in a sculpture mounted on top of a boat hull.

buoyancy until equilibrium is reestablished and the centers of gravity and buoyancy are aligned.

A condition of equilibrium is that if the vessel is tilted, the center of gravity of the object and its contents must be located such that the forces of weight and buoyancy tend to restore the vessel to an upright position, rather than causing it to continue to overturn. In figure 16.2, if the vessel is tilted, a new center of buoyancy is established that creates a moment tending to restore the vessel to an upright position. The tilting also causes the center of gravity of the whole vessel to shift and create an overturning moment that tends to capsize the vessel. If the vessel's center of gravity is low, the restoring moment is greater than the capsizing moment and the vessel rights itself. If the center of gravity is very high, then the structure tends to continue to overturn soon after tilting begins to occur. Any off-center weight also contributes to overturning. Similar considerations of equilibrium would suggest that narrow hulls also contribute to a susceptibility to overturning.

In ship design, these ideas are reflected in the idea of a *metacenter*, where lines passing through the centers of buoyancy and gravity intersect (point M in figure 16.2). If the center of gravity of the vessel is above this point, the vessel is unstable, when points are coincident the vessel is in neutral equilibrium, and when the center of gravity is beneath this point the vessel is stable. Note that while vessels are most susceptible to overturning in the transverse direction, similar considerations apply to the stability of a vessel in its long direction (its "trim").

In vessels with keels, a weighted keel lowers the center of gravity and thus lends stability to the floating object. As a boat starts to overturn, reactive forces from the water pushing against the surface of the keel are also developed that tend to resist overturning.

Forces in Floating Vessels

Forces that are developed on floating vessels are quite complex. Briefly, several primary types of forces exist. There are local forces due to static water pressure acting transversely to the surface of the hull. These forces increase with increasing depth and are resisted by the plates (and supporting ribwork, if necessary) comprising the hull. For small sculptures, these forces are generally negligible. For larger works, they may be significant.

Another set of forces act on the whole structure and stem from wave-induced variations in the distribution of the buoyancy forces present, the vessel's motions, vibrations, and so forth. For example, a long hull may be temporarily suspended between high waves at its bow and stern. Very large bending moments and shear forces are consequently induced in the whole hull of the vessel that tend to break it much like a beam. Whole portions of the hull may be cantilevered in other wave conditions. The bending moments and shear forces induced must be resisted by the hull acting as an integral unit. Even under still water conditions, unevenness in the distribution of weight along the hull may set up significant bending moments and shear forces as well.

17 Landforms, Earthworks, and Earth-Related Structures

17.0
Michael Heizer, *Effigy Tumuli Sculpture.*

The shaping of land has long been perceived by architects and landscape architects as a vital design act. More recently the possibilities inherent in landforms and earthworks have attracted many sculptors. Perspectives have ranged widely, and so has the commensurate technology. Some works that have dealt with issues of siting, access, and view have innovatively employed the well-documented technology of landscape architecture for the creation of elements such as paths and berms. In other cases, artists such as Walter De Maria and Robert Morris have constructed works in which traditional technology of this type has seemingly played little role (except perhaps as a larger focal metaphor against which some of these works react).

The works of sculptors such as Robert Smithson, Robert Morris, Herbert Bayer, and Mary Miss—to name but a few—have reached an interesting level of maturity. The connection of works by individuals such as Smithson and Morris with larger societal issues of technology, ecology, and land reclamation is useful to bear in mind, since this perspective helps in understanding the setting, scale, and material constructs of at least some of their works (surely not others). Robert Morris's *Untitled* reclamation project in King County, Washington (fig. 17.1), is representative of this type of earth sculpture. Michael Heizer's *Effigy Tumuli Sculptures* near Ottawa, Illinois, were built on the site of an abandoned coal strip mine. Reclaimed land areas often involve extensive areas of fill. Land fill remains a common method for some towns to dispose of garbage (wastes, often put in a pit, are simply covered up) and undoubtedly will provide settings for future works. In other cases, land has been carefully built up with good materials to new profiles for general leveling or drainage purposes. In large landform sculptures, the land shapings are normally fairly gentle and encompassing.

In contrast to these large landform sculptures, *Field Rotation* by Mary Miss or *Dark Star Park* by Nancy Holt involve the interplay between the land and built works on the land, shading over into what was once more exclusively the domain of the architect and landscape architect.

17.1
Robert Morris, *Untitled*. This
gentle work with the landscape
was done as a reclamation pro-
ject in King County, Washington.

In some cases earth-related structures are built to provide an interface between the earth and some built structure put on top of, or built into, the earth. Some of these interface structures might be primary parts of the overall design; others might simply be necessary supporting elements. The end retaining walls of Michael Heizer's *Complex One/City* (fig. 17.2) obviously form an integral part of the overall design. The end walls cut off and retain the earth mound. Walls of this type experience complex laterally acting forces from the retained earth and are subject to overturning and sliding as a unit. Failure can also occur in the concrete wall itself.

Less conspicuous but equally important earth-related structures include the foundation elements of outdoor works. Reasons for using foundations are obvious—one of the foremost being that a heavy sculpture can sink into soft ground. As the stressed soil beneath a heavy sculpture consolidates, the work can dig into the earth, tilt erratically, or even overturn. If the ground settles unevenly beneath the structure—a phenomenon called "differential settlement" —the effect might be to cause parts of the structure to bend or twist, resulting in cracking or even parts breaking off. Carefully designed foundations can prevent this. Characteristics such as soil consolidation are of concern in relation to the design and siting of other sculptural types as well. Richard Serra's *Wright's Triangle* (fig. 8.6), for example, was originally intended to be sited so that it could be viewed from above. The extremely heavy weight of the work coupled with poor soil conditions at the site, however, posed a danger of bearing stress failures in the soil beneath the sculpture. These considerations necessitated that the sculpture be placed at a second location. The original view was lost; new accesses and views had to be devised. Serra was an active participant in this relocation.[1]

Of concern in all of these different landform works and earth-related structures are the characteristics and structural properties of earth materials themselves. There are many types of earth materials, including various forms of rock, clay, sand, and gravel. There is a corresponding large range in the physical characteristics of the materials and ways of working with them. Questionable ground materials include natural soft clays, silts, and peat. Consolidation and differential settlements underneath foundations can be consider-

able when these materials are present. Soil-related problems also include erosion induced by wind or water run-off. The more mechanical properties of different types of stone and other earth materials are addressed in chapter 18 as part of a more general discussion of materials. This chapter will focus more on the works themselves.

Large Landforms

General Characteristics
Many landform sculptures do not incorporate any built structures other than the land itself. Land is often sloped or shaped by acts such as grading, cutting, and filling— acts that require careful thought since natural forces tend to flatten out slopes that are built too steeply. Gentle slopes can be made that naturally retain their integrity over time. Robert Morris's *Untitled* reclamation project in King County, Washington, executed in 1979 on the site of an abandoned gravel pit, demonstrates this kind of sloping. The concentric rings have no sharp inclines. Once made, these slopes were seeded, helping to stabilize them by preventing erosion.

Prior to shaping any site, it is obviously necessary to understand the existing topography. Site information can be obtained in a variety of ways involving standard surveying techniques. Elevations of different points on a site are measured and the results depicted, typically through the use of contour maps where each line represents a constant elevation. Closely spaced contour lines mean that ground slopes are quite sharp; widely spaced contour lines indicate slight slopes. Peaks, valleys, ravines, and other typical land features have characteristic contour patterns. Associated slopes (or grades as they are often called) are measured in terms of the relative amount of rise or fall with respect to the horizontal. A 1:10 slope is the same as a 10 percent slope.

Determining appropriate slopes for landforms can be quite complex, and is strongly dependent on the existing topography of the site and its intended use. Important factors include whether people will walk on the site, water run-off considerations, and maintenance issues (e.g., mowing). In situations where there are strong functional mandates to be met, such as the inclusion of pathways or vehicular access routes, these constraints may actually dictate slope profiles.

Slopes for different situations are typically as follows. Pedestrian walks may slope up to 12 percent, but a maximum of 8 percent is preferred. Wheelchair access ramps are constrained by law to a 7 percent maximum slope in many communities. Fields used for play are in the 1 to 5 percent range. When vehicular access is needed, publicly accessible streets may slope up to around 10 percent, but a maximum of 8 percent is preferred. Private streets may slope up to 20 percent, but a maximum of 12 percent is preferred.

Slopes intended to be mowed are normally limited to a maximum slope of around 25 percent because of limitations on mowing equipment; unmowed slopes can be quite steep (up to 100 percent when planted with special dense ground covers). Additional functional considerations in the design of large landforms often include the need to drain sites (to prevent stagnant water pools or muddy spots from developing) or to divert existing water run-off channels (ditches, streams) into new locations. Carrying water in ditches or swales (broad, shallow ditches) presents special problems since their longitudinal slopes must be carefully maintained between maximum and minimum ranges (e.g., 2 to 15 percent longitudinally, with a maximum of 10 percent desirable). Swales with gently sloping sides are often used since they can be mown. It is also necessary to slope the ground away from installed structures for general water run-off purposes (at least a 2 percent grade).

Creating Large Landforms
Specially shaped earthworks can be created either by shaping natural earth materials alone (by cutting, filling, compacting, or grading) or by introducing some sort of external stabilization device (retaining walls, surface coverings, meshes, geotextiles) that would allow shapes to be formed that are not otherwise possible.

The shapes possible using earth materials alone are strongly influenced by the physical characteristics of the existing site materials. These characteristics include properties such as internal cohesion, degree of moisture saturation, and angle of repose.[2] New profiles can be created by cutting into the existing topography, but any inclined surface of unretained earth is naturally subjected to forces that tend to flatten it out—either barely perceptibly over time or more dramatically as in the case of a landslide. The incline will eventually assume a particular slope defined by the angle of repose of the material for the prevailing moisture content present.

In many cases it is necessary to alter the existing topography through the deliberate filling in of sites to create new profiles. As with cuts, there are limitations in the steepness of the slopes created when fills are made with natural materials. In all cases, the technical quality of the profile created is particularly dependent on the type of fill material used and the specific way it is put into place. *Controlled fill* may take place with a view toward building on the site. Surfaces are carefully prepared and water diversion ditches or drains possibly added. Well-graded inert fill material is subsequently added in thin layers, each compacted. Controlled fill sites are not necessarily problem-free, but are generally quite good sites for earthwork or other large outdoor sculptures. It is generally best not to build immediately even on a well-compacted controlled-fill site, since some settlement invariably takes places (particularly with wet cohesive soils).

Uncontrolled fill, by contrast, can consist of virtually anything (poor-quality clays, industrial wastes, etc.) that is simply dumped in place and leveled. Industrial and other wastes are typically covered with a thin layer of soil. Compaction rarely if ever takes place. These kinds of fills are extremely problematic to build upon. Newly placed uncompacted fill will unevenly and substantially settle under its own weight. Anything built on top of this material will have to follow accordingly. Large rigid sculptures might twist or tilt as a unit. Differential settlements underneath large rigid sculptures could lead to cracking and other structural problems. Earthwork structures could differentially settle and might show signs of soil cracking, consolidation pockets, or other distress.

For very large sculptures that are to be built on sites known to have poor natural soil conditions or uncontrolled fill, it is always possible to remove the poor ground by earth-moving equipment and replace it with good, compacted fill. Sometimes poor ground can be improved directly by compacting it with heavy roller equipment, by vibrating, or by dynamically consolidating it using heavy equipment that drops huge weights on the ground. All of these techniques are extremely expensive. An alternative to ground improve-

17.2
Michael Heizer, *Complex One/
***City*. This work hinges on the use**
of reinforced concrete retaining
walls.

2
The angle of repose is the angle
naturally formed by a material
when it is continuously piled
into a mound and allowed to
settle (see chapter 18). There
are different angles for different
materials.

ment techniques is to use a specially designed foundation. It is possible to drive foundation piles through the poor material to better bearing soil or rock, or to use specially designed stiff raft foundations (typically made of reinforced concrete). These alternatives will be discussed more extensively below.

Chemicals pose an increasing problem in uncontrolled landfill sites. Decomposition of organic material may result in potentially hazardous concentrations of methane or carbon dioxide. Other chemicals in soils contaminated by industrial wastes can attack metal or even concrete in foundations. Sites suspected of contamination should be carefully tested before being built on. Cleaning up hazardous sites is a major problem. When contamination is assessed to be minor, not hazardous to health and posing a risk to structural members or foundations only, then some resistance to chemical attack can be provided through techniques such as treating exposed surfaces of structural elements with coatings (e.g., pitch epoxy) or using separating membranes (e.g., flexible plastic sheets or rigid plastic sleeves).

Excessively sharp slopes can be stabilized by a number of techniques involving the use of geotextiles (tough sheets designed not to degrade over time when embedded in wet soil) interspersed through the fill in layers, or by some sort of surface covering. A landform project of quite a different type uses geotextile material as a primary part of the sculpture. Gary Dwyer's proposal for *Mea Culpa* suggests the use of a two-inch-thick fibrous erosion control mat to create an enormous work along the Elkhorn fault scarp. The work is based on ogham, the ancient Celtic alphabet that uses an axial line with a series of transverse markers to form letters and words. Words would be marked on the land; with the shifting of adjacent ground planes, the transverse markers would be shifted to form new configurations and perhaps new words.[3]

Rammed Earth Sculptures

A special form of earthwork is made by specially compacting (ramming) earth until it becomes very dense. The rammed earth technique for making structures is quite old. Particularly interesting rammed earth houses were constructed in France in the seventeenth century. *The Other*

Side of the Earth by Richard M. Brown (fig. 17.3), installed at the De Cordova Museum and Sculpture Park in Lincoln, Massachusetts, from 1989 to 1990, provides an excellent recent example of a rammed earth structure (the illustration shows one part only; a similar piece is on the other side of the hill so that the wall conceptually passes through the hill).

Formwork not unlike that used for casting concrete shapes is typically used in creating rammed earth shapes. The formwork needs to be fairly substantial since the earth material is compacted into place. The material itself needs to possess high internal cohesion (which rules out many materials such as sand). The soil is normally placed in layers, often with an integral matrix of some other binding material (ranging from straw to various types of synthetic fibers). Layers are sequentially compacted.

With time and exposure to the elements, rammed earth constructions degrade. Surface erosion from wind or rain is common. Normal contractions and expansions of earth masses (e.g., due to temperature effects) can lead to cracking in the compacted mass. Water can collect in these cracks and cause subsequent deterioration of the compacted mass. Freeze-thaw cycles can cause even more cracking to develop (water freezes, expands, opens cracks more, and melts—thus leaving a wider crack to collect even more water as the cycle repeats).

The shapes of many rammed earth structures seem to invite observers to walk or sit on them. These actions, however, cause particular damage to rammed earth structures in the form of indentations and cracks. Sharp corners can be easily broken off.

Foundations and Anchors

Bearing Foundations

Foundations are designed to distribute the loads from a large work into the ground in such a way as not to overstress the ground and thus avoid unwanted soil consolidation or differential settlement, which might in turn cause structural distress in the supported sculpture. Not all structures need substantial foundations. Many of the light wood structures by Mary Miss, for example, are more or less simply placed on top of the ground. Others require only small pad footings. The larger and heavier the structure and the more it is intended to be a permanent rather than a temporary installation, the more likely are serious foundations to be needed.[4]

Soil considerations that are particularly important include the bearing capacity of the soil and the degree to which it settles over time. The *bearing capacity* of a soil describes its ability to carry applied forces without excessive immediate consolidation, and is thus a measure rather like allowable stress for other materials (see chapter 18). When the bearing capacity of a soil is exceeded due to the weight of the structure and small bearing area, the structure may dig into the ground, as happened with *Wright's Triangle*. Properly designed foundations can avoid such problems.

There are several ways of distributing applied forces into the ground. The most common technique is to distribute applied loads throughout a large surface area of soil, thus reducing the bearing force on the soil to a point where the soil can carry it without excessive consolidation. This is what the simple concrete pad, spread footing, or strip footing does, but this is also the principle underlying more complex and extensive raft foundations.

In relatively small outdoor sculptures (e.g., those of about human size), there is hardly ever a need to calculate footing sizes. Typically the normal size that would be put in to level the work and provide a base to build on suffices. As works get to be very large, however, it may be necessary to assure an adequate foundation size. Clearly the size required depends on the weight of the sculpture and the allowable bearing stress of the soil. Either high applied loads or weak soil bearing capacities dictate large footing sizes. These sizes are relatively easy to determine.[5]

Once the overall plan dimensions of a footing are determined, it is necessary to make sure that the footing itself does not crack or otherwise fail while performing its function of distributing the load. A simple spread footing experiences forces that tend to cause it to bend in the manner of a double upside-down cantilever beam. A reinforced concrete footing tends to crack due to the tension stresses associated with the bending phenomenon and the low capacity of concrete to resist tension. A grid of reinforcing steel is consequently put in the tension zone to prevent this kind of failure from occurring. The amount and spacing of this steel depends on the magnitude of the applied loads and the size of the footing.

3
Gary Dwyer, "The Power under Our Feet," *Landscape Architecture*, May/June 1986, pp. 65–69.

4
While it might be generally argued that "temporary" installations do not need serious foundations while "permanent" ones do, there are exceptions. Christo's temporary *Valley Curtain* provides an excellent case in point (see the photographs of the cable foundations in figure 10.1).

5
Assume that one leg of a very large sculpture has a force of 6,400 lbs in it and that the allowable bearing capacity of the soil is only 400 lbs/ft^2. The required area of a footing would be: area = load/allowable bearing capacity, or $A = 6,400$ lbs/(400 lbs/ft^2) = 16 ft^2. Thus a 4 ft × 4 ft foundation would be needed.

Richard M. Brown, *The Other Side of the Earth:* the rammed earth sculpture just after initial installation

The sculpture some time after installation

17.3
Richard M. Brown, *The Other Side of the Earth*. Part of the concept of this rammed earth installation is the expectation that its appearance will change over time due to the natural effects of aging and weathering. The technology used in making the work is particularly innovative.

Sculptures resting on footings placed literally on top of the ground are normally subjected to some amount of movement due to soil movements beneath the footing. These movements might come from expansion and contraction of the soil due to varying moisture conditions, or, in many parts of the country, due to freeze-thaw cycles. Consequently, footings on major works are often installed well into the ground—below the frost line—in a prepared excavation. The bottom surface of the footing is designed to rest on undisturbed ground that is not sensitive to the freeze-thaw movements in soil near the surface.

In some large works there may be a choice of using a series of individual spread footings or a single larger foundation, typically called a raft or mat (fig. 17.4). Usually the choice depends on how close individual spread footings would be to one another (if they get very closely spaced, it is often easier just to tie them together into one large mat). Very poor soil conditions often dictate the use of a large mat as a way to provide a relatively nondeformable base for a rigid structure. In these situations, rafts must be specially reinforced to deal with the various forces involved.

When ground conditions are especially poor and loads are very high, driven piles must occasionally be used. Usually these are found in larger structures only. Piles are driven through weak ground until they either hit ground with a high bearing capacity or begin to carry the loads by the action of friction alone (between pile perimeters and adjacent soil). Typically clusters of piles are driven and topped

The sculpture after extended
natural aging and weathering.

A mixture of topsoil, clay, water,
and straw was compacted with a
gasoline-powered tamper.

The formwork consisted of pine 2
in. x 4 in. members, plywood,
expanded metal lathing, and
molding plaster. The plaster lining
absorbed moisture from the
compacted soil to provide an easy
separation of the formwork from
the compacted soil.

off with a reinforced concrete cap. Frequently they are bat-
tered (driven in at slight angles to one another). Battering
particularly helps in stabilizing the top cap with respect to
wind or earthquake forces. These forces, transmitted
through the superstructure down to the pile cap, tend to
cause it to slide sideways—a phenomenon that battering
the piles helps prevent. Obviously, battering piles is necessary at best for very large structures. Piles can be designed
to resist not only downward forces, but upwardly directed
tension forces. A tall tower, for example, might actually
need to be tied down by piles to prevent it from overturning
due to laterally acting wind forces (see chapter 2). Piles can
be made of many different types of materials. Timber, steel,
and reinforced concrete piles are common.

Ground Anchors

In many cases it is necessary to transfer a tension force into
the ground. The sloped guy cables supporting Christo's
Running Fence (fig. 9.3), for example, develop tension
forces within them when they serve their function of stabilizing the fence. Uplift and associated sliding forces can be
resisted by cables simply attached to a large, heavy block on
the ground. Alternatives to this brute force method exist in
the form of different types of ground anchors (fig. 17.4). For
light forces, there are various devices that actually screw
into the ground. For heavier loads, more complex devices
exist. The underlying principle of any ground anchor of this
type is to mobilize the weight of the earth itself in resisting

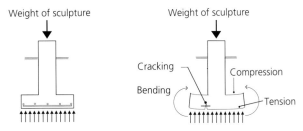

Weight of sculpture

Weight of sculpture

Cracking

Compression

Bending

Tension

Bearing stresses on soil

Reinforced concrete footings distribute point forces over larger soil area. Reactive forces cause bending in the footing. Steel reinforcing is needed to prevent cracking.

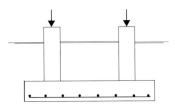

Raft or mat foundations are used for larger structures.

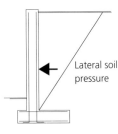

Lateral soil pressure

Retaining walls

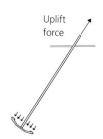

Uplift force

Ground anchors resist uplift forces

17.4
Suitable for most large-scale sculptures, simple spread footings distribute point loads onto a much wider area of soil. This reduces the bearing stresses on the soil to a sustainable value. Piles could be used beneath spread footings to carry even higher loads if necessary. Raft foundations work similarly but are much bigger and more appropriate for very large scale works. A ground anchor or tension piles are used when uplift forces are present.

the uplift or sliding forces. For exceptionally large tension forces, ground anchors can be extremely complex and involve multiple tension rods with ends buried back into the ground in a splayed fashion. Christo's *Valley Curtain* (fig. 10.1) utilized extremely heavy-duty ground anchors tied into bedrock to resist the forces of the main cables.

Walls

Freestanding Walls

Freestanding walls have long been used to define space in the landscape or serve as focal elements. Structurally, walls must be designed not to overturn or slide as a unit due to wind, earthquake effects, or their own imbalances; nor to crack up or otherwise fail due to these effects; nor to sink into the ground under their own dead weight. Walls can be made of a host of different materials, which in turn affect how stability and strength are assured. The wall can be specially configured, sunk into the ground, or supplied with special wide strip footings.

The basic need to prevent a wall from overturning or sliding can be effectively accomplished by paying careful attention to its configuration. If planar walls are configured so that wall planes or wall segments are frequently placed orthogonally to one another, then each wall braces the other. A number of the light wood structures by Mary Miss derive their stability from their orthogonally placed wall planes. These structures often simply rest on top of the soil. In long linear walls, placing short orthogonal wall segments periodically along the length of the wall in more or less buttresslike fashion achieves the same end.

Curving a wall also increases its stability. The old serpentine wall has a remarkable ability to resist overturning by virtue of its configuration. Richard Serra's various curved steel planes derive their stability from their curvatures. The tilted steel planes would naturally be unstable if the walls were straight or only slightly curved. Heavy steel structures of this type normally require a concrete footing beneath them to distribute the loads into the ground. Curving the wall also reduces the need to tie the wall down to any footing beneath it (but it's always good practice to do so anyway since lateral forces can also tend to cause a wall to slide off of its footing).

Straight walls without transverse elements can be used as well, but special care must normally be taken with respect to the way the wall meets the ground. Walls using vertical timbers can be stabilized by burying their ends in the ground (a relatively temporary solution since eventually timber rots when exposed to moisture in the earth). The series of walls containing the slanted air column defined by the cut holes in *Untitled* by Mary Miss (fig. 5.1) are each made of two vertical timbers with their ends buried in the ground, which in turn stabilize horizontally placed timbers. A number of walls are built in this general way (fig. 17.6).

In masonry or reinforced concrete, low wide forms can often be stable due to their own proportions and dead weights. Since common wall materials can be extremely heavy, strip footings are often used to distribute wall loads into the ground. The use of a wide strip footing integrally connected to the wall can also prevent overturning in exactly the same way that an expanded base and/or a heavy pedestal can prevent a singular form, such as a statue, from overturning.[6] Typically strip footings are made of concrete and connected to the wall by steel reinforcing.

Unless building in an almost vernacular vein (e.g., low unmortared stone walls) where movements or cracks are not a problem, it is usually advisable to use a strip foundation under any heavy finished wall so that the weight of the wall is adequately carried. Differential settlements associated with overstressed or poorly prepared (e.g., unconsolidated) soil can cause a wall to crack up along its length.

Strip footings on major finished walls are usually sunk below the frost line to prevent destructive movements and differential settlements associated with freeze-thaw cycles in the soil. Usually it is best to center the strip footing directly under the wall so that the forces developed at the interface between the footing and the ground are uniformly compressive. Eccentric load placement on a footing is possible but may generate some problems.

Retaining Walls

Retaining walls are common devices in sculpture as in landscape architecture. Retaining walls differ from freestanding walls in that they hold back earth materials on one side. There are many ways of making them. Parallel wood posts simply buried in the ground can work in temporary situations (the ends rot away over time). Steel sheet piling driven

17.5
Richard Serra, *Clara-Clara*. Walls are naturally stable if sufficiently curved in plan.

6
All of the stability principles discussed in chapter 5 apply to walls as well. Usually a unit length of wall (e.g., one foot) is considered in determining the applied and resisting moments in such analyses.

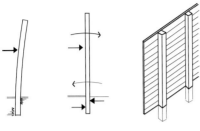

Forces developed on ground   Buried ends

17.6
Burying the end of a column in the ground stabilizes the member and prevents it from overturning. For timber columns this approach is useful only for temporary installations, since buried ends tend to degrade with time.

7
Note that if the wall were actually made of a rigid continuous material, such as reinforced concrete, and formed a complete circle, it would inherently form a very strong structure that would easily resist the forces from the soil mass. In this case, the ring would more uniformly compress instead of the top bowing inwardly. Morris's structure, however, appears to be made of individual vertical elements that do not provide this continuous rigidity in the circumferential direction. The top ring serves this function.

into the ground can also be used to make vertical wall planes. Most retaining walls, however, are made of reinforced concrete. Common reinforced concrete types include the gravity wall, the cantilever wall, and the counterfort wall. Retaining walls are subjected to lateral pressures from the retained earth that tend to cause them to slide or overturn (figs. 17.7 and 17.8). These same forces can also cause walls to bend, crack and fail.

Common retaining walls of the gravity or cantilever types are normally drawn in section because that is the way their structural actions are often conceived. The wall is imagined to continue indefinitely in the longitudinal direction. The importance of the plan configuration of a wall, however, cannot be fully appreciated in these terms. *Field Rotation* by Mary Miss (fig. 17.9) is built into the ground and utilizes retaining walls all around its periphery. In this work most of the wall surfaces are made of horizontally placed members. Long walls made with members of this type are naturally subjected to overturning. The overall wall configuration, however, is such that short segments of the wall are orthogonally placed with respect to adjacent wall planes. These short segments serve as buttressing planes that prevent overturning or sliding of the longer wall. Individual horizontal members of the wall may be thought of as spanning between braced wall segments. Forces associated with the retained soil still tend to cause bending and bowing in these horizontal members. Tie-back cables attached to buried ground anchors minimize these effects.

Circular Pit with Troughs by Mary Miss (fig. 17.10) further clarifies the importance of plan configuration. The circular ring forms a structure naturally resistant to the inwardly directed lateral pressures of the soil. Instead of a wall section providing a resistance to overturning, the entire structure is mobilized as a compression ring. As noted in chapter 12, curved plates of this kind can be extremely strong when sufficiently curved.

In Robert Morris's *Observatory* (fig. 17.11), the nearly circular ring at the top of the vertical wall plane on the interior of the ring mound serves a valuable stabilizing function for the wall. When the soil mound exerts lateral forces on the vertical wall plane (apparently composed of discrete vertical elements), the tops of the wall elements tend to deform inwardly.[7] Wall bases are stabilized by the ground. The

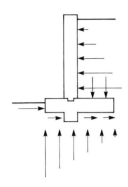

Forces acting on the retaining
wall

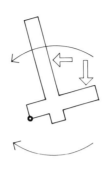

Overturning and balancing
moments

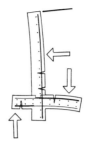

Minimum steel placement

17.7
**Lateral pressures are induced
on retaining walls that tend to
both slide and overturn them.
Extending the footing in front
of the wall and mobilizing the
weight of the earth over the
back part of the footing help
stabilize the wall and keep it
from overturning. Bending is
developed in both the vertical
wall and the footing, which
necessitates the use of steel
reinforcing at critical regions.**

8
Perhaps the most common
time for a retaining wall to fail
by overturning or sliding is after
a heavy rain when the soil is
sodden.

upper deformation tendency is resisted by the upper circumferential ring, and compressive forces are correspondingly
induced in the ring. A complete ring would naturally be
quite strong in compression and capable of resisting applied
forces from the wall tops. The incomplete nature of the ring
poses a problem (a cut ring naturally loses much of its
strength). The two stiff transverse retaining walls at the
entry, however, help reestablish the strength of the ring by
serving as surrogate ring connection pieces. The cut ring,
however, then exerts forces on the retaining walls near
their tops and tends to cause them to collapse toward each
other. These walls must be designed to resist forces of
this type.

Bearing in mind the importance of overall configuration,
it is useful to look in more detail at the nature of the forces
that act on a retaining wall. These forces stem from the tendency of an unrestrained soil mass to slip downward along a
plane described by the soil's angle of internal friction. The
sliding earth delivers a diagonal thrust against any wall
intended to prevent the sliding from occurring. The horizontal component of this downward force tends to cause a wall
to both overturn and slide. The higher the wall, the greater
is the sliding wedge of earth and, consequently, the greater
is its horizontal component that tends to cause sliding and
overturning. Any additional heavy object atop the soil near
the wall, e.g., an automobile or a tree, can add to the forces
normally associated with the soil sliding. Additional forces
can also be induced by the pressure of water or moisture in
the soil itself, particularly when the structure extends below
the ground water line.8 (Installing drains at the base of the
wall serves to reduce forces on the wall.) All of these effects

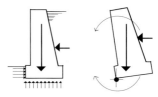

17.8
This retaining wall derives its stability from its massiveness.

9
Equivalent pressures (w') can be determined for different soil types. Well-drained gravel has a value of about 20 lbs/ft², average earth around 30 lbs/ft², wet sand around 50 lbs/ft², and mud around 100 lbs/ft².

10
See the discussion in chapter 5. In the case of a retaining wall, the overall applied force acting on a unit length that tends to cause overturning is given by $F = \frac{1}{2}w'h$, where w' is the equivalent distributed soil pressure and h is the wall height. The factor of $\frac{1}{2}$ comes from the fact that the distributed load varies from zero to a maximum, so an average value is used. This force is considered applied at one-third of the way up from the bottom of the wall (at the centroid of the triangular load area), which reflects the fact that there is more force near the bottom of the wall than at the top. The moment that tends to cause overturning is given by $M_{applied} = (\frac{1}{2}w'h)(h/3) = w'h^2/6$. In a gravity wall, the moment available to resist overturning is given by $M_{resisting} = W \times (d/2)$, where W is the weight of the wall per unit length and d is the base width. If $M_{applied} > M_{resisting}$ the wall will overturn. If $M_{applied} < M_{resisting}$ the wall will not overturn. A safety factor should be used in designing to prevent overturning.

are sometimes modeled into a single lateral distributed force (called the equivalent fluid pressure) acting against the side of the wall that varies from zero near the top to a maximum value at the base of the wall.[9] The triangular distribution of forces follows from the original triangular wedge model. When the wall is low, the wedge is small and little force is exerted on the wall. Increases in height and associated mass accumulations lead to linearly increasing lateral forces, as shown in figure 17.7.

Gravity walls of the type shown in figure 17.8 resist these sliding and overturning forces through a combination of their proportions and their dead weights (in much the same way that a sculpture with a heavy base resists overturning).[10] The shorter, wider, and heavier the wall, the better able it is to resist lateral forces.

Cantilever walls of the kind shown in figure 17.7 are more sophisticated than gravity walls in that they mobilize the weight of the earth itself to help prevent overturning. Overturning cannot occur in a wall of this type unless the stem of the wall underneath the retained earth either lifts the earth mass on top of it or breaks off. The longer the stem, the more stable is the wall. The weight of the stem itself also helps prevent overturning, as does the extended toe of the footing on the front side of the wall that extends

17.9
Mary Miss, *Field Rotation*. The walls of this work derive their stability from both tie-backs into the surrounding ground and the judicious presence of short transverse wall segments that stiffen the longer walls.

17.10
Mary Miss, *Circular Pit with Troughs*. The rings derive their stability and resistance to lateral earth pressures from their closed configuration. The complete rings naturally form a stable structure.

the base width of the structure.[11] These structures are quite efficient.

In designing cantilever walls, care must be taken to assure that the bending moments induced in the structure by the forces associated with the retained soil do not cause any part of the structure to fail. Bending stresses can be quite high in the back and vertical stems, as well as in the extended toe. In reinforced concrete walls, special steel reinforcing is introduced to prevent the wall from cracking due to these bending stresses. Steel is placed where the tension stresses associated with bending are the highest (fig. 17.7). Hence a lot of steel is typically placed where the stems and toes connect. In addition to transverse steel in the section, longitudinal steel is also placed along the length of the wall to prevent cracking from occurring along vertical planes.

There are many variants of the basic cantilever design. The extended front toe, for example, need not always be used, wall thicknesses are sometimes varied, and so forth. Presumably the two concrete walls evident in Herbert Bayer's *Mill Creek Canyon Earthworks* (fig. 17.12) are cantilever walls without front toe planes. This work also illustrates the obvious point that retaining walls need not be of constant height. Bayer's work is particularly elegant in a purely technical as well as a visual sense—the longitudinal slope of the wall height matches the natural slope of the earth behind it, which is presumably at or near the angle of repose for the mound material itself.

11
In evaluating whether a wall like this will overturn, the extended toe distance and weights of the stem and earth mass are calculated in as part of the resisting moment when considering whether $M_{applied}$ is equal to, less than, or greater than $M_{resisting}$.

Forces on rings

Forces on retaining walls

Counterfort walls are similar to cantilevered retaining walls but have transverse buttressing vertical planes placed periodically along their lengths. They function as basic cantilever walls in terms of the way they resist overturning. The periodically placed vertical planes dramatically increase the stiffness of the vertical walls, however, and reduce dependence on wall thickness and related reinforcing steel to carry the bending moments induced in the stems by the soil forces. The need for steel reinforcing, however, is not eliminated. The counterfort wall also has many variants. The buttressing vertical planes may either be placed on the outside of the wall or buried in the soil mass.

Many other types of retaining walls can be devised as well. A particularly interesting approach is to provide point supports to the wall by a series of ground anchors of one form or another that are drilled into the earth horizontally. These point supports stabilize the wall with respect to overturning and sliding and also serve to reduce the bending moments present in the wall. Wall thicknesses, steel amounts, and lengths of horizontal stems can all be correspondingly reduced. A variant on this approach that is particularly useful when retaining filled earth is to build layers of heavy-duty geotextiles into the earth and then connect the walls to the geotextiles.

17.12
Herbert Bayer, *Mill Creek Canyon Earthworks*. The cantilever walls are subjected to lateral forces and overturning tendencies from the soil. The walls are generally sloped in correspondence with the angle of repose of the soil (see chapter 19).

Materials

Michael Heizer, *Dragged Mass Geometric* (installation view, Whitney Museum of American Art, 1985).

18.0
Robert Smithson, *Closed Mirror
Square.*

18 Material Types and Properties

The nature of materials plays an intrinsic role in sculpture, either directly as an influence on form via a consideration of material characteristics and fabrication processes, or indirectly—perhaps even as part of a quest to disassociate the materiality of a work from other intents. The necessity of taking some position toward materials, however, has proven unavoidable. And why not, after all, since physical sculptures must be made of something or they would not exist.

Physical sculptures can be made from virtually any material. The properties of the material selected and the way it can be worked normally inform the specific shaping or the assemblage of a sculpture; alternatively, a determined intent to create a precisely conceived form may severely limit the selection of materials available for use.

Common sculptural materials include those that are naturally found in their fundamental organic or inorganic states and those that are essentially synthetic in nature. Various woods and stones are typically directly used in their natural states. Other materials are processed to a greater or lesser extent before they assume their common forms (metals such as copper are derived from copper-bearing ore, for example, through a heating process), and many are combined with other materials during these processes to produce new materials with unique characteristics (bronze is a combination of copper and tin, for example). Many materials are highly synthetic and are formed as a result of physical and chemical interactions between constituent ingredients. Many of the newer materials—plastics—fall into this category.

Associated with each type of material are certain physical properties that affect both the way a sculptor can work with the material and what forms can be made with it. The physical properties of a material are those that are intrinsic to the material itself at the atomic or molecular scale, and include factors such as strength, ductility, and hardness. Materials may be homogeneous with respect to these properties or may internally vary in some organized or random way. These characteristics in turn affect very directly the suitability of a material for carving, modeling, or assemblage.

From a structural perspective, two broad categories of material properties are of interest. First, there are the mechanical properties of different materials that stem from their internal constituency or makeup. A primary property, *strength* (a measure of the relative ability of a material to carry internal stresses), has already been introduced in chapter 2. Other properties, such as brittleness, ductility, and malleability, are equally important. *Brittle* materials exhibit virtually no visible deformations prior to failure when stressed. Many brittle materials can carry compressive stresses well, but fail easily when subjected to tension, bending, or torsional stresses. Failure occurs seemingly instantaneously and without prior visual warning. Cast iron and glass are brittle materials. *Ductile* materials undergo large, normally visible, deformations as the material is loaded to near failure, but retain their ability to carry loads while these deformations occur. Ductile materials normally have a significant ability to carry tension stresses as well as compressive stresses. Steel is a ductile material. *Malleable* materials are those that can be easily beaten into thin sheets. Malleability and ductility are not the same thing. Lead is a highly malleable material that has little ductility. Other properties such as hardness or optical qualities (transparency, reflectivity, etc.) may be important as well, depending on the application.

There are also important properties associated with the performance of a material over time. Certain materials are particularly prone to corrosion or other time-dependent effects that might seriously weaken a structural member or a connection. On the other hand, materials such as concrete may actually gain strength with time. Materials may weather in particular ways that may be desirable, such as the beautiful patina that can develop on copper; or undesirable, such as the loss of surface detail in sandstone carvings due to erosion from wind or rain.

It is impossible to discuss all of the important characteristics of materials in this brief coverage and only the more salient points will be addressed. This chapter introduces different materials and their characteristics; the following chapter focuses more explicitly on the mechanical properties of different materials and defines measures such as "strength" in detail.

Metals

Metals have long been used in sculpture. Most metals commonly available—copper, iron, bronze, brass, gold, silver, lead, aluminum—have been used at one time or another. There are many different methods for working with different metals to produce sculptural forms. One classic method involves casting molten metals directly to make sculptural forms. Another method involves first making basic geometric shapes (bars, plates, sheets, rods) and subsequently working them via various hammering and heating processes—thus making wrought objects. Repoussé involves the hammering of very thin sheets into complex three-dimensional shapes. Which technique is most suitable depends greatly on the actual physical properties of the material— the subject of this chapter—in relation to its intended use.

Metals are usually classified as ferrous (containing iron) or nonferrous. Steel, wrought iron, and cast iron are all ferrous metals, while aluminum, copper, tin, brass, and bronze are nonferrous metals. Many of these metals are actually *alloys*, or composite materials. Bronze contains copper and tin, for example, while brass consists primarily of copper and zinc. The precise composition of a metal strongly affects its mechanical properties, such as strength or ductility, and the way it can be fabricated or subsequently worked with by a sculptor. For example, steel differs in chemical composition from cast iron primarily in terms of its lower carbon content. Cast iron is a hard, brittle material that withstands heat quite well. Steel has much more ductility and malleability than cast iron, but cannot be easily cast and must be rolled or otherwise formed. Steel is intrinsically stronger and less prone to exhibiting large deformations when stressed than are materials such as copper.

The precise way a metal is cast or rolled, worked by hammering, or subsequently treated by processes such as annealing also strongly affects its final properties. Hammering metals into thin sheets, for example, typically increases the hardness of the metal while at the same time increasing its brittleness and sensitivity to fracture. Consequently, elements are often heated to certain temperatures and slowly cooled (a process called annealing), which toughens the metal and again makes it more ductile. These different mechanical and heat treatment processes will be introduced in more detail below in connection with steel, but similar processes are used with many different metals (the precise way they affect the materials, however, varies).

Metals can and do deteriorate through phenomena such as corrosion. The term "corrosion" generally refers to the deterioration of a metal by chemical or electrochemical reaction with its environment, which is often accompanied by the development of a surface oxide or incrustation. Corrosion is a general phenomenon affecting most metals. Platinum, gold, and copper are among the less corrosive of metals, while plain iron is among the more corrosive. Corrosion is discussed more extensively below.

Steel
Basic material characteristics and production. Steel consists primarily of iron, carbon, silicon, phosphorus, and manganese. The amount of carbon present in steel varies from near zero to about 1.5 percent. A steel with low carbon content is ductile and malleable. Increasing the carbon content increases hardness and enables steel to be more castable, but also decreases ductility. Other elements are added to improve workability or impart specific properties to the final steel (e.g., small amounts of silicon increase the strength of steel without affecting its ductility).

There are several procedures for manufacturing steel. Commonly, a blast furnace is first used to separate iron from iron-bearing ores that contain many other minerals as well. This first product from a furnace is called pig iron. A furnace is charged with iron ore, limestone, and coke in layers and heated to very high temperatures. Molten pig iron settles to the bottom and is tapped off to harden into ingots or pigs; slag and other impurities float to the top and are removed. Oxygen in the iron ore is the oxidizing agent that combines with the silicon, manganese, and phosphorus also normally present to produce the slag, and with the carbon present to produce a carbon dioxide gas. The pigs are then fed into an electric or open hearth furnace, along with further limestone and scrap iron, for further refining and oxidizing until impurities are reduced to desired percentages. Heating is also continued until the carbon is removed to a level below that eventually desired. Later additional carbon is added

through a recarburizing process (ferromanganese with coal, coke, or charcoal is added to the metal in the ladle) until the desired level is reached. Melting points of various steels are in the 2,600° to 2,800° range. Molten steel is again tapped off to be formed into ingots by a rough press. A roughing mill converts the ingots into various large shapes (billets, blooms, and slabs). These primary elements are then run back and forth under intense pressure provided by large rollers, which further shapes them into bars, structural shapes, sheet products, and so forth. This rolling can take place with either hot or cold shapes. Billets are used to make bars, wires, and seamless pipe. Blooms are used to make structural shapes (wide-flange beams, channels, angles). Slabs are used to make plates, cold rolled sheets, and large-diameter welded pipe.

The primary components (plates, pipes, structural shapes) are produced in major steel plants and become the elements that a sculptor, architect, or engineer, has available to work with. A specific design using these elements is actually made in a local steel fabricating yard, where these basic components are further worked. There is a close relation among the type and physical dimensions of the primary steel elements, an appropriate fabricating process, and the actual shapes and forms that can be created. Large pieces can be cleanly cut, holes drilled or punched, members curved, surfaces given special treatments, and so forth. Large plates, for example, can be given simple curves by running them through large rollers (fig. 18.1). Thinner sheets can be stamped or pressed into three-dimensional shapes.

Various types of steel suited to particular purposes can be made using the processes described. Common ductile steel used in building construction is made using a carbon content on the order of 0.25 to 0.29 percent and has a minimum yield strength of 36,000 lbs/in². Much higher-strength steels are also available. Steel is intrinsically a stiff material and highly resistant to deformations (it has a high modulus of elasticity; see chapter 19). Steel used for molded castings (common in big machine parts) has a significantly higher carbon content, and is consequently harder but more brittle than common building steel.

Various alloying elements can be introduced to alter the properties of the final steel. Stainless steel, for example,

Ute Rothenberg, *Lazy Wave*

Rolling mill

18.1
Fabrication of curved steel plates. Flat plates are run through a rolling machine to curve them.

which tends to resist corrosion better than normal steel, is made by adding from 10 to 30 percent of chromium to basic steel. Nickel is often added as well. Small amounts of copper are often added to improve resistance to atmospheric corrosion, or when the steel is to be used primarily lfor sheet metal products. Special weathering steel has also been developed (often called Corten after an original brand name) that acquires a protective oxide coat with time that inhibits rust and corrosion. The oxide coating has a deep sepia tone. The coating itself is fragile and can be easily scratched or marred—marks that cannot be easily removed or covered. During rains, some of this oxide coating is carried away and can stain surfaces below the steel. This steel is usually recommended only for places where maintenance via painting is a problem due to the inaccessibility of the members (e.g., towers) and where the material is not likely to be scratched and its stains will not be a problem.

Normal building steel can be easily bolted, riveted, or welded. Welding stainless steel requires special techniques to avoid destroying the "stainless" character of the metal, but is possible (see chapter 14).

Effects of mechanical and heat treatments. The final character of metals is greatly affected by various mechanical and heat treatments. Ancient treatments, such as hammering and tempering, have long been used to affect the properties of metals and reduce flaws present. Many of the heat and mechanical rolling processes used today lead to the same ends.

These treatments affect the crystalline structure of metals at a very basic level. Of interest here is the distinction between coarse- and fine-grained crystalline structures. Fine-grained structures are generally preferable because of increased yield strengths and toughnesses. Grain structures are affected by both cooling rates and working processes. Big steel ingots fresh from a furnace that are allowed to cool in air will tend to have fine-grained structures in external layers and coarse-grained structures internally. Recrystallization takes place during hot rolling (a working process) and alters the grain structure of an ingot to a more uniform size distribution. Cold rolling further breaks down the grains and leaves the material in a harder and stronger state, albeit stressed somewhat since recrystallization cannot occur at low temperatures. Large steel shapes, such as wide-flange

1
See Massimo Leoni, "Observations on Ancient Bronze Casting," *The Horses of San Marco* (n.p.: Olivetti, 1977).

beams, are rarely cold-rolled because of their size and the difficulty of the process. They are hot-rolled instead. Smaller products, such as wire, are typically cold-drawn to achieve a smaller grain size and higher strength. Hammering processes can have similar results on grain sizes as rolling processes, but are suitable only for smaller pieces.

Affecting grain structures through cooling rate variations is accomplished through traditional means of quenching, normalizing, and annealing. *Quenching* is a process suitable for small elements only. Quenching is often done in an iced brine. It is the most rapid means of cooling available and is quite drastic (cracking and distortions can easily occur). The process changes the character of the metal significantly, producing a steel material called martensite that is extremely hard and quite brittle. Internal stresses produced by the process (by differential cooling rates of different parts of the element) are high. Further treatments, notably *tempering*, are carried out to improve the toughness of the material. In tempering, the material is reheated to a moderate temperature to allow some recrystallization to occur, but not to a level that results in a loss of strength and hardness.

Normalization is controlled cooling in still air, after first moderately reheating the metal to achieve some recrystallization. The resulting fine-grained structure produces a steel slightly harder and stronger than annealed steel. Big sections, however, cannot be normalized because their cooling rates are too low.

Annealing is a process of heating and slowly cooling that is used to toughen and reduce the brittleness in steel. It can be done at any stage in the process of making the metal and can be applied to fairly large sections. In addition to reducing the grain from a coarser to a finer state, it can also relieve internal stresses resulting from cold working. Annealing is done quite slowly. Heating takes place gradually and a form of recrystallization slowly takes place. Overheating can be detrimental and can lead to weakness and brittleness. Cooling is also done slowly. Annealed steel has a higher ductility than normalized steel and is easier to machine, but has a lower yield strength.

These same processes are used to affect the qualities of other metals as well. Many respond similarly to steel; others may be affected differently. For example, rapid cooling of bronze causes it to become softer rather than harder.

Bronze

Bronze has traditionally enjoyed great popularity as a sculptural medium. Bronze has a high structural strength, approximating that of normal structural steel, and is a tough metal that resists abrasion well. It is relatively easy to work with and takes a good finish. It has a high resistance to atmospheric corrosion. Pieces can be soldered, riveted, or bolted together.

Bronze is an alloy consisting primarily of copper and smaller amounts of tin. The addition of tin to copper increases the strength, hardness, and durability of the metal. Varying small percentages of other metals, zinc and often lead, are sometimes added (although major amounts of zinc begin to produce brasses). Lead lowers the melting point of the bronze. Aluminum bronze results when aluminum is alloyed with copper. The term cast bronze refers to shapes formed by the solidification of molten bronze in a mold, while wrought bronze refers to shapes formed by heating bronze and then working it by rolling or hammering.

There are many ways in which bronze can be cast, with the sand mold and lost wax processes, described below, being common. Most larger castings are made hollow, which reduces the amount of material needed and helps prevent excessive metal shrinkage during cooling (which in turn might cause distortions and even cracking). Sand-casting processes yield less intricate forms but are more suitable for larger pieces and more repetitive castings. Forms of the lost wax process described below can yield intricate castings, but the process is easiest for relatively small pieces and is not particularly suitable to making large numbers of repetitive copies, although many large pieces have surely been made this way (see fig. 18.2).[1]

Sand mold processes can be used for repeated castings. In the sand mold process, a plaster positive is made of an original clay model. Within a casting frame or "flask," fine casting sand is subsequently dampened and packed around the plaster reproduction, which is then removed. Highly three-dimensional objects may require sectioning the casting and preparing several individual flasks that are eventually clamped together. Grooves are cut into the sand beds to provide gates for the flow of the molten bronze and vents for the eventual escape of the gases produced during casting. A larger feeder channel for the molten material is also

18.2
The casting of a bronze equestrian statue of Louis XIV in 1695 by the City of Paris. A variant of the lost wax method of casting was used. The description given here is adapted from the account provided by Bouffand in 1743.

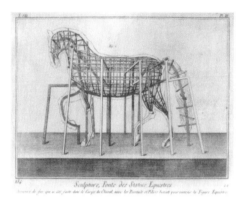

A plaster model was made from a clay original. A casting countermold of fitted plaster blocks that could be disassembled was made from the plaster model.

The blocks were brushed with hot wax to varying thicknesses. The wax linings were removed to obtain a wax model exactly like the plaster statue. Sections were reassembled so that the iron framework to support the internal core could be made.

The external mold was made by gently applying successive layers of *luto* over the wax. In this case the *luto* was a mixture of Chatillon earth, dung, ground broken white crucibles, dried urine, and egg whites. *Luto* models easily and does not crack when drying. Four layers were used. Twenty additional layers of *luto* with added cloth clippings were applied. Fuller's earth was added and the whole wrapped in iron bands to give it the necessary stiffness and strength. Walls were then built and the remaining space filled. The assembly was moderately heated to melt the wax.

The core was made of sand, dung, and cloth clippings. The intricate wax sections were applied to the core. Runners and vents were fixed by means of hollow wax rods.

The mold was again heated until red in color. It was then cooled and buried with only three feeder gates protruding. A basin for the molten metal was made above the gates. The casting metal came from old cannons, copper, brass, tin, and an ingot from the casting of the statue of Sextus Marius.

cut into the sand. The feeder channels, vents, and gates are all interconnected. The sand mold is then dried and hardened in an oven. For hollow castings, a carefully fitted inner core is made as well (moist sand or other materials are often shaped over a metal armature). The inner core is suspended within the disassembled primary mold by means of various small rods or nails. The flasks are reassembled. The metal flask is then put in a casting pit and molten bronze continuously poured into it. Initial hardening can shortly occur. Flasks are removed and inner cores pulled out. Surface finishing then takes place.

Processes for making smaller, more intricate sculptures are more complex. A brief look at how some of Degas's last works were cast is illustrative. Degas had left many wax and clay originals in his studio at his death, which were hidden from the advancing Germans during the First World War. Under the direction of Degas's friend, the sculptor Bartholomé, many were subsequently selected for casting in bronze. The process chosen because of its fidelity was the *cire perdue* or lost wax technique, to be executed by A. Hebrard, a great master of his day. A piece mold in plaster was made from each wax or clay original. Original plaster models were then cast from these molds to serve as the basis for the limited edition of twenty-two copies of each work. Twenty-two negative molds of thick elastic gelatine or glue were consequently made from every original plaster model. A mold consisted of two halves, which when put together contained a void in the shape of the work. Its inside was coated with a layer of hot wax, then filled with a core of fire-resisting material. Wax appendages were added to form the gates and the vents. Since the wax was to be melted out in an oven, pins held the cores suspended in the mold. Heating melted out the wax. Molten bronze was poured in, the mold broken away, and a bronze replica awaited touch-ups (e.g., removal of attached channels and vents of bronze).[2]

The method described above is only one of many different forms of the lost wax process, ancient in its origins. Perhaps the most basic method used from antiquity to the present that is capable of producing finely detailed small works consists of making a model out of wax and covering it with an outer shell of fine refractory clay or newer synthetic material impervious to heat. Feeder gate tubes are

2
This process is described in John Rewald, *Degas Sculpture* (New York: Harry Abrams, 1956), p. 28.

inserted through this shell for later pouring in the molten bronze, and vent tubes for the escape of gases produced during the casting. If the outer shell is of clay, it is air-dried and then heated until the wax dissipates. Molten bronze is poured into the cavity. The outer shell is chipped away or otherwise removed after cooling. A solid bronze piece results. This method is suitable for small works only and destroys the original wax carving. A variant of the method is designed to produce larger, hollow works. A rough clay core is first made and covered with wax, which is then subsequently carved in the final image. Various pins or separators are added to maintain the relative placement of the clay core and the final outer shell after the wax is burned away. The outer shell is added, along with vents and gates. Drying, heating, and adding the molten bronze follows. The outer shell is chipped away. The inner core is scooped out, in configurations where voids allow access to it. Sometimes the sculpture is cast in pieces, which allows direct removal of the core.

A more involved process designed to yield repeated castings involves making a rough wax image to establish the size and shape of the work to be cast. An inner core of refractory material (and armature if necessary) is then made. Wax is brushed on and then carved to the intricacy desired in the final casting. A master mold (often of plaster) especially designed for easy removal is made from this carving. The inside of this master mold is coated with wax until the desired thickness of the final casting is obtained, and the mold is then reassembled. A core (often of liquid clay) is added. The mold is then removed and the new wax image is carefully retouched. Vents and feeders, also made of wax, are attached. Layers of refractory clay are gently brushed or poured over the wax to form the inner surface of the external core, which is subsequently completed with refractory sand packed inside of a flask. The assembly is subsequently heated to dry the shells and dissipate the wax. Molten bronze is poured through feeders, with gases escaping out through the vents. The flask and shells are removed, the feeders are cut off, and the surface of the final casting retouched and refinished as necessary. The master mold can be used again to make new copies. A variant of this process involves the use of an elastomeric material in the master mold (as described previously). Given the complex history of bronze, innumerable variants of these basic approaches as well as other techniques have been developed.

Today, a whole series of different kinds of materials, often synthetic, can be used as substitutes for the various moldings and casting enclosures described above. The process, however, is largely the same.

The way bronze is treated after casting the molten material is quite important. When bronze is allowed to cool slowly it can become quite hard but brittle. Rapidly cooling molten bronze will cause it to become softer and more malleable. The material thus significantly differs from steel in these respects.

While an excellent material if used properly, bronze is susceptible to many problems associated with corrosion when material properties, casting techniques, or final environments are not properly controlled. A major problem related to poor casting techniques can be the porosity of the walls. Moisture can be transmitted through the walls of a casting even if direct cracks or passages are not present. Sloppy casting (blowholes), shrinkage voids, or even pieces of plaster left over from the molding process can cause this kind of porosity. External moisture associated with rains or high humidity can thus reach the inside of a work, accumulate there, and cause destructive corrosive reactions to occur. Internal condensation can cause similar accumulations of moisture inside a work. Migration of this moisture through the walls to the outside can result in efflorescence and the consequent deposition of whitish minerals on external surfaces.

Copper, Brass, and Lead

Copper occurs naturally in its elemental form and in sulfide and oxide ores. To make pure copper from sulfide ores, concentrated ores are sent through a roasting process in which impurities, slag, carbon dioxide, and oxygen are removed; the resulting copper is then subjected to electrolytic refining to form pure copper, and the copper is cast into various ingot and billet forms. Wire, sheet, and other products are subsequently made.

Copper is a highly ductile and malleable material that can easily be bent, formed, forged, stamped, and soldered. Copper's corrosion resistance is excellent. Oxides form and coat the surface, which slows corrosion. Copper is one of the "noblest" metals with respect to the phenomenon of electrolysis (described below). It behaves like a cathode with respect to other metals it touches and hence is protected by the other metals at their expense. Copper is resistant to most acids.

Brass is fundamentally an alloy of copper and zinc. Brass is generally harder than copper and can withstand abuse better. During manufacture it can be easily shaped. Generally, brass weathers well and resists corrosion well, even though its zinc content can lead to some problems.

Lead is a highly malleable but nonductile material that is easy to work and has good weathering properties. On exposure to atmospheric conditions, a protective coating of lead carbonate forms. Lead may undergo electrolytic corrosion if it comes into contact with copper.

Cast Iron and Wrought Iron

Two iron-based metals, cast iron and wrought iron, were widely used prior to the development of steel and remain in use for special purposes. Cast iron has a much higher carbon content than steel. It was originally obtained by reducing iron ore using charcoal and then coke. The molten material absorbed carbon from the coke, thus rendering the metal castable and the final material hard but brittle (and susceptible to shattering). Compressive strengths of this material are high, but tensile strengths are very low. As the name implies, it is typically cast into molds. In the sand-casting process, a model of a sculptural work is first made (of wood or occasionally clay or plaster). Molds are made by packing special refractory sand around a shape much like the traditional processes used for bronze castings. The level of detail obtainable is usually fairly low due to the mold medium, and would not have the same finish qualities as bronze or other traditional sculptural metals.

Wrought iron has a long and impressive history of use in building, particularly in fences and similar traceries. It is an ancient material. In contrast to cast iron, it has a relatively low carbon content. The material was originally obtained by reducing iron ore in open pits and beating in the resulting nuggets and slag by hand. The low carbon content and incorporated slag yielded a highly ductile material with both high compressive and tensile strengths that was readily workable via hammering and forging, but was not castable.

Later processes varied pig iron to produce wrought iron, and more mechanized processes were developed to produce larger pieces. Rolling techniques similar to those described for steel were used to produce common flat, round, and square shapes suitable for subsequent fabrication. The material has good resistance to corrosion. The "wrought iron" used by many craft blacksmiths today is actually a form of mild steel.

Aluminum

Aluminum is a lightweight but strong and highly versatile material capable of serving many of the same functions as steel, although it is not as intrinsically stiff. Aluminum can be used to make structural members, rods, sheets, tubes, wires, and so forth.

Aluminum is made by first obtaining aluminum oxide from the ore (found principally as bauxite), often by means of a reduction furnace that involves the application of high charges of electricity (and is consequently highly energy intensive). Various alloying elements may be added during the latter steps of the process to impart certain desired properties. For example, corrosion resistance (already good) can be further improved through the addition of manganese. Materials obtained during manufacture are subsequently rolled or extruded through dies to form specific products.

Aluminum weighs only about one-third as much as steel. Its failure strengths may match those of common structural steels. However, its inherent stiffness or resistance to deformations (as reflected by its low modulus of elasticity value; see chapter 19) is about one-third that of steel. This makes aluminum about three times as susceptible as steel to deflections when used as a structural element (it is this lack of intrinsic stiffness that helps prevent its more widespread use in lieu of steel in larger engineering constructions). Temperature expansions and contractions are about double those of steel.

A reactive material, aluminum nonetheless resists corrosion because a thin coating of aluminum oxide develops on exposed surfaces to seal off the material beneath. Once it is sealed, further corrosion is minimized. In unpolluted atmospheres, aluminum may be left unpainted. Still, aluminum may corrode in the presence of some substances, such as fresh damp cement paste or metals such as copper or iron (especially if chloride ions are present). Paints containing copper or lead may be harmful. Further protection can be obtained through processes such as anodizing, in which aluminum is electrolytically coated with protective oxides of various colors.

Welding is possible but is difficult, partly because of the oxide film that must first be removed. Arc welding with an inert gas shield that excludes atmospheric oxygen and nitrogen is possible (see chapter 14). Any anodizing makes welded connections virtually impossible, so other forms of connections must be used.

Corrosion and Related Problems in Metals
Corrosion is a commonplace occurrence in any metalwork. In metal sculptures corrosion can be particularly destructive. Structurally, members or connections can be seriously weakened by the deterioration associated with corrosion. A good example of structural dangers caused directly by corrosion is provided by Alexander Milne Calder's *William Penn* in Philadelphia. The statue sits on top of Philadelphia's City Hall tower and was originally connected to its base by a series of wrought iron bolts (fig. 18.3). These bolts were obviously critical in keeping the statue in place; without them it would surely have overturned and fallen from its precarious perch when subjected to even relatively low winds. With time, the original wrought iron bolts corroded severely. The white dots at the base of the statue are evidence of this corrosion. The corrosion penetrated beyond the bolt heads and nuts and attacked the bolt shafts, severely weakening them. As a consequence, the stability of the statue was potentially endangered, creating a major public safety issue. The bolts were replaced in the early 1970s and the statue was rendered secure.[3] In *William Penn*, the source of the corrosion was electrolytic in nature, stemming from the juxtaposition of two dissimilar metals—a complex phenomenon long appreciated but poorly understood until present times.

Surface deterioration of several forms can also occur. In bronze an initial conversion of surfaces to a form of copper sulfate can first occur, followed by streaking and black scab formation, then by the spread of pitting, and finally by the conversion of all exposed surfaces to sulfate.

Dealing with corrosion is a major problem faced by

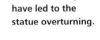
Bolt failure might have led to the statue overturning.

Alexander Milne Calder, *William Penn*

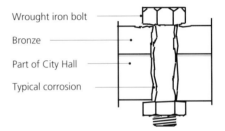
Wrought iron bolt

Bronze

Part of City Hall

Typical corrosion

The strengths of the bolts connecting the base of the statue to the top of the tower were significantly reduced by the effects of corrosion.

18.3
Corrosion is a common problem in metals. Problems with corrosion may have serious structural implications. The problem with the connecting bolts on A. M. Calder's *William Penn* was corrected during a major restoration effort.

3
This example is drawn from an article by Andrew Lins in Virginia N. Naude, ed., *Sculptural Monuments in an Outdoor Environment* (Philadelphia: Pennsylvania Academy of Art, 1985). This excellent publication documents many issues and problems associated with the conservation of outdoor sculpture.

conservators and others. For example, consider the *Rhinoceroses* executed in 1937 that were placed outside the biological laboratories on the Harvard University campus (fig. 18.4). In recent years, the rhinos suffered from a problem common in the placement of bronze in exterior urban environments. Acid rain had attacked the bronze surface of the rhinos, etching the surface and producing a light green copper sulfate corrosion product in an irregular pattern. The presence of this copper sulfate on any bronze sculpture not only affects the appearance of the sculpture but also promotes the further corrosion of the sculpture's exterior surface and ultimately results in loss of surface detail. This chemical reaction when combined with sooty air may also produce a black film in areas adjacent to the green weathering product. If this corrosion is not prevented, serious aesthetic damage will occur. Eventually structural damage may also occur. Poor detailing can create conditions where corrosion develops. The rhinos also suffered from a water condensation problem in their hollow interiors. No weep holes (small drain holes in areas where water could collect) were originally provided, nor was any provision made for adequate natural ventilation of the interior. Condensation eventually accumulated a significant amount of water (approximately 10 gallons!) inside the lowest portions of the rhinos' interior (the belly and the feet). Some of this accumulated water actually migrated through the casting to the surface of the sculpture (a process known as efflorescence) and caused the deposit of whitish discoloring minerals to appear on the surface. This can be noticed at the foot of the rhino in figure 18.4. In recent restoration work, the surfaces of the rhinos were cleaned and refinished. Weep holes were provided in the belly and feet to drain any further condensation that might develop.[4]

The causes of corrosive phenomena are extremely complex and will not be treated in depth here. Ultimately, the causes are traceable to imperfections within the crystalline lattice structure of metals. Under certain conditions— exposure to air and water and the juxtaposition of dissimilar materials—the atomic bonding forces of the lattice become unstable, which in turn leads to a deterioration of the metal. Although all corrosive phenomena are ultimately the same, it is nonetheless useful to describe corrosive effects with respect to oxidation, electrolytic corrosion, and acidic corrosion.

18.4
Katherine Ward Lane Weems, *Rhinoceroses.* **The pair of bronze rhinos, executed in 1937, experienced considerable damage due to corrosion. The statues were recently restored.**

Katherine Ward Lane Weems, *Rhinoceroses*

Lack of ventilation and weep holes allowed condensation to accumulate inside, causing corrosion.

Corrosion and efflorescence occurred at the foot of the rhinoceros where water gathered.

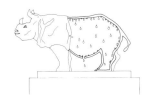

Weep holes were installed during restoration.

4
Information on the rhinos was made available through Mr. Henry Lie of Harvard University's Conservation Department, located in the Fogg Art Museum.

Oxidation. The internal metallic bond that gives materials such as bronze or iron their strength is fundamentally unstable in an oxygen-containing atmosphere at normal temperatures. Metal atoms near the surface of a form are normally reactive and tend to combine with oxygen molecules in the air to produce a metallic oxide. The rate of oxide formation depends of many factors (e.g., the permeability of the oxide coating to metallic and oxygen ions). The oxide may be tightly or loosely bound to the metal. When impermeable and tightly bound, the oxidized surface itself prevents further oxidation from occurring beneath the surface. In some materials, the rate of oxidation decreases very quickly and the material reaches a more or less steady state. Lead, zinc, chromium, and many aluminum products exhibit these properties and are thus widely used in exterior environments. In many cases, alloying elements are added to a base material to produce a protective film. Nickel or chromium is often added to iron for this reason. The addition of certain amounts of carbon to steel to affect other mechanical properties, however, can lead to a softening of the surface, since carbon oxidizes more quickly than steel.

Acidic corrosion. When exposed to moisture or an aqueous solution, metal ions on a surface and ions in the solution tend to react with one another. Positive metal ions may leave the surface of the metal and enter the solution, leaving a slight negative charge on the remaining metal. This process continues until remaining electrons set up a sufficient negative voltage to oppose further release of positive ions. Or a converse reaction could occur in which material from the solution is deposited on the surface of the metal. These processes normally continue until a state of dynamic equilibrium is reached due to a balancing of electrical charges in the adjacent materials.

When metals are exposed to certain highly acidic environments, the steady state dynamic equilibrium noted above cannot be reached because of the excess concentration of ions in the acid. Corrosion will continue as the two adjacent environments seek to reach a steady state.

Electrolytic corrosion. This process is similar to that described for acidic corrosion. In this case, however, the change in potential that disrupts the steady state condition and leads to corrosion arises from the joining of two dissimilar metals. One of the metals has a lower negative potential on the electrolytic scale than the other, which gives rise to an exchange of ions: one metal becomes an anode, and the other a cathode. Electron flow is from the anode to the cathode. Zinc and copper connected in a solution containing sulfates, for example, will produce an electron flow from the zinc to the copper. The zinc (the anode) will tend to dissolve, creating zinc salts.

The results of electrolytic phenomena are commonplace and very evident when dissimilar metals are placed in contact with one another. Securing copper sheets with steel nails will result in the steel corroding rapidly. This phenomenon is particularly a problem in many sculptures. Highly detrimental corrosion occurred between the copper enclosure skin of the Statue of Liberty and the attachments to the puddled iron armature (see the discussion on the statue in chapter 15).

The electrolytic phenomenon is complex and can even occur within the same material. The rusting of steel, for example, is chiefly electrolytic, with the anodes and cathodes being different parts of the same member—parts that are different because of slight nonuniformities in makeup, junctures of grain boundaries, and variations of this sort.

Electrolytic corrosion can cause surface pitting. A scratch in an oxide coating can cause the coating to behave as a cathode with respect to the base metal. In steel, rust builds up on the cathodic mill scale while cavities form in the metal underneath. The small surface area of a scratch intensifies the anodic action, causing pitting to develop.

Related issues. Casting and assembly techniques can strongly influence rates of corrosion. Surfaces that have fine-grained structures and are relatively homogeneous tend to be more corrosion-resistant than larger-grained structures. Fine-grained structures often occur when cast metals first hit a mold (in thin castings, fine-grained structures can exist more or less throughout). As subsequent material solidifies during the casting of thicker pieces, grain structures become larger. Larger crystal dendrites are formed that are relatively pure, with intergranular eutectic formations between. In a corrosive environment, the purer dendrites often stand up quite well, but the intergranular formations are subjected to attack and consequently etched away. Thus the relative thickness or thinness of a casting can affect its resistance to corrosion. Sand-cast pieces whose surfaces have been chased and hammered often have improved resistance to corrosion due to the compression of the grain structure on the surface.

Rates of corrosion are faster where pieces are joined together. When thin pieces are broken off thick castings, corrosion can occur on the broken face since the larger-grained internal structure may be exposed directly to a corrosive atmosphere.

High stresses can induce corrosion in some alloys, including steel. High stresses are naturally accompanied by high deformations (and often microscopic cracks), which lead to a form of material dissimilarity, and, in turn, corrosion. Areas around bolts or rivets are often highly stressed and become problems. In addition, stress concentrations can cause cracks that expose internal structures to a corrosive atmosphere.

Timber

Wood is a natural material composed of cellulose fibers, which occupy about two-thirds of the bulk, and a binding matrix, lignin. Timber consists of softwoods (from coniferous trees) and hardwoods (from broad-leafed trees). The latter contain relatively more cellulose and are usually, but not always, denser, harder, and stronger than softwoods, and likewise harder to shape.

Unseasoned green wood contains great amounts of moisture (60 percent or more). Subsequent seasoning (drying) stabilizes moisture-related movements in wood (shrinkage on drying can be quite high), makes wood less susceptible to fungus attack (fungus typically requires at least 20 percent moisture to grow), and allows some chemical preservative to be used. The strength of wood varies with the slope to the grain. Longitudinally along the grain, wood has great strength. Perpendicular to the grain, bonding is very weak and the material lacks strength.

Wood is durable material if protected from fungus and related decay. Moisture-related dry rot, propagated by spores, is the most serious form of fungus-related decay, since it leaves the material friable and without strength. Once started, dry rot is difficult to eradicate. Infected areas must be cut out. Wet rot is similar but occurs in much damper environments. On the other hand, wood constantly submerged underwater can last indefinitely if not exposed to marine borers, and wood kept dry can last indefinitely

(hence the reason for the covering of older timber truss bridges). Alternating cycles of wetting and drying particularly cause wood to decay.[5] Various preventive preservative treatments are possible (pressure treatments work best).

Glass

Ordinary glass is silica-based, although various other materials are added to improve strength, surface luster, and other qualities. Ingredients are mixed and melted at temperatures around 2,500°F. The molten mass is cooled to a thick, viscous state around l,800°F, at which it can be worked. In this state glass is quite ductile. Masses of glass can be permanently joined to other equally hot masses. Many glasses are annealed (cooled slowly over time in a steadily cooling environment) to prevent fracture during cooling. On final setting, glass becomes a hard, brittle material that has a high degree of permanency under normal conditions.

Typical working techniques include molding and shaping glass while in a molten state, casting it into special molds, cutting it, or various surface treatments (etching, sand blasting, engraving). Cutting and engraving depend upon a mechanical abrasion process. Etching is a relatively rough process involving exposing surfaces to caustic acids (hydrofluoric acid). Protective coatings are applied where no surface etching is wanted.

Colors in glass result from the addition of specific metals or oxides. The presence of lead increases the luster of glass but also makes it relatively soft and readily cuttable into unique shapes.

The hardness of glass varies with its composition. Older soda glass is quite soft and contains sodium carbonate, while hard glass contains potassium oxide. Flint glass contains lead oxide.

5
Witness the decay common in wooden pilings in tidal areas. Above and below the tide levels, the pilings are often in reasonable shape. But at zones where wetting and drying cycles constantly occur, the wood is often decayed.

The strength of normal glass is very dependent on the effects of surface imperfections. Strength can reduce with age, particularly by increases in surface imperfections due to chemical attack or natural abrasion. Surface flaws can be chemically removed to a certain extent to increase strength. A more common approach is to toughen glass by use of a heat treatment. Glass is heated uniformly until plastic and then quickly cooled by air jets. Outer layers contract and harden first upon cooling. As the thicker inner core cools, the contraction effect causes compressive stresses to be developed in the outer layers of the glass, which tends to close microscopic flaws and make the glass stronger (particularly when subjected to bending stresses with their associated tension stress components). The recent widespread development of laminated glass has also improved the strength of planar glass sheets. Parallel glass sheets are bonded with a tough clear plastic membrane between them.

Most current glass is fairly resistant to the effects of atmospheric pollution, except when significant hydrofluoric acids are present in the atmosphere. Certain alkalis found in cement or paint strippers can also attack glass.

Plastics and Fiberglass

The term "plastic" is broad and ambiguous. It is generally used to describe the finished products made from various synthetic and some natural resins. Plastics are generally divided into thermoplastics and thermosetting plastics. Thermoplastics usually have significant flexibility. Thermoplastics include common insulating plastic around wires and many plastic films. Thermosetting plastics are normally quite rigid. "Bakelite" was one of the earliest thermosetting plastics produced. Common epoxies are also thermosetting plastics.

Most plastics are synthetically made. Many substances called monomers have relatively simple molecular structures, but usually exist only in gaseous or liquid form. To make them into solids, their molecular size must be increased. This can be done through a process called polymerization. Small molecular structures are linked together until a material with a larger molecular weight is obtained and a consequent degree of rigidity is achieved. Polymerization is essentially a chemical process typically involving the use of initiator sub-

stances. Various catalysts, plasticizers, and stabilizers are also used in making plastics.

If no cross-links occur between the long molecular chains created during polymerization, then the material becomes a thermoplastic. Solid at room temperatures, thermoplastics can soften upon heating. This characteristic can be used to advantage to mold and shape the material. Thermoplastics always retain, however, their temperature sensitivity. By contrast, if cross-links are formed between the molecular chains created, then the material becomes a thermosetting plastic. Thermosets are rigid materials because of their three-dimensional bonding. They are not softened by heat (but they can decompose under heat).

Plastic fabrication processes depend strongly on the specific plastic used. Common techniques include basic molding and extruding methods. Casting, pressure forming, rotational molding, drawing and extruding, dip molding, vacuum forming, and a host of other specific techniques have been developed. Compression and injection molding are common. In the former, plastic pellets are heated to a liquid state, poured into a mold cavity, and then pressed. Curing occurs under pressure. In injection molding, a ram or screw forces hot, soft plastic into one or more cavities connected by sprues. Curing again occurs within the molds.

Both thermoplastics and thermosetting plastics can be reinforced with fibrous networks—such as glass fibers (at the microlevel glass fibers can be very strong). Liquid resins surround and cure around fibers under little pressure and normally at room temperature (although heating typically speeds up the curing process). Normally reinforced plastics are molded. One technique uses a base mold that is lined or covered with fibrous material; the resin is then poured or otherwise applied. A second technique simultaneously blows chopped up fibers and resin directly onto a surface mold. A third technique places chopped fibers and resins in a vacuum mold. The vacuum draws the materials together, which are then pressed. Matched dies may be used to get finished surfaces on two sides. Fiberglass is widely used both for new sculptures (e.g., many by Shingu) and for restoration work. Interestingly, the original bronze *Horses of San Marco* were so subject to atmospheric corrosion that they are now housed in a museum, with fiberglass replacements in their place.

Plastics can be selected or even designed to meet specific requirements. A thermoplastic such as an acrylic (a plastic based on acrylic acid) has good weathering and light diffusion properties. Various epoxies, silicone, and polyvinyl chloride also have good weather-resistant properties. Transparent plastics include acrylics, polycarbonates, and others. Plastics with high ductility include acrylics and nylons. Plastics are available that expand from a liquid state and solidify (usually they are foaming and often based on styrene). Various elastomers (plastics that have a rubbery state) are capable of extreme elastic deformation. A wide range of adhesives are also plastic-based.

Virtually all plastics decompose in fire. Some are quite flammable. They may emit noxious gases and smoke during the process. Due to the high hazards involved, great care must be taken with the selection and use of plastics for larger-scale works, particularly in enclosed areas.[6] The greatest fire hazard is usually from foamed or sheet plastics.

The structural strengths and stiffnesses of plastics vary enormously. Thermosets can be quite stiff and strong, although not in the same league with metals. Plastics can be used structurally, albeit typically for minor elements or light loading conditions. Their unit strengths are typically not high, and their inherent stiffness (modulus of elasticity value) is low. But they can be used quite effectively in sheetlike fashion with the geometry of the sheet itself imparting strength and rigidity to the form. Even if they had been available at the time, Gustave Eiffel could probably never have made the great internal structure of the Statue of Liberty out of plastic elements, but Bartholdi might have used one form or another of glass fiber–reinforced plastic for the covering forming the lady herself. Recall that reinforced plastics were used for the enclosing surface of the rotating elements on Shingu's *Echo of the Waves* (see chapter 1).

Stone

The long historical use of stone in sculpture has provided many insights into the question of which stone should be used for which purpose. There is also direct evidence about how well different types of stone have fared in different structural and climatic environments. The basis for selecting a stone for a particular application has many dimensions.

Properties such as ease of carving, workability, type and appearance of surfaces, and so forth are of obvious importance. Mechanical and weathering properties can be of equal importance in many instances.

The primary mechanical property of interest in stone is that it is strong in compression and weak in tension. This characteristic limits the use of stone to certain sizes and types of forms. Large shapes in which bending is present are particularly prone to cracking associated with the tensile component of bending stresses. This might be the case in stone sculptures with projecting (cantilevered) parts, or when a stone piece spans between two supports (bending stresses would be associated with the dead weight of the stone mass itself). Again recall that shapes that work at a small scale may not work at a large scale due to the nonlinear increase of the mass of an object with linear increases in scale. Hence a small shape with projecting parts might work in stone, while a larger version might not. The history of sculpture is rife with examples of these scale effects, particularly in stone.

Weathering issues are much more diverse, but hinge around the effects of water and air environments on exposed stone surface. General durability and resistance to erosion are of crucial importance, as are changes in surface texture and appearance over time. Wind and water can cause physical erosion. Water can seep into cracks and expand during freezing, thus causing more cracking (an effect accentuated during rapid cycles of freezing and thawing). This same general effect can occur within the rock itself, with absorbed water undergoing freezing and thawing actions. Rocks with minimal pore space (granite, for example) resist this kind of internal action best. Chemical weathering when rocks are exposed to water saturation takes many forms, but is often associated with hydrated salt production and subsequent decomposition of certain rock types. Surface dissolution in limestones and marbles is

6
In the building industry, there are many severe restrictions placed on the use and characteristics of plastics in habitable areas because of the extreme fire danger.

common. Hydrous expansion can also occur, which leads to decomposition.

Further degradation can occur through pollution effects. The acidic content of water and pollutants in the air can cause chemical erosion. High levels of sulfur dioxide and tri-oxide are particularly troublesome. If resistance to these phenomena over time is important in sculpture placed in an outdoor environment, granite is one of the few stone types that are appropriate for use. Biological processes, such as fungal or bacterial infestations, can also lead to premature dissolution of rock surfaces.

Precise mechanical and weathering properties of stone are naturally dependent on the exact type of stone used. Several major types will be briefly discussed below. The clas-sic breakdown of rocks into igneous, sedimentary, and metamorphic types is a useful starting point.

Igneous

Igneous rocks are formed directly from molten magma. Slow cooling produces a hard coarse-grained crystalline material such as granite and granodiorite. More rapid cooling pro-duces a finer-grained material, such as basalt.

Both granite and basalt have excellent durability and do not abrade or erode easily. Granite has minimum pore space and resists physical weathering processes (freeze-thaw actions). Absorption and moisture movement are virtually negligible. Igneous rocks have a high silica content and are thus reasonably resistant to environmental pollution. Their compressive strengths can be quite high. They have no natu-ral bedding planes and are thus difficult to work with when it comes to carving intricate or highly detailed shapes. Advances in mechanical cutting and finishing devices, how-ever, make it possible for simple geometric forms (including thin planar sections) to be made rather easily.

Sedimentary

Sandstone and limestone are common sedimentary rocks. They are typically created through an accumulation (typically sedimentation) of particulate materials, organic remains, or chemical precipitates, which are deposited in beds in an aeolian or subaqueous environment. The resulting stone can be relatively hard or soft, depending on type and con-stituency. Particulates may be cemented together with

materials such as calcium carbonate , silica, clay, or iron oxide. Sandstones are formed when grains of silica (fre-quently pure quartz) are deposited. A highly durable mate-rial is made when silica is a bonding agent. Calcareous sandstones are usually adequately strong, but not as resis-tant to atmospheric pollution. Clay-cemented sandstones are of low durability. Sandstone is easy to carve and has been widely used throughout the world (recall the great sandstone carvings in India and other places). Limestone is particulate calcium carbonate or calcium magnesium car-bonate of organic origin, possibly including fossils. Traver-tine is a form of limestone formed by chemical precipitation of the carbonate.

The sedimentation beds in these kinds of rocks form planes of inherently weak bonding, which yields anisotropic strength characteristics. It is consequently very easy to split or otherwise work with the material along these planes. On the other hand, these same planes are inherently prone to structural failure. On exposure to the atmosphere, erosion can occur between bedding planes and cracks can develop. Moisture penetration and concomitant freeze-thaw effects can occur, with subsequent flaking off of large planar ele-ments. (The deterioration of the brownstone buildings in New York and other locations, for example, is directly linked to these effects.) Sedimentary rocks are best used with the bedding planes laid so that the exposure of their ends is lim-ited (often this means using them with their beds horizontal and not as vertical cladding). Most sandstones and lime-stones have a relatively poor resistance to weathering. Direct dissolution may occur under constant water saturation, albeit slowly. Protective patinas may form, particularly in limestones. Resistance to atmospheric pollution is low, since sulfur dioxides dissolved in rainwater create sulfuric acids, which accelerate the dissolution process and destroy protec-tive patinas. Limestones may form hard films of calcium sul-fate on exposure to air pollution, which may in turn flake off due to differential thermal movements within the material or due to the crystallization of salts beneath the film.

Compressive strengths are generally much less than for either igneous or metamorphic rocks (about one-third to one-half as great). Moisture absorption rates are much higher than for their igneous or metamorphic counterparts.

Metamorphic

These are rocks of either igneous or sedimentary origin that have been changed by exposure to enormous heat and pressure, thereby increasing their crystallinity. Marble, slate, serpentine, and quartzite are common metamorphic rocks. Marble is essentially a form of limestone with other materials (such as iron) incorporated and recrystallized under the action of heat and pressure. Slate results from pressurized and shaped mudstone. Serpentine—frequently mistaken for marble—is a magnesium-rich silicate rock of igneous origin that has been altered. Quartzite is essentially recrystallized limestone.

The heat and pressure processes may form flake-shaped crystals and cause particular alignments of the crystals that rarely coincide with possible original bedding planes. These cleavage planes result in a fissile rock.

With the remarkable exception of marble, sculptural use of metamorphic rocks is not widespread. Marble is strong in compression but weak in tension, a fact that has commonplace implications in sculpture (fig. 18.5). Some harder varieties of marble have been used externally. Nonetheless, in external environments, most marble varieties easily lose their polish, are susceptible to atmospheric pollution, and degrade with time. The compressive strength of marble is fairly high and often comparable to igneous rocks. Marbles are sensitive to heat. Many fine marble statues have been destroyed during fires. Marbles will eventually succumb to constant water saturation. Protective patinas of insoluble materials may form, as often happened in many ancient Greek and Roman marbles. But degradation processes are vastly accelerated by waterborne or airborne atmospheric pollution. Sulfur dioxides dissolved in rainwater create sulfuric acids which in turn accelerate the dissolution processes. Protective patinas may be destroyed by these attacks. Carbonate-based marbles may be detrimentally attacked by fungi and bacteria as well.

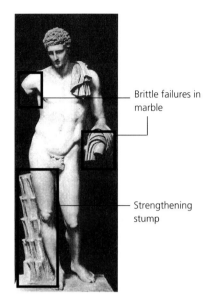

Brittle failures in marble

Strengthening stump

Mercury

18.5
Marble is capable of carrying high compressive stresses, but fails quite easily in a brittle manner when subjected to tension stresses. Projecting pieces are often subjected to bending (with its associated tension stresses), which results in their being broken off. The stump evident in this statue was a device commonly used by Roman sculptors to give added strength to figures and help prevent their being broken off at their bases.

Soils

The term soil is generally used to describe unconsolidated layers of material derived from rock and organic (vegetable) materials. Soils are often classified in terms of their component percentages of gravel, sand, silt, and clay (listed in

Robert Smithson, *Closed Mirror Square*

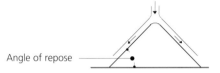

Angle of repose

order of decreasing grain size), as well as the presence of organic material. Loam, for example, is a combination of sand, silt, and clay in nearly equal amounts and also contains some organic matter. Hardpan is a dense, cohesive, rocklike soil that does not significantly soften when wet. Mud is a mixture of silt or clay with water. Gumbo is a sticky fine-particled sandless clay known to expand and contract greatly with variations in moisture content, and also known to be particularly difficult to build upon.

Plasticity and cohesiveness are terms commonly used in descriptions of soil properties. Plasticity generally refers to the ability of a soil to be molded or to distort without major rupture or cracking. A cohesive soil is one in which particles tend to form a mass because of both intermolecular attraction and capillary action of soil moisture. Cohesive soils generally swell when wet and shrink as they dry. Polygonal surface cracking in dry weather is often associated with shrinkable clay. Noncohesive soils are composed of finely weathered rock particles, such as sand; such soils do not possess plasticity. Different soils are experimentally tested to determine their allowable bearing capacities.[7] Rock or stone values are quite high, while those for clays and noncohesive sands and gravels can be much lower. For large projects, it is common to make on-site investigations (making borings by drilling, extracting samples, and testing these samples) in order to determine the precise characteristics of the site ground materials. As described below in connection with foundation design, these values can then be used to design

18.6
Granular material assumes a natural slope when freely piled, defining the material's angle of repose. Different soils have different angles of repose.

[7]
Results are usually expressed in terms of an allowable "force/unit area" measure (in lbs/ft^2 or kN/m^2). Some clays, for example, have allowable bearing capacities of between 1,000 and 1,500 lbs/ft^2.

appropriate ways for a large sculpture to interface with the ground.

Robert Smithson's elegant *Closed Mirror Square* (fig. 18.6) demonstrates another particularly important characteristic of soils and granular materials—that there is a characteristic slope a material naturally assumes when stacked. Different materials will slope differently. An important measure in this regard is called the *angle of repose*. The angle of repose defines the shape that a specific material naturally assumes when it is continuously piled into a heap (such as when soil is dumped from a truck and slumps into a pile). It is measured between the naturally sloping surface and a horizontal ground plane. Different materials will have different angles of repose depending on their internal cohesion and other factors, such as the presence of moisture. Typical damp sand, for example, assumes an angle about 35° to the horizontal, while very wet clay assumes a shallower angle of 15° or so. Many common soils for building earthworks average around 33°. In general, damp materials will withstand the steepest slopes. Consistently wet or dry clays, silts, or loams will have shallower angles.

Terra-Cotta, Tile, and Other Masonry

Baked and unbaked clay in the form of brick, tile, or terra-cotta have long been used in a sculptural context. Simple drying of shaped clay can yield works of surprising longevity—as witnessed by the several unbaked clay sculptures still existing from the seventh and eighth centuries (Nara period) in Japan—as long as they are kept in protected environments. Drying and then baking artifacts in a kiln, however, changes the basic nature and structure of the material, rendering it much harder and more durable. There are a seemingly endless variety of fired-clay artifacts and processes, only a few of which will be cursorily addressed here.

Terra-cotta is an Italian term that generally means "burned earth"—thereby potentially describing a whole host of artifacts. As commonly used, however, the term refers to repetitively made artifacts carefully shaped out of very high quality clay that are fundamentally sculptural in nature (as contrasted to flat tiles). In one typical process, a clay original is carefully sculpted and a plaster negative

made (or a negative of some stronger material depending on the intricacy of the detail and the number of units to be made). Clay is pressed into the mold, by hand or press. Thin elements are often stiffened by making ribs on opposite sides of final exposed surfaces. Units are air-dried and removed from negatives, followed by various trimming, smoothing, and other detail renewal operations. A thin slip is often applied (a water-based mixture containing suspended clay particles) and allowed to dry. Various glazes may be applied to obtain different colors or finishes, and the units are fired in a kiln. Depending on the finish desired, multiple glazing and firing operations may take place. Some shrinkage invariably occurs during the drying and firing processes.

Tiles are similar in nature but may be produced in a more repetitive fashion (due to their simpler geometries) via either hand-molded or mechanized pressing processes. It is useful here to distinguish between tiles used primarily for surface coverings and those intended for structural applications. As surface coverings, the real glory of these tiles lies with the kinds of final surface colors and textures that can be obtained. Many of the more complex and beautiful tiles are often structurally fragile and not very durable. Briefly, the surface-making processes are highly dependent on whether monochromatic or polychromatic results are desired. An essential issue is that different glazes (salts or oxides of one type or another—cobalt, copper, etc.) that are ultimately associated with different colors and finishes have different optimal firing temperatures for obtaining their maximum lusters, which highly complicates the firing processes. In one ancient process, air-dried tiles are covered with a thin slip and fired to a biscuit color. A glaze is applied and fired to its optimum temperature. The process is then repeated. In order to expedite the process, different glazes may be applied simultaneously and a compromise firing temperature selected. Many highly sophisticated variants of these processes have evolved over the years with the aim of maximizing the number and type of colors possible, as well as their luster. Often resulting tiles are relatively fragile in a structural sense and suitable only for interior surface coverings where the underlying structure carries all loads. Tiles with hard durable surfaces can be devised for exterior surface applications, but their surface intensities and qualities may not match those of interior tiles.

Thicker tiles may be made for use as structural elements, usually without special surface finish and with lesser quality control than for surface tiles. Structural tiles can be used in remarkable ways. By overlapping tiles in certain ways, for example, rigid surfaces that have stiffnesses comparable to thin reinforced concrete shell surfaces may be built up. The architect Antonio Gaudí and others have used tile assemblages of this type to create remarkable structures of major dimensions.

Common bricks can be made by hand by pressing clay into molds or by automated pressing processes. Bricks are kept from sticking by watering or sanding the molds—producing water-struck or sand-struck brick. The tactile quality of resulting surfaces is remarkably different. Extrusion processes are also widely used, in which stiff clay is forced through a die to form a ribbon which is then cut by wire. Wire-cut brick is common; it offers little control over surface qualities other than simple forms of combing or roughening. Various grades of brick are available based on their ultimate durabilities and resistance to weathering. Glazes may be applied before firing to give hard enamel-like finishes. A host of wonderfully different bonding patterns may be used in laying bricks into larger assemblies. When used as veneers in large expanses, layers may be of single brick thickness as long as they are tied back into a support by means of ties or cross-laid bricks. Self-standing and/or load-bearing walls typically demand cross-bonded layers of two or more brick thicknesses. In such instances, specially sized bricks are often needed at corners. Particular problems include *efflorescence* —white soluble salts that frequently appear on wall surfaces. Efflorescence normally consists of calcium and magnesium sulfates leached out of bricks by water. It can be stopped only by careful material selection and by preventing the passage of moisture through bricks.

Concrete

Concrete is primarily a carefully proportioned mixture of cement, fine and coarse aggregates (sand, small rocks), and water. In most cases, concrete is created *in situ* (cast in place). The cement, water, and aggregates are first mixed together, then the mixture is poured into formwork (often around preplaced reinforcing steel rods) where it hardens with time. Formwork is subsequently removed.[8]

Upon initial mixing, the cement and the water begin to react with one another to produce a matrix that hardens with time, encasing the inert aggregates. The reaction between the cement and water is chemical in nature (heat is given off during this reaction). Initial setting occurs quickly, within an hour or so, but significant strength is not achieved until much later (the strength of concrete typically increases with time). Since the reaction between the cement and water is chemical in nature and does not depend on atmospheric elements, setting can occur under water as well as in the air.

The mechanical properties of concrete, including its strength, are dependent on the specific type of cement used, the relative ratio of water to cement, curing conditions, and other factors. Increasing the amount of water in the mix relative to the amount of cement present, for example, decreases strength. Resultant compressive strengths can be quite high, but strengths in tension are invariably low. Concrete does exhibit some creep (time-dependent deformation), a property that can cause problems in large structures.

Special lightweight concretes can be created by using aggregates such as vermiculite or expanded shale. Various colors and finish types are possible. Occasionally various additives are used to the basic mix to impart certain desired properties.

Ingredients

Cements can be either natural or artificial. Natural cements were used quite early, made from materials such as volcanic ash. Artificial cements (now typically called Portland cements) were introduced in the nineteenth century and are now almost exclusively used in making concrete. Mixtures of limestone, clay, shale, or even oyster shells and other seemingly unlikely materials are ground into a powder, calcined (heated and dried at very high temperatures until partial fusion takes place), and again ground into a fine powder. Different ingredients yield different physical and chemical properties for the cement, including its color, hardening rate, and strength.

There are several primary types of cement typically available, including normal cement, sulfate-resisting cement, low-heat cement, and high early strength cement. Normal cement is used for most applications. Sulfate-resisting cement (including high-alumina cement) helps concrete resist degradation caused by sulfate attacks. Some groundwater contains sulfates that attack foundations. Atmospheric pollution is also associated with sulfates. Low-heat cement has a low heat of hydration and is often used in situations where the heat generated by setting could otherwise lead to cracking associated with thermal expansions and contractions (this might be the case in massive constructions like dams or very large foundations). High early strength cement sets quickly. Initial strengthening occurs about twice as fast as normal concrete, but tails off quickly and soon is comparable to normal cement. It has a high heat of hydration and is not suitable in many cases (e.g., for large concrete masses).

Aggregates typically consist of both fine and coarse materials (e.g., sand and rocks). They are inert and are simply bound into the matrix formed by the cement and water. Aggregate selection does, however, affect the workability of the mix, ease of placement, resistance to freeze-thaw cycles, and other considerations. Certainly coarse aggregates should be no larger than will conveniently fit between closely spaced reinforcing bars or between bars and formwork.[9] A controlled distribution of progressively sized aggregates is typically used to help prevent voids from forming in the final mix.

While aggregates are typically clean sand, gravel, or rocks, other inert materials may be used as well. Expanded shale, expanded perlite, or vermiculite is often used to make lighter-weight concrete. Slag from steel mills, various natural shells, and a host of other ingredients have been used to make concrete. Resultant mixtures, however, are not always problem-free. Many materials are not really inert and reactions can occur between the cement and the aggregates that attack the aggregates. Final strengths and resistance to freeze-thaw cycles can be detrimentally affected as well. Nevertheless, many good concretes have been made using aggregates other than sand and rocks.

The water used must be clean (drinkability is the test often used). Seawater can be used but is not recommended. Its use can lead to corrosion problems in embedded steel, and efflorescence can create unsightly salt deposits on surfaces.

Admixtures are various liquids or solids added to a mix to alter its workability during mixing or its final physical proper-

18.7
Robert Smithson, *Amarillo Ramp*.
The idea of a material's angle
of repose applies to large-scale
works as well as small-scale ones.

8
Alternative processes do exist wherein aggregates are placed first and a cement-water mixture is then forced into interstitial spaces by high-pressure pumping. These specialized processes can be useful but require special equipment (see the following discussion on the Picasso-Nesjar cooperation).

9
Common aggregates are rarely larger than 1½ inches in diameter and typically smaller when used directly as the sculptural medium.

ties, including color. A typical admixture is an air-entraining agent derived from resins, oils, or other ingredients. Minute disconnected bubbles are developed in the mix, which improves workability, resistance to freezing and thawing, resistance to abrasion, and resistance to sulfate attacks. Accelerating agents such as calcium chloride can be added to increase the quickness of setting. Retarding agents reduce the speed of setting. Coloring agents are natural or synthetic mineral oxides, or even finely pulverized natural marbles, granites, and other materials. Care must be taken with the use of admixtures since adverse effects can occur. For example, accelerating admixtures can cause deterioration of embedded aluminum or galvanized steel pieces in a final concrete structure.

The color of the final concrete can be altered by using different types of cement during the mixing phase. White concrete, for example, can be obtained by using white Portland cement and light-colored aggregates. Color variations can be obtained through the use of aggregates such as crushed quartz, marble, or even ceramic materials. Color pigments can be added during mixing as well.

Concrete Mixing and Finishing
Wide variation is possible in the relative amount of cement, water, and aggregates used in a concrete mix. Early mixing techniques often called for proportions by volume of something like one part cement, two parts sand, and four parts coarse aggregate, with sufficient water added for workability. More recent methods of determining mix proportions pay more attention to the the precise ratio of the relative amounts of water and cement used in a mix. This is because the water-cement ratio of a mix has been found to be the single factor that governs the strength and durability of the resultant concrete. Concretes made with low water-cement ratios are stronger than those made with higher ratios.

By weight, typical water-cement ratios now used range from a low of around 0.30 to a high of 0.70. Normal values are around 0.5. Mixes with lower water-cement ratios are stiff and hard to work with but can result in concretes with high strengths. (Care must be taken to assure that sufficient water is present to allow the cement to hydrate completely.) Conversely, mixes with high water-cement ratios can be easy to mix and work with but can result in lower strength concrete. Concrete exposed to severe atmospheric conditions should be made with lower water-cement ratios to increase its durability. In precisely designed mixes, the moisture content that may be present in the sand aggregate is taken into account in determining the amount of water to be added to a mix. Admixtures are typically added only after the basic cement, water, and aggregates have been initially mixed together.

Various empirical techniques, such as the slump test, are often used to estimate the workability and associated water content of a mix. Mix is placed in an inverted cone with an open end and leveled off. The cone is raised and the amount that the mix sags downward (slumps) is measured. Watery mixes simply spread outward, while stiff mixes do not slump at all. A good mix has a limited amount of slump.

The way a concrete mix is left to harden, or cure, can dramatically affect the properties of the final concrete. Strength, abrasion resistance, freeze-thaw resistance and other properties continue to increase as long as hydration continues to occur between the cement and water in a mix. This hydration can continue over a long period of time as long as there is moisture present in and around the concrete and temperatures are favorable. Hydration can stop if moisture is absent within the mix. Hydration can also stop at the surface of a mix due to evaporation (surface deterioration can follow). Thin sections particularly tend to dry out quickly after casting.

Curing methods for preventing moisture from leaving the mix include leaving formwork in place, using waterproof membranes, applying waterproofing compounds, and other techniques. Curing methods for supplying additional moisture to the surface of a mix during the hardening period include sprinkling the surface with water or using some sort of wet covering material (burlap).

Hydration is accelerated in warmer temperatures and slowed when the temperature is near freezing. While the heat of hydration itself (due to the chemical reaction between the cement and water) generates adequate heat so that concrete can be cast in temperatures somewhat below freezing, the practice is far from desirable since curing is slowed significantly. Ideally, a warmer environment is either naturally present or provided during curing.

In general, reasonable curing can be accomplished in anywhere from three days to two weeks, although a full month of curing is needed to bring concrete close to its full potential compressive strength.

Various finishes can be obtained on the final concrete by different final surface treatments. The float finish is common. Wood or rubber floats are used to smooth the surface just after the concrete has begun to set. Floating brings mortar (cement paste and sand) to the surface, fills in low spots, and covers large aggregate pieces. Trowel finishes create a smoother and more polished finish. Broomed finishes roughen the surface. Exposed aggregate finishes can be created by washing away cement paste and fine aggregates from the floated surface of the setting concrete, or, occasionally, by embedding larger aggregates into the surface after casting and washing away excess mortar.

Colored minerals, crystals, or other materials can be sprinkled onto the surface and bonded by floating.

Strength Properties of Final Concrete

As already noted, the strength of concrete critically depends on the ratio between the amount of water used during the mix process and the amount of cement present. Mixes with low water-cement ratios tend to produce stronger concrete than mixes that use more water. The strength of concrete is also time-dependent. Concrete tends to increase in strength rapidly for a short period after casting and then more slowly with time. Freshly cast concrete is quite weak. After it sets for about a month it reaches an appreciable proportion of its final strength.

In many large works, it is often necessary to have a specific quantitative measure of the strength of a concrete batch. This is done in the following way. A cylinder of concrete of specified dimensions is cast and allowed to set for a given number of days. To measure the compressive strength of the specimen, the cylinder is then placed in a load-testing machine and subjected to increasing loads until it crushes. The stress (load/area) at failure is then calculated. Typical concrete failure strengths in compression are in the 3,000 lbs/in^2 to 5,000 lbs/in^2 range (as measured 28 days after casting), although much stronger concretes are easily possible. Strengths in tension are much lower, typically around a tenth or so of the compression strength. Consequently, plain concrete is best used when only compressive forces are present. The poor strength of concrete in tension necessitates the use of reinforcing steel in structures where the presence of bending or some other structural phenomenon

leads to the development of tension stress fields (see the discussion on this point in chapter 9).

Picasso and Nesjar's Concrete Sculptures

As with most other materials, there are many different ways of making and working with concrete. The concrete works by Picasso and Nesjar provide an interesting case in point.

Picasso's concrete sculptures are unusual in many ways, not least in how they were actually made. Picasso's engagement with sculpture throughout his life was long and profound. One series of works consisted of small-scale models of metal or cardboard. The planar surfaces of these were manipulated into evocative three-dimensional forms by cutting them into distinctive shapes, folding them, and finally painting them. He sought to create these same forms at a much larger scale. It was not until he was seventy-six, however, when he met the Norwegian artist Carl Nesjar, that he found the appropriate opportunity and technique. This same meeting also led to the execution of several of Picasso's drawings in concrete wall engravings.

Nesjar introduced Picasso to Naturbeton ("nature concrete"), a set of concrete processes developed by Erling Viksjo, Nesjar's architect mentor. Naturbeton is based on a process in which formwork is packed with aggregate. Grout (a cement, fine sand, and water mixture) is then pumped into the form. The mortar contains aluminum powder to help prevent shrinkage during curing. After the formwork is removed, the surfaces are cut into in varying degrees to expose different textures of aggregate. A concrete engraving process, called Betograve, involves cutting by high-pressure, fine-nozzled sandblasting. This technique eventually provided a means of translating the broad areas of shading or delicate lines of Picasso's sketches into a large-scale built work.

When Picasso expressed great interest in the process, Nesjar developed the technique further by substituting crushed silicate for natural sand, thereby obtaining a finer cut. He provided close-up photographs showing the width and depth of lines obtained, as well as different-sized aggregates. Picasso agreed to the execution in this medium of several of his drawings, *Beach Scene*, *The Fisherman*, *The Satyr*, *Dancing Calf*, and *Centaur*, as concrete engravings for a government building in Oslo. Nesjar began by trying to execute the sandblasting for the figures of the satyr, dancing calf, and centaur from direct projections of Picasso's original sketches. Finding the results unsatisfactory in their composition and quality of line, he decided to recompose the drawing, removing the centaur figure, and not to use projections. Instead, only a large grid and a picture of the original served as guidelines for the sandblasting. The work that resulted maintained the gesture of the original. Ultimately Picasso agreed: "The two figures are right: three would have been wrong."[10]

This initial collaboration established the basic working method for later projects. With each new commission, Picasso would develop a sketch or maquette. Nesjar would then pick an appropriate size and color of aggregate, manage the construction of the formwork and pouring of the mixture, and finally execute the engravings, all in a way that maintained the spirit of the original idea, without necessarily directly copying or working from projections of the original sketches or models. At times he had to reproportion the work to suit concrete (*Profiles*, Marseille).[11] Usually original contours of the sculpture had to be adjusted according to the shape of formwork and needs dictated by the placing of reinforcing rods (*The Bather*, Chicago).[12] Nesjar documented each phase thoroughly, at times even with movies, for Picasso's approval to ensure that the work was consistent with Picasso's intent and sensibilities.

The Bather (fig. 18.8), built in 1974 in Chicago, provides a good example of some of the details of the construction process. The sculpture essentially consists of four shaped concrete planes, each eight inches thick. A concrete foundation slab with three short (one and a half foot) columns projecting from it was first poured using conventional concrete. Heavy reinforcing steel in the columns was extended four feet above the column tops to tie in later with the reinforcing inside the sculpture.[13] The formwork itself was of plywood backed with wood studs. Single front planes were first made on a temporary surface. Nesjar created a grid on these panels and roughly cut the plywood planes to the intended outline. These shapes were hoisted into place by a crane and joined. The projecting steel was bent into the right position. Nesjar then made final contour corrections to the plywood shapes, adjusting for perspective and scale. Identical back formwork sections were made using the front sections as a guide and then moved out of the way to make

room for the placement of the reinforcing steel. The reinforcing steel itself was in the form of a continuous mesh of crossed bars near the exterior and interior faces.[14] It was positioned by steelworkers, and the mesh was tied and welded to the steel projecting from the base columns. The back forms were then positioned eight inches behind the front forms using snap ties. Pine crosspieces were added to create a box to hold the aggregate. Granite aggregate (about one-half inch in diameter) was packed into the box by hand around the reinforcing steel. It was pounded by hand as well as mechanically vibrated. A grout mixture (cement, water, and sand) was then pumped into box at high pressure through a series of holes drilled at intervals in the formwork. Holes were plugged immediately when the nozzle was moved. Pressure was carefully regulated so as not to cause the formwork to loose its shape or even pull apart completely. The grout was allowed to cure for three days, then the forms were stripped away. Minor grouting was done to smooth the surface where snap-ties had been connected. Nesjar then drew his interpretation of Picasso's lines onto the concrete, first in charcoal and then with wax crayons in several colors. The slow process of surface cutting by fine sandblasting then started, to be completed about a month later. An acrylic sealer was used to coat the entire sculpture to protect the surface.

Many other works followed a similar construction sequence. Note that there is nothing particularly easy about the process of placing the coarse aggregate first (and around reinforcing steel at that) and then pumping grout into the interstitial voids between aggregate pieces. A more conventional process would be to mix the coarse aggregate with the cement, water, and sand to obtain a more or less fluid mixture and to pour this mixture into the formwork, allowing the fluid nature of the mix to surround the reinforcing steel. It remains an open question whether the Naturbeton process was ultimately critical to creating the basic underlying concrete shape, as opposed to carefully controlled conventional casting techniques. On the other hand, the specific type of cutting away achieved by fine sandblasting the surface of the basic shape is not really achievable through other abrasion or casting techniques.

In collaborating with Nesjar in over thirty-seven projects, Picasso never directly participated in the siting or building of any of the Betograve works. In fact, he saw only one of them (*Wall of Castile*). He apparently considered the works to be neither mere enlargement of his models nor the creation of new sculptures. Picasso followed the development of a work but did not hold Nesjar strictly to the original expression, understanding the collaboration as fundamentally an act of translation in which he relied heavily on Nesjar in works that would ultimately bear his own name. Nesjar was clear about his own role as a translator and interpreter, yet he understood that there are certain things that cannot be translated: "My role is comparable to that of a musician before the score of a genius…. There are certain things on a piece of paper that a sandblasting hose will not do on a piece of concrete…. The minute you start to copy in concrete what, in this case, Picasso did in pencil, then you are on the wrong track…. You recreate in one medium with respect for the other medium … otherwise it's going to be dead."[15]

Picasso, *The Bather*

Reinforcing steel, formwork, and formwork ties

18.8
Carl Nesjar executed many of Picasso's designs in reinforced concrete. A fine-nozzled sand-blasting process called Beto-grave was used for final surface engravings.

Other

There are a host of materials available other than those described—think of the wonderful thirteenth-century statues at Sanjusangendo temple in Kyoto, Japan, made of layers of lacquered hemp cloth. This ancient material—interestingly not subject to corrosion, moisture, or dry rot—belongs to a class of materials called composites, which are essentially new materials made by utilizing two or more materials together, usually in a carefully controlled way such that the strength, stiffness, or other mechanical property of the final product is superior to that of its elemental constituents. The glass-reinforced plastics noted earlier are actually best considered as a composite material. Reinforced concrete is likewise a composite material. Various other new composite materials have recently become available.

Sandwich panels and laminates are invariably layered and bonded. In sandwich panels, the strongest, hardest, or stiffest material is used on the outside, and softer, weaker, materials on the inside. Many building materials, for example, have stiff outer planes (say aluminum sheets) and cores of soft insulating material—the result is strong, lightweight, resistant to abrasion, and thermally efficient.

10
Sally Fairweather, *Picasso's Concrete Sculptures* (New York: Hudson Hills Press, 1982), p. 61. My discussion here is largely drawn from this extensive and excellent work on the relationship between Picasso and Nesjar.

11
Ibid., p. 83.

12
Ibid., p. 141.

13
In order for forces to be transmitted from the steel in the top part of the sculpture to the foundation, the steel must be effectively continuous. When construction demands require use of discontinuous steel, this continuity can be achieved by using long overlaps between rods, tying them together, and casting the concrete around them. Welding them together also certainly achieves continuity but is not always necessary if the laps are long enough.

14
Reinforcing of this type must be placed near each surface so as to best resist bending stresses (see chapter 9), but it cannot be placed at the surface itself. There must be sufficient concrete covering the reinforcing steel to bond to it and protect it, and the concrete must not spall or split off. The covering obviously cannot be thinner than the diameter of the coarse aggregate used. In some cases where fire protection is important, coverings must be made even thicker.

15
Fairweather, *Picasso's Concrete Sculptures*, p. 61.

19.0
David Smith, *Cubi XX*.

This chapter focuses on creating a more careful definition of the properties of materials that are particularly important in a structural context, and expressing these properties in a way that is useful in sizing or shaping a member.

Of primary concern are the strength and rigidity properties of materials as they relate to the different kinds of internal stresses induced in a member (tension, compression, bending, shear, torsion). The fundamental concept of stress as an internal force intensity per unit area that is caused by the action of an external load on a member has already been introduced. Typically these internal stresses are dependent on the nature and magnitude of the external loading and the size and shape of the member itself, and would exist at the same levels no matter whether the material used was steel, cast iron, bronze, or whatever.[1] Whether or not the material used will be capable of carrying these internal stresses without rupturing or otherwise failing is dependent on the strength and rigidity characteristics of the material. Some materials are obviously stronger than others. Barnett Newman's *Broken Obelisk* (fig. 1.1) works in steel, but would be doubtful at best in plastic and impossible in stone. How, then, to characterize more rigorously the strength and rigidity of different materials so that one can know a priori whether a member is potentially subject to failure because of the attributes of the material?

Strength and Rigidity

One way of describing strength and rigidity properties of materials is in relation to the stress levels that are present in the material. In a simple member loaded in tension, as the magnitude of the applied force is increased, the stress level present in the member increases as well. As the material in the member is subjected to higher and higher stress levels, the material will eventually fail in some way. One measure of the strength of a material is the stress level, or force intensity per unit area, that is present *at the time* of failure. The strength of a particular piece of material can be deter-

[1]
Exceptions to this general observation certainly exist, particularly insofar as self-weights vary; in the case of materials that do not have homogeneous mechanical properties (such as concrete); or in the case of certain structures with many redundant members ("hyperstatic" structures). Nonetheless, the observation remains useful.

mined experimentally. A member having a known cross-sectional area, for example, can be loaded in tension by simply pulling on it (with weights or some sort of jack) until it pulls apart. When the applied force present at the time of failure is known, it is possible to work backward to determine the stress level present in the material at the time of failure.

The actual behavior of a loaded member, however, can be quite complex. A typical piece of structural steel subjected to a tension force, for example, would carry increasing stress levels accompanied by relatively small deformations (typically not visible to the eye) until it would begin to pull apart, or *yield*, at around a stress level of 36,000 lbs/in² (about 250 MPa or Newtons/mm²). This value is commonly called the *yield stress* of steel. Steels with higher or lower yield stresses are also found in use.[2] At the yield point the steel begins pulling apart but does not actually physically separate. After this point, the member can still carry some additional external loads. Eventually the member would actually physically separate, but only after extremely large deformations have occurred and at a slightly higher stress level than the yield stress. Once the stress level in the steel increases beyond the yield point and the material begins pulling apart, the deformation levels are quite high and often visible to the eye. The material is said to be in the *plastic range* in this event. In steel minor increases in load-carrying capacity can still occur before the material finally physically separates.

The deformations that take place can also be quantified. The term *strain* is used to describe deformations per unit length in the material.[3] The steel undergoes relatively small deformations (typically not visible to the eye) prior to yielding. The strain present is directly proportional to the stress present (if the stress level doubles, so does the strain level). A material is said to be *linearly elastic* when this type of direct proportionality between stress and strain exists. Engineers often describe this linearity between stress and strain by means of a measure called the modulus of elasticity.[4]

The general relations between stress and strain described above are frequently depicted on a diagram called a stress/strain curve (fig. 19.1). Different materials exhibit stress/strain curves that are quite unlike one another. Aluminum can have similar ultimate strengths to steel, but tends to deform more under loading (as evidenced by the slope of the stress/strain curve) and has no sharply defined yield point as has steel. Cast iron can be quite strong and stiff, but again has no defined yield point, nor does it exhibit any plastic deformations under loading prior to failure. The stress/strain curve shown is for cast iron as loaded in compression. Cast iron would fail at considerably lower stress and deformation levels when loaded in tension. Concrete has a lower strength in compression (and also does not exhibit any plastic deformations prior to failure). Plain concrete, for example, might have ultimate failure stresses on the order of 3,000 to 6,000 lbs/in² or more when used in compression (although much higher strengths are easily possible). But concrete is notoriously poor when subjected to tension stresses, and might fail at values as low as 200 to 400 lbs/in². Yield and failure stresses for different materials can be experimentally determined, as can their associated modulus of elasticity values useful for describing deformations.

Ductility, Brittleness, Temperature Effects, Fatigue, and Stress Concentrations

An important feature of the strength and stiffness of a material is whether or not the material is *ductile* or *brittle*. A ductile material is one like steel in which very large, typically visible, deformations take place in the plastic range prior to failure. A brittle material is one like cast iron or concrete in which failure occurs without significant prior deformations. Ductility is greatly desired in structural materials because the large deformations give prior visual warning to impending collapse. A ductile steel member will sag or droop greatly (and visibly) in an overstressed condition before it actually physically ruptures or breaks apart. A brittle cast iron member, however, can collapse quite suddenly and completely as soon as it is overstressed and before the member even looks like it is in trouble or about ready to give way. It would simply fracture without any warning. Consequently, cast iron members are rarely used any longer as large-scale beams or tension members.

Often materials are subjected to large temperature swings. *Temperature changes* can alter the characteristics of a material in many ways, including making it either more brittle or more ductile. With low temperatures, steel can become quite brittle. With increasing temperatures, the ductility of steel increases. Very high temperatures can cause an irreversible change in the material itself (called a phase change) that drastically alters its properties. At approximately 700°F, for example, a steel member can no longer support its own dead weight. Curiously, changing the rate of load application on most materials also changes their characteristics. The ultimate strength of a steel cable that is quite rapidly loaded (such as an elevator cable) is much higher than that of one that is gradually loaded. On the other hand, a constant cycling of a load (on again, off again) can potentially lead to undesirable fatigue effects that can cause premature failure.

Time-dependent material properties also affect the strength and rigidity of structural materials. The term *creep* refers to deformation with time. The phenomenon of creep is extremely important in the design of sculptures made of certain materials. Many fine forms have been made that look quite superb when initially constructed but lose their elegance with time as parts begin to droop under their own dead weight. Many plastics display significant creep and will thus continue to deform slowly over time. A plastic piece serving as a beam in bending, for example, will instantaneously deflect a certain amount under load due to the basic elasticity of the material. With time, however, the measured deflections will continue to increase (or creep) as long as the load is present. Other materials, such as steel, display virtually no creep. Unfortunately, there is really nothing that can be done to reverse creep effects.

Another factor affecting the strength of a material is the phenomenon of *fatigue*. Fatigue can develop in any member subjected to rapidly varying and alternating cycles of tension and compression, causing the member to fail at lower stress levels than a member subjected to a more or less static load condition. A simple paper clip can be broken apart by rapidly bending it back and forth, whereas bending it only once or twice does not affect it. Fatigue failures must be guarded against in structures with parts that vibrate or move, such as those with motors attached to them. Airplanes, for example, are structures in which fatigue stresses are particularly dangerous. For most sculptures, fatigue stresses are obviously not a problem, but the phenomenon should be borne in mind in the design of any sculpture with rotating parts. Keeping stress levels quite low can solve most problems of this type in common sculptures.

2
Differences are associated with the different physical makeup of the steel itself, e.g., the presence of greater or lesser amounts of carbon and other ingredients (see chapter 18).

3
If a tension member of length L stretches an amount ΔL, then the strain (ε) present is given by $\varepsilon = \Delta L / L$. Strain is consequently measured in "inches/inch" or "mm/mm." Hence it is often called a dimensionless quantity. More precisely, strain is defined as a ratio of the deformed size of an object to its original size.

4
The modulus of elasticity (E) in the linearly elastic range of a material is defined by E = stress/strain, or $E = f/\varepsilon$.

In certain circumstances, premature failures can be caused by what are known as *stress concentrations*. Higher than average stresses typically exist around the very tip of any crack in a material, which in turn can cause the crack to propagate farther. Stress concentrations are usually not particularly a problem in ductile materials, such as steel, since the ductility mitigates the crack propagation. They can, however, cause problems in brittle materials such as cast iron or even some cast acrylics. Rounding or filleting internal corners and otherwise detailing to avoid places where cracks tend to open up helps prevent stress concentrations.

Allowable Stresses

When designers are sizing a large-scale structure, particularly a structure that people walk by and under, it is important to define exactly how close to failure to allow the internal stress level to come. If it is known that a material such as steel has a yield stress level of 36,000 lbs/in² in tension, this measure can be used to determine whether or not the actual tension stress level produced in a member by an external load is excessive.[5] There is no sense, however, in allowing the actual stress level present in the material to come very close to the yield or failure stress level, since minor unexpected overloads might cause failure. It is thus common to define and utilize a specific *factor of safety* to ensure that there is an adequate margin of safety present in the final member.

One way of incorporating an appropriate factor of safety into the design of a member is not to allow the stress level present in the material to exceed a certain safe value. This safe value is called the *allowable stress* ($F_{allowable}$) for the material. An allowable stress is simply some percentage of the expected yield or failure stress level of a material. Stresses in steel, for example, are often limited to allowable stress values that incorporate a factor of safety of 1.5. Thus $F_{allowable} = F_{yield}/1.5 = 0.66F_{yield}$.[6] The actual stresses in a member caused by an external loading are then limited to this amount. If it is found that the stresses present in a loaded member exceed the previously specified allowable stress, then the member may not be used. The dimensions of the member should then be increased until the actual stress levels present are equal to or less than the allowable

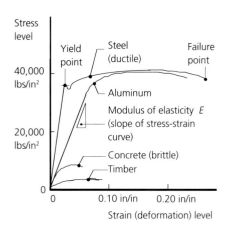

19.1
Typical stress-deformation properties for different materials. Materials with sharply sloped initial curves are quite stiff and resistant to deformations. Steel exhibits ductile behavior and stretches significantly prior to actual failure by pulling apart. Materials such as concrete exhibit brittle behavior: little deformation takes place prior to failure.

stress level for the material used. In sizing simple members, it is possible to use allowable stresses directly in determining member sizes.[7]

Factor of safety values other than the 1.5 noted above are occasionally used. The less certain a designer is about the quality of material used, e.g., its failure stress level, the higher is the factor of safety used. Higher safety factors, for example, are used in the design of wood members, since wood tends to be a more variable material than steel with respect to its strength qualities.

The allowable stress used in the design of a member is also dependent on the exact type of stress present (tension, compression, bending, shear, bearing, torsion) in relation to the characteristics of the material used. As already noted, some materials have different properties depending on the type of stress present. For virtually all materials, allowable stresses for most stress states are expressed as some constant percentage of the yield or failure stress—with different percentages for different force states and material types. The allowable stress for compressive stress states is not a constant value but varies with the effective length of the member in relation to its cross-sectional properties (long slender members have considerably lower allowable stresses than short compact members). Exact formulations for allowable stresses in compression members are quite complex and generally beyond the scope of this book.

For steel, allowable stresses in tension and bending are generally similar and quite high (e.g., $F_{allowable} = F_{yield}/1.5 = 0.66F_{yield}$). Allowable stresses in shear are somewhat lower than those for tension or bending (e.g., around $0.4F_{yield}$ versus $0.66F_{yield}$). Allowable bearing stresses are also quite high. The frequent slender proportions of steel compressive members, however, often make it necessary to use low allowable stresses.

For cast iron, allowable stresses in both tension and bending are quite low (bear in mind that bending involves a tension stress field). Allowable compressive stresses can be high as long as members are short and compact. Wrought iron, by contrast, is better able to carry tension and bending stresses than cast iron.

For timber, allowable stresses in tension and bending are comparable and reasonably high (e.g., $F_{allowable} = 1,200$ to 1,600 lbs/in²). Timber is particularly sensitive to shear stress failures parallel to the grain, however, and allowable

5
Assume that a steel rod having a cross-sectional area of 0.5 in² supports a 5,000 lb weight. The weight of 5,000 lbs produces an actual tension stress level of the following: $f = P/A = 5,000$ lbs/0.5 in² = 10,000 lbs/in². Since the steel would not fail until it reaches a stress level of 36,000 lbs/in² it is evident that the member would *not* fail by pulling apart in tension. In this example there is even an appreciable reserve of extra strength (the actual stress level of 10,000 lbs/in² is much less than the failure stress level of 36,000 lbs/in²).

6
In the specific case of the steel rod of 0.5 in² cross section loaded in tension, $F_{allowable} = 0.66F_{yield} = 0.66 \times 36,000 = 24,000$ lbs/in². Thus the member could actually support a load of 12,000 pounds safely ($P = A \times F_{allowable} = 0.5$ in² × 24,000 lbs/in² = 12,000 lbs).

7
Suppose that we need to know the cross-sectional area ($A_{required}$) of a steel bar needed to carry a tension load of 48,000 lbs. The area can be found directly: $A_{required} = P/F_{allowable} = 48,000$ lbs/(24,000 lbs/in²) = 2.0 in². A bar 1.0 by 2.0 inches would work: the internal stress level present would be 24,000 lbs/in², which is exactly equal to that allowed.

stresses for timber can consequently be quite low (e.g., $F_{allowable}$ = 150 to 200 lbs/in²). Allowable bearing stresses that act parallel to the length of the grain are quite high, but bearing stresses that act perpendicular to the length of the grain are quite low. Timber often crushes locally due to bearing stresses that act perpendicular to the grain structure. Allowable compressive stresses are high in short, compact members. Laminated timber (planar elements glued lengthwise) typically has higher allowable stress values than does plain sawn timber (splits or checks that might exist in one of the laminates are glued against another laminate, thus long splits are minimized).

For concrete, allowable stresses in both tension and bending are quite small—to the extent of being considered negligible in a structural design context (hence the need for reinforcing steel to carry any tension stresses present). In compression, concrete can be quite strong. Allowable shear stresses are much lower in concrete.

Allowable Deformations

Usually most design criteria relate to limiting stresses rather than deformations, even though the two phenomena are closely related. One reason is that there is rarely clarity in defining what constitutes an acceptable deformation. Another is that the context of a member is extremely important in defining allowable deformations.

For members in tension, such as steel, deformations are rarely actually visible to the naked eye. By contrast, for members in bending (such as a common beam), the downward deflections that result from the strains in the material are often quite visible. Visible deflections are usually to be avoided since they generate unease on the part of viewers or their droopiness is simply unsightly. (Just because a member visibly deflects, however, does not mean that it is not strong enough to support loads. A member may sag excessively but still be quite safe.) In building design, deflections in beams are usually limited to some value such as 1/240 to 1/360 of the span of the beam. Designing to meet these restrictions usually means the resulting structure will not have deflections that are visually apparent. For given loading and structural geometries, deflections can be minimized either by increasing member dimensions or by using materi-

als that have inherently high stiffnesses (a stiff material exhibits little strain at high stress levels).

In dealing with material properties to control deflections, structural engineers make great use of a measure discussed earlier—the modulus of elasticity (E)—in describing the inherent stiffnesses of different materials. This measure is also used in calculating exact deformations or deflections that might be present in structural elements. The higher the modulus of elasticity of a material, the more inherently resistant the material is to deformation. Steel has a higher E value than does aluminum or plastic, and is consequently a stiffer material less susceptible to deformations. Assuming similar span and loading conditions, steel members would deflect considerably less than aluminum or plastic members.[8]

8

The modulus of elasticity of steel is E_S = 29,300,000 lbs/in^2 (about 204,000 MPa), that of aluminum is E_A = 11,300,000 lbs/in^2, while that of some plastics can be as low as E_P = 500,000 lbs/in^2. If similar-sized tension members made of each of these three materials were subjected to identical loads, then the members would deform or pull apart in amounts relative to these values. The steel member would deform the least, aluminum next by a factor of E_S/E_A or about 3, and the plastic the most by a factor of E_S/E_P or about 60.

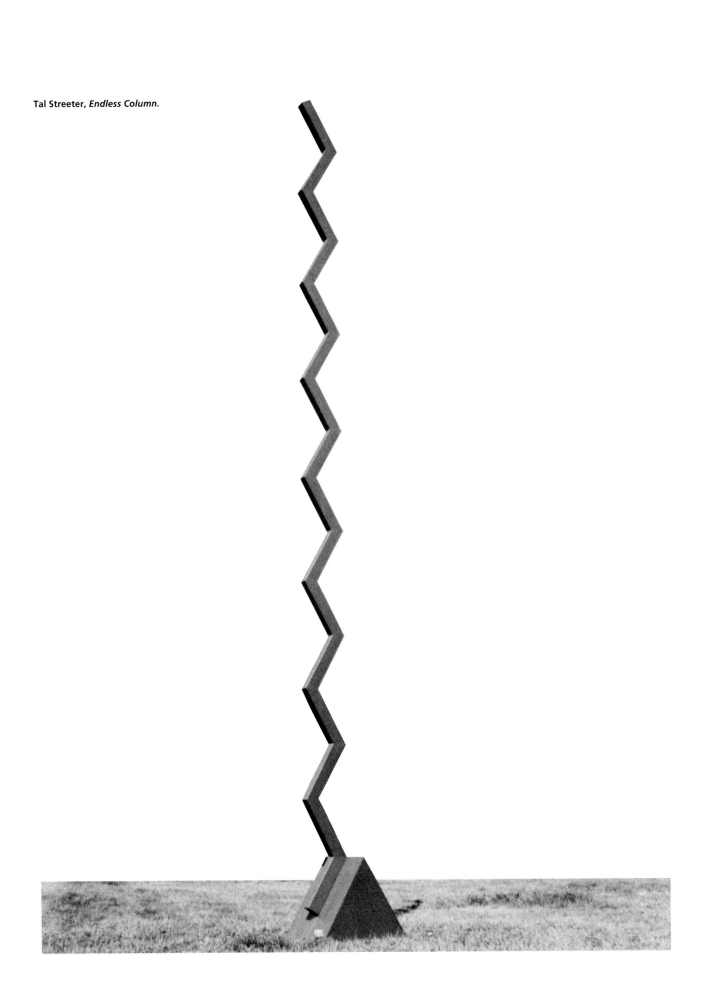

Tal Streeter, *Endless Column.*

Observations

6

20.0
Sol LeWitt, *13/11*.

One aspect of designing structures in relation to sculpture rather than architecture, engineering, or aerospace is refreshingly different—traditional structural design objectives and constraints such as efficiency, lightness, or cost rarely dominate the structural attitudes assumed. Seldom is there any special need, for example, to make a sculpture as lightweight as possible for the task at hand—as might be *the* fundamental design criteria in an aerospace application. The role of structure in the context of sculpture is radically different. There is thus seemingly little particular reason to explore how to shape sculptural forms so that they not only are structurally viable (in terms of strength and stability) but also satisfy some more abstract idea of structural efficiency. Nonetheless, criteria of efficiency or structural elegance possess an intellectual interest, and a book of this type must address the question of *how* to shape forms with respect to such criteria *if* one should want to do so.

Principles: Simple Forms

The first task is to broadly define the characteristics of structures and structural components that are of interest with respect to criteria of efficiency such as relative lightness, strength, and rigidity. These characteristics are quite general and apply to "structures" found in any field (from the plant and animal kingdoms to the world of sculptures). Discussions about specific elements and forms in past chapters of this book have already brought into focus many design principles that are of relevance in this connection. Here these principles will be summarized in a more abstract form. For clarity, these principles are presented more or less as postulates. There are no absolute truths here, and exceptions can certainly always be found. Nonetheless, the general principles noted are surprisingly useful in understanding structures.

1 The lightest-weight structures for carrying a given load in space are those that consist exclusively of tension or compression elements and whose member sizes are varied in proportion to the forces present within them. (Of the three primary force states—tension, compression, and bending—structures that carry loads by a bending action may be common but are not efficient.)

a In tension/compression assemblies, the use of tension members should be maximized and the use of long compression members minimized. (As has been seen, the load-carrying capacity of an element in tension is independent of its length. Long compression members, however, are potentially subject to buckling, a phenomenon that reduces efficiency and increases required member sizes.)

b Tension members may be any length. The length of compression members should not be longer than that associated with the transition point between crushing and buckling for the member (hence compression members should be fairly short). There is no particular structural value in reducing lengths below this point.

c In tension/compression assemblies, forces are usually reduced and stiffnesses increased when the maximum depth of interconnected elements is oriented in the direction of the load (as is typically the case, for example, in a common truss found in a building or a bridge). Varying total structural depths of such assemblies in response to the bending moment distributions present in the structure will also result in benefits.[1]

2 If structures are to carry loads via a funicular action (e.g., arches, cables) and thus be in a state of either tension or compression, the geometry of the structure cannot be arbitrary but depends on the type and distribution of the loading present.

a The presence of uniformly distributed loads along the length of the structure requires shapings that are parabolic in nature.

b The presence of a series of concentrated point loads requires that the structure be composed of linear segments with nodal points beneath the load points.

c Combined (distributed and point) loadings require structures with peaked curves. The degree of curvature depends on the relative magnitudes of the uniform versus point loads that are present.

d A corollary of (c) is that the shape of a funicular structure must change beneath any loading for the structure to carry loads by tension or compression. If no shape change occurs, bending will develop within the structure.

3 The use of members carrying loads by bending, twisting, or other actions should be minimized. (This is nothing more than a variation of the first point.)

a Lengths of members in bending or twisting should be minimized. (Reducing member lengths reduces bending moments.)

b The overall magnitudes of the bending moments present in a structure can be reduced and member stiffnesses increased by using fixed or rigid connections to connect a member to other parts of the structure. (Some adverse bending moments are consequently created at the connections. Members and connections must designed accordingly)

c Members in bending should have their cross-sectional shapes organized so that the bending occurs about the strong axis of the member. (This typically implies that the deepest dimension of the member is aligned with the direction of the load.)

d Members subject to twisting are best made of closed-form compact shapes (e.g., box-shaped cross sections).

4 Frameworks of line-forming members are stiffest and most capable of carrying high external loadings when arranged in triangulated configurations.

a Fully triangulated assemblies may use simple pin-connected joints.

b A few concentrated loads are best carried by a uniquely designed triangulation pattern of a limited number of members with node points directly beneath the loads. Loads acting on members between node points are to be avoided.

c Space frameworks based on repeating geometries are most efficient when carrying uniformly distributed loads acting over a large area. These same frameworks are not well suited to carrying concentrated loads. Concentrated loads are best carried by uniquely designed configurations of a limited number of linear elements.

d Triangulation patterns that minimize the length of compressive members (see above) and maximize the length of tension members are usually highly efficient.

e Flexible cables can be used to carry tension forces within frameworks, but they must be carefully placed so that there is no requirement that they carry only compressive forces under any type of changing load condition. Use of cables often necessitates a certain level of redundancy in the number of members used to achieve stability.

5 Frameworks with nontriangulated configurations have members subject to combined force states (bending, shear, tension, and/or compression) and thus require larger member sizes than in triangulated configurations. (But nontriangulated configurations are extremely versatile in their application.)

a Nontriangulated frameworks must normally use rigid joints between all members. (Only occasional use can be made of a few carefully placed pin-connected joints.)

b Less adverse bending is developed in shorter members than in longer members.

6 Rigid structures made of surface-forming elements (plates, shells) are typically best suited for carrying uniformly distributed loads as opposed to concentrated point loads.

a Surface-forming structures in compression and/or tension are more efficient than those subjected to bending. This often implies the use of special curved shapes rather than flat planes. (Flat plates loaded perpendicular to their faces will be subject to bending.)

b Doubly curved convex surfaces typically provide very stiff structures. If the convexity is directed toward the applied loading, the structure tends to be mostly in compression. A concave shape would tend to be mostly in tension.

c The stiffness and strength of a doubly curved surface increases with increasing surface curvatures (decreasing radii or sharper curves).

d The presence of concentrated point loads on surface-forming structures normally introduces adverse bending. Folding or peaking surface shapes directly beneath point loads, or introducing ribbed stiffeners, mitigates adverse effects.

7 Flexible surface-forming membranes are also best suited for carrying distributed rather than concentrated forces, but normally must be prestressed via internal pressurization or external jacking forces to be viable.

a An optimum level of prestressing exists. The stability of the flexible surface (and its resistance to wind-induced fluttering) increases with increasing prestressing, but excessive prestressing makes designing the membrane itself more difficult.

1
With respect to the more general issue of shaping and positioning elements, Mitchell studied the shapes of minimum-weight structures consisting of both tension and compression elements in 1904 and devised a series of abstract systems usually now called "Mitchell structures" or "Mitchell frameworks." These frameworks often consist of curvilinear nets with specific elements orthogonal to one another.

b Point loads are best distributed into a membrane via cables or load distribution caps.

8 As the scale of a structure increases, funicular structures and triangulated frameworks become increasingly more efficient than members in bending. In very small scale structures, members in bending are among the simplest and easiest to use.

These principles are useful in guiding designers to create more viable structures and in understanding what features characterize structures that are technically well designed. None of these principles, however, are sacrosanct, since design constraints and opportunities that arise from the specific shape and context of the structure must invariably take precedence over abstractions; and not all of the rules are provable in the strictest sense of the word. Hence they should perhaps be considered guidelines rather than rules. Nor are they comprehensive, since they focus more on elements and primitive forms than on complex assemblies of diverse elements (although some mention is made of aggregations). For example, if specific fields such as building design are considered, it is evident that there are principles that relate to how hierarchies of commonly used elements are best organized (e.g., surface-forming elements are optimized prior to supporting collector members). In the animal world, dynamic and kinematic factors become extremely important and introduce additional considerations that are often of overriding importance. In the plant world, light-gathering and other objectives often dictate the way forms evolve and the structures that consequently support them.

On a very general level, if there were a single axiom to best characterize an overall strategy for organizing primitive forms and elements so as to make viable and effective structures, it might be as follows: For earthbound structures, *structural efficiency is obtained when all loads and forces are channeled to the ground as directly as possible.* Indirect or extended load paths contradict this principle. This does not mean that such load paths cannot be used, merely that resulting forms are rarely efficient or of any theoretical interest from a purely structural perspective.

On a more specific level, application of the principles noted leads to structural forms that are simple and straightforward. Forms shaped according to these structural princi-ples are gently curved, peaked, or are otherwise shaped. They rarely consist of stark right-angled forms.[2]

Assemblies: "Structures" versus "Stable Geometries"

In considering the structural rightness of *assemblies* of structural elements (rather than focusing on the constituent elements), a major intellectual issue that has been lurking about previous parts of this book is whether using certain types of regular shapes based on repetitive geometries has any intrinsic structural virtue—or whether principles for the most appropriate overall shaping of a form for structural purposes stem from a different source. There are many different types of member assemblies that are based on one or another type of repetitive geometry. Sol LeWitt's *13/11* (fig. 20.1) is perhaps an extreme example. Analogous forms based on familiar polytopes (two-dimensional polygonal forms) or polyhedra (three-dimensional polygonal forms such as tetrahedra) are surely possible as well.

Certainly repetitive geometries of this type can result in viable structures. Building structures based on this same arrangement can be found by the score, and nature provides the honeycomb and other forms based on the repetition of elemental forms. The visual attributes of such patterns often seem to be associated with the very *idea* of "structure." This is quite common, for example, in architecture: architects wanting an effect of "technology" in their designs often simplistically resort to the use of "space frames" and other structures based on repeating geomtries. It does not follow, however, that what seems to look "structural" axiomatically has desirable structural characteristics.

On a general level, the design principles noted above suggest nothing in repetitive geometrical assemblies that makes them especially attractive as "structures" (as opposed to what might merely be called "stable geometries"). There are losses in structural performance when forms are determined solely on the basis of repetitive geometries and without equal emphasis on creating unique member configurations in response to known loading conditions. Many of these repetitive patterns intrinsically contradict the general principle of channeling loads to the ground as quickly as possible, or varying member sizes in response to the forces actually present, as a way of achieving high structural performance.

On the other hand, in specific situations there may be some reason for leaning toward more generalized structural responses associated with repeating geometries. Surely for this to be the case, the expected loading conditions would have to be best characterized as distributed rather than concentrated loads. Generalized responses become even more desirable when locations of expected loads are not known a priori, as is often the case with environmental loads. Repetitive geometries are also of interest for other technical but nonstructural reasons (honeycombs surely don't assume their forms for structural reasons). Considerations of construction process, buildability, and mass production all may well support the use of repetitive geometries.

"Tensegrity" structures warrant special mention in this context. They are exciting, but are they desirable forms as structures per se? They may be quite interesting expositions of the balance between tension and compression forces as literally manifest through a physical assembly (as surely are many of Kenneth Snelson's works), but it does not necessarily follow that these physical arrangements have any special quality to them that gives them a unique status when compared to any number of other structural approaches. To be sure, members *are* in a state of either pure tension or pure compression, and bending is thus absent. In this regard tensegrity structures *share* (but do not uniquely possess) a desirable characteristic of many different types of triangulated and nontriangulated frameworks. The idea of "continuous tension/discontinuous compression" underlying the tensegrity concept is also undoubtedly of interest from other points of view. Certainly it *seems* like it ought to be an important concept, but its true dimensions lack clarity. Asserting that it somehow yields preferable structures remains a dubious proposition at best, and certainly an unproven one.

The idea of tensegrity structures being "overbraced by one," explored in chapter 11, may be more fruitful theoretically; at least it ties tensegrity structures in with a much larger class of frameworks, familiar in the engineering world, that are sometimes characterized as "hyperstatic" structures, and which are known to be interesting. Hyperstatic structures have a controlled redundancy of carefully

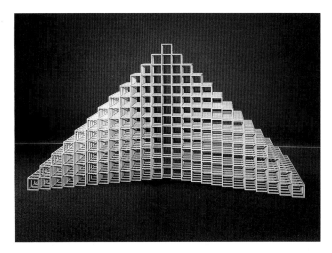

20.1
Sol LeWitt, *13/11*.

2.
There is a highly curious association of right-angled forms with an "engineering" or "technological" view of built objects. Perhaps this view was fostered by architects such as Mies van der Rohe who adopted such a language in their buildings and defined them in relation to technology. Few associations could be more misleading. Clearly the structural design principles listed all point *away* from the use of right-angled forms.

placed members. Current thinking suggests that hyperstatic structures may well be better or more efficient at carrying loading patterns that are highly changeable than are simpler nonredundant triangulated networks, while the latter are better at carrying steady state or nonchangeable loading conditions. A common bridge truss, for example, is subjected to changing load patterns as traffic moves across it, although the dead weight of the structure itself is a nonchangeable loading condition. A short-span truss where dead loads are small in relation to movable live loadings may thus be a particularly suitable candidate for the use of a hyperstatic framework; while a long-span truss where unchangeable dead loads are very high in relation to live loads may not be (a simpler nonredundant triangulation configuration may be preferable).

It should be stressed that these observations do not imply that there is anything wrong with approaches based on repeating geometries or tensegrity ideas; but it is important to differentiate clearly between the virtues of a "geometry" and those of a "structure." It is intellectually suspect to ascribe to clever geometrical constructs special structural virtues because of visual characteristics or other rationales without explicit considerations of the types of forces that are present, material properties, and so forth.

Scale Effects

The general precepts noted at the beginning of this chapter made little reference to the scale of a structure. Scale issues—the relationship between the size of an object and the relative proportions of its constituent members—are among the most important of all issues in the shaping of physical forms. A number of interesting arguments developed in diverse fields to deal with the changing proportions of forms give surprisingly useful insights into why some animate and inanimate objects have the shapes they do, and, in turn, what might be some guiding principles for the shaping of objects. These arguments address such wonderful issues as why elephants have different forms and proportions from small dogs, and why dogs are proportioned differently from grasshoppers.

Briefly, the central thesis is that any overall change in the scale of a solid object will naturally entail or suggest a non-

linear reproportioning of its constituent elements. As solid objects increase in absolute size, their forms and constituent elements tend to become bulkier. As solid objects decrease in absolute size, their forms and elements may tend to become lighter and capable of being made of more tracery-like pieces. (In art and literature as well as in folk wisdom, these general principles have often been intuitively followed: giants or ogres, for example, are invariably portrayed as beings with enormously thick limbs and compact bodies rather than as lithe or delicate creatures—with the latter proportions largely reserved for woodland elves and other small beings.) The constituent members of the objects involved are proportioned primarily on the basis of the physical forces that act upon them—either because of their origins in nature or because of a specific intent on the part of a designer. Thus the thesis at best applies only tenuously to the proportioning of sculptures, where the design intent may be quite different. Surely a sculptor can create a piece in the shape and appearance of an elephant at the size of the grasshopper. But it is less clear that a piece exactly proportioned as a grasshopper, and made of real materials, could easily be made to work at the size of an elephant. It is in the latter connection, not the former, that the thesis becomes useful. A further limiting consideration is that the thesis applies most clearly to objects that are essentially characterizable as solid throughout, and not as open frameworks composed of individual members.

The importance of scale effects in the form of solid structures was commented upon quite early by no less a personage than Galileo Galilei in his *Dialogue Concerning Two New Sciences*. In observing shipbuilders working at the Venetian Arsenal, he noted that they employed "stocks, scaffolding and bracing of larger dimensions for launching a big vessel than they do for a small one . . . in order to avoid the danger of the ship parting under its own heavy weight, a danger to which small boats are not subject." He thus touches on one of the critical ingredients of the argument—that of the self-weight of an object and how its importance in the sizing of an element (in this case the stocks, scaffolding, and bracing) changes with changes in the scale of the object. The discussion continues with Galileo requiring that one of the discoursers, Salviati, illustrate the principle by sketching a series of bones of different proportions that would yield increases in strength proportionate to increases in weights. The conclusion drawn is that there is a size limit beyond which a structure of a particular form would be unable to carry its own weight, thus introducing the concept that strength and size are not necessarily linearly related. Galileo's observations were subsequently explored and extended by many others, perhaps most eloquently in D'Arcy Thompson's *On Growth and Form* (first published in 1917). Thompson's original discussions "On Magnitude" or "On Form and Mechanical Energy" remain classic in the field, although new understandings of biological processes have necessitated that the work be revised. Subsequently, many of the same basic ideas on the importance of scale have been treated in purely mathematical ways in many different fields. These works clearly point out the importance of scale in the proportioning of an object. Three salient issues become clear in these discussions. The first is that the self-weight of an object changes more rapidly than changes in the linear dimensions of an object. The second is that measures of the strength of most objects do not vary directly with their size (for example, doubling the dimensions of an object does not necessarily double its strength). The third is that, as an object becomes larger, the net internal forces induced in the object because of environmental loads (wind, earthquake, snow) become sufficiently large as not to be negligible, as they occasionally are in small objects.

First look at the question of the self-weight of a solid object by considering some very simple examples in depth. For simple geometric forms, such as spheres or cubes, the volume of the form varies by the cube of its governing linear dimension (the side of a cube or the radius of a sphere). The weight of a solid homogeneous object is the unit weight of the material (expressed as a certain number of pounds per cubic foot or kilograms per cubic meter) multiplied by the volume of the object. Thus the weight of a simple cube or sphere also increases or decreases directly according to the cube of the governing linear dimension (since the unit weight of the material remains constant). For example, if the linear dimensions of a solid cube or sphere of a certain type of material are doubled, then its weight is increased by a factor of eight; if tripled, by a factor of twenty-seven.[3] Obviously the converse is true as well; halving the linear dimensions of a cube or sphere decreases its weight by a factor of eight. Clearly the way the weight of an object

3
Thus the volume V_1 of a cube of side d_1 is $V_1 = d_1{}^3$ and that of a sphere of radius R_1 is $V_1 = (4/3)\pi R_1{}^3$. For a new cube of doubled dimensions, $V_2 = (2d_1)^3 = 8d_1{}^3 = 8V_1$. Or if the linear dimensions are increased by a factor of three, weights increase by a factor of twenty-seven: $V_3 = (3d_1)^3 = 27d_1{}^3$.

changes more rapidly than changes in linear dimensions must have a strong impact on the design and final proportions of any supporting structure.

Again consider a simple solid cube, this time suspended from a circular steel rod. The question is how the required size of the rod is affected by scale changes. As noted in chapter 9, the strength of a member in tension depends directly on its cross-sectional area and on the tensile properties of the material itself (expressed in terms a certain strength per unit area). For this discussion, the tensile properties of the material in the rod may be considered constant; then the load it can ultimately carry is directly dependent only on the cross-sectional area of the rod—which is in turn dependent on the diameter of the rod. Now consider a circular rod having a diameter designed to be *exactly* large enough to support a solid cube of certain initial dimensions. If the linear dimensions of the whole system were simply doubled, the weight of the suspended cube would increase by a factor of eight, but the area of the rod would increase only by a factor of four since its area increases by the *square* of its diameter. Hence its strength would also increase only by a factor of four. The rod of doubled linear dimensions would be too small for the new weight and would fail. The supporting structure, in this case the rod, must be reproportioned. Obviously the linear dimensions of the rod would have to be more than doubled, and the rod will be bigger and bulkier relative to the cube than before.[4] The whole system would look quite different from its scaled-down counterpart.

Similar arguments could be made for more complex structural elements. The strengths and stiffnesses of other structural elements—such as beams or columns—do not vary directly with increases or decreases in linear dimensions, but behave in a more complex way.

These observations about scale enhance the understanding of forms. Most sculptors intuitively adopt suitable proportioning systems for the general scale range at which they work, and do not try to translate a specific form from one scale to another. While the principles are rarely realized in an intellectual sense, manifestations can easily be seen in a spectrum of works. For example, Michael Heizer's *Complex One/City* (fig. 17.2) and David Smith's *Australia* (fig. 5.2) both represent proportioning systems entirely appropriate for their respective scales. Given the principles discussed

here, it is easy to see that Heizer's work could be executed at the scale of Smith's work, but not vice versa.

The need to make proportions of objects bulkier as linear dimensions are increased applies only when scale changes for solid volumes are considered. If increases in volumetric size can be accomplished without the weight of the object changing as rapidly as was discussed, then constituent elements can again have more delicate proportions. This is indeed what certain structural forms seek to do. Aggregations of three-dimensional triangulated networks (the "space frames" of chapter 11) provide one example. By composing a larger volume of a specifically configured network of light tension and compression elements, rigid shapes can be made quite large without excessively large increases in the overall weight of the object. Member sizes in a bar network may still be quite large in an absolute sense, but may appear quite slender relative to the whole object.

4

The strength of a supporting circular rod in tension is given by $W = F \times A$, where $A = \pi d^2/4$ and F is the allowable stress of the material. Since the dimensions of the cube are doubled, its weight (and the strength of the supporting rod) must be increased by a factor of eight (see note 3): $W_2 = 8W_1$. Hence the cross-sectional area of the rod must also be increased by a factor of eight: $A_2 = W_2/F = 8W_1/F = 8A_1$. Substituting this into the formula for area, we get $A_2 = \pi d_2^2/4 = 8(\pi d_1^2/4)$, hence $d_2^2 = 8d_1^2$ and $d_2 = \sqrt{8}d_1 = 2.83d_1$. The rod dimensions thus must increase by more than a factor of two.

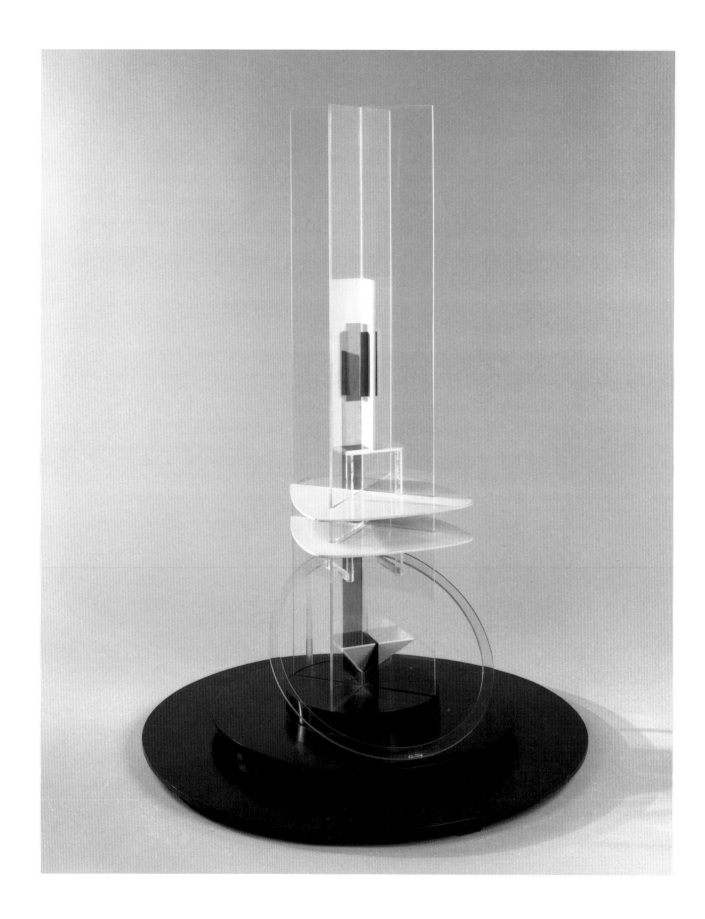

21 Structural Rightness and Imagery

On Rightness

Each field of endeavor in our world seems to have its own variant of the quest for the holy grail. In structures there is what might be called the "quest for structural rightness" (to borrow a phrase from L. B. Rogers's *Sculpture*).[1] "Structural rightness" refers to the shaping of material forms in a way that best seems to satisfy our intuitive or learned sense of how an object should be shaped to be consistent with the set of externally imposed conditions and laws that define its context. Certain forms have repeatedly struck many individuals as being natural, logical, or right. Forms found in nature often seem this way—a theme explored by D'Arcy Thompson in *On Growth and Form*. But many feel that the same sense of rightness can be found in objects deliberately shaped by humans as well, such as the shapes of the hulls of racing sloops or aircraft. Most discussions, however, deal with forms found in nature or in architecture, and few examine the underlying causes for the perception. What can we say about the specific shapes, attributes of shapes, and spatial relationships that convey this perceptual sense of structural rightness?

A general aspect of forms that seem to possess this sense of rightness is that they can be visually understood as single objects and are *shaped according to, and clearly manifest, some internal ordering system* or set of principles. This characterization is not unlike Rogers's argument that the perception of a sculpture as satisfactory involves not only noticing part and surface variations but also relating the variations within some internal rationale. This process builds up an appreciation of the form as a single object having a unitary character; Rogers holds that there are specific form attributes that contribute to this appreciation.[2] In the case of natural forms, the ordering principles are associated both with the forms' environmental context and with their evolutionary and biological growth. Growth issues, in particular, can be a dominant influence, as Thompson and others have so eloquently illustrated. The hull of a racing sloop, or that of an aircraft, feels right because it clearly manifests its

1
L. B. Rogers, *Sculpture* (New York: Oxford University Press, 1969).

2
Ibid.

21.0
Naum Gabo, *Column*.

designer's response to certain ordering principles demanded by the object's unique functions and environmental context.

An interesting characteristic of many forms of this type is that their precise shapes change subtly along their different dimensions according to the mandates of the internal ordering system present. These subtle shape changes are quite apparent in forms found in nature and are evident as well in man-made forms. The nonarbitrary origin of these shape variations is often perceptually apparent, even if the precise nature of the more fundamental ordering system is itself unknown or not fully understood. One reason may well be that the shapes assumed often follow curves describable in simple mathematical terms—curves that are common and repeatedly seen in different manifestations of which observers retain a perceptual memory. The shape of a ram's horns can be described in terms of a logarithmic spiral, for example, and the arch of a bridge can be shown to be that of a simple parabola—generic shapes well known to describe many natural and man-made objects. Is not the whirlpool a spiral, and does not a vine occasionally drape itself parabolically? One does not need to know exactly how to describe these forms mathematically to appreciate their perceptual qualities. These familiar shapings, in turn, are the direct consequence of an internal ordering system—the logarithmic spiral of a ram's horn, for example, is ultimately a consequence of constant growth patterns. The spin of a whirlpool is ultimately related to the motion of the earth itself (recall that whirlpools spin in different directions in the northern and southern hemispheres). The evocative recall of the human figure in many of David Smith's seemingly abstract metal sculptures is an example of a work imparting a recall ordering of yet another type, an ordering related to innate biological consciousnesses.

Following this general line of thinking, the idea of structural rightness should involve the shaping of a complete form in accordance with an ordering system derived from more abstract principles. A form having a sense of rightness thus strongly suggests these principles via the precise shaping of the form, which has perceptual qualities that can be appreciated even if the more abstract basis of the originating ordering system is not fully understood or even consciously perceived by the observer.

It is useful to look at examples of ordering systems in more detail. Sometimes the associated shaping stems from

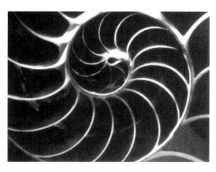

The shape of the nautilus stems from growth principles based on the need for self-similarity along its length.

The shape of this nineteenth-century lenticular truss at Binghamton, New York, results from deliberately varying the depth of the structure to match the bending moments present along its length.

Antoine Pevsner, *Oval Construction:* the form of this sculpture is based more directly on mathematically defined surfaces and has no internal ordering system that is initially generated by a growth or structural principle.

21.1
Internal ordering systems.

natural phenomena. It is known, for example, that there is no lack of spiral shapes in nature. From the shell of a *Nautilus pompilius* to a ram's horn, the shape is commonplace (fig. 21.1, top). In broad terms the spiral is a curve whose radius of curvature continually increases from a single point of origin. Most such shapes in nature are equiangular or logarithmic spirals, which possess the unique mathematical characteristic of what might be called "continued similarity" along their length.[3] In a mathematical sense, the *shape* of the spiral remains unchanged along its length. As a shell grows from a single point, it widens and lengthens in the same unvarying proportions. This is perhaps the most simple growth law of nature. Each new growth component is increased in size from its predecessor, but its *shape* is not affected. In a structure of this type, both its newness and its oldness can be viewed simultaneously *within* a special geometric context—a rather staggering thought. Note that humans can never be viewed in this way; they grow not from a fixed point but by the simultaneous magnification of all parts in all directions. Hence, human forms could never be spirally shaped.[4]

An example of shaping according to an ordering system in bridges is provided by the lenticular form introduced in the nineteenth century (fig. 21.1, center). This shape is designed to effectively utilize materials by varying the structural depth of the structure in direct response to the magnitude of the external bending moment present at a point (see chapters 9 and 10). For a uniformly distributed load, the bending moment that is present and that the structure must carry varies parabolically. Structural depths are consequently varied parabolically as well to reflect the intensity of the bending moment present at any point along the length of the structure. Where bending moments are the highest, so is the depth of the structure. The classic arch is also based on this principle. In the lenticular shape, part of the varying structural depth is placed below a horizontal reference line.[5] In the classic arch, the varying depth is placed completely above a horizontal reference line.

Often the resulting shapes can be described in simple mathematical terms. Many sculptors have used mathematical models as a basis for their work. Works such as Antoine Pevsner's *Oval Construction* or Naum Gabo's *Translucent Variation on a Spheric Theme* are certainly of interest as studies of space. But are they of interest as studies of order-

[3] The mathematics of this shape are beyond the scope of this book, but the following can be observed: As the curve extends from a fixed point, the arc intercepted between any two radii drawn from the point is always the same.

[4] This subject has been eloquently explored by D'Arcy Thompson, *On Growth and Form* (Cambridge: Cambridge University Press, 1961), p. 179, among others.

[5] The theory behind the lenticular structure is discussed in greater detail in Schodek, *Structures*, p. 172.

ing systems? Doubtful. Simply because a shape can be conveniently described mathematically or has some interesting topological property does not axiomatically mean that it has any inherent interest vis-à-vis internal ordering systems. The latter not only involve theoretical precepts or shape-forming factors from mathematics but typically spring in some way from the physical world. The fascination of the spiral in nature, for example, stems not solely from its mathematical geometry but also from its coupling with physical forms that grow over time in a self-similar way.

A sense of structural rightness may also be dependent on the spatial relationships among a form's components. This often occurs when there is some degree of congruence between purely visual and purely structural precepts. For example, there are visual concepts of balance that are not at all unlike structural concepts of balance. One of Calder's mobiles not only is in a state of careful physical balance but is also visually perceived as a statement of balance because of the relative sizes and placements of different components in space. The visual perception of a single object appearing to rotate about a point is congruent with the actual tendency of an object to do so, with imbalance being the consequence in both cases. Restoration of both visual and actual sense of balance is accomplished in both cases by the placement of an object that tends to provide an equal and opposite counterrotation. The analogies between physical and perceptual balance can also be seen in the ordering of the members at the tops of many of the great wood temples of Japan that are expressive of a strong visual symmetry—a symmetry that is perfectly at ease with the actual state of the balance of forces present there.

Some distinction should be drawn, however, between visual symmetry and the physical balancing of actual objects. The former deals with general shape and spatial relationships only. The latter deals not only with these but also with the actual mass characteristics of the material used. Consequently, it is perfectly conceivable that a sculpture made of several different materials having different densities or unit weights could be in a state of physical balance without the presence of an obvious visual balance. To a typical observer it might not appear structurally right, although a structural fanatic might view it with far more fascination because of the intellectual interest associated with a more complex view of the world and the forms of

physical objects than that stemming from a purely visually based understanding.

While the general sense of structural rightness applies to all objects, some sculpture engages another dimension of the issue because of its representational aspects. When a sculpture aims to represent some object, such as a form found in nature, the perceptual quality of structural rightness can stem from a visual association with the object represented or from the specific qualities of the actual object created by the sculptor. This is an interesting circumstance. Sculpture made to represent realistically human, natural, or artifactual forms is clearly not subject to the same contextual forces or circumstances that contributed to the shaping of the actual forms themselves. Yet it may still be held accountable in a purely perceptual way: the sense of structural rightness in a work can be lost by either a poor or a strained representation of the proportions and shapes of a perceptually familiar object (recall, for example, the issue of the unsatisfying distorted posture of *Guardian with Lantern* in figure 4.8) or by apparent contradictions of physical laws in the represented object. This does not mean that there is anything wrong here if the design intent is not simple realism and is successfully carried off. The shapes of Alberto Giacometti's sculptures of men, such as *Tall Figure* (fig. 5.4), have little to do with precepts à la D'Arcy Thompson but display their own visual integrity. But even these representations have to be in a state of true physical balance. The fact that they visually suggest balance and stability as well is of obvious interest in connection with this discussion of rightness.

Exchanged Imagery

One aspect of the art historical study of sculpture addresses the general symbiotic relationships in the development of art, science, and technology. Notably in the Renaissance one finds connections between the emerging science of the day and the arts—connections that are often evident within the lives and works of individual artist-scientists. More recent examples can also be identified of how the broad field of endeavor now commonly called the arts has contributed to the development of the general field of technology (most obviously that part of technology dealing with technique).

In many instances the arts have in some way contributed to the development of the sciences as well, though these connections are much less clear and obvious. There is little doubt of the converse influence—that the products and ideas of the age of science and engineering have dramatically impacted the arts, either directly in terms of technique and materials, or indirectly through their impact on society or by serving as an inspiration or point of departure for a variety of artists. The visual power of structural forms created for other purposes—such as bridges or buildings—has been sufficiently strong to cause them to be a source of imagery in the works of different sculptors. This is the subject of the remainder of this discussion.

It is useful to look at the design goals of such engineering structures as a way of understanding how their basic nature differs from objects as they are commonly created by sculptors. In bridge and building design in particular, a certain visual aesthetic has come to be associated with the idea of a structure. In these fields the scale of the objects and the demands placed on them require that extremely serious attention be paid to how they carry applied loads (snow, occupants, etc.), far more so than is necessary in any but the largest of sculptures. Typically associated with these structural demands are a host of other functional requirements. Bridges must carry pedestrians or vehicles from one point to another. Certain dimensional clearances must be maintained, as well as grades on the roadways and so forth. While there are of course higher aspirations in architecture than pure functionalism, buildings must by and large still serve the purposes of habitation or commerce and provide a well-tempered environment. There are thus strong pragmatic functional as well as purely structural demands that must be accommodated in the design of a bridge or a building. To state that sculptures serve no function is manifestly silly, but it may be stated that the functions that many do serve are of a more abstract quality (whether iconographic, symbolic, simply space-defining, or whatever). To be sure, there are some sculptors who have deliberately sought to deny even these more abstract qualities as a point of departure in their works, as there are many architects who have sought to make their works almost exclusively self-referential and to escape from functionality completely. Still, it can still be argued that the design requirements and intents for buildings and bridges are normally different from the design requirements and intents for sculpture. Issues of scale and functionality are important.

Bridges and buildings also differ from sculptural artifacts in the priority placed on efficiency and optimization. This is most evident in bridge design but also to a limited extent in the design of building structures. In the majority of cases, the design ethic of bridge builders is most directly linked with the efficiency of the objects they create. Although many early engineers were certainly concerned with what might be best termed the handsomeness of their works, as was the case with John Roebling, and many others have since been directly concerned with the appearance of their works, the normal overriding purpose of a bridge from the perspective of most design engineers is to span from one point to another and carry all applied loads in a safe and efficient manner, *not* to be a visual exploration of the concept of connection or some equally abstract notion. Consequently, in a bridge, an efficient structural form with a functional purpose normally dominates the visual image and symbolizes the whole bridge itself. As to efficiency, one measure of this is the relative weight or volume of material needed to support a given applied load in space. Thus many bridges are designed to carry their required loads using the absolute minimum volume of material possible in the structure itself. The degree to which this type of design goal is achieved frequently forms the basis for the structural engineer's own sense of the elegance (or lack thereof) of the resulting structure. Pursuit of this value of efficiency as a basis for establishing form has led to the recurrent and widespread use of several particular arrangements of material in space. For example, certain truss forms—specific triangulated patterns of rigid elements—have been known by bridge designers since their development in the nineteenth century to be highly efficient structures, and consequently have found wide use in bridges. Other shapes, notably the arch form, have repeatedly surfaced whenever value has been placed on the efficient use of material to carry certain uniformly distributed loads.

Interestingly, many of these same forms that were derived originally on the basis of function and efficiency are commonly thought to possess that sense of structural "rightness" discussed earlier. This is not surprising, for achieving efficiency requires that the forms be shaped according to a strongly defined internal ordering system, which is normally visually evident in a powerful way. In the case of the arch, for example, the depth of the structure varies directly with the magnitudes of the internal bending moments present along its length, with the resultant shape that of a parabola—a form with strong perceptual characteristics.

While the intent of many of these structures may originally have been utilitarian, their powerful visual forms provide a strong source of imagery for artists in several disciplines, including sculpture. At the very basic level of the structural element, we have seen that the familiar I-beam is a form derived in an engineering context solely for reasons of efficiency (the specific distribution of material in the cross section optimizes the capacity of the material present to carry external loads by bending; see chapter 9). This same shape has become almost symbolic of engineering and appears in the works of many sculptors. Anthony Caro's *Homage to David Smith* provides a striking example of this evocative shape (fig. 9.1).

Another primary architectural and engineering form, the arch, is infrequently used as a direct structural element in sculptural applications. More often it is the symbol of the arch that is evoked. The arch in Tatlin's *Monument to the Third International* (fig. 15.9) is used more in this spirit. (Even if the monument had actually been constructed in gargantuan proportions, its structural behavior would still be more like that of a trussed framework with an arch shape cut out of it than that of an arch supporting loads above it—see the discussion of this work in chapter 15.) Several of Armajani's sculptures, such as *Skyway Bridge* (fig. 11.2) or parts of his more recent work at the Walker Art Gallery in Minneapolis, clearly have their inspirations in truss structures and seek to explore them in what is apparently a fairly literal way. But to the structuralist they are only one-dimensional explorations, dealing with certain visual characteristics of triangulated patterns but not conveying any of the strong form-making ideology and intent that underlie the shaping of the original truss forms themselves. (This is not to say that those types of explorations are necessarily wrong. Armajani's forms are striking and convey much to many.)

In addition to engineering structures such as bridges and the like, structures in buildings have also provided a source of imagery in sculpture in a much broader sense.

Developments in the broad domains of architecture and sculpture have of course historically been closely linked. The rise of modern architecture at the beginning of this century, with its seemingly transparent objects and open forms that reduced distinctions between inside and outside, finds its parallels in sculpture of the same period. Certainly the work of Naum Gabo, Antoine Pevsner, and others sought a clarity that would reveal an inner structure and point to an unambiguous geometry, a process that often involved the dematerialization of the outside of an object. Points of direct interface between the fields, such as occurred at the Bauhaus, are well known. It has even been suggested that some of Pevsner's work, exemplified by the *Developable Column* (1942), has more specific referents in the shell structures of twentieth-century engineers such as Nervi or Candela who constructed soaring surface forms in reinforced concrete.[6] While this connection is tenuous at best, there was certainly a shared infatuation with certain geometries that were largely unused in both architecture and sculpture prior to the modern movements in both fields.

There are other broad similarities in the architectural and sculptural fields, particularly in attitudes toward the material reality of created objects. In each field there are advocates of a direct expression of what Tatlin called a "culture of materials," and others who give no heed to these considerations or actively oppose them. Certainly the difference in attitude between Tatlin, who actively sought a material culture, and Gabo, who was at odds with Tatlin's move into "real space and real materials," broadly exemplifies the debate in the sculptural field. One of literature's great confusions is here. Gabo's efforts to achieve a formal clarity of interpretation led to the use of the term "constructivism" to describe his works, the same name already adopted to describe works more akin to Tatlin's. The two schools were, of course, ideologically opposed. As applied to Gabo and like-minded sculptors, the term has more a geometric connotation than one of material reality. Although Gabo is known to have trained in engineering, mathematics, and the sciences, many of his actual works were surprisingly fragile and susceptible to breakage. A similar difference in attitude could be identified in the architecture of the same period, as could a confusion in identifying formally based and geometrically oriented attitudes with material-based ones.

There are many instances in which visually powerful structural forms that emerged in building design have formed a basis for the imagery of structure in sculpture. In the works of some architects, a special assembly is often provided, distinct from other building parts, to create an entity clearly identified as a "structure" to carry the applied loads. A consequence of this disaggregation of building parts is that the "structures" are then more susceptible to shaping in terms of specific design intentions vis-à-vis structural theory and efficiency objectives. This assembly is in turn sometimes celebrated as the dominant imagery of whole buildings. Oldenburg's *Batcolumn* (fig. 15.5) has been described as having its inspiration in such a celebrated building structure, in this case that of the John Hancock Building in Chicago.[7]

Even when not celebrated, however, separate structural assemblies are frequently provided in buildings. The reasons for this separation between structural and other building parts are many. One reason can be a deliberate design philosophy that seeks to render parts visually autonomous. Elements with different roles are give different physical and visual identities. Other reasons can be more pragmatic. One classic form that resulted from the specific design intent of separating the "structure" from the "skin" of a building is generally referred to as a frame structure (see chapter 11). The frame is an arrangement of specially connected beams and columns reduced to its simplest essence. The frame structure was developed in the latter part of the nineteenth century in connection with the emergence of high-rise buildings. It subsequently became so widely used that it became for a time a dominant visual image of engineering accomplishment in the reach skyward. It is thus not surprising that this structure has become a form of icon. The general referent of a frame can be seen in the works of several sculptors. It has been convincingly argued, for example, that the work of Gustav Klutsis (associated with Russian constructivism) strongly suggests the influence of this type of engineering structure. His *Three Dimensional Construction* (c. 1920) is a case in point.

Nonetheless, utilitarian engineering structures often seem to provide sculptors with more sources of imagery than do the structures of buildings. The latter are usually not visually dominant as objects in their own terms and consequently less likely to serve as points of reference. Another

6
Rogers, *Sculpture*, p. 86.

7
Fuchs, *Oldenburg*, p. 14.

reason is perhaps that the structural mechanisms provided for carrying applied loads in buildings have historically been treated in a variety of ways and with many different design intents. Certainly building structures often comply far less with efficiency criteria than do bridges because of other design priorities on the part of the architect. A consequence is the shaping of structural elements for a multiplicity of purposes rather than for a single clear objective. Building structures are often already heavily laden with their own referents; this prior lading, in turn, makes building structures less susceptible to use as a source of imagery in other fields.

A particular element, the column, provides an example of this point. The engineering sense of "column" (discussed in chapter 9) is a relative newcomer next to its architectural meanings. While it could be argued, for example, that the columns in the great works of ancient Greece and Rome originally evolved from humble and pragmatic earlier timber constructions, the ideas driving their development and visual expression certainly had other origins as well. An extreme example is found in the caryatid, a particular form of embellished column-like support (fig. 21.2). Caryatids allegorically symbolize the burden carried by the women of Caryae. The burden was the weight of their shame. This column was used in public buildings of the time in order that the sin and punishment of the people of Caryae might be known and handed down to posterity. The general idea of the personalization of columns was later extended by Vitruvius, with the Doric order having a referent in the strength of men, the Ionic in the woman, and the Corinthian in the maiden. Bramante incorporated an allusion to the assumption made by Vitruvius that the Doric order evolved from a timber prototype in the form of trunks of trees. His design for the cloister of S. Ambrogio included classical stone columns covered with carved representations of the stumps of sawn-off branches. By Sebastiano Serlio's time the language of columns had evolved into a set of classical rules for designing classical buildings that only hazily reflected any of the technical origins of the orders. All such architectural meanings have little to do with buckling effects and other physical phenomena that form the basis for a view of the column as a physical object subjected to an axial force. The former are also of only doubtful interest for abstract interpretation in a purely sculptural context, for they are already laden with layers of interpretations that are largely self-referential to architecture.

Some columns, of course, manifest the more technical origin of their forms. The latticed and wide-flange column forms illustrated in figure 21.2 are rather late developments that are again based on an idea of structural efficiency. It is also only later that some sculptors began to explore the dimensions of the idea of the column. Some common themes do appear. *Repeatability* of shapes along an axis, for example, is an important design attitude for the pragmatic engineer. *Axiality* is necessary to carry loads directly from one point to another without introducing the bending that would invariably develop with deviations from linear forms. Repeatability of form is of interest in an engineering context not so much for visual reasons or inherent structural value but because it makes for economies in production and assembly. The idea of shape repeatability along an axis is common in sculptural explorations of columns as well. In sculpture this theme is well illustrated in Brancusi's *Endless Column* with its strong visual sense of geometric repetition axially directed upward and its suggestion of infinite extensibility. Tal Streeter's *Endless Column* is a variant on this theme. Many of Kenneth Snelson's explorations suggest the same extensibility evident in Brancusi's column, but are also coupled with a sense of the balancing of forces and the process of construction. Fox notes in his essay on Snelson that his columns are "expressive of a desire to transcend material limitations, to traverse vast expanses of space."[8] Be this as it may, the fundamental axial theme is present in Snelson's columns.

The idea of endlessness is a well-explored topic in the sciences and mathematics as well as in sculpture (few people have not seen the symbol ∞). It is, however, rarely visually manifest in specific engineering structures. Also, the pragmatic columns of the engineering world are typically constituent parts of a larger whole in which they serve the role of transferring or transmitting something (usually forces) from one element to another. The endless columns of Brancusi and his successors stand in contrast to their engineering counterparts with their preoccupations with infinite extensibility and stand-alone uniqueness. In an engineering sense, these sculptures are more akin to towers than to columns. Towers are by nature self-standing and self-contained

Caryatid

Corinthian column

Penn Station, New
York (latticed column)

Steel wide-flange
column

21.2
Columns and columns.

Constantin Brancusi,
Endless Column

Tal Streeter,
Endless Column

Kenneth Snelson,
X Column

Naum Gabo, *Column*

structures; they transmit or carry no forces other than their own dead weights and environmental loads; and they also have reasons for being that cause them to seek the sky.

Gabo's *Column* stands in marked contrast to the other examples shown in figure 21.2. Not surprisingly, it is a probing of the interior of the object through the formal interactions of planes and lines, and a dematerialization of the exterior. But the centralization around the core still suggests the fundamental idea of the column. In a seemingly curious way, imagery of the type found in Gabo's explorations is not at all antithetical to the idea of the column in the engineering theory and underlying mathematics of column shaping. Concepts such as the radius of gyration and moment of inertia of column sections are, in a broad sense, nothing more than theoretical ways of exploring the ordering of material in space about a core point (with obviously different objectives and methods) that lead to similar conclusions.

In general, however, most attempts to explore the imagery of engineering or architectural forms seem to take as a premise the need to strip the original form of its original pragmatic functionality and to substitute a highly abstract functionality or iconographic significance. These abstractions rarely reflect any inherent structural logic based on structural principles in the original forms, but rather seek to use them as a way of exploring other ideas, albeit ones that are often related.

While one flow of imagery is from structures used in building design to sculptures, the converse flow occurs as well. Many building structures are often described as having sculptural qualities—by this is often meant structures with continuous or free-flowing shapes seemingly not immediately based on functional dictates. This limited interpretation of "sculptural qualities" is of course naive or simplistic at best, given the richness of the field of sculpture. On other occasions, specific bodies of work—such as that of the Russian constructivists—have attracted the interest of architects and formed the basis for many design proposals. In light of the fact that many of the constructivists drew some of their own imagery from engineering structures to begin with, this return transference is well worth briefly exploring.

The reasons for the attraction of architects to the work of Russian constructivists are many and complex. One of the simpler may be that many of the works from this movement exhibit particularly interesting visual explorations of the

potential of both materials and assemblages that were originally, according to some writers, at least partly derived from basic engineering works. Thus the fascination with these forms from the Russian constructivist movement seems to be associated with the *perceived* potential of these works to serve as even higher-order visual images of what actual building construction could ultimately aspire to be. Exactly *why* these images should serve as a direction of aspiration, of course, has never been particularly clear or adequately explored.

The explorations of the constructivists freed engineering forms from the strong functional and efficiency-oriented determinants that had provided an ideological design basis for these forms in the first place. The move by some architects to adopt and reinterpret these forms from the constructivist movement in sculpture, returning them to a context that may place strong functional and use demands on them, is curious at best as an architectural intent and nonsensical at worst.

The direct application of constructivist forms as literal building structures is also curious from another point of view. Others have convincingly documented that the constructivist movement was founded in a particular artistic attitude directed toward "the merging of art and life through mass production and industry" that was in turn linked to a specific ideology of the culture of the future. Indeed, the first group of sculptors to explicitly call themselves constructivists basically considered their work to be in contrast to art and aestheticism, which they considered corrupting. Bearing in mind the postrevolutionary context of Moscow in 1922 at the time of the first great exhibition of constructivist work, the adoption of constructivist imagery for essentially aesthetic purposes by architects (many with staid middle-class origins) working in the context of a capitalistic society is somewhat ironic. Viewed in this particular context, more recent architectural fashions that are in turn based on evolved "deconstructivist" concepts—both in the world of physical artifacts and the world of symbols—become equally curious. The transfer of imagery from architecture to sculpture discussed earlier is more understandable and convincing. The fundamental nonutilitarian aim, the absence of strong pragmatic functional dictates (including needs to enclose space), the traditional license in the field, and other facets of sculpture certainly allow for broader interpretations of structural imagery than are often tenable in architectural explorations of sculptural imagery.

In completing this brief tour, it is also relevant to note that some sculptural works were directly proposed as prototypes for large buildings, a point of obvious interest in a book of this type. The Russian constructivist Vladimir Stenberg, for example, commented that his works were conceived as explorations toward the realization of actual buildings.[9] Even Gabo thought of his *Column* as a small version of a larger structure. The reality is that Stenberg's sculptures could probably never have been made to work as serious large-scale load-carrying structures without changing their fundamental character. The role of a structure as the prime device for carrying loads to the ground is not convincingly articulated, and certainly there are scale problems. Tatlin's *Monument to the Third International* discussed in chapter 15 bears mention here again. The approach of putting the symbol of the structure on the outside wrapping and making it visually dominant, while the truly significant structure is on the inside and is thought of as essentially nonexistent, is a difficult notion to say the least. It was argued previously that at the scale of a real multistory building this attitude critically compromises the proposal. Here it is argued that in the same sense that architecture is not sculpture, sculpture is not architecture. A sculptural interpretation of a structure at a small scale is not necessarily the same as a real structure at a large scale.

There is too much theoretical content to the field of structures to assume that the only sculptural approach possible must be one based on a literal interpretation of structure and adoption of only its visual imagery. Nor must visual interpretations of physical principles be stripped of any true understanding and reflection of the reality of these principles. The thoughtful explorations of Gabo and others often attempted a visual interpretation of engineering forms, but ultimately only partly explored the principles underlying the forms (albeit this was never their declared intent). Imagery was addressed, but not theory. Addressing theory requires dealing with the internal ordering systems that are present in many referent structural works, and not just the adoption of more obvious imagery.

Although it has been argued that sculpture is not architecture and architecture is not sculpture, the recent preoccupation with public art has hastened the interaction

21.3
Georgii Stenberg's *KPS 58 NXIII* may convey what to many is a convincing image of engineering structures, but it does not convey the essence of the generative principles underlying real structures.

9
Christina Lodder, *Russian Constructivism* (New Haven: Yale University Press, 1983), p. 70.

between architecture and sculpture and softened distinctions between the two fields. There is urgent need for developing a serious dialogue on this topic.

A Closing Comment

Most of this book has focused on elucidating technical principles that are relevant in the design of sculpture, either to assure the basic stability and structural integrity of a work or more generally as a dimension for informing its shaping. I have argued more implicitly that a conscious consideration of technical dimensions may be a positive force in improving sculpture. Knowing something about the nature of structural principles may yield valuable insights into the shaping of a work, in the same way that a knowledge of how to work with specific materials has already proven its value. From this perspective, a very positive view emerges of the role of technical principles in sculpture, with a clear suggestion of how best to achieve this goal: sculptors can indeed become fully knowledgeable about the technical dimensions their work, and technical dimensions can then masterfully inform the shaping and execution of a work at the choice of the sculptor. This paradigm of the assimilation of technical principles and knowledge has been met many times in the past by sculptors particularly attuned to the materiality of their works, with positive results.

There may be implicit limits, however, in at least some situations to how far this paradigm can be reasonably propagated. As sculptures become larger in scale and are placed in more complex environments, as new materials come to the fore, as sponsors' demands increase for improved technical performance and longevity (as well as related guarantees), and as the body of theory concerning the physical behavior of objects increases in sophistication, the paradigm of the willful, all-knowledgeable and all-controlling individual becomes harder and harder to achieve. Voluntary interactions of sculptors and others (e.g., engineers, material specialists) provide another form of paradigm based on the not unreasonable assumption that in this day it is not really possible for any individual to possess complete mastery over many diverse skills and bodies of knowledge. Bringing together the very best talents from different fields may well produce the best product, as long as a basis for understanding is there.

Appendix 1
Case Study of *Echo of the Waves*

Discussions of the technical dimensions underlying this sculpture are provided in chapter 1 and chapter 7. The following timeline gives the sequence of events in the development and implementation of the sculpture in front of the New England Aquarium in Boston.

1976: Plaza design including fountain, paving, and sculpture completed by architect and all preliminary approvals obtained.

1978–1979: Site contracting company completes plaza. Sculpture canceled due to cost.

1980: Client requests architect to reevaluate sculpture for plaza. Sculptor contracted for design.

1980–1981: Sculptor designs sculpture.

1982, April: Consulting engineer prepares foundation design based on sculpture. Site contractor estimates cost of foundation.

July: Drawings arrive at architect from sculptor.

August: Consulting engineer evaluates proposed structure and requests engineering research firm be retained to analyze structure for dynamic effects due to wind. Bearing specialist evaluates proposed design and determines that bearing system must be redesigned.

September: Engineers determine that proposed structure will not satisfy existing building code requirements and begin redesign of structure in steel. On recommendation of engineers, architect begins investigation of fiberglass-reinforced plastic for skin. Bearing specialist advises architect that they cannot take on fabrication due to contractual liabilities. Composite materials firm is asked to fabricate the skin.

October: Architect asks composite materials firm to evaluate building the entire sculpture out of fiberglass-reinforced plastic. The same bearing specialist prepares bid documentation for structure and prepares sample steel joint.

November: Architect receives evaluation from composite materials firm and decides to build sculpture in fiberglass-reinforced plastic with a steel mast because of material cost and weight. Bids are taken for fiberglass-reinforced plastic work. Another firm is selected to fabricate the structure and skin.

December: Architect asks engineering research firm to continue structural investigations. Bearing specialist continues design of T arm bearing and machining.

1983, January: Representatives from fabricator meet with bearing specialist and engineering research firm to review construction. Engineering research firm discovers wings will generate greater stress than anticipated. Wing truss and slope of front wing tail must be redesigned and surface perpendicular to main wing must be added. All changes are approved by sculptor. (Details of this phase of the project are discussed more extensively in chapter 7.)

February: Fabrication of mast and main wings begins. Engineering research firm evaluates stress on front wing and finds structure satisfactory.

March: Fabricator begins front wings. Architect meets with Boston Building Department, Zoning Department, Redevelopment Authority, Committee on the Arts, and Engineering Department to obtain final clearances. Bearing specialist observes work in progress at fabricator.

April: Fabricator completes mast and sends it to riggers. Fabricator continues work on main and front wings and begins machining for T arm. Architect meets with site contractor and site paver to coordinate site work. Architect and bearing specialist inspect work at fabrication plant. Engineering research firm reviews site construction.

May: Sculptor, architect, and bearing specialist go to fabricating plant to balance sculpture to ensure correct movement. Front wing balanced on its own axle, then attached to main wing. Both wings then balanced on the T arms.

1983: Installation of sculpture at site. Strain gages attached to the sculpture by the engineering research firm to monitor the initial performance of the sculpture under actual conditions.

Principal project participants: New England Aquarium, Boston, Mass. (client); Susumu Shingu (sculptor); Cambridge Seven Architects, Cambridge, Mass. (architect); LeMessurier and Associates, Cambridge, Mass. (engineers); Littleton Research and Engineering, Littleton, Mass. (engineers); Welch, Walpole, Mass. (bearings and machining); Composite Engineering, Inc. (materials consultant); Design Evolution 4, Inc., Lebanon, Ohio (fabricator); J. F. White Contracting, Newton, Mass. (site contracting); T. G. O'Connor Co., Boston, Mass. (site paving); Shaughnessy and Ahern, Co., South Boston, Mass. (riggers).

Appendix 2
Additional Notes on Loading Conditions

Live and Dead Loads

Chapter 3 briefly explored the types of loads that a sculpture experiences. There it was noted that in the structural design of sculptures it is necessary to consider both self-weights, or dead loads, and live loads that result from the sculpture's environmental context. This section examines these loadings in greater detail.

Determining the magnitude of the dead load of an object is normally a straightforward, but tedious, task. It involves determining the volume of a form and then multiplying this volume times the unit weight of the material used. Volume estimates are made from direct linear measurements of the work itself. Unit weight values are readily available for most materials,[1] but can be determined experimentally for more unusual materials.

Magnitudes for common live loadings (occupancy loads, snow loads, etc.) on structures are experimentally determined and tabulated in common reference sources. Live loads are often expressed in terms of a force per unit area acting on a surface. A portion of a sculpture supporting people moving across it (as is the case in Siah Armajani's "bridge" in Minneapolis) might be designed for anywhere between 60 and 100 pounds per square foot depending on the design context. The magnitude and distribution of the total force experienced by a sculpture carrying a live loading of this type is subsequently obtained by considering the size and shape of the area over which the distributed live loading acts.[2]

Much of the available information on magnitudes of live loadings has been determined for use in building or bridge structures. Much of it can be adapted, however, for use in connection with the design of sculptures.[3] Snow loads can be a particular problem on some large works, particularly those having extensive surfaces or pockets that would allow snow to build up. Snow is hardly ever a problem, however, in smaller works. In potentially problematic larger works, the first step in determining snow loads is to investigate past records in the area of interest. Typically reasonable design

[1]
For example, steel has a weight of 492 pounds per cubic foot.

[2]
For example, assume that a flat horizontal part of a large public sculpture measures 4 feet by 5 feet in plan and is intended to support people. Also assume that the local building code requires that the design be capable of supporting a live loading of 100 lbs/ft². The horizontal platform would have to be designed to carry a total downward force of 2,000 lbs. (The area of the platform is 4 ft × 5 ft = 20 ft². The total force acting downward is therefore 100 lbs/ft² × 20 ft² = 2,000 lbs.)

[3]
See, for example, Schodek, *Structures*, chapter 3.

values are contained in applicable building codes local to the area. Design values are typically expressed in terms of a force per unit area for a particular location. In the northern part of the United States, for example, typical design values might be on the order of 40 or 50 pounds per square foot. Design values in southern areas are considerably less, e.g., 0 to 10 pounds per square foot. Once the design value is determined, the corresponding applied forces are obtained by multiplying the design force per unit area value times the expected area over which the snow would act.

Wind Loads

Wind forces can cause a sculpture to overturn or slide off its base. Determining the magnitudes of wind-induced pressure or suction forces and predicting whether undesirable dynamic movements will occur are extremely complex undertakings. Pressure or suction forces depend on the velocity of the wind, the mass density of the air, the geometrical shape, dimensions, and orientation of the structure, the exact location of the point considered on the piece, the nature of the surface the wind acts on, and the overall location and setting of the work.

Determination of design wind forces on a new structure in a specific location usually involves several steps, including a determination of the maximum wind velocity that might be expected in the place where the structure is located. Design wind velocities in coastal areas, for example, might be considerably higher than those inland because of the threat of hurricanes. These design velocities, ranging anywhere from 60 to 120 miles per hour, are also based on what is known as a 50-year recurrence interval for the proposed location—meaning that a wind of the velocity the sculpture must be designed to resist is not likely to occur more than once every 50 years (occasionally other recurrence intervals are used). While designing for such a rare large wind may seem conservative, and a sculpture may well be in place only a year or two, designing for long recurrence intervals of this type has proven to be important for typical outdoor structures since temporary structures have a habit of remaining. Selecting an appropriate design velocity is important since the magnitude of wind forces varies according to the square of the velocity of the wind. Thus, as

the wind speed doubles, wind forces increase by a factor of four.

Once the design wind velocity has been selected, the next step is to determine what force a wind of this velocity would exert on an object of a specific shape. For some common forms (spheres, cylinders, cubes, etc.), basic principles of fluid mechanics enable the prediction of pressure or suction forces that might exist on the object as a function of the velocity of the wind. These formulations usually involve the use of what is called a shape coefficient that relates force to velocity. Shape coefficients vary for different geometrical forms, but are commonly tabulated in design manuals.

For some common forms typically found in building construction, wind loadings have been previously determined and tabulated. Wind forces would be expressed in terms of a force per unit area acting on a surface. A tall building, for example, might feel a pressure force of 20 to 30 pounds per square foot against one face during a storm having winds of 90 to 100 miles per hour. The structure of the building would then be designed in response to this force.

Shapes of sculptures are often so varied that resort must be made to wind-tunnel testing if one really wants to be sure of the magnitudes and distributions of the pressures and suctions that might exist. Depending on the size of the sculpture, this process involves putting either the whole piece or a reduced scale model inside a wind tunnel and subjecting it to a specified wind velocity. Pressure and suction measurements are made via sensors placed at selected points on the object. Occasionally strain gages are also placed on the object to record deformations that can then be used to estimate stresses that exist in the structure itself. This general process is a complex one, but it does yield reasonable results. The process is, however, a very expensive one and must be done by specialized professionals.

Earthquake Forces

Earthquake forces are among the most difficult to predict due to their complex origins and the way local geological conditions modify ground motions. Several different scales are used to describe earthquake magnitudes or intensities, most commonly the Richter scale and the Modified Mercalli scale. The former describes the general amount of energy released during an earthquake while the latter describes the intensity of an earthquake as perceived at a specific point on the ground.

Maps depict the locations of earthquake-prone areas. Some areas are well-known, e.g., parts of California, Japan, or Turkey. But a very appreciable seismic hazard often not appreciated by the general public exists in other areas, e.g., Boston, Massachusetts, Charleston, South Carolina, and St. Louis, Missouri, to name a few. Precise locations must be checked to obtain design values for expected earthquake intensities and motion characteristics.

Earthquake ground motions are complex and involve accelerations in the horizontal and vertical directions. These ground motions cause various types of forces to be developed within structures that are inertial in character (the magnitudes of the forces developed consequently depend on the mass of the structure—the heavier the structure, the greater are the earthquake forces developed within it). These forces can cause a sculpture to slide off its base, to overturn, or to physically break apart. (See the discussion on overturning effects in chapter 5.)

In larger structures that might be dangerous if overturning or member failure due to earthquakes should occur, the process of determining the design earthquake forces begins with a determination of the probable seismicity of the area in which the work is to be located. The forces themselves are subsequently predicted on the basis of either a simplified static model largely based on the classical Newtonian formulation of the relation between forces, masses, and accelerations (i.e., $F = ma$), with the resultant force simply considered applied to the structure as a static (nonmoving) applied load, or a more complex dynamic formulation in which the structure is modeled as an assembly of springs and masses that vibrate in a complex mode. The latter approach is clearly a task for an engineer. The type of analysis used depends upon the size and physical make-up of the structure, a judgment that is again best made by an engineer.

Other Forces

Depending on the specific configuration of the sculpture, it might also be necessary to design for certain concentrated loads that might develop as a consequence of people hanging onto or swinging from a projecting element. Common sense is often used to predict values for loadings in these cases. The trick in these situations is to imagine anything possible that a person might do or cause to be done to a work and design accordingly.

Appendix 3
Additional Notes on Designing
Structural Elements in Bending

As generally discussed in chapter 9, the steps in determining the exact required size of a beam are as follows: (1) determine the loading on the beam, (2) determine reactions (forces at connections), (3) determine the shear forces and bending moments present (maximum values and distributions along the length of the member), (4) select a material with known allowable stresses, (5) estimate a beam size based on maximum forces and material properties as described below.[1]

Assume that a 4 inch × 8 inch timber beam cantilevers out 10 feet (120 inches) and supports a load of 1,000 lbs at its free end. Assume that the allowable stress of the timber in bending is 1,500 lbs/in². Is the beam safe in bending? First, find the bending moment: $M = P \times L = 1,000 \text{ lbs} \times 120 \text{ in} = 120,000$ in-lbs. The bending stress is given by $f = Mc/I$. M is known. The moment of inertia I needs to be calculated, as does the distance c, which is measured from the centroid to the outer face of the beam. The moment of inertia for a rectangular beam measured in inches is given by $I = bd^3/12 = (4)(8^3)/12 = 171$ in⁴. The c distance is simply $d/2 = 8/2 = 4$ in. Hence, $f = Mc/I = (120,000)(4)/171 = 2,807$ lbs/in². Since this is the actual stress developed on the outer face of the beam at the base of the cantilever, the beam is not safe since the allowable stress is only 1,500 lbs/in². A new size should be tried.

Estimate a new size by setting $I/c = M/f_a$ where f_a is the allowable stress. Define the section modulus $S = I/c$. Hence $S_{required} = M/f_a = 120,000/1,500 = 80$ in³. $S = I/c = (bd^3/12)/(d/2) = bd^2/6$ for a rectangular beam. Thus, $bd^2/6 = 80$ in³ or $bd^2 = 480$ in³. Any combination of b and d^2 that yields 480 will work. If $b = 4$, $d^2 = 120$ and $d = 10.95$ in. A beam 4 inches × 11 inches would work and carry the load without excessive bending stresses.

Determining design bending moments for other loading conditions is problematic. A common beam of span L simply supported at its ends and carrying a uniform load w along its length experiences a midspan moment of the following: $M = wL^2/8$. If $L = 10$ ft (120 in) and $w = 240$ lbs/ft (20 lbs/in), then $M = (20)(120^2)/8 = 36,000$ in-lbs. Is the 4 in × 8 in

1
See Schodek, *Structures,*
chapter 5.

beam used above adequate in bending for this condition? Find the actual bending stress: $f = Mc/I = (36,000)(4)/171 = 842$ lbs/in². This actual stress value is less than the allowable value of 1,500 lbs/in², so the member is adequately sized in bending. Other forces exist in beams of this type. The reactions at either end ($R = wL/2$) cause shear forces and bearing stresses to develop in the member. The maximum shear V present anywhere equals the reaction: $R = V = wL/2 = (20)(120)/2 = 1,200$ lbs. The maximum shear stress in a rectangular beam occurs at its centroid and can be shown to be $f_v = (3/2)V/A = (3/2)(1,200)/(4)(8) = 56$ lbs/in². This value is quite small in comparison with safe values for timber of around 150 lbs/in². The bearing stresses that exist between the end of a beam and its support are given by $f_{bg} = R/A_{interface}$. Say the beam sits on a 3-inch-wide wall. Thus: $f_{bg} = 1,200/(3)(4) = 100$ lbs/in², which is less than allowable values of near 400 lbs/in². Deflections for beams like this assume the form $\Delta = wL^4/384EI$, where E is the modulus of elasticity of the material (see chapter 19). Deflections would be found to be very small and not a problem.

If steel members are used, not only are allowable stresses different, but it is also typically more difficult to find the moment of inertia value for odd-shaped sections such as wide-flange beams. Values tabulated for common sections are available.

Appendix 4
Advanced Methods of Structural Analysis

Many sculptures are highly complex and difficult to analyze structurally. The analysis techniques discussed in this book are necessarily simplified and are only developed to a limited extent. When a large-scale sculpture really demands intensive structural investigation by an engineering office, it is entirely probable that more sophisticated computer-based structural analysis techniques will be used. These powerful techniques enable a structural engineer to determine the forces and moments present within highly complex forms with a great degree of confidence.

Advanced analysis techniques are invariably computer-based. One set of techniques, called *matrix displacement* methods, form the basis for common structural analysis programs. Most applicable to framed structures, these methods treat joint displacements as unknown values to be found. Once found, member forces are determined by considering the various stiffnesses of the different members. For continuous surfaces, such as shells or plates, an alternative analysis approach is based on what are known as *finite-element* techniques. The surface is divided into a mesh of many smaller elements having their own stiffness and strength properties. An advanced computer-based analysis technique then solves for the forces in the various elements.

All of these techniques typically require that the geometry and physical characteristics of the structure be known beforehand and treated as inputs into the analysis program. The outputs of these programs are usually displacements of nodes, axial forces, shears, and moments. This information is then used to determine if the sizes of the members actually used are sufficiently large to carry the stresses involved (available programs rarely do this directly). Many different types of programs are available that accomplish different analysis goals.

Most engineering offices make use of one or more of these formulations and would typically use them in the analysis and design of any complex large-scale sculpture. Programs of this type are very useful to an engineer, but they are by no means panaceas for the novice designer. Certainly they are limited in the sense that they only analyze a structure and in no way actually design or shape a configuration. The results of an analysis can be used to infer appropriate design changes to improve the behavior of a structure, but the changes are still primarily developed in a directly human way.

Photograph Credits

© Estate of David Smith/Visual Artists and Gallery Association,
   New York, 1992, 5.2, 5.7, 5.8, 6.10, 12.6, 19.0
Estate of Robert Smithson and Courtesy of John Weber Gallery, N.Y.,
   18.0, 18.6, 18.7
Smithsonian Institution, Archives of American Art, 5.7, 5.8, 12.6
Kenneth Snelson, 2.4, 11.20, 11.21
Storm King Art Center, 1.3; 2.3; 5.1, 5.7, and 5.8 (Gift of the Ralph E.
   Ogden Foundation; Jerry L. Thompson, photographer); 6.9 (Gift of
   Muriel and Philip I. Berman; Jerry L. Thompson, photographer); 1.0,
   8.2, 11.21, and 12.0 (Jerry L. Thompson, photographer); 8.0 and 8.7
   (Gift of the Ralph E. Ogden Foundation); 11.11; part 6 opening and
   21.2 (Purchased with the aid of funds from the National Endowment
   for the Arts)
Western Washington University, art allowance from Arntzen Hall and the
   Environmental Studies Center, the National Endowment for the Arts,
   and the Virginia Wright Fund, 8.6 (Carl Root, photographer)

Requests for permission for reproductions were sent to the artists,
agents, and/or photographers of other works shown, but replies were
not received.

Note: The structural analyses shown for several of these works are strictly
the interpretation of the author. There is no implication that the artists
were interpreting structure in their work in any way.

Index